Victor Duruy

History of Rome and the Roman Empire

From its origin to the establishment of the Christian empire

Victor Duruy

History of Rome and the Roman Empire
From its origin to the establishment of the Christian empire

ISBN/EAN: 9783337173692

Printed in Europe, USA, Canada, Australia, Japan

Cover: Foto ©ninafisch / pixelio.de

More available books at **www.hansebooks.com**

BARBARIANS.

By VICTOR DURUY,

MEMBER OF THE INSTITUTE, EX-MINISTER OF PUBLIC INSTRUCTION, ETC.

TRANSLATED BY M. M. RIPLEY AND W. J. CLARKE.

EDITED BY

THE REV. J. P. MAHAFFY,

PROFESSOR OF ANCIENT HISTORY, TRINITY COLLEGE, DUBLIN.

Containing over Three Thousand Engravings, One Hundred Maps and Plans,
AND NUMEROUS CHROMO-LITHOGRAPHS.

VOLUME I. — SECTION I.

PUBLISHED BY
C. F. JEWETT PUBLISHING COMPANY
BOSTON.

EDITOR'S PREFACE.

IT is the duty of those who offer to the public so large a work on a subject already treated in English books, to justify its position and explain the principles followed in translating and editing it. Strange to say, though some of the greatest English historians have devoted themselves to Roman history, there does not exist any standard English work on the whole subject. Portions of it have been thoroughly handled, but a complete survey is not to be found except in little handbooks; so that the Englishman or American who wants as a work of reference for his library a history of Rome down to the close of its pagan days, has hitherto been unable to find it. Even if he can read French and German, he will encounter the same difficulty; nor is it in any way satisfactory to supply the want by two or three special histories. No doubt the English edition of Mommsen's History, the large work of Merivale, and the incomparable Gibbon cover the ground, but they cover it writing from widely different standpoints, in various styles, and without any general index which could enable the ordinary reader to find any fact required. Moreover, the very original and suggestive work of Mommsen on the early history of Rome is totally unsuited for ordinary readers and for ordinary reference, inasmuch as he treats with silent contempt most of the popular stories, and re-arranges the remnants of tradition according to new and peculiar principles of his own. To a public ignorant of his special researches, — his *Römische Forschungen* and *Römisches Staatsrecht*, — the History, published without references or explanations, must be often quite unintelligible.

The account of the early reforms in the Constitution, and of the relations of the Three Assemblies, are so totally opposed to the accounts in ordinary English histories, that the thoughtful reader is completely at a loss to find out when all these novelties were discovered, or how they are to be justified. An edition of this fine book, with some such information in foot-notes, would have made it a work of far greater value; for it represents a school of thought which is as yet quite foreign to England, and which, under the able expositions of Rubino, Mommsen, Soltau, and others, bids fair to displace the views of Niebuhr, even when corrected and modified by Schwegler, Lange, and Clason.[1] But as yet these matters are within the field of controversy; and to assume all his own views as proved may indeed be admitted as lawful in the historian, but cannot be regarded as satisfactory in a work professing to give all the facts of Roman history.

The broad difference between the older school of Niebuhr and that of Mommsen is this: that while Niebuhr sifts tradition, and tries to infer from it what are the real facts of early Roman history, Mommsen only uses tradition to corroborate the inferences drawn concerning early Roman history from an analysis of the traditional facts and usages still surviving in historical days, and explained as survivals by critical Roman historians. Thus, the usages in appointing a dictator or consul lead him to infer that of old the kings were appointed in like manner, these magistrates having taken the place of the king. Such researches are naturally only of value in reconstructing early *constitutional* history.

The work of Duruy does not adopt this method, and stands on the ground of Niebuhr, or rather of Schwegler, whose valuable History, like that of our own Thirlwall, is regaining its real position after some years of obscuration by a more brilliant, but not impartial, rival. Indeed, the newer critical school in Germany cannot yet, and perhaps never will, furnish a real history of early Rome, such as Niebuhr's, Ihne's, Schwegler's, or the present, but only acute and often convincing essays on the Constitution. It was beyond my duty to introduce these newer views by way

---

[1] The first glimpse of these new lights in English is to be found in Mr. Seeley's Introduction to his edition of *Livy*; Ihne's *Essay on the Roman Constitution* and his *History* are original and independent labors on the general lines of Niebuhr.

of foot-notes, even though often convinced of their truth; for I undertook to edit Duruy's great work, and not to supply anything more. Accordingly I have confined myself here and there to mentioning a fact or suggesting a different view of some event, but have avoided stating any conflicting theory. Additional books of reference, however, and these principally of the newer school above described, have been sometimes cited, and a great deal has been done to improve another capital feature of the book, — the illustrations. In this respect Duruy's book stands alone, giving the reader all kinds of illustration and of local color, so as to let him read the history of Rome, as far as possible, in Italy, and among the remains of that history, with all the lights which archæological research can now afford us. In many places I have left out a cut which seemed of little authority, and supplied from photographs (collected in Italy and Sicily) better and truer pictures. I have had recourse to contemporary art, and given some ideal pictures of great events in Roman history, as imagined by artists learned in the local color and the dress of the period. Here and there I have also ventured to curtail the descriptions of battles, which are borrowed from the ancient historians, as they were composed from purely rhetorical considerations, and have no claim to accuracy. Enough, and more than enough, has been left to show the views of these patriotic historians. It is a perpetual cause of offence and annoyance in the extant classical historians, that instead of giving us some intelligible account of military movements, they supply us with the most vulgar and often absurd platitudes concerning tactics, and with the invented harangues of the respective leaders.

I will add, in conclusion, that the publishers have met all my demands and requirements with the largest liberality. So far as they are concerned, everything has been done to make the book the best and the most complete which has yet appeared on Roman history.

TRINITY COLLEGE, DUBLIN.

TABLE OF CONTENTS.

VOLUME I.

INTRODUCTION.

THE PRE-ROMAN EPOCH.

		PAGE
I.	Geography of Italy	17
II.	Ancient Population of Italy — Pelasgians and Umbrians	44
III.	Etruscans	60
IV.	Oscans and Sabellians	88
V.	Greeks and Gauls	106
VI.	Political Organization of the Ancient Nations of Italy	116
VII.	Religious Organization	122
VIII.	Summary	132

FIRST PERIOD.

ROME UNDER THE KINGS (753–510 B. C.). FORMATION OF THE ROMAN PEOPLE.

CHAPTER I.

TRADITIONAL HISTORY OF THE KINGS.

I.	Romulus (753–716)	137
II.	Numa (715–673)	146
III.	Tullus Hostilius (673–640)	150
IV.	Ancus Marcius (640–616)	156
V.	Tarquin the Elder (616–578)	157
VI.	Servius Tullius (578–534)	161
VII.	Tarquinius Superbus (534–510)	166

CHAPTER II.

CONSTITUTION OF ROME DURING THE REGAL PERIOD. — PRIMITIVE ORGANIZATION.

I.	Sources of Roman History	181
II.	Probable Origin of Rome	185
III.	Patricians and Clients	189
IV.	Senate and King; Plebeians	194

CHAPTER III.

RELIGION AND RELIGIOUS INSTITUTIONS.

	PAGE
I. The Public Gods	199
II. The Domestic Gods	206
III. The Manes	210
IV. Naturalism of the Roman Religion and Formal Devotion	216
V. Sacerdotal Colleges	222
VI. Public Festivals	232

CHAPTER IV.

CHANGES IN RELIGION AND CONSTITUTION UNDER THE THREE LAST KINGS.

I. The Gods of Etruria at Rome; Reforms of Tarquin the Elder	235
II. Reforms of Servius Tullius	239
III. Tarquin the Proud; Power of Rome at this Epoch	250

CHAPTER V.

MANNERS AND CUSTOMS.

I. Character of Ancient Roman Society	255
II. Private Manners	260
III. Public Manners	267

SECOND PERIOD.

ROME UNDER THE PATRICIAN CONSULS (509–367 B. C.). — STRUGGLES WITHIN — WEAKNESS WITHOUT.

CHAPTER VI.

INTERNAL HISTORY FROM 509 TO 470 B. C.

I. Aristocratic Character of the Revolution of 509; the Consulship	272
II. The Tribunate	279
III. The Agrarian Law	288
IV. Right of the Tribunes to accuse the Consuls and to bring forward Plebiscita	294

CHAPTER VII.

MILITARY HISTORY OF ROME FROM THE DEATH OF TARQUIN TO THE DECEMVIRS (495–451 B. C.).

I. The Roman Territory in 495; Porsenna and Cassius	299
II. Coriolanus and the Volscians; Cincinnatus and the Aequians	308
III. War against Veii	315

TABLE OF CONTENTS.

CHAPTER VIII.

THE DECEMVIRS AND CIVIL EQUALITY (451–449 B.C.).

I. Bill of Terentilius	319
II. The Decemvirs (451–449)	327
III. The Twelve Tables	331

CHAPTER IX.

EFFORTS TO OBTAIN POLITICAL EQUALITY (449–400 B.C.).

I. Re-establishment of the Tribunate and Consulate	341
II. New Constitution of the Year 444	344
III. Struggle for the Execution of the New Constitution	348

CHAPTER X.

MILITARY HISTORY FROM 448 TO 389 B.C.

I. Conquest of Anxur or Terracina (406)	352
II. Capture of Veii (395)	356
III. Capture of Rome by the Gauls (390)	362

CHAPTER XI.

MILITARY HISTORY FROM 389 TO 343 B.C.

I. Rebuilding of the City; the Roman Legion	369
II. Return of the Gauls into Latium; Manlius; Valerius Corvus	373

CHAPTER XII.

ACCESSION OF THE PLEBEIANS TO CURULE OFFICES.

I. The Licinian Laws: Division of the Consulships	380
II. The Plebeians gain Admission to all Offices	384

CHAPTER XIII.

THE AGRARIAN LAW AND THE ABOLITION OF DEBT.

I. Agrarian Law of Licinius Stolo	398
II. Laws on Debt	403
III. The Aerarii; Censorship of Appius (312)	406

THIRD PERIOD.

WAR OF ITALIAN INDEPENDENCE, OR CONQUEST OF ITALY (343–265 B. C.).

CHAPTER XIV.

WAR WITH THE SAMNITES AND LATINS (343–312 B. C.).

		PAGE
I. First Samnite War; Acquisition of Capua (343–341)	. . . . .	412
II. The Latin War (340–338)		417
III. Second Samnite War (326–312)		425

CHAPTER XV.

COALITION OF THE SAMNITES, ETRUSCANS, AND SENONES (311–280 B. C.).

I. Third Samnite War (311–303)	438
II. Second Coalition of Samnites, Etruscans, Umbrians, and Gauls (300–290) . .	445
III. Coalition of the Etruscans and Senones; War against the Lucanians (283–281)	456

CHAPTER XVI.

WAR WITH PYRRHUS (280–272 B. C.).

I. Rupture with Tarentum; First Campaign of Pyrrhus in Italy (282–278) .	460
II. Pyrrhus in Sicily; Capture of Tarentum (272)	470

CHAPTER XVII.

ORGANIZATION OF ITALY BY THE ROMANS.

I. The Freedom of the City, and the Thirty-Five Tribes	476
II. Municipia, Prefectures, and Allied Towns	483
III. Colonies and Military Roads	488
IV. Religious Supremacy; Rome governs, and does not administer	497

CHAPTER XVIII.

INTERNAL STATE OF ROME DURING THE SAMNITE WAR.

I. Manners	500
II. The Constitution; Balance of Forces	502
III. Military Organization	509
IV. Recapitulation	523

FOURTH PERIOD.

THE PUNIC WARS (264–201 B. C.).

CHAPTER XIX.

CARTHAGE.

	PAGE
I. Commercial Empire of the Punic Race	525
II. Carthaginians and Liby-Phoenicians; Commercial Policy of Carthage	533
III. Mercenaries	538
IV. The Constitution	541

CHAPTER XX.

THE FIRST PUNIC WAR (264–241 B. C.).

I. The Treaties between Rome and Carthage (509–279)	549
II. Operations in Sicily (264)	552
III. Maritime Operations; Landing of the Romans in Africa (260–255)	560
IV. The War is carried back into Sicily (254–241)	568

CHAPTER XXI.

CONQUESTS OF ROME AND CARTHAGE BETWEEN THE TWO PUNIC WARS (240–219 B. C.).

I. Roman Expeditions outside of Italy and into Gallia Cisalpina	581
II. Carthage; Wars of the Mercenaries; Conquest of Spain	603

CHAPTER XXII.

INTERNAL STATE OF ROME IN THE INTERVAL BETWEEN THE TWO PUNIC WARS.

I. Commencement of Roman Literature; Popular Games and Festivals	612
II. Changes in Manners, Religion, and Constitution	625

CHAPTER XXIII.

THE SECOND PUNIC WAR UP TO THE BATTLE OF CANNAE (218–216 B. C.).

I. Hannibal in Spain	648
II. Hannibal in Gaul · Crossing of the Alps	660
III. Hannibal in Cisalpine Gaul; Battle of Ticinus; Battle of Trebia (218)	665
IV. Thrasimene (217); and Cannae (216)	669

LIST OF FULL-PAGE ENGRAVINGS.[1]

VOLUME I.

	PAGE
Autium, View of	426
Appian Way, the	494
Ardea, Remains found at	172
Aventine, the (present state)	324
Bâal-Hammon, Temple of (ruins)	536
Cannae, Battle-field of	684
Castel d' Asso, Valley of	84
Cenis, Mont	660
Chastity, Temple of (restoration)	396
Circello, Monte	30
Cloaca Maxima	160
Coins, bronze, table of	630
Concord, Temple of (restoration)	386
Courage " " "	602
Erete, Mount	482
Fortune, Temple of (restoration)	376
Geese of the Capitol	366
Girgenti, Temple at (remains)	560
Human Sacrifices	68
Jupiter Stator, Temple of (restoration)	146
Liris, Fall of the	380
Metapontum, Harber of	112
Naples and Mount Vesuvius	26
Nemi, Lake	344
Norba, Walls of	54
Nymphaeum of Egeria	150
Ravenna, Canals and Pine Forest of	36
Roman Campagna	40
Romulus, Wall of (remains)	144
Rosa, Monte	18
Spoleto, View of	676
Sybaris, Plain of	118
Terni, Cascade of	454
Terracina, Rock of	250
Tiberina, the Insula	176
Tivoli, Temple at	124
Tomb, called that of Aruns	302
" Etruscan	60
" of the Horatii	154
Valley of Tombs near Norchia (restoration)	444
Veii, City of (restoration)	354
" Vases found at	358
Viso, Monte	664

[1] Facing the pages indicated.

ALPHABETICAL INDEX

TO

TEXT ILLUSTRATIONS, INCLUDING MAPS AND PLANS.

VOLUME I.

	PAGE		PAGE
Acarnania, coin of	592	Antoninus Pius, coin of . .	17
Adoration before a tomb . . .	211	" " " " .	340
" gesture of	212	Apollo, the Pythian . . .	361
Adria, *as libralis* of . . .	29	" priest of . . .	636
Aediles, plebeian (coin) . . .	298	Apollonia, coin of . . .	591
Aeneas carrying Anchises . . .	139	Appian Gate (restoration) . .	494
" (coin)	140	" Way	408
Aesculapius "	637	Aquinum, coin of	492
Aeserniu, coin of	492	Archigallus, an	640
Agathocles " "	555	*Argentarii*	630
Ager Romanus (map) . . .	302	"	633
Agrigentum, coin of . . .	557	Ariminum, *as* of	373
" " "	559	Arretium, earthenware of . .	446
" (plan) . . .	558	Arvalis, Frater	225
Alatri, wall of	91	*As* in rude metal (actual size) . .	248
Alba, extinct volcanoes about (map) .	39	" double, of Camers . . .	77
Alba Fucentia (plan) . . .	447	" *libralis* of Adria . . .	29
Alba Longa, coin of	89	" " " Ariminum . . .	373
Alexander I., King of Epirus, coin of .	425	" " " Tuder . . .	57
Alexander II. " " " (gem) .	470	Astarte	565
Alphabets :		Atellane figures	621
Early Roman (Latin) . .	182	Athlete, victorious . . .	624
Etruscan	63	Augur	237
of Central Italy . . .	61	Augurinus, coin of . . .	349
of Northern Italy . . .	113	Aulus Postumius (coin) . . .	179
Alps and Apennines, limit of the (map)	39	Aurunca, wall of	96
Alsium, tumuli at	493	Aventine, wall of the . .	323
Altar (tomb at Pompeii) . . .	287		
" (domestic)	206	Beak-head of a ship (coin) . .	561
Ancilia, or Shields of Mars (coin) .	149	Bellona (priest of) . . .	419
" " " " (gem) .	224	Beneventum, coin of . . .	471
Ancona, coin of	110	Black stone, the (coin) . .	639
Ancus Martius, traditional portrait of .	157	Boii, coin of the	594
Anna Perenna (coin) . . .	284	Bronze arms	14
Antigonus Gonatas, coin of . .	472	" " and tools . . .	69
Antistia, *gens*, " " . . .	168	" candelabra	303

ALPHABETICAL INDEX TO TEXT ILLUSTRATIONS.

Bronze jewels	70
" "	72
" vases	71
" vessels	84
Brundusium, coin of	493
Brutus (bust in the Capitol)	174
Brutus, L. Junius (coin)	277
Bulla	209
" young man wearing the	209
Buxentum, coin of	33
Cabeiri	51
"	52
Cadiz, coin of	531
Caeles Vibenna and Mastarna	240
Caere, vase of	165
Cales, coin of	423
Camarina, coin of	461
" " " (early period)	545
Camers, double *as* of	77
Camillus	231
Campagna, Roman, cattle of the	40
" " flint weapons found in	42
Cannae, ruins of	683
Capitoline Hill (restoration)	251
Capua, coin of	103
Carthage, aqueducts of	528
" cisterns "	529
" coin of	532
" " "	532
" " "	533
" " " (gold)	533
" (plan)	527
" ports of	534
Carthaginian art, remains of	543
" *ex-voto*	539
" warrior	605
Castor, temple of	178
Caudine Forks, valley of the	432
Cephaloedium, coin of	569
Ceres	308
" (found at Ostia in 1856)	281
Chariot-races, genii of	623
Chastity, altar of (coin)	307
Chickens, the Sacred	437
Chimaera	66
Cinerary Urns	257
Circe, Ulysses, and Elpenor	93
Circeii, wall of	170
Civic crown (coin)	325
" " with laurel-leaves (coin)	325
Claudia dragging the vessel of Cybele	639
Cloaca Maxima	252
Clusium, black vases of	85
Clusium, black vases of	86
Coins, table of (bronze), see full-page illus	
" " " (gold)	632
" " " (silver)	631
Colony, coin of a	488
" (ground plan of lands for)	489
Comic actor	622
Concord (coin)	125
Consul between two fasces (coin)	273
Corcyra, coin of	591
Cosa " "	492
Corsica and Sardinia (map)	589
Cossura, coin of	536
Crotona " "	111
Cucumella, the	83
Cumae, coin of	109
" cave of the Sybil of	171
Cybele (coin)	641
" "	647
Decius Mus (coin)	415
Decurions, coin of the	490
Demetrius Poliorcetes (coin)	472
Demons leading away a soul	129
Denarius, silver	581
" " of Antoninus Pius	340
Diana, or the Moon (cameo)	618
" with the hind	247
Dii Penates (coin)	149
Dioscuri "	179
Duillius, rostral column of	563
Elea, coin of	111
Elephant (*ex-voto*)	541
Elephants, African (gem)	580
" (coin)	473
" (gem)	466
Elysian repast	213
Entella, coin of	559
Ercte, coin of	575
Eryx, remains of the town of	576
" Mount, view from	577
Escutcheons, patrician	192
Etna, from Taormina	582
Etruria, Southern (map)	317
Etruscan alphabets	63
" archer	378
" chimaera	66
" cups	258
" figure with four wings	66
" figures	64
" funeral urn	458
" gorgon	65
" helmet of Lucumon	78

ALPHABETICAL INDEX TO TEXT ILLUSTRATIONS. 21

Etruscan jewels and earrings	. .	73
" Mars		443
" mirror		93
" sideboard		254
" standard-bearer . .		440
" tomb (the Cucumella)	.	83
" warrior		378
" " . . .		440
" "		597
" vases (comic scenes from)	.	618
" " " " "	.	619
Eugubine tables, fragment of	. .	58
Fabia, *gens*, coin of . .	.	190
Fabius Pictor (coin) . .	.	614
Faesulae, walls of . .	. .	595
Falerii (old gate of citadel)	. .	350
Fasces (coin) . . .	.	273
Faun of Praxiteles . .	. .	203
Faustulus (coin) . .	.	141
Feronia " . .	.	204
Fides " .	. .	222
Flora " . .	.	623
Flute-player	.	436
Fortuna (statue in the Vatican)	.	201
" Virilis, tetrastyle temple of		202
Frater Arvalis . . .	.	225
Frentani, coin of the .	.	98
Furia, *gens*, tomb of the .	.	600
Futile (vase of the Vestals)	.	227
Gabii, treaty with (coin) .	.	181
Gallic chariot		452
" *torquis*		379
Garlands of leaves around a temple (coin)		221
Gaul, wounded		376
Gaulos (coin of)		536
Gauls		364
Gela, coin of		462
" " "		556
Gladiator (gem) .		625
Good Success (coin) .		124
Greek tomb-reliefs . .		578
Grinder, statue of the .	.	175
Group from the Villa Ludovisi	.	599
Hannibal		652
Haruspex (bas-relief) .		671
Heracleia, coin of .		466
Ilicetas, " "	.	461
Hiero II. " " .		553
Honor and Virtue (coin) .	. .	603
Hope		305
" (cameo) . .		316
Horatia, *gens*, coin of . . .	.	176
Horatius Cocles (medallion) .	.	176
Issa, coin of		592
Italy (coin)		17
Janus (coin)		149
" "		135
Juno		672
" Lucina (coin) . .	.	163
" Moneta " . .	.	630
" nursing Hercules . .		200
" of Herculaneum . .		236
" Sospita (coin) . .	.	422
Jupiter, head of . . .	.	127
" (intaglio) . . .	.	347
" Capitolinus, temple of (coin)	.	251
" Feretrius, ruins of temple of	.	354
" of Herculaneum .	.	236
Knight holding his horse (coin)		411
Lacinian Cape, the . .	.	463
Lares		207
" (coin)		271
Larinum, coin of . .		681
Laus " " . .	.	111
Lectisternium (coin) . .		234
" seat for a .		387
Liberty (coin) . . .		524
Libya, coin of . .		533
Lilybaeum, coin of .		548
Lipari " " . .		555
Lucania " " .		104
Lucumon's helmet .		78
Maccus		621
Malta, coin of . .		535
Mamertines, the, coin of .	.	556
Mamilia, *gens* " " .		179
Marcellus (coin) .		602
Marcia, *gens*, coin of		150
Mars (coin) . .		199
" sacrifices to . . .		126
Matri Magnae (coin) . .		204
Merchant vessel under sail (gem)		426
Mercury		613
" found at Palestrina		196
Messina, coin of .		553
" Straits of (map)	.	554
Metapontum, coin of .		33
" ruins of the temple of	.	107
Metellus (coin) . . .		560
Milestone		278

ALPHABETICAL INDEX TO TEXT ILLUSTRATIONS.

Minerva of Herculaneum	236
Municipium, coin of a	484
Naples, coin of	485
Navius, miracle of (coin)	160
Nola, coin of	485
" vase of	651
Nomentum, bridge of	234
Nuceria, coin of	486
Numa Pompilius, traditional figure of	147
Nuraghe of Sori	530
Ops (coin)	124
Order of battle (plan)	517
Paestum, coin of	426
Palatine, ancient substructions of	188
Palladium, the (coin)	228
Pallor "	156
Paludamentum	673
Panormus, coin of	571
Pelasgic remains	47
Pharos, coin of	593
Phintias " "	461
Pilum	515
Ploughman	260
" Tuscan	69
Po, present state of the coast south of (map)	30
Pomegranate (*ex-voto*)	541
Pontine Marshes, present state of (map)	32
Populonia, coin of	36
" " "	76
Praeneste, bronze group found at	259
" chest " "	480
" " lid of " "	615
" Phoenician cup found at	300
Praxiteles, the Faun of	203
Priest of Apollo	636
" presenting incense-box	336
Prisoner (gem)	308
Ptolemy IV., Euergetes (coin)	603
" Philadelphus "	472
Punic ships, figures at prow of	538
Puteal of Libo (coin)	259
Pyrrhus	465
" coin of	464
Regillus, Lake, battle of (coin)	179
Regulus "	506
Rhea Sylvia "	141
Rhegium, coin of	557
Roman bracelet	146
" camp (plan)	518
" galley	562
Roman horse-soldier	513
" soldier	511
" "	512
Rome, followed by a magistrate	351
" seated upon the Seven Hills (coin)	180
" and the She-wolf (coin)	142
Romulus, traditional figure of	143
Rostra, the (coin)	422
Rostral columns	563
Rutulians, coin of the	90
Sabines, rape of the (coin)	186
Sacred tree,	216
Sacrifice, instruments of	223
Sacrifices, human	375
Saguntum, remains of theatre of	656
Salian priest (coin)	149
Samnite horseman	442
" warrior	100
" "	440
" "	441
Samnium, coin of	101
Santa Maria di Leuca, Cape	23
Sardinia, coin of	530
Saturn, temple of	148
Saturnus	138
" (coin)	138
Scipio Barbatus, tomb of	448
Segesta, coin of	557
Selinus " "	571
" remains of	573
" temple of (frieze)	568
" " " (metope)	570
" " " "	572
" " " "	574
" " " archaic metope	579
Servilius Ahala, coin of	348
Servius Tullius, *agger* or rampart of	161
" " " " (section)	163
" " wall of	162
Sezze	313
" ruins of a temple near	314
She-wolf of the Capitol	626
Shield, votive	459
Shrine, entrance of a	123
Sicily, coin of	552
" (map)	550
Sidon, coin of	530
Signia, gate of	169
Stola	266
Suessa, coin of	423
Sun-dial	628
Suovetaurilia	233
"	507

ALPHABETICAL INDEX TO TEXT ILLUSTRATIONS. 23

Sutrium, amphitheatre of . . .	372
Sybaris, coin of . . .	45
Sylvanus (coin)	262
Tanit, the goddess . . .	539
" " " temple of . .	542
Taormina, theatre of	586
" view of	587
Tarentum, coin of . . .	485
" harbor of (plan) . .	462
Tarpeia (coin)	145
Tarpeian rock	335
Tarquius, tomb of the . . .	179
Tatius, traditional figure of . .	146
Tauromenium, coin of . . .	575
Tente " " . .	98
Teatro Greco, Taormina . .	590
Temesa, coin of	215
Terina, " "	102
Terminus, the god . .	119
Terror (coin)	156
Thrasimene, Lake (map) . .	674
Thunderbolt with eight forks (coin) .	127
" " twelve " " .	127
Thurii, coin of the . . .	104
Tiber (coin)	204
Toga, Roman in a	133

Torquis, Gallic	379
Triquetra, the (coin) . . .	553
Tuccia, the Vestal	229
Tuder, as of . . .	57
" coin of	57
Twelve gods, altar of the . . .	678
" " " bas-reliefs of .	677
Tusculum (restored) . . .	303
" (present state) . .	304
Veii, city of (plan)	306
Venus Erycina (coin) . . .	564
Venusia, coin of	23
Vesta (coin)	221
" "	234
Vestal " " . . .	227
Vestals " "	230
Victory, statue of . . .	680
Volaterra, gate of . . .	81
Volscians, coin of the . . .	92
Vulcan of Elba, the . . .	128
War-vessel with beak-head (gem) .	444
" " " double beak-head (coin)	561
Women spinning . . .	261
Youth (coin)	125

INTRODUCTION.

THE PRE-ROMAN EPOCH.

I.

THE GEOGRAPHY OF ITALY.

COIN OF ANTONINUS REPRESENTING ITALY.[1]

HORACE was afraid of the sea; he called it *Oceanus dissociabilis*, the element which separates; and yet it was, even for the ancients, the element which unites.

Looking at the mountains which run from Galicia to the Caucasus, from Armenia to the Persian Gulf, from the region of the Syrtes to the Pillars of Hercules, we recognize the higher parts of an immense basin, the bottom of which is filled by the Mediterranean. These limits, marked out by geography, are also, for antiquity, the limits of history, which never, save towards Persia,

---

[1] The letters TR. POT., an abbreviation of *Tribunicia Potestas*, signify the tribunician power with which the Emperors were invested; the letters COS. III. mean that Antoninus was, or had been, Consul for the third time; and S. C. that it was by order of the Senate, "Senatus Consulto," that the piece of money was coined. Antoninus having had his third Consulship in A. D. 140, and the fourth in 145, the medal was issued during one of the years which intervene between these dates. The Senate of the Empire only coined bronze money. The first *trib. pot.* dated from the day of the prince's accession: since Trajan's time, all are dated from the 1st of January; hence the number of the *trib. pot.* gives the number of the years of the reign.

departed far from the coasts of the Mediterranean. Without this sea, the space it occupies would have been the continuation of the African Sahara, — an impassable desert; by means of it, on the contrary, the people settled on its shores have interchanged their ideas and their wealth; and if we except those ancient societies of the distant East which always have remained apart from European progress, it is around this coast that the first civilized nations have dwelt. Italy, therefore, by its position, between Greece, Spain, and Gaul, and by its elongated shape, which extends almost to the shores of Africa and towards the East, is in truth the centre of the ancient world, — at once the nearest point to the three continents which the Mediterranean washes and unites. Geography explains only a portion of history; but that portion it explains well, — the rest belongs to men. According as they show in their administration wisdom or folly, they turn to good or evil the work of nature. The situation of Italy, therefore, will easily account for her varied destinies in ancient times, and in modern up to a recent period; it will account for the vigor and energy she manifested outside her limits, so long as her inhabitants formed a united people, surrounded by divided tribes; later, for the evils which overwhelmed her from all points of the horizon, when her power was exhausted and her unity destroyed, — it accounts for Italy, in a word, mistress of the world around her, and Italy. the prize for which all her neighbors contend.

There is another important consideration. If the position occupied by Italy at the very centre of the ancient world favored her fortune in the days of her strength, and procured her so many enemies in the time of her weakness, was not this very weakness, which at first delivered the peninsula to the Romans, and after them, for fourteen centuries, to the stranger, chiefly due to her natural conformation?

Surrounded on three sides by the sea, and on the fourth by the Alps, Italy is a peninsula which stretches towards the south in two points; while at the north it widens into a semicircle of lofty mountains, above which towers majestically, with its sparkling snow, the summit sometimes called by the Lombards "La Rosa dell' Italia." The summit next in height to Mont Blanc is this Monte Rosa; it is not six hundred feet lower than the

MONTE ROSA

giant of Europe.[1] Italy, then, is in part peninsular, and in part continental, the two regions being distinct in origin, configuration, and history. The one, a vast plain traversed by the great river whose alluvia have formed it, has been in all ages the battle-field of European ambitions; the other, a narrow mountain-chain, cut into deep ravines by countless torrents, and torn by volcanic shocks, has almost always had an opposite destiny.

This peninsula is the true Italy, and it is one of the most divided countries in the world. In its innumerable valleys, many of which are almost shut off from the outside world, its population grew into that love of independence which mountain races have manifested in all time; but, with it, into that need of an isolated life which so often endangers the much-loved liberty: in every valley, a state; for every village, a god. Never would Italy have emerged from obscurity had there not been developed in the midst of these tribes an energetic principle of association. By dint of skill, courage, and perseverance, the Roman Senate and its legions triumphed over physical obstacles as well as over the interests and passions which had grown up behind their shelter, and united all the Italian peoples, making of the whole peninsula one city.

But, like the oak half-cleft by Milon, which springs together when the strength of the old athlete gives way, and seizes him in turn, Nature, for a time conquered by Roman energy, resumed its sway; and when Rome fell, Italy, left to herself, returned to her endless divisions, until the day when the modern idea of great nationalities accomplished for her what, twenty-three centuries earlier, had been done by the ablest statesmanship, served by the most powerful of military organizations.

By her geographical position, then, Italy was destined to have an important share in the world's history, whether acting outside her own territory, or herself becoming the prize of heroic struggles. Nor is Rome an accident, a chance, in the peninsula's history; Rome is the moment when the Italian peoples, for the first time united, obtained the object promised to their joint efforts, — the power which springs from union. Doubtless History has often been compelled to say with Napoleon: "Italy is too long and too much divided." But

[1] Mount Elbourz, in the Caucasus, is now known to be the highest (eighteen thousand five hundred feet).

when from the Alps to the Maltese Channel there was but one people and one interest, an incomparable prosperity became the glorious lot of this beautiful land, with its two thousand miles of sea-coast, its brave population of sailors and mountaineers, its natural harbors and fertile districts at the foot of its forest-covered hills, and its command of two seas, holding as it did the key of the passage from one to the other of the two great Mediterranean basins. Between the East, now breaking up in anarchy, and the West, not yet alive to civilization, Italy, united and disciplined, naturally took the place of command. This phase of humanity required ten centuries for its birth and growth and complete development; and the story of these ten centuries we call the History of Rome.

A modern poet gives in a single line an exact description of this country, —

"Ch' Apennin parte e 'l mar circonda e l' Alpe." [1]

That portion of the Alpine chain which separates Italy from the rest of Europe extends in an irregular curving line from Savona to Fiume, a distance of about seven hundred and fifteen miles; the breadth of this mountain mass is from eighty to ninety-five miles in the region of the St. Gothard and the Septimer (the Pennine Alps), and rather more than one hundred and sixty miles in the Tyrol [2] (the Rhaetian Alps). The perpetual snows of these high summits form huge glaciers, which feed the streams of Upper Italy, and trace a glittering outline against the sky. But the watershed, lying nearer Italy than Germany, divides the mass unevenly. Like all the great European mountain-chains,[3] the Alps have their more gentle slope towards the North, — whence have come all the invasions, — and their escarpment towards the South, — which has received them all.[4] Upon the side of France and Germany the mountains run to

---

[1] "Which the Apennine divides, and the sea and the Alps surround."

[2] From St. Gothard to the Straits of Messina, Italy measures 625 miles, with a mean breadth of from 88 to 100 miles; in area, 185,000 square miles.

[3] With the exception of the Caucasus, whose northern slope is much steeper than that of the south.

[4] This is true, especially for the Maritime, Cottian, Graian, and Pennine Alps; but the Helvetian and Rhaetian Alps send forth to the south long spurs, forming the high valleys of the Ticino, of the Adda, the Adige, and the Brenta. Geographically, these valleys belong to Italy (canton of the Ticino, the Valteline, and part of the Tyrol); but they have always been inhabited by races foreign to the peninsula, which have never protected her against invasions from the north.

the plain by long spurs, which break the descent, while from the Piedmont side Mont Blanc appears like a wall of granite, sheer for about ten thousand feet down from its summit. Man stops at the foot of these cliffs, on which hold neither grass nor snow; and Northern Italy, having little Alpine pasture-land, is not like the Dauphiné, Switzerland, and the Tyrol,[1] defended by a race of brave mountaineers.

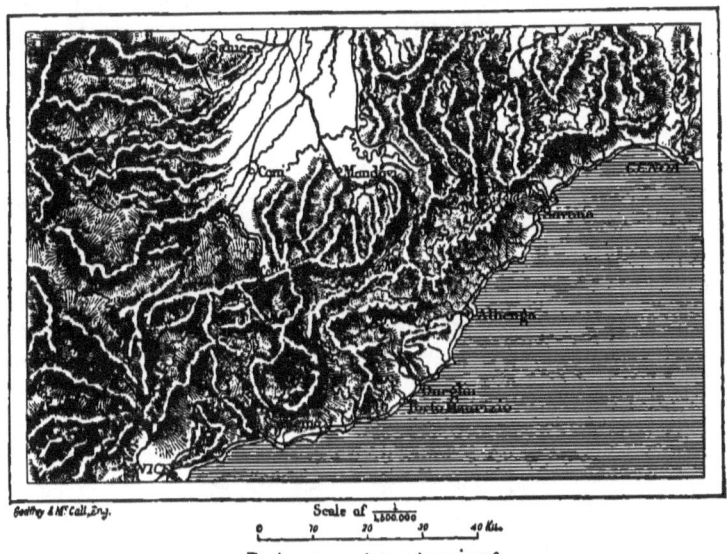

THE LIMIT OF THE ALPS & APENNINES.[2]

This difference between the incline and extent of the two sides indicates one of the causes which insured the first successes of the expeditions directed against Italy. Once masters of the northern side, the invaders had only a march of a day or two

---

[1] These Alps are covered with beautiful forests, which Venice at the time of her power turned to profit; intractable mountaineers live there, like the inhabitants of the Sette Communi. One of the characteristics of the Julian Alps is the number of grottos and subterranean channels which they embrace. From the River Isonzo to the frontiers of Bosnia there are more than a thousand; and the natives of the country say that there are as many streams below the soil as there are over it. Channels of this kind, when not filled with water, afford an entry into the Sette Communi.

[2] The question of the boundary between the Alps and the Apennines has been long a subject of debate; the engineers have decided it by making a railroad above Savona over the Col d' Altase, which is not sixteen hundred feet in height, whence one descends into the famous valleys of the Bormida and the Tanaro.

to bring them into the richest country.[1] Thus Italy has never been able to escape from invasions or to keep aloof from European wars, despite her formidable barrier of the Alps, with their colossal summits, "which, when seen close," said Napoleon, "seem like giants of ice commissioned to defend the approach to that beautiful country."[2]

The Alps are joined, near Savona, by the Apennines, which traverse the whole peninsula, or rather, which have formed it and given it its character. Their mean height in Liguria is 1,000 mètres (3,275 feet); but in Tuscany they are much higher, where the ridges of Pontremoli, between Sarzana and Parma, of Fiumalbo, between Lucca and Modena, of Futa, between Florence and Bologna, attain the height of 3,300 to 3,900 feet. Thus Etruria was protected for a long time by these mountains against the Cis-Alpine Gauls, and for some months against Hannibal.

The highest summits of the whole chain of the Apennines are to the east of Rome, in the country of the Marsians and the Vestini: Velino, 8,180 feet; and Monte Corno, 9,520 feet, whence can be seen the two seas which wash Italy, and even the mountains of Illyria, on the eastern shore of the Adriatic. At this height a peak of the Alps or the Pyrenees would be covered with perpetual snow; in the climate of Rome it is not cold enough to form a glacier, and Monte Corno loses its snow at the end of July; but it always preserves its Alpine landscape, with the bears and the chamois of great mountains.

Three branches separate at the west from the central chain, and cover with their ramifications a considerable part of Etruria, Latium, and Campania. One of these branches, after sinking to the level of the plain, rises at its extremity in a nearly detached rock forming the promontory of Circe (Monte Circello), where is shown the grotto of the mighty sorceress. Tiberius, who on the question of demons believed neither in those of the past nor in those of the present, had a villa built near this dreaded spot.

[1] Augustus understood it; and in order to defend Italy, he carried the Roman outposts as far as the Danube. Marius also had gone beyond the Alps to meet the Cimbri; while Catulus, who wished only to defend the Italian side, was forced to retreat without a battle behind the Po. Thus it was not in the mountains, but behind the Adige, that General Bonaparte established his line of defence in 1796.

[2] Cicero, *de Prov. Consul.* 14, said more simply: "Alpibus Italiam muniverat antea natura, non sine aliquo divino numine."

THE GEOGRAPHY OF ITALY.

From the eastern side of the Apennines there are only some hills detached, which descend straight towards the Adriatic. But, like Vesuvius on the opposite coast (3,948 feet), Monte Gargano forms, over the Gulf of Manfredonia, a solitary group, of which one summit rises to the height of 5,283 feet. Ancient forests cover this mountain, ever beaten by the furious winds which toss the Adriatic.

Below Venosa (Venusia) the Apennines separate into two branches, which surround the Gulf of Taranto; the one runs through the land of Bari and Otranto, and ends in a gentle slope at Capo di Leuca; the other forms, through the two Calabrias, a succession of

COIN OF VENUSIA.[1]

undulated table-lands, one of which, the Sila, 4,910 feet[2] high, is not less than fifty miles long from Cosenza to Catanzaro. Covered

CAPE SANTA MARIA DI LEUCA.

formerly with impenetrable forests, the Sila was the shelter of fugitive slaves (Bruttians), and was the last retreat of Hannibal in Italy. Now fine pastures have partly taken the place of

[1] On the obverse the head of Jupiter; on the reverse, an eagle bearing a thunderbolt; the letters AE (AES) signify that the piece is bronze money, and the five ooooo that it was a quincunx, that is to say, that it weighed 5 oz., — the *as libralis*, or Roman pound, weighing 12 oz. Rome never struck the quincunx; it was found only in the South of Italy.

[2] The highest top of the Sila, the Monte Nero, is nearly six thousand feet high.

these forests, whence Rome and Syracuse obtained their timber. But the temperature there is always low for an Italian country, and notwithstanding its position in latitude 38°, snow remains during six months of the year.[1] Still farther to the south, one of the summits of the Aspromonte measures 4,368 feet high. Furthermore, while beyond Capo di Leuca there is only the Ionian Sea, beyond the lighthouse of Messina we come to Etna and the triangle of the Sicilian mountains, — an evident continuation of the chain of the Apennines.

The two slopes of the Apennines do not differ less than the two sides of the Alps.[2] On the narrow shore which is washed by the Upper, or Adriatic, Sea, are rich pasture-lands, woody hills, separated by the deep beds of torrents, a flat shore, no ports (*importuosum litus*),[3] no islands, and a stormy sea, inclosed between two chains of mountains, like a long valley where the winds are pent in, and rage at every obstacle they meet. On the western side, on the contrary, the Apennines are more remote from the sea, and great plains, watered by tranquil rivers, great gulfs, natural harbors, numerous islands, as well as a sea usually calm, promote agriculture, navigation, and commerce. Hence a population of three distinct and opposite kinds: mariners about the ports, husbandmen in the plains, and shepherds in the mountains; or, to call them by their historical names, the Italiotes and Etruscans, Rome and the Latins, the Marsians and the Samnites.[4]

Yet these plains of Campania, of Latium, of Etruria, and of Apulia, notwithstanding their extent, cover but a very small part of

---

[1] Bruguière, *Orographie de l'Europe*.

[2] However, Apulia, with its extinct volcano, its great plains, its Lake Lesina, its marshes, situated to the north and to the south of Mount Gargano; beyond this the marshy but extremely fertile lands watered by the Gulf of Taranto; lastly, the numerous harbors of this coast, — reproduce some of the features of the western coast.

[3] All the islands of the Adriatic, with the exception of the unimportant group of the Tremiti, are on the Illyrian coast, where they form an inextricable labyrinth, the resort of pirates, who have in all times levied contributions on the commerce of the Adriatic.

[4] All the extinct as well as active volcanoes are west of the Apennines, except Mount Vultur in Apulia. It is these numerous volcanoes which have driven the sea far from the foot of the Apennines, and have enlarged this coast, whereas the opposite shore, where not a single volcano is to be seen, is so narrow; whence come also those lakes in the midst of ancient craters, and perhaps a part of the marshes. It is known that in 1538 the Lucrine Lake was changed into a marsh by a volcanic eruption. The lowest part of the Pontine Marshes is on a line joining Stromboli to the ancient craters of Bolsena and Vico.

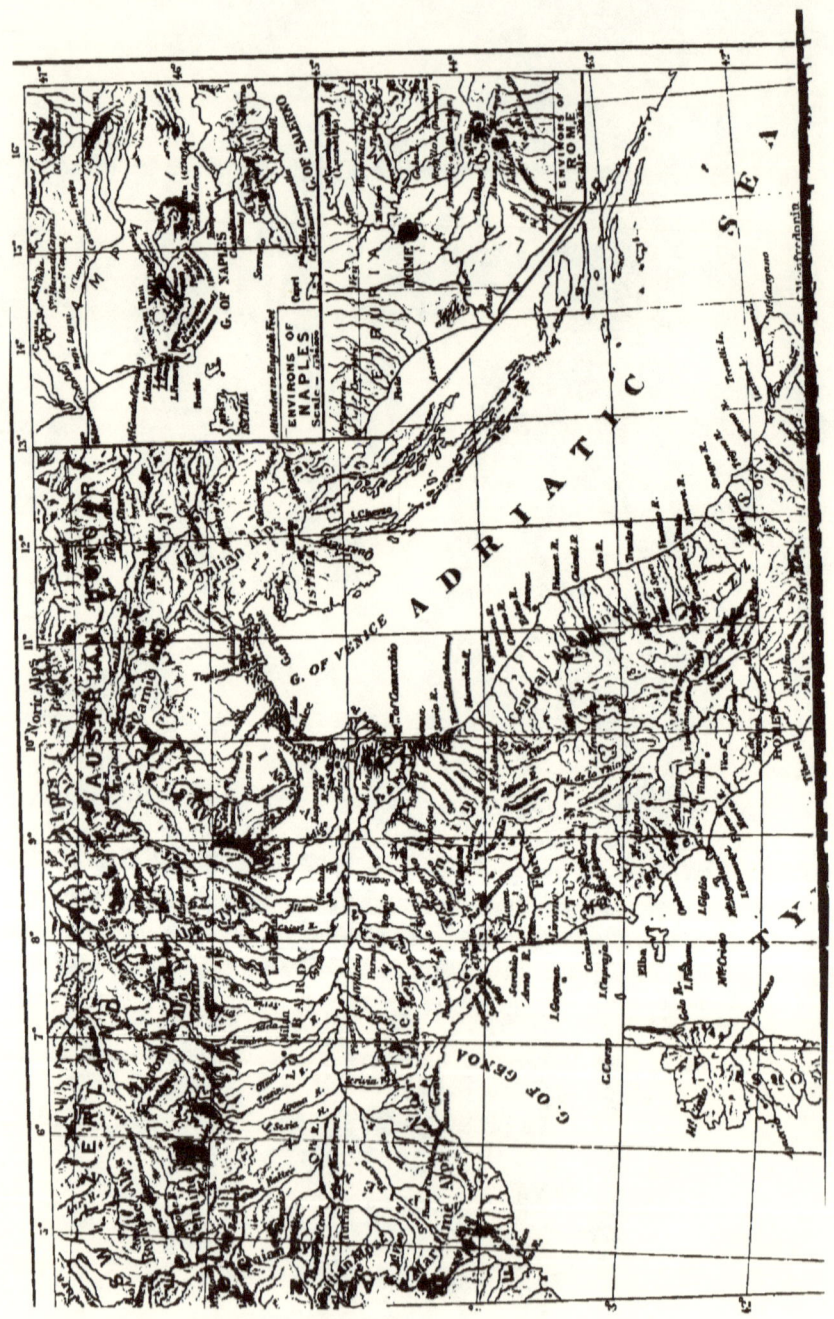

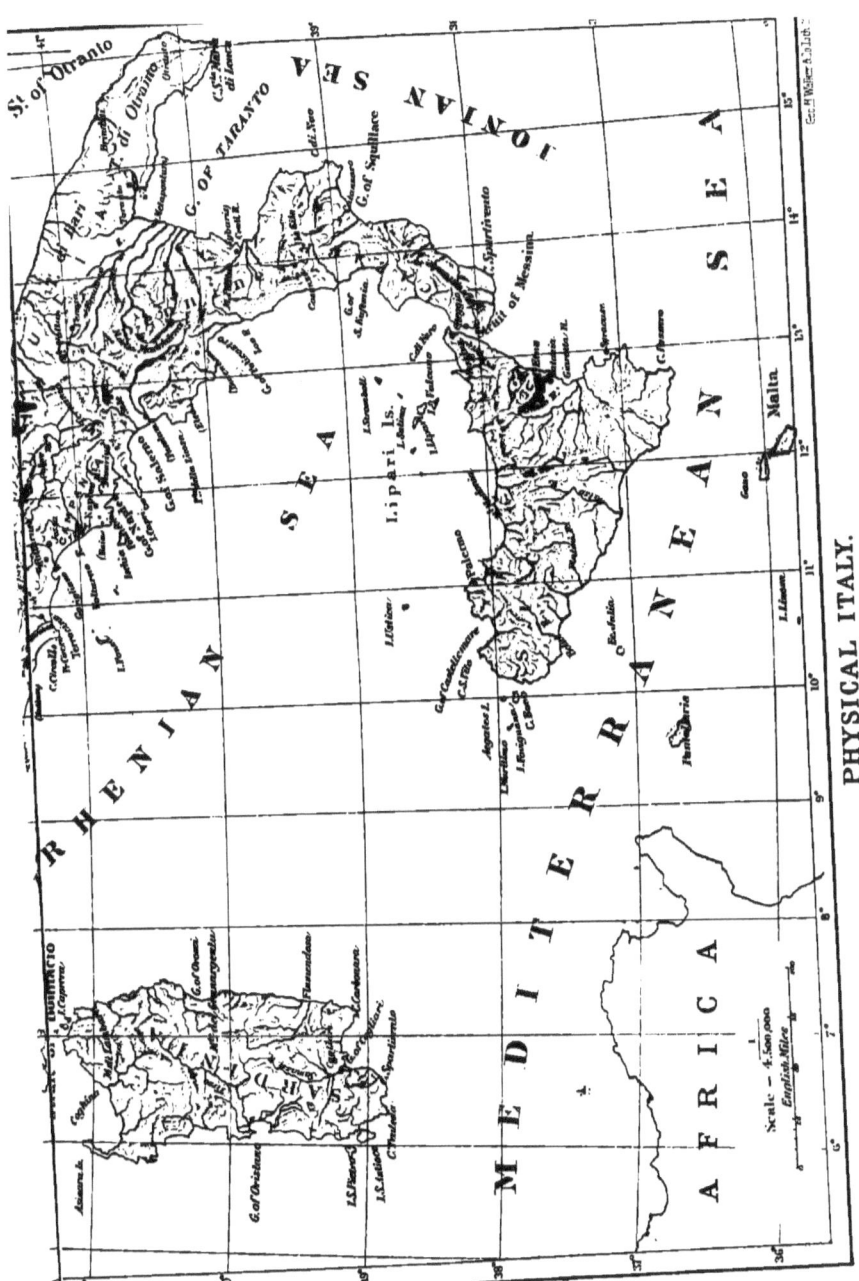

PHYSICAL ITALY.

a peninsula which may be described generally as a country bristling with mountains and intersected by deep valleys. Why need we wonder at persistent political divisions in a country so divided by Nature herself? — Aelian counted up as many as 1,197 cities, each of which had possessed, or aspired to, an independent existence.

The Apennines possess neither glaciers, nor great rivers, nor the pointed peaks of the Alps, nor the colossal masses of the Pyrenees. Yet their summits, bare and rugged, their flanks often stripped and barren, the deep and wild ravines which furrow them, all contrast with the soft outlines and the rich vegetation of the sub-Apennine mountains. Add to this, at every step, beautiful ruins, recalling splendid traditions, the brightness of the sky, great lakes, rivers which tumble from the mountains, volcanoes with cities at their foot, and everywhere along the horizon the sparkling sea, calm and smooth, or terrible when its waves, lashed by the Sirocco, or by submarine convulsions, buffet the shore, and beat now upon Amalfi, now upon Baiae or Paestum.

Europe has no active volcanoes but in the peninsula and islands of Italy. In ancient times, subterranean fires were at work from the Carinthian Alps, where are found some rocks of igneous origin: these reach as far as the Island of Malta, a part of which has sunk into the sea.[1]

The basaltic mountains of Southern Tyrol and of the districts of Verona, Vicenza, and Padua; near the Po the catastrophe of Velleja buried by an earthquake; in Tuscany subterranean noises, continual shocks, and those sudden disturbances which made Etruria the land of prodigies; on the banks of the Tiber the tradition of Cacus vomiting forth flames,[2] the gulf of Curtius, the volcanic matter which forms the very soil of Rome, and of all its hills, the Janiculum excepted; the streams of lava from the hills of Alba and Tusculum; the immense crater (thirty-eight miles in circumference), the sunken edge of which shows us the charming lake of Albano and that of Nemi, which the Romans used to call

---

[1] The *Travels* of Major de Valenthienne. The volcanic action used to reach still farther in the same direction. Many extinct volcanoes and lava are found in the regency of Tunis towards El-Kef (Sicca Veneria). Cf. *La Régence de Tunis*, by M. Pelissier de Reynaud.

[2] This legend is true so far as concerns the recollection of the volcanic eruptions of Latium, but it is false in placing them on the Aventine, the abode of Cacus.

the Mirror of Diana; the legend of Caeculus building at Praeneste walls of flames; the enormous pile of lava and debris on the sides of Mount Vultur;[1] the islands rising from the sea, of which Livy speaks; the Phlegraean fields, the ancient eruptions of the Island of Ischia, of Vesuvius, and of Etna, and so many extinct craters, —all these show that the whole of Italy was once situated on an immense volcanic centre.

At the present time the activity of the subterranean fires seems to be concentrated in the middle of this line, in Vesuvius, whose eruptions are always threatening the charming towns which insist on remaining close to this formidable neighbor; in Etna, which, in one of its convulsions, tore away Sicily from Italy;[2] and in the Lipari Islands, situated in the centre of the seismic sphere of the Mediterranean. In the north we find only craters half filled up,[3] —the volcanic hills of Rome, of Viterbo, and of St. Agatha, near Sessa; the hot streams and springs of Tuscany; the fires or "hot springs" of Pietra, Mala, and Barigazzo; and lastly those of the "Orto dell' Inferno," the Garden of Hell.[4]

Before the year 79 A. D. Vesuvius appeared to be an extinct volcano; population and culture had reached its summit; when, suddenly reviving, it buried Herculaneum, Pompeii, and Stabiae under an enormous mass of ashes and dust. In the year 472, according to Procopius, such was the violence of the eruption, that the ashes were carried by the winds as far as Constantinople. In 1794 one of these streams of incandescent lava, which are sometimes eight miles long, from 300 to 1,200 feet in breadth, and from twenty-four to thirty feet in depth, destroyed the beautiful town of Torre del Greco. Stones were hurled to the distance of 1,300 yards; vegetation far away was destroyed by mephitic gases; and within a radius of ten miles people went with torches at midday.

[1] Tata (*Lett. sul Monte Volture*), considers this extinct crater as one of the most terrible of pre-historic Italy.
[2] The name of the town of Rhegium (now Reggio), on the Strait, signifies "rupture."
[3] Lakes Avernus, Lucrine, Albano, Nemi, Gabii, Regillo, San Giuliano, Bracciano, etc. Earthquakes are still frequent in the neighborhood of Belluna and Bassano.
[4] With regard to the "Salse" of the neighborhood of Parma, Reggio (di Emilia), Modena, and Bologna, which are also called volcanoes of mud, we must not confound them with true volcanoes, although they possess some of the features of volcanic eruptions. In the Salse, carburetted hydrogen, the inflammable gas of the marshes, predominates.

NAPLES AND MOUNT VESUVIUS.

Humboldt has observed that the frequency of the eruptions varies inversely with the size of the volcano. Since the crater of Vesuvius has diminished, its eruptions, though less violent, have become almost annual. Its terrors are no more, its curiosity remains. Rich travellers come from all parts, and the Neapolitans, who have short memories, while exhuming Herculaneum and Pompeii, say of their volcano, "It is the mountain which vomits gold."

In 1669 the inhabitants of Catania had likewise ceased to believe in the old tales of the fury of Etna, when an immense stream of lava came down upon their town, passed through the walls, and formed in the sea a gigantic mole in front of the harbor Fortunately this formidable volcano, whose base is 113 miles in circumference, from whose summit there is a view of 750 miles in extent, and which has grown, by excessive piles of lava, to the height of 10,870 feet, has very rarely any eruptions. Stromboli, on the contrary, in the Lipari Islands, shows from afar by night its diadem of fire, by day a dense mantle of smoke.

Enclosed between Etna, Vesuvius, and Stromboli, as in a triangle of fire, Southern Italy is often shaken to her foundations. During the last three centuries no less than a thousand earthquakes are recorded, as if that part of the peninsula were lying on a bed of moving lava. That of 1538[1] cleft the soil near Pozzuoli, and there came forth from it Monte Nuovo, 450 feet high, which filled up the Lucrine Lake, now only marked by a small pond. In 1783 the whole of Calabria was wrecked, and forty thousand people perished. The sea itself shared these horrible convulsions; it receded, and then returned 42 feet above its level. Sometimes new islands appear; thus have risen one after another the Lipari Islands. In 1831 an English man-of-war, on the open sea off the coast of Sicily, felt some violent shocks, and it was thought she had grounded: it was a new volcano opening. Some days after an island appeared, about 230 feet high. The English and the Neapolitans were already disputing its ownership, when the sea took back in a storm the volcano's gift.[2]

[1] Livy speaks (iv. 21) of numerous earthquakes in Central Italy and in Rome itself in 434. The overflowing of the Alban Lake during the war with the Veientines is perhaps due to an event of this kind.

[2] In these same parts the cable from Cagliari to Malta was twice broken in 1858 near Marctimo by submarine eruptions.

For Southern Italy the danger lies in subterranean fires; for Northern and Western Italy it lies in water, either stagnant and pestilential, or overflowing and inundating the country and filling up the ports with sand. From Turin to Venice, in the rich plain watered by the Po, between the Apennines and the Alps, not a single hill is to be seen; and consequently the torrents, which rush down from the belt of snowy mountains, expose it to dreadful ravages by their inundations.[1] These torrents have, indeed, created the whole plain, by filling up with alluvial deposits the gulf which the Adriatic Sea had formed there, and whose existence is proved by the remains of marine animals found in the environs of Piacenza and Milan,[2] as well as by the sea-fish which still haunt its lakes.

Springing from Mount Viso, and rapidly swelled by the waters which run down from the slopes of the Alpine Giant,[3] the Po is the greatest river of Italy, and one of the most celebrated in the world. If it had a free outlet into the Adriatic, it would open to navigation and commerce a magnificent territory. But the condition of all rivers flowing into seas which, like the Mediterranean, have no tides, renders them unfit for sea navigation. The Italian torrents bring to the Po quantities of mud and sand, which raise its bed,[4] and form at its mouth that delta before which the sea recedes each year about 220 feet.

Adria, which preceded Venice in the command of the Adriatic, is at the present day more than 19 miles inland; Spina, another

---

[1] ". . . Sic aggeribus ruptis quum spumeus amnis,
Exiit oppositasque evicit gurgite moles,
Fertur in arva furens . . .
Cum stabulis armenta tulit."
VERGIL: *Aeneid*, ii. 496.

[2] Ramazzini believed also that the whole country of Modena covers a subterranean lake. This would explain the prodigy, which startled the whole Senate, of fish which came forth from the earth under the ploughshare of the Boian peasant. Near Narbonne there had also been a subterranean lake, where they used to fish with a lance. Cf. Strabo, IV. i, 6. They are found in many places.

[3] The height of Mount Viso is 12,550 feet. The tributaries of the Po: on the right bank, the Tanaro, the Trebbia, whose banks have been the scene of great battles; the Reno, where was the Island of the Triumvirs; on the left bank, the Ticino, the Adda, the largest tributary of the Po, the Oglio, and the Mincio.

[4] Napoleon I. thought of having a new bed dug for the Po; for in its present state imminent dangers threaten the country which it traverses in the lower part of its course, where the rising of its bed has caused a rise in the level of the waters, which overflow the surface of the country.. (De Prony, *Recherches sur le Système hydraulique de l'Italie*.) During the last two centuries only, M. de Prony has calculated the prolongation of the delta by 230 feet a year.

great seaport, was in the time of Strabo 30 stadia from the coast, which in former times it used to touch;[1] and Ravenna, the station of the imperial fleet, is now surrounded by woods and marshes. Venice, also, has too long suffered the channels of its lagoons to be stopped up by the alluvium of the Brenta. The port of Lido, from which the fleet which carried forty thousand Crusaders went forth, is now only navigable for small boats, and that of Albiola is called the "Porto secco" (dry port).

The north-east extremity of Italy is surrounded by a semicircle of mountains, which send forth to the Adriatic several streams, whose ravine-beds afford an easy defence against any invasion from the Julian Alps. Of all these obstacles the last and most formidable is the Adige, a broad and mighty river at its very departure from the mountains.

In peninsular Italy

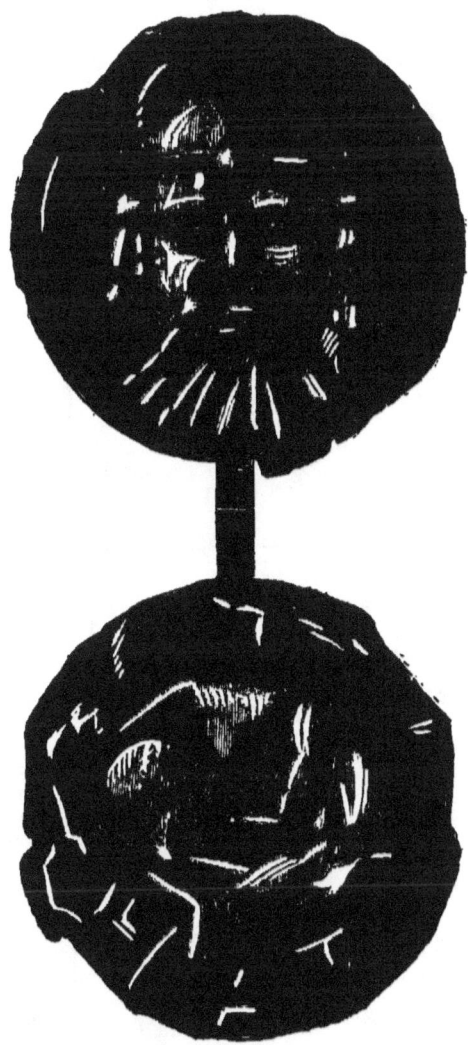

AS OF ADRIA.[2]

[1] Strabo, V. i, 7. It had a treasure-house at Delphi, and is conjectured to be the present village of Spina.

[2] We cannot say whether this medal, one of the beautiful bronzes of the French National

the Apennines are too near both seas to send them great rivers. However, the Arno is 75 miles long, and the Tiber 190 miles. But this king of ancient rivers is sad to look at. Its waters, constantly filled with reddish mud, cannot be used for drinking or bathing; and in order to supply the deficiency, numerous aqueducts brought into Rome the water of the neighboring mountains. Hence one of the characteristics of Roman architecture: triumphal arches and military roads for the legions; amphitheatres and aqueducts for the towns. Moreover all the watercourses of the Apennines have the capricious

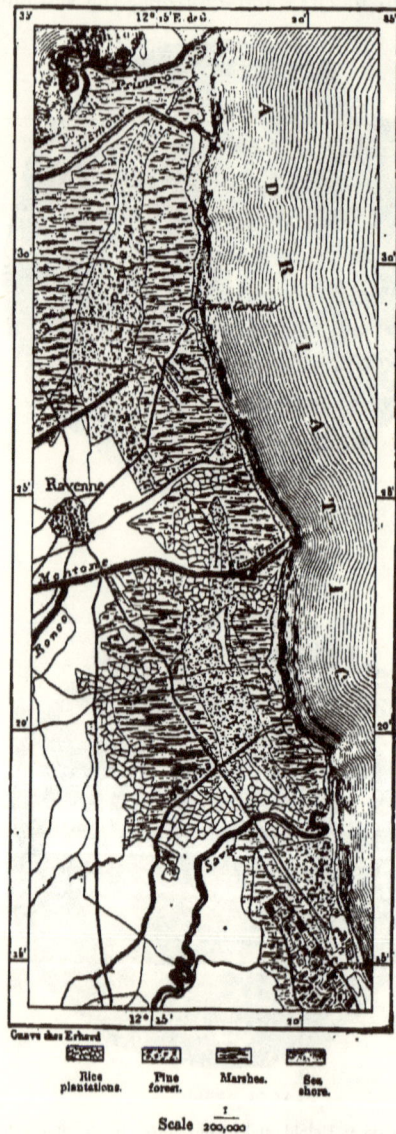

PRESENT STATE OF COAST TO THE SOUTH OF THE MOUTHS OF THE PO.

Collection, and which bears the head of a bearded Bacchus, belongs to Adria on the borders of the Po, or to that of Picenum. The character of the three letters on this piece, H A T (for Hadria), shows that it cannot be earlier than the third century before our era. The "as" denoted with the Romans the monetary unit. It ought exactly to weigh a Roman pound; that is, exactly twelve ounces, or 288 scruples, — whence the name *as libralis*. The real weight, however, on the average, is not more than ten ounces. The Romans have without doubt kept to this usage, because ten ounces of bronze were worth in Italy a scruple of silver, or $\frac{1}{288}$ of a silver pound. (Mommsen's *Hist. of Roman Coinage*.)

[1] The Adige, 250 miles in length, the Bacchiglione 62, the Brenta 112, the Piave 129, the Tagliamento 33, the Isonzo 56.

MONTE CIRCELLO.

character of torrents:[1] wide and rapid in spring-time, they dry up in summer, and are at all times almost useless for navigation.[2] But how beautiful and picturesque is the scenery along the banks of their streams, and in the valleys where their tributaries descend! The waterfalls of Tivoli, the most charming of sights, make a delightful contrast to the wild grandeur of the Roman campagna; and near Terni, at the Cascade delle Marmore, the Velino falls into the Nera from a vertical height of 540 feet, then rushes in cataracts over the huge bowlders which it has brought down from the mountain.

All the lakes of Upper Italy are, like those of Switzerland, hollow valleys. (Lake Maggiore, 39 square miles; Como, 35; Iseo, 14; Garda, 34), where the streams from the mountains have accumulated till they have found in the belt of rocks and land the depression whence they have made their escape and given rise to rivers. Those of the peninsula, on the contrary, filling up ancient craters or mountain basins, have no natural outlets, and often threaten, after long rains, or the melting of the snow, to inundate the surrounding country: such were the overflowing of Lake Albano, the signal of the downfall of Veii, and those of Lake Fucino, which at times rose 54 feet, and has lately been drained. There are others, as Lake Bolsena, a kind of inland sea, 25 miles round, and the famous Trasimene Lake, resulting from an earthquake.[3] The rains have filled up these natural cavities, and as the neighboring mountains are low, they supply just sufficient water to compensate the loss produced by evaporation. There

---

[1] Often and often in the Middle Ages Florence—which, by the way, was built on a dried-up marsh—was near being carried away by the Arno; in 1656 Ravenna was flooded by the Ronco and the Montone; and in the last century Bologna and Ferrara have many times been on the point of coming to blows, as the Provençals and Avignonnais did, on the subject of the Durance, to decide the spot where the Reno should join it. Thanks to the numerous cavities where during the winter the water of its sources stores itself, the Tiber does not sink much at its summer level.

[2] Other watercourses of peninsular Italy: at the west, the Magra, the boundary of Tuscany and Liguria, 36 miles in length; the Chiana, the Nera, and the Teverone (Anio), tributaries of the Tiber; the Garigliano (Liris), 70 miles; the Volturno, 83; the Sele; the Lao: at the east, the Pisatello (Rubicon); the Metauro; the Esino; the Tronto, 56 miles; the Pescara (Aternus), 83; the Sangro, 83; the Biferno, 58; the Fortore, 81; and the Ofanto, 114.

[3] There is some doubt on this point for the Lake of Bolsena, which some travellers (Dennis, *Etruria*, i. 514) and some learned men (Delesse, *Revue de Géol.* 1877) regard as a crater.

hardly issue from them even insignificant rivers. Lake Trasimene, at its greatest depth, does not reach 30 feet, and it will soon have the fate of Lake Fucino.

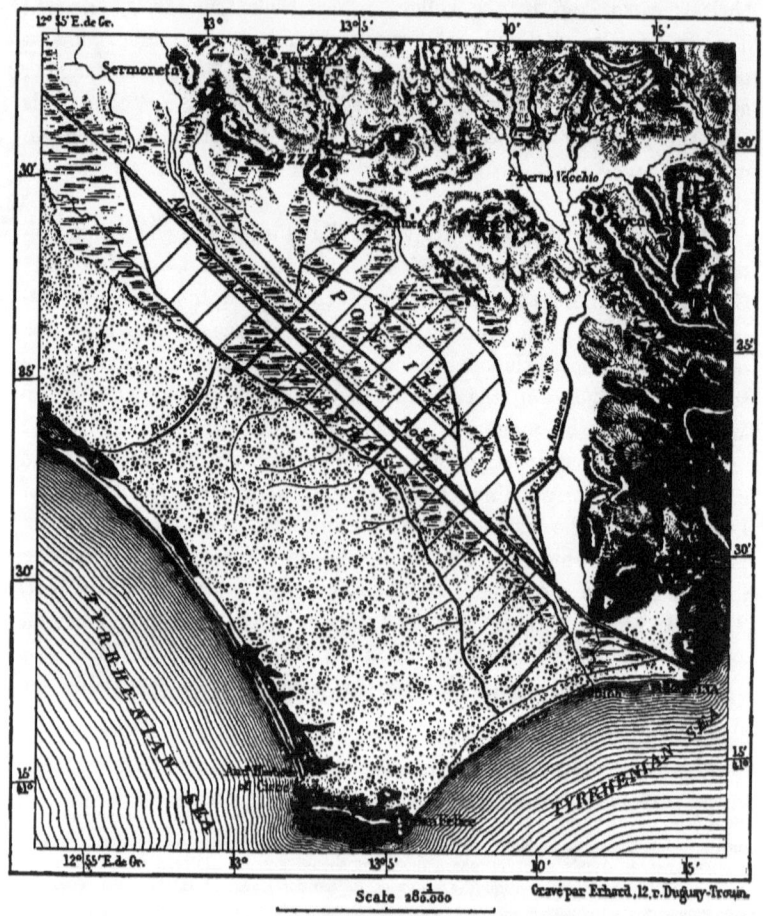

THE PRESENT CONDITION OF THE PONTINE MARSHES.

Stagnant waters cover a part of the coast to the west and to the south: it is the realm of fever. The younger Pliny speaks of the unhealthiness of the coasts of Etruria, where the Maremma, which the Etruscans had once drained, was reappearing. In Latium the sea formerly reached to the foot of the mountains of Setia and Privernum, about 9 miles in from the present coast:[1] from the time of Strabo the whole coast from Ardea to Antium was marshy and unhealthy; at Antium the Pontine Marshes commenced. Campania had the marshes of Minturnae and of Linternum. Farther south, the Greeks of Buxentum, of Elea, of Sybaris, and of Metapontum had to dig thousands of canals to drain the soil before putting in the plough. Apulia, as far as Mount Vultur, had been a vast lagoon, as well as the country around the mouths of the Po, fully 100 miles south of its modern mouth.[2] Lombardy also was for a long time an immense marsh, and to the Etruscans are attributed the first embankments of the Po. The banks of the Trebia, the territories of Parma, of Modena, and of Bologna, had not been drained till the works of Aemilius Scaurus, who during his censorship (109 B. C.) made navigable canals between Parma and Placentia.[3] There is nothing so charming and so treacherous as those plains of the "Mal'aria," — a clear sky, fertile land, where an ocean of verdure waves under the sea-breeze; all around there is calm and silence; an atmosphere mild and warm, which seems to bring life, but carries death. "In the Maremma," says an Italian proverb, "one grows rich in a year, but dies in six months."

COIN OF BUXENTUM.

COIN OF METAPONTUM.[4]

". . . . La Maremma,
Dilettevole molto e poco sana."[5]

How many peoples, once flourishing and powerful, are sleeping

---

[1] De Prony, *Descr. Hydrog. et Hist. des Marais Pontins*, pp. 73 and 176.

[2] Pliny, *Hist. Nat.* iii. 20; Cuvier, *Disc. sur les Révolutions du Globe*, p. 216.

[3] In 187 B. C. the Consul Aemilius Lepidus continued the Flaminian Road from Rimini to Bologna and to Placentia, and from thence to Aquileia, ἐγκυκλούμενος τὰ ἕλη (Strabo, V. i. 11). In the year 160 B. C. the Consul Cethegus received as his province the duty of draining the Pontine Marshes (Livy, *Epitome*, xlvi).

[4] On the obverse, this medal bears the head of the hero Leucippos, the founder of the city; on the reverse, an ear of corn with a bird on the leaf.

[5] Very delightful and very unwholesome.

here their last sleep! Cities also can die, — *Oppida posse mori*, said the poet Rutilius, when contemplating, fifteen centuries ago, the crumbling ruins of a great town of Etruria.

To restrain and direct their streams was then for the Italians not only a means, as with other people, of gaining lands for agriculture, but a question of life and death. These lakes at the summit of mountains, these rivers overflowing their banks every spring, or changing their beds, these marshes, which under an Italian sun so quickly breed the plague, compelled them to constant efforts. Whenever they stopped, all that they had conquered with so much trouble reverted to its pristine state.[1] To-day Baïae, the delightful retreat of the Roman nobles; Paestum, with its fields of ٭. ٭s so much beloved by Ovid, — *tepidi rosaria Paesti;* rich Capua, Cumae, which was once the most important city of Italy, Sybaris, which was the most voluptuous, are in the midst of stagnant and fetid waters, in a fever-breeding plain, "where the decaying soil consumes more men than it can feed." Pestilential miasma, solitude, and silence have also conquered the shores of the Gulf of Taranto, once covered with so many towns; leprosy and elephantiasis in Apulia and Calabria exhibit the hideous diseases of the intertropical regions traversed by "untamed waters." In Tuscany 120 miles of coast-line, in Latium 82 square miles of land, have been abandoned to poisonous influences. Here the wrath of man has aided that of Nature. Rome had ruined Etruria and exterminated the Volscians. But water invaded the depopulated country; the malaria, extending gradually from Pisa to Terracina, reached Rome herself; and the Eternal City expiates now, in the midst of her wastes and her unhealthy climate, the merciless war waged by her legions.[2] At the point where but lately the Maremma of Tuscany and that of the States of the Church join, the saddest of solitudes meets the eye: not a hut nor a tree to be seen, but huge fields of asphodel, — the flower of the tomb. One day, about fifty years ago, a vault, hidden under the grass, gave way under the heavy tread of an ox: it was a funeral chamber. Excavations were prosecuted. In a little time 2,000 vases and

---

[1] Muratori (*Rer. Ital. Script.* ii. 691, and *Ant. Ital. diss.* 21) has shown how quickly the drained lands become marshy again as soon as cultivation is suspended.

[2] Cicero, *de Rep.* ii. 6, said of Rome: "Locum . . . . in regione pestilenti salubrem;" and Livy, v. 54, "saluberrimos colles."

other objects of art were discovered,[1] and Etruscan civilization was reclaimed from oblivion.

The name of the rich city which had buried so many marvels in its tombs is not mentioned by any of the Roman historians, and must have remained unknown but for an inscription which mentioned its defeat and the triumph of its conqueror.[2] The Vulcientes had fought the last battle for Etruscan liberty. How heavy were the hands of Rome and of Time, and how many flourishing cities they have destroyed! But again, how many wonders does the Italian soil reserve for the future, when the malaria is expelled, and the towns it has slain shall deliver up their secrets.[3]

Bordering on the great Alps, and reaching to Africa, Italy has every climate, and can have all kinds of culture. In this double respect she is divided into four regions: the Valley of the Po, the slopes of the Apennines turned towards the Tuscan Sea, the plains of the Peninsula, and the two points in which it terminates.[4]

[1] M. Noël des Vergers has narrated with eloquence the emotion he felt when, in an excavation that he made in the same necropolis of Vulci: "At the last blow of the pick, the stone which formed the entrance to the crypt gave way, and the light of the torches illumined vaults where nothing had for more than twenty centuries disturbed darkness and silence. Everything was still in the same state as on the day when the entrance had been walled up, and ancient Etruria arose to our view in the days of her splendor. On their funeral couches warriors, covered with their armor, seemed to be resting after the battles they had fought with the Romans or with our ancestors, the Gauls; forms, dresses, stuffs, and colors were visible for a few minutes; then all vanished as the outer air penetrated into the crypt, where our flickering torches threatened at first to be extinguished. It was a calling up of the past which lasted not even the brief moment of a dream, and passed away, as it were, to punish us for our rash curiosity.

["Like that long-buried body of the king
Found lying with his urns and ornaments,
Which, at a touch of light, an air of heaven,
Slipped into ashes, and was found no more."

TENNYSON: *Aylmer's Field*.]

While these frail remains crumbled into dust in contact with the air, the atmosphere became clearer. We then saw ourselves surrounded by another population due to the artists of Etruria. Mural paintings adorned the crypt all round, and seemed to come to life with the flash of our torches."

[2] *Fast. Capit.*, ad ann. 473. Triumph of T. Coruncanius in 280 for his victories over the Vulcientes and Volsinienses.

[3] Those unhealthy countries, where a thick vegetation covers the ruins, protect so well against curiosity even the monuments which are there, that a century ago the temples of Paestum were not known, and also a few years ago, the curious necropolis of Castel d' Asso, of Norchia, and of Soana.

[4] In antiquity Italy abounded more in woods and marshes, and the winter was colder. [This is proved, for historical times, not only by allusions like Horace's "Vides ut alta stet nive candidum Soracte," etc., but by the researches of Hehn in his well-known work on the spread of domestic animals and plants in antiquity. — *Ed.*]

INTRODUCTION.

Calabria, Apulia, and part of the coast of the Abruzzi have almost the sky and the productions of Africa: a climate clear and dry, but scorching; the palm-tree, which at Reggio sometimes ripens its fruit, the aloes, the medlar, the orange, and the lemon; on the coast the olives, which are the source, as formerly, of the wealth of the country; farther up, for two thousand feet, forests of chestnut-trees covering a part of the Sila. But from Pisa to the middle of Campania, between the sea and the foot of the mountains, the malaria reigns; the soil is abandoned to herdsmen, and although very fertile, waits for the labor of man to produce its old return. Already in Tuscany tenant-farming is driving back the Maremma, and the land is peopled again wherever it is drained.

Above these plains, on the first slopes of the Apennines, from Provence to Calabria, there extends the district of the olive, the mulberry-tree, the arbutus, the myrtle, the laurel, and the vine.

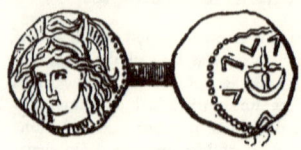

COIN OF POPULONIA.[1]

This latter grows so freely that it may be seen reaching the top of the poplars which support it; and in the time of Pliny a statue of Jupiter used to be shown at Populonia carved in a vine-trunk. Farther up, on the mountain, come chestnut-trees, oaks, and elms; then fir-trees and larch. The summer snow and the freezing wind remind one of Switzerland, but for the flood of dazzling light from the Italian sky.

But it is in the Valley of the Po, when coming down from the Alps, that the traveller receives his first and most pleasant impressions. From Turin, as far as Milan, he keeps in view the line of the glaciers, which the setting sun colors with brilliant tints of rose and purple, and makes them glitter like a magnificent conflagration spreading along the sides and on the summits of the mountains. In spite of the vicinity of the perpetual snow, the cold does not descend far on this rapid slope; and when the sun bursts forth in the immense amphitheatre of the Valley of the Po, its rays, arrested and reflected by the wall of the Alps, raise the tem-

---

[1] On the obverse, the head of Minerva with helmet; on the reverse, a crescent and a star with the word PVPLV written from right to left in Etruscan characters. *Puplu* was the commencement of the name Populonia.

CANALS AND PINE-FOREST OF RAVENNA.

perature, and scorching heat succeeds suddenly the cold air of the lofty summits. But the number of the streams, the rapidity of their courses, the direction of the valley, which opens on the Adriatic and receives all its breezes, cool the atmosphere, and give Lombardy a most delightful climate. The inexhaustible fertility of the soil, enriched by the deposits of so many rivers, causes everywhere a very rich vegetation. In one night, it is said, grass which has been cut shoots up afresh;[1] and the land, which no culture exhausts, never lies fallow.

Such is the general aspect of Italy, — a land of continual contrasts: plains and mountains, snow and scorching heat, dry and raging torrents, limpid lakes formed in ancient craters, and pestilential marshes concealing beneath the herbage once populous cities. At every step a contrast: the vegetation of Africa at the foot of the Apennines; on their summits the vegetation of the North. Here, under the clearest sky, the malaria, bringing death in one night to the sleeping traveller; there, lands of inexhaustible fertility,[2] and above, the volcano with its threatening lava. Elsewhere, in the space of a few leagues, sixty-nine craters and three entombed towns. At the north, rivers which inundate the lands and repel the sea; at the south, earthquakes opening unfathomable depths or overthrowing mountains. Every climate, every property of the soil combined, — in short, a reduced picture of the ancient world,[3] yet with its natural peculiarities strongly marked.

[1] " Et quantum longis carpent armenta diebus
    Exigua tantum gelidus ros nocte reponet."
                              VERGIL: *Georgics*, ii. 201.
Varro (*de Re rust.* i. 7) said more prosaically, " In the plain of Rosea let fall a stake, to-morrow it is hidden in the grass."

[2] In Etruria and in some other parts of Italy the land produced 15-fold, and elsewhere 10-fold (Varro, *de Re rust.* i. 44). The fertility of the ground of Sybaris, like that of Campania, was proverbial: it used to be said that it returned 100-fold. [And even now the traveller is delighted with the sudden display of rich pasture in the Valley of the Crati, and with the splendid herds of cattle roaming through its meadows and forests. Nowhere in Southern Italy is there such verdure. — *Ed.*]

[3] This can be maintained without any systematic survey. Has not Italy the sun of Africa; the valleys and mountains of Greece and Spain; the thick forests, the plains, the marshes of Gaul; indented coasts and harbors like Asia Minor; and even the valley of the Nile in that of the Po? Both are the product of these rivers, with their delta, their lagoons, and their great maritime cities, Adria or Venice, Alexandria or Damietta, according to the age. " The Veneti," says Strabo (V. i. 5), "had constructed in their lagoons, canals and dikes like those of Lower Egypt." In another passage Ravenna recalls to him Alexandria. See in the fourth chapter of the sixth book the different causes he assigns for

In the midst of this nature, capricious and fickle, but everywhere energetic for good as for evil, there appear peoples whose diversity of origin will be stated in the following pages; but we know already, by the study of the Italian soil, that the population, placed in conditions of territory and climate varying with each canton, will not be moulded by any one of those physical influences whose action, always the same, produced civilizations uniform and impervious to external influences.

In this general description of Italy we have only glanced in passing at the hills of Rome, which, notwithstanding their modest size, surpass in renown the proudest summits of the world. They deserve careful study. The earth is a great book, wherein science studies revolutions beside which those of man are but child's-play. When the geologist examines the soil of Rome and its environs, he finds it formed, like the rest of the peninsula, from the twofold action of volcanoes and water. Remains have there been found of the elephant, the mastodon, the rhinoceros, and the hippopotamus, — proving that at a certain period of geological time Latium formed a part of a vast continent with an African temperature, and one in which great rivers ran through vast plains. At another epoch, when the glaciers descended so far into the Valley of the Po that their moraines were not far from the Adriatic, the Tuscan Sea covered the Roman plain. It formed in it a semicircular gulf, of which Soracte and the Promontory of Circei were the headlands.[1]

At the bottom of this primordial sea volcanoes burst forth, and their liquid lava was deposited by the water in horizontal beds, which, at the present day, from Rome as far as Radicofani, are found mingled with organic remains. When this lava has become solidified by time and the action of water, it becomes the *peperino*, the close-grained *tufo* of which Rome, both under the Kings and the Republic, was built. When the lava remains in a

the superiority of Italy. It has even been established that all the geological formations are represented in Italy; and although mining operations are not well prosecuted, they give rise to an annual exportation of 600,000 tons of the value of 100 millions (of francs).

[1] It is considered that the Campagna di Roma from Civita Vecchia to Terracina is 91 miles in length, and that from the Mediterranean to the mountains its breadth is more than 27 miles. As far inland as Rome, the mountains are in some parts distant only from three to five miles. The Anio falls into the Tiber at less than three miles' distance from Rome.

granulous state it produces the *pozzolana*, from which was made the tenacious cement of the Roman walls. Of this *pozzolana* the Seven Hills, on the left bank, are formed. The Capitol alone is

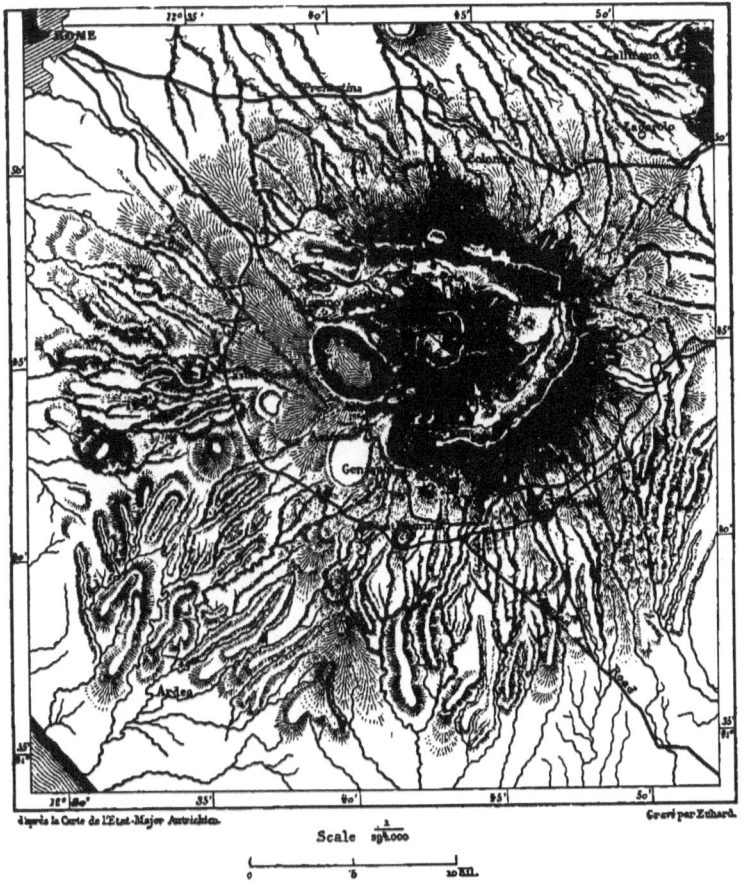

EXTINCT VOLCANOES ABOUT ALBA.

almost entirely composed of a porous *tufo;* a more solid substance seemed needed for the hill which was destined to be the throne of the world.[1]

When the formidable volcanoes of the Alban Hills had lifted

[1] Ampère, *L'Histoire Romaine à Rome,* i. 8.

Latium above the sea, the lava which came from their craters spread over the sides of the mountain, and one of the hot streams descended across the new plain as far as Capo di Bove.[1] From this lava, when consolidated, Rome procured the flagstones with which she paved the Appian Road, and which remain to this day.

The Roman campagna, formed in the midst of waters, whose gentle undulations or level surface it reproduces in turn, changed afterward by the volcanoes of the Alban Hills, is furrowed by little hills and low ground, — "a humpy soil," said Montaigne, whose

CATTLE OF THE ROMAN CAMPAGNA.

cavities are filled with fresh water. Once they were limpid lakes: now they are unhealthy pools;[2] and a learned man, Brocchi, attributes to the influence of the *aria cattiva* the gloomy, violent,

---

[1] Brocchi, *Dello stato fisico del suolo di Roma.* Capo di Bove is the part of the Appian Road where is the tomb of Caecilia Metella, the frieze of which bears heads of oxen, in remembrance of the sacrifices made before the tomb.

[2] The season of [malaria] fever [typhoid, now so common, is apparently a new scourge to the city, arising from modern causes — *Ed.*] extends from June to October. Horace especially dreaded the autumn (*Od.* II. xiv. 15; *Sat.* II. vi. 19; see also *Ep.* I. vii. 5). M. Colin, the chief physician of the French army, attributes the malaria in the Campagna di Roma less to the effluvia of the marshes, since the Pontine Marshes do not reach so far, than to the exhalations from a soil, very fertile and untilled, under a sky of fiery heat during the day-time, from July to October, and comparatively very moist and cold during the night. (*Traité des fièvres intermittentes,* 1870.)

VIEW OF THE ROMAN CAMPAGNA.

and irritable temper of those who carry in their veins the germs of the fever of the Maremma. This has been noticed by all travellers; while, under a beautiful sky, and on the shore of the bright sea of the Gulf of Naples, the people are merry, playful, and noisy, the people of Rome, on the other hand, in the midst of their majestic and stern country, are gloomy, silent, and prompt with the knife. We shall find this harshness of character running through the whole history of Rome; for though man may call himself intelligent and free, the surrounding influences of nature impress their mark upon him, and for the majority this mark is indelible.

We might assert the same influences for all animals alike; for the buffaloes and great oxen with formidable horns, which wander about the country of Roman campagna are as savage as the herdsmen who drive them; and it is dangerous for a stranger to venture near them.

While the volcano was furnishing Rome with indestructible paving for her military roads, the waterfalls of Tivoli, larger then than they are now, and the waters of the neighboring lakes, saturated with carbonic acid or sulphurated hydrogen, formed the *travertino*, — a light and whitish limestone, which hardens in the air and takes warm and orange-colored tints. With this stone Rome built all her temples, the Coliseum, and other monuments of the Empire.

The architecture of a nation depends on the materials which it has at hand. The bricks give London its dulness, while Paris owes its elegance to the French limestone, so easy to handle. Marble made Athens sparkling with beauty. Rome was severe with her grayish *peperino*, massive with her *travertino* cut in large blocks, until the time came when she was able, with the costly marbles unloaded at Ostia, to indulge in all the splendors of architecture; "so that her very ruins are glorious, and still does she retain, in her tomb, the marks and image of her empire" (Montaigne).

The Tiber was much larger than it is at the present day; for it received then all the Chiana, perhaps a part of the Arno, and carried to the sea, with the streams of the Sabine territory, those of a great part of the Tuscan Apennines. A large and

INTRODUCTION.

deep lake once covered the site of Rome; and on the Pincian, Esquiline, Aventine, and Capitoline Hills, fluvial shells are found, 130 to 160 feet above the present Tiber.

The river, barred probably by the Hills of Decimo, had accumulated its waters behind that obstacle, which at length it succeeded in sweeping away.

Man appeared early on this soil. In the post-tertiary strata of the basin of Rome his remains are found, and some cut or polished flints along with the bones of the *Cervus elephas*, of the reindeer, and of the *Bos primigenius*.[1] Implements of stone were followed, as everywhere, by implements of bronze. Man, then armed, was able to contend against the fauna, and afterward against Nature herself. But many centuries passed before his efforts produced any useful effects.

In the first days of Rome the Forum, the Campus Martius, the Velabrum, the valley between the Aventine and the Palatine Hills (*Vallis Murcia*), which ultimately the Circus Maximus filled up entirely, — in short, all the low-lying lands at the foot of the Seven Hills, — were marsh lands, where the river often returned, and where it still returns. It is from a slough that the most beautiful city in the world was destined to rise.

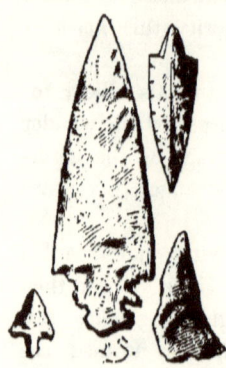

FLINT WEAPONS FOUND IN THE ROMAN CAMPAGNA.[2]

For the purpose of self-defence the Capitoline and Aventine were secure refuges; but in order to live and spread, she must descend from the hills and overcome the wandering or stagnant waters over which already the malaria began to hover. Fever had early an altar on the Palatine, where they attempted, by prayer and sacrifices, to charm away its fatal influence.[3] But though superstitious, the people were also energetic. What they

---

[1] *Bull. de l'Inst. arch.*, 1867, p. 4, and the *Atlas*, viii. 38. M. Capellini believes he has found quite recently (1870) in Tuscany traces of Pliocene man.

[2] *Atlas de l'Inst. archéol.*, viii. 36.

[3] For the Latins the Fever was the God Februus, to whom was consecrated the month of February, during which purificatory sacrifices were offered; hence the verb *februare*, to purify. [Yet surely it seems strange that so healthy a month should be chosen for this purpose. It may be connected with ceremonies at the end of the old year, when the 1st of March was New Year's Day. — *Ed.*]

asked from the gods they were ready to demand from their toil; and this struggle against Nature prepared the way for the struggle against men. In this work of improving the Roman soil they

ARTICLES IN TERRA-COTTA FOUND IN THE ENVIRONS OF ROME.[1]

were helped by the Etruscans, who knew how to drain marshy plains and to build imperishable monuments for the leading away of subterranean waters. The entrance of Etruscan art into Rome was a geographical necessity, as also was the laborious and rough life of the first Romans. With art many also of the civil and religious institutions of Etruria migrated to Rome.

[1] *Atlas de l'Inst. archéol.*, viii. 37.

II.

THE ANCIENT POPULATION OF ITALY—PELASGIANS AND UMBRIANS.

ITALY has not, like France, England, Germany, and Scandinavia, preserved numerous traces of a race anterior to the epoch in which man had learned to furrow the earth with implements of metal; at least, as far as our researches have reached, it seems to have possessed only in certain spots what has been called the age of stone.[1] Separated from the rest of the world by the Alps and the sea, it was peopled later than the vast countries of easy access which lie on the east, north, and west of its mountains. But when these regions were once inhabited Italy became the country of Europe where the greatest number of foreign races have met together. All the surrounding nations contributed their share in forming the population; and each revolution which disturbed them produced a new people. The Sicanians were formerly derived from Spain; now they are identified with the Pelasgic Siculi.[2] But from Gaul came the Ligurians, the Senonian, the Boian, the Insubrian, and the Cenomanian Celts; from the great Alps, the Etruscans; from the Julian Alps, the Veneti; from the eastern coast of the Adriatic Seas and from the Peloponnesus many Illyrian and Pelasgic tribes; from Greece, those Hellenic tribes which came in so great numbers into Southern Italy as to give to that part the name of Great Greece; from Asia Minor, the Lydian Pelasgians; lastly, from the coasts of Syria and Africa, the more certain colonies which Tyre and Carthage established in the two great Italian islands.[3] And if we were to trust to the patriotic pride of one of her historians,[4] Etruria would owe to

---

[1] However, prehistoric discoveries occur daily in the Campagna di Roma, in Tuscany, and from the Valteline, as far as Leuca, at the extremity of Italy, where M. Botti Ulderico has discovered grottoes which have served as shelters for primitive man.

[2] Cf. Benloew, *Études Albanaises*.

[3] [We may add at least Agylla (Caere), in Etruria, whose name, as Mommsen has shown, declares its origin. — *Ed.*]

[4] Micali, *Storia degli antichi popoli Italiani*, i. 142; cf. Fréret, "Recherches sur l'origine et l'histoire des différents peuples d'Italie," *Hist. de l'Acad. des inscr.*, xvii. 72-114.

Egypt and the distant East her religious creeds, her arts, and her sacerdotal government.

Italy was, therefore, a common asylum for all the wanderers of the ancient world. All brought in with them their language and their customs; many preserved their native character and their independence, until from the midst of them there should arise a city which formed at their cost her population, her laws, and her religion,— Rome herself, the asylum of all races and of all Italian civilizations![1]

All the Italian races belonged to the great Indo-European family, which came from the high regions of Central Asia and gradually peopled a part of Western Asia and the whole of Europe. When they penetrated into the peninsula, they had already arrived at that degree of civilization which stood midway between the pastoral, or nomad, and the agricultural, or settled, state. The most ancient geographical names are a proof of this: Oenotria was the country of the vine; Italy (*vitulus*), that of oxen; the Opici meant "laborers of the fields;" and the first means of exchange were cattle, *pecus*,— whence *pecunia*. Sybaris, like Buxentum, seems to have wished to preserve this remembrance. One of her coins bears on both sides the image of an ox.[2]

COIN OF SYBARIS.

The most ancient of these nations seem to have belonged to

---

[1] We must say that these questions of origin and relationship are among the historical controversies which are still being argued every day. The evidence for and against is so mixed, that both sides can accumulate contrary quotations and interpretations, so that this mass of doubtful proofs rather fatigues than enlightens the mind. Niebuhr says, as regards one of these peoples: "What abuses of imagination were not indulged in with regard to the mysteries and wisdom of the Pelasgians! Their very name is an abomination to the truthful and serious historian. It is this disgust which kept me from making any general references to that people, lest I might open the floodgates for a new deluge of writing about this wretched subject." But later on he himself could not resist "that inclination which led him, like most of his countrymen, to guess out lost history;" and the Pelasgians obtained from him sixty pages.. The most recent and complete work on the ancient populations of Italy is that of Schwegler (*Römische Geschichte*, i. 154–384). [A valuable book, obscured, like our Thirlwall, by the brilliancy of a more passionate, but less trustworthy, rival. — *Ed.*]

[2] Some Samnite coins, struck during the Social War, have also *Vitelu* inscribed in place of *Italia*. It is perhaps in a letter of Decimus Brutus to Cicero (*Fam.* xi. 20) that the earliest mention is made of the name of Italy as applied to the entire peninsula as far as the Alps.

the mysterious race of the Pelasgians,[1] whom one finds confusedly at the commencement of so many histories, though there is nothing left of it but its name and its indestructible buildings. After having carried its industry and activity into Greece and its islands, into Macedonia and Epirus, into Italy, and perhaps into Spain, the race disappeared, pursued, according to the ancient legend, by the celestial powers, and suffering endless misfortunes.

At the commencement of historic times nothing but uncertain remains of that great people are found, as we discover, in the bosom of the earth, the mutilated remains of primitive creations. It is a whole buried world, — a civilization arrested, and then calumniated by the victorious tribes after they have destroyed it. Their altars were stained, they say, with the blood of human sacrifices, and, in a vow, they offered a tithe of their children. The priests directed at their will the clouds and tempests; they summoned the snow and the hail, and by their magic power they changed the form of objects; they were acquainted with fatal charms; they fascinated men and plants by their glance; on animals and on trees they poured the deadly water of the Styx; they knew how to heal, and how to compose subtle poisons. Thus in the mythologies of the North the Goths have consigned the Finns, whom they had dispossessed, to the extremities of the earth under the forms of industrious dwarfs and of formidable magicians. Like the Pelasgians, the Finns open mines and work metals; and it is they who forge for the Odinic gods the invincible shackles of the wolf Fenris, as Vulcan, the Pelasgic god, had made, for new divinities also, the chains of Prometheus.

It seems, then, that there were at the north and at the south of Europe two great nations who knew the earliest arts, and commenced this struggle against physical nature which our modern civilization continues with so much success. But both were subdued and cursed after their defeat by the warlike tribes, who looked upon work as servile labor, and made slavery the law of the ancient world.

In Italy, where, their first colonies settled at a remote epoch, the Pelasgians covered, under various names, the greater part of the coast. At the north, in the low plains of the Po, and along

---

[1] "Pelasgi primi Italiam tenuisse perhibentur" (Serv. in *Aen.* viii. 600).

PELASGIC REMAINS.

1. Bovianum. 2. Volaterrae. 3. Lista. 4. Olivano. 5. Veii. 6. Signia. 7. Arpinum.

the western coast from the Arno, there were Siculi, the founders of Tibur, a district of which was called the Sicelion;[1] at the southwest, the Chonians, Morgetes, and, above all, Oenotrians, who had, like the Dorians of Sparta, public meals; at the south-east, Daunians, Peucetians, and Messapians, divided into Calabrians and Salentines, and said by tradition to come from Crete; at the east, lastly, Liburnians, of that Illyrian race which we must perhaps identify with the Pelasgic.[2]

The Tyrrhenians were probably one of these Pelasgic nations. According to a Greek tradition which agrees with Egyptian records, they came from Lydia. "In the days of King Atys, son of Manes, there was a great famine throughout the land of Lydia. The King resolved to divide his kingdom into two equal parts, and made his people draw lots to decide which part should remain in the land, and which should go into exile. He was to continue to rule over those who remained; the emigrants were to have his son Tyrsenus as their chief. The lots were drawn; and those who were destined to depart came down to Smyrna, built ships, put in them the necessaries of life, and went in search of a hospitable land. Having coasted for a long time, they reached the shore of Umbria, where they founded the towns which they inhabit to this day. They discontinued the name of Lydians, and called themselves Tyrseni, after the name of their king's son, who had acted as their guide."[3] These towns, of which Herodotus speaks, were built to the north of the mouth of the Tiber, and consequently very close to Rome. They were Alsium, Agylla or Caere,[4] Pyrgi,

[1] There is still near Tivoli a *valle di Siciliano*.
[2] From a number of testimonies it seems to result that people of the Illyrian race covered the whole of the eastern coast of Italy exactly opposite Illyria, while the western shore was occupied by Pelasgians; and Micali (ii. 356) identifies these two peoples. This is also the opinion of Dalmatian critics, who have found a strong analogy between the Oscan, which is akin to Latin, and the remains of the ancient Illyrian, preserved in the dialect of the Skippetars. Grote admits the relationship of the Oenotrians, the Siculians, etc., with the Epirotes. "All," he says, "have the same language, the same customs, the same origin, and can be comprised under the name of Pelasgians." He adds, "They were not very widely separated from the ruder branches of the Hellenic race" (*History of Greece*, iii. 468). The Pelasgic influence can be recognized in the oldest religion of Rome, especially in the worship of Vesta, and is found in the Sibylline books, which recommended the building of a temple to the Dioscuri, the worship of the Bona Dea, and the sacrifice of two Gauls and two Greeks. Lastly, Samothrace, the centre of the Pelasgic religion, had her relationship with Rome acknowledged by the Senate. Cf. Plut., *Marcellus*, 30.
[3] Herodotus, i. 94; Dionysius of Halicarnassus, *Antiq. Rom.*, i. 27-30.
[4] Dionysius of Halicarnassus (*Ibid.* i. 20) makes Pisa a Pelasgian city.

which was their port, Tarquinii, which played so great a part in Roman history, and perhaps, at the mouth of the Arno, the city of Pisa, the population of which spoke Greek.

The story of Herodotus is fabulous, but it may allude to a real emigration. In the time of the Emperors this tradition was national both at Sardis and in Etruria.[1] Whatever be their origin, the Tyrrhenian Pelasgians possessed a power which spread far their name; for notwithstanding the conquest of the country by the Rasena, the Greeks never recognized any people between the Tiber and the Arno but "the glorious Tyrrhenians,"[2] and the Athenians have consecrated, in the beautiful frieze of the Choragic Monument of Lysicrates,[3] the memory of the exploits of one of their gods against the pirates who came forth from the harbors of Tyrrhenia.

But while admitting the existence of these Tyrrhenians, it is not necessary to sacrifice the Etruscans to them. The Romans, who certainly had not learnt it from the Greeks, called the Rasena, their neighbors, Tusci or Etrusci,[4] and the Eugubine tables, an Umbrian monument, also call them Turscum,— a plain proof that the name of the Tyrrhenians was national also in Etruria. What can this native use of two names mean, if not the co-existence of two nations? After the conquest the Tyrrhenians were neither exterminated nor banished; their name even prevailed with foreign nations, as in England the name of Anglo-Saxons over that of the Norman conquerors; and the subsequent progress of Etruscan power appeared to be that of the ancient Tyrrhenians.

The Pelasgians, then, formed along the western coast of the peninsula a first stratum of population, which was soon covered by other nations. In the midst of these new races the ancient masters of Italy, like the Pelasgians of Greece, lost their language, their manners, their liberty, and even the remembrance of what they had been. Nothing remained of them but the Cyclopean walls of Etruria and of Latium, enormous blocks of stone, set without cement, which have withstood the ravages of time as well

---

[1] Tac. *Ann.*, iv. 55, and Strabo, V. i. 2.
[2] Hesiod, *Theog.*, 1015 and 1016.
[3] [Pictured in Stuart and Revett's *Antiquities of Athens*, and since in all the histories of Greek art; it dates from 335 B. C.— *Ed.*]
[4] The Greeks said Τυρρηνοί and Τυρσηνοί: whence from the Etruscan form, Turscum, we easily arrive at Tusci, Etrusci, and Etruria.

as of man.[1] Some Pelasgians, however, escaped; and yielding to the impulse for invasion which was at work from north to south, gained by slow degrees the great island to which the Siculi gave their name, and where the Morgetes followed them.[2] Those who preferred the rule of the foreigner to exile, formed in many parts of Italy an inferior class, who rested faithful, in their degradation,

THE CABEIRI.

to that habit of labor which was one of the characteristics of their race. In Oenotria the low or servile occupations, that is to say, all arts and manufactures,[3] fell to their lot, as in Attica, where the building of the citadel of Athens was intrusted to them; so that the much-vaunted Etruscan arts, the figures in bronze[4] or

---

[1] "At Segni the walls, composed of enormous blocks, form a triple enclosure. At Alatri we still see a Pelasgian citadel. The walls are 40 feet high, and some stones are 8 to 9 feet long. The lintel of one of the gates of the town is formed of three blocks placed side by side. These stones have been carefully cut, and set with skill. The joining of the stones is perfect. It is a work of giants, but of clever giants." — AMPÈRE: *L' Histoire Romaine à Rome*, i. 135. For the description of these monuments see Abeken, *Mittel Italien vor den Zeiten Römischer Herrschaft*.

[2] Thucydides (vi. 2) shows the Siculi fleeing into Sicily before the Opici.

[3] It is to Temesa (Tempsa, in Bruttium) that the Taphians came to exchange brass for glittering iron (*Odys.*, I. 184). In the time of Thucydides, the Siculi still inhabited this town. *Stephanus Byz.* (sub voce χίοι) says that the Italian Greeks [Italiotes] treated the Pelasgians as the Spartans did the Helots.

[4] According to tradition it was the Pelasgic Telchines — half men, half sprites — who

terra-cotta, the drawings in relief, the painted vases,[1] like those of Corinth, etc., would be the work of the Pelasgians, who remained as slaves and artisans under the Etruscan Lucumons.

Their religion was as obscure as their history. It was con-

THE CABEIRI.

nected with the worship of the Cabeiri of Samothrace, Axieros, Axiokersa, Axiokersos, and Casmilos, cosmic deities, personifications of earthly fire and celestial fire, — the religion of a nation of miners and smiths. Later on the Cabeiri were identified with Greek divinities. Thus on a famous Hermes of the Vatican, Axiokersos is associated with Apollo-Helios, Axiokersa with Venus, and Casmilos, "the ordainer," with Eros. Axieros, the supreme god, remained above the trinity who emanated from him.

It has been said that all the ancient religions have been the worship "of nature naturalizing (*naturantis*), of nature naturalized (*naturatae*)." The expression is barbarous, but it is just. Of these religions the first belonged to simple naturalism; the second have given rise to anthropomorphism, in which all terminate. The Cabeiri being considered the cause of things, the symbol of generation played an important part in their figurative worship and

had discovered the art of working metals, and who had made the first images of the gods. Niebuhr has remarked the singular coincidence which exists in Latin and in Greek between the words for a house, a field, a plough, husbandry, wine, oil, milk, oxen, pigs, sheep, apples (he could have added *metallum, argentum, ars*, and *agere*, with their derivatives, *abacus*, etc.), and generally all the words concerning agriculture and a peaceful life; while all the objects which belong to war or hunting, *duellum, ensis, sagitta, hasta*, are denoted by words foreign to Greek. This fact is explained if we consider that the peaceful and industrious Pelasgians formed the foundation of the population in Greece and Italy, especially in Latium, where the Siculians remained mingled with the Casci. [Niebuhr's acute remark anticipated what Pictet and others have shown to result from the common Aryan, not Pelasgian, ancestry of Greeks and Romans before they settled in either country. The common roots indicate what culture each race brought with it into its adopted home. — *Ed.*]

[1] [We must not forget the direct importation of these things from Attica. — *Ed.*]

history. On a Tusco-Tyrrhenian mirror of the fourth century before our era, two of the three Cabeiri, transformed into the Dioscuri, Castor and Pollux, are seen in the act of killing the youngest under the eyes of Venus, who opens the cista in which the remains of the god are to be placed, and in the presence of the wise Minerva, calmly and serenely witnessing his death, which is no real death. Life in reality comes from death; the god will revive when Mercury has touched him with his magic wand.

The initiation into the mysteries of the Island of Samothrace remained an act of deep piety with the Romans as with the Greeks. Rome was, by the legend, even put in direct relation with the Pelasgic island.[1]

The Palladium and the Penates, carried away by Aeneas from the flames of Troy, to be the pledge of power to the Eternal City, were taken by the Pelasgian Dardanus, it is said, from Samothrace to the banks of the Scamander, whence they passed to Rome.

Vesta, the goddess of the inextinguishable fire, who played so great a part in the Italian religions, must also have been a deity of the Pelasgians; but she belonged to all the people of the Aryan race, for she was the feminine representative of the Agni of the Vedas.

The Pelasgians, and those who imitated their method of building, rendered a service to the pretended descendants of the Trojans which has not been sufficiently noticed. The Cyclopean walls, with which they surrounded so many towns of Central Italy, saved Rome in the Second Punic War, by preventing Hannibal from occupying a single one of those impregnable fortresses which defended the approaches to the "Ager Romanus." During sixteen years the great Carthaginian held little beyond the enclosure of his camp.[2]

For two centuries the Pelasgians had the mastery of Italy; when the Sicanians, expelled from Spain by a Celtic invasion, and some Ligurians, who had come from Gaul,[3] spread themselves along

[1] See the *Revue archéol.* for December, 1877.

[2] See plate of the walls of Norba. Twenty centuries ago this town, taken and burned down by Sylla, ceased to exist; but its walls are the most curious Italian specimen of the architecture called Cyclopean. The town was built on a declivity commanding the Pontine Marshes. The enclosure remains almost entire; it has no tower to defend the foot of the wall, but the principal gate is flanked by two quasi-bastions.

[3] For a long time the Ligurians were believed to be Iberians. "Their language is Indo-European," says M. d'Arbois de Jubainville (*Les Premiers Habitants de l'Europe*) ; " it is

the shores of the Mediterranean from the Pyrenees to the Arno. In Italy they occupied, under various names, a great part of Cis-Alpine Gaul and the two slopes of the Northern Apennines. Their constant attacks, especially those of the Sicanians,[1] who had advanced farthest south, forced the Siculians to leave the banks of the Arno. It was the beginning of the disasters of that nation, which pretended to be indigenous, in order to prove its right to the possession of Italy.

When, four centuries later, the Etruscans descended from their mountains, they drove the Ligurians from the rich valley of the Arno, and confined them within the banks of the Macra. However, bloody fights still took place for a long time between the two nations, and notwithstanding their advanced post of Luna, the Etruscans were unable to maintain themselves in peaceable possession of the fertile lands watered by the Serchio (Ausar).[2]

Not far, on the San Pellegrino, the highest summit of the Northern Apennines (5,150 feet), and in the impracticable defiles from which the Macra descends, the Apuans dwelt, who, from their lofty mountains, watching the roads and the plain, gave neither truce nor respite to the merchants and traders of Tuscany.

Divided into as many little states as they had valleys, and always in arms against each other, these nations preserved, however, the general name of Ligurians and some of the customs common to all their tribes, — respect for the character of the *fetials*, and the custom of proclaiming war by ambassadors. Their manners also were alike everywhere. They were those of poor mountaineers upon whom nature had bestowed courage and strength, in place of the wealth of a fertile soil.[3] The women labored, like the men, at the hardest work, and hired themselves out for the harvest in the neighboring countries, while their husbands traversed the sea in their frail ships as far as Sardinia and Africa, to the detriment of the rich merchants of Marseilles, of Etruria,

---

Celtic," adds M. Maury (*Comptes Rendus de l'Acad. des Inscript.*, 1870). M. Ern. Desjardins discusses this question in the second volume of his *Géographie ancienne de la Gaule*, and arrives at the same conclusions.

[1] Thucydides (vi. 2) admits the Sicanians as an Iberian tribe, ὡς δὲ ἡ ἀλήθεια εὑρίσκεται.

[2] The country of Lucca watered by the Serchio is called the garden of Tuscany, which is itself one of the most fertile countries of Italy.

[3] "Assuetum malo Ligurem." — VERGIL, *Georgics*, ii. 168.

WALLS OF NORBA.

and of Carthage.¹ They had no towns, except Genoa, their common market, but numerous small villages, hidden in the mountains, where the Roman generals never found anything worth taking. A few prisoners, and long rows of chariots loaded with rude arms, were ever the only ornaments of their triumphs over the Ligurians.²

Few people had so high a reputation for hard work, for sobriety, and valor. During forty years their isolated tribes held in check the Roman power in their mountains, which succeeded in overpowering them only by forcing them away from that ungrateful soil,³ where they saw famine ever threatening them, but where they possessed that which they esteemed their chief good, their liberty.

At the other extremity of Cis-Alpine Gaul dwelt the Veneti. The two nations are contrasted, like their countries. In the midst of those beautiful plains, fertilized by the mud of so many rivers, under the mildest climate of Italy, the Veneti, or the "victorious,"⁴ as they were called, exchanged their poverty and valor for effeminate and timid manners. They had, it is said, fifty towns, and Padua, their capital, manufactured fine woollen stuffs and cloths, which, by means of the Brenta and the port of Malamocco, they exported to distant countries; their horses were in great demand for the Olympic races, and they travelled to Greece and Sicily to sell the yellow amber which they obtained from the Baltic. Their industry and commerce accumulated wealth, which often tempted the pirates of the Adriatic. But never were they seen in arms; and they accepted disgracefully, without battle, without a struggle, the Roman domination: a luxurious life had early sapped their courage.

Having entered Italy with the Liburnians of Illyria, or having come, perhaps, from the borders of the Danube,⁵ the Veneti had been driven into the mountains of Verona, of Trent, and Brescia,

---

¹ Poseidonius (ap. Strab. III. iv. 17, and Diod. v. 39). The descendants still go to the coasts of Sardinia and Algeria to get fish and coral, which the Ligurian Sea does not afford them, because of the depth of its water near the coast.

² Livy, xl. 34.

³ Forty thousand Apuans, the bravest of the Ligurians, were transported into the country of the Hirpini; and thirty times, if there is no mistake in the text of Pliny (iii. 6), the Ingaunians were compelled to change their abode. "Ingaunis Liguribus agro tricies dato." [This is the Asiatic system of μετοίκισις, which we know from early Greek and from Hebrew history. — *Ed.*]

⁴ This is the sense given by Hesychius to the word Heneti, sub voce 'Ενετίδας πώλους.

⁵ Mannert declares them to be of Slave origin.

by the Euganei, who had possessed the country before them, and who had given their name to a chain of volcanic hills between Este and Padua.

To the north of the Veneti, the Carni, probably of Celtic origin, covered the foot of the mountains which have taken their name, and some wild Illyrians had taken possession of Istria.

At a period probably contemporaneous with the invasion of the Ligurians, the Umbrians[1] (*Amra* — the noble, the brave) arrived, who, after bloody battles, took possession of all the countries possessed by the Siculi in the plains of the Po. Pursuing their conquests along the Adriatic, they drove towards the south the Liburnians, who left only a few of their number (Praetutians and Pelignians)[2] on the banks of the Prexara, and penetrated as far as Monte Gargano, where their name is still preserved.[3] At the west of the Apennines they subdued a part of the country between the Tiber and the Arno.[4] The Sicani, who had settled there, found themselves involved in the ruin of the Siculi, and many bands of these two nations united and emigrated beyond the Tiber. But they met there with new enemies; the natives, encouraged by their disasters, drove them gradually towards the country of the Oenotrians, who, in their turn, forced them to go with the Morgetes, and find a last asylum in the island which they called by their name. The Sicanians shared a second time their fate, and passed after them into Sicily.[5]

Heirs of the Pelasgians of the north of Italy, the Umbrians ruled from the Alps to the Tiber on the one side, and as far as Monte Gargano on the other. They divided this vast territory into three provinces: Isombria, or Lower Umbria, in the partly inun-

---

[1] The Gallic origin of the Umbrians accredited by antiquity, has been revived by modern writers. But the inscriptions found in Umbria, on the frontier, it is true, of the Sabine country, tell of a Latin tongue; we must then connect the Umbrians with the Sabellian Osci. Pliny (iii. 14) says of them, "gens antiquissima Italiae." The recent works of M. Bréal have proved that Umbrian was an Italian dialect, — which, after all, does not solve the ethnological question. M. Ern. Desjardins makes them a Ligurian people; M. d'Arbois de Jubainville makes them akin to the Latins.

[2] Ovid, who was himself Pelignian, gives to these people a Sabine origin (*Fast.*, iii. 95).

[3] Scylax (*Periplus*, p. 6). See the map of the kingdom of Naples by Rizzi Zannoni. At the centre of the group of mountains are found, besides the "Valle degli Umbri," other localities named Catino d' Umbra, Umbricchio, Cognetto d' Umbri (Micali, i. 71).

[4] The Umbro takes its name from them.

[5] Dionys. (i. 73) and Thucydides (vi. 2) fix this migration as having taken place two hundred years after the Trojan war, — of course without certainty.

PELASGIANS AND UMBRIANS.

dated plains of the Lower Po; Ollumbria, or Upper Umbria, between the Adriatic and the Apennines; Vilumbria, or Maritime Umbria, between the Apennines and the Tyrrhenian Sea.

Like the Celts and the Germans, they dwelt in open villages in the middle of the plains, disdaining to screen their courage behind high walls; but therefore exposed after a defeat to irretrievable disasters. It is said that when the Etruscans came down into Lombardy, the Umbrians, being conquered, lost at one blow three hundred villages. However, in the mountainous cantons of Ullumbria, after the example of the Tyrrhenian cities which were in the neighborhood, their towns were built on the summits, and surrounded with ramparts;[1] thus Tuder, close to the Tiber; Nuceria, at the foot of the Apennines; Narnia, on a rock which commands the Nar; Mevania, Interamna, Sarsina, Sentinum, etc., which by their construction

LIBRAL AS OF TUDER.[2]

are proof of a more timid, but also more advanced, civilization.

[1] These fortifications are perhaps the work of the Etruscans, for Umbria remained subject to them for a long time. "Umbria vero pars Tusciae" (Serv. *in Aen.* xii. 753). Livy (v. 33) says, without any restriction, that the Tuscan empire embraced the whole width of Italy, from sea to sea.

[2] Tuder (Todi) or, as it is called on the money, TVTERE, was early an important city. What is left of the walls resembles, in its greater regularity and absence of rudeness, those of Volaterrae and Perusia. It will be observed that its money, which dates perhaps from the fourth century B. C., is of remarkable elegance.

For three centuries the empire of the Umbrians gained for that people a reputation of great power; but it was broken by the Etruscan invasion, which deprived them of the plains of the Po and of Maritime Umbria, where the attacks of the Tyrrhenians,

FRAGMENT OF EUGUBINE TABLES (FROM IGUVIUM).[1]

who remained masters of a part of the country, had shaken their power.

Shut in from that time between the Apennines and the Adriatic, they were there subject to the influence and even to the rule of their neighbors. Etruscan characters are seen on their coins; they are found, too, on the tables of *Iguvium*, together

[1] M. Bréal, the learned author of the work entitled *Les Tables Eugubines*, has been kind enough to give me this passage from Table V. in both Etruscan and Latin characters. It contains two decrees given by the brotherhood of priests who caused the Eugubine tables to be engraved. The first decree, of which only the end is here reproduced, is in Etruscan letters; the second is in Latin letters; but the language of the two documents is the same, it is Umbrian. We only give a transcription of the commencement : —

"Ehvelklu feia fratreks ute krestur panta muta adferture si.
Rogationem faciat fratricus aut quaestor quanta multa adfertori sit.
Panta muta fratru Atiiediu mestru karu pure ulu benurent.
Quantam multam fratrum Attidiorum major pars qui illuc venerint
adferture eru pepurkurent herifi, Etantu mutu adforture si.
adfertori esse jusserint [quantam] libet, tanta multa adfertori sit."

The date of these two passages may be placed between the first and second centuries before the Christian era, but the language of them is much older.

with some words which appear to belong to the language of the Rasena; and finally, the soothsayers of Umbria had no less reputation than the Tuscan augurs.[1]

Oftentimes they banded together against the same adversaries. Thus the Umbrians followed the Etruscans to the conquest of Campania, where the towns of Nuceria and Acerrae recall by their names two Umbrian cities; and they took part in the great expedition against the Greeks of Cumae.[2] When Etruria understood that the cause of the Samnites was that of all Italy, Umbria did not abandon her at that last hour; sixty thousand Umbrians and Etruscans stretched on the battle-field of Sutrium bore witness to the ancient alliance, and perhaps blending, of the two peoples. Finally, when the loss of liberty left them no other joy than pleasure-seeking and effeminacy, they were devoted to these, and remained united still in the same reputation for intemperance.[3] Both, too, had had the same enemies to resist, Rome and the Gauls; with this difference, — due to the position and direction of the Apennines, which protected Etruria against the Gauls, and Umbria against Rome, — that the latter had first come to be more dreaded by the Etruscans, as no barrier separated them, and the former by the Umbrians, whose country opened into the Valley of the Po. The Senones invaded a considerable portion of it, and always struck across Umbria in their raids towards the centre and south of the peninsula.

The Umbrians were divided into numerous independent tribes, of which some dwelt in towns, others in the country. Thus while the mass of the nation made common cause with the Etruscans, the Camertes treated with Rome on a footing of perfect equality; Ocriculum also obtained the Roman alliance, but the Sarsinates dared to attack the legions alone, and furnished the consuls with two triumphs. Pliny still counted in his time in Umbria forty-seven distinct tribes;[4] and this separation of the urban and rustic populations, this passion for local independence, this rivalry between towns, was always the normal state of the

---

[1] Cic., *de Divin.*, i. 41.
[2] Strabo, V. iv. 3; Pliny, *Nat. Hist.*, iii. 5; Dionysius, *Ant. Rom.*, vii. 3.
[3] " Aut pastus Umber aut obesus Etruscus." — CATULLUS: xxxix. 11. On the dissoluteness of Etruscan manners, see Theopompus, in *Athenaeus*, xii. 14.
[4] Pliny, *Nat. Hist.*, iii. 14.

Romagna, of the marches of Ancona, and of almost the whole of Italy. In the fifteenth century, just as in ancient times, there were in the Romagna communities of peasants entirely free, and all the towns formed jealous municipalities.[1] Thus it happened that this energetic race, which had no knowledge of the litigious spirit of the Romans, and with whom might settled right,[2] — these men, that Napoleon declared to be the best soldiers in Italy, have, thanks to their divisions, submitted quietly to the ascendency of Rome, and came ultimately to obey the weakest of governments.

III.

THE ETRUSCANS.

OUR Western civilization has its mysteries, like the old East; Etruria is to us what Egypt was before Champollion. We know very well that it was inhabited by an industrious people, skilled in commerce, art, and war, rivalling the Greeks at the same time that they were under their influence, and for a long time powerful and formidable in the Mediterranean; but this people has disappeared, leaving us for its riddle an unknown language for a proof of what it once was, innumerable monuments, vases, statues, bas-reliefs, ornaments, objects precious both for workmanship and for materials, — a people rich enough to bury with its chiefs the means wherewith to pay an army or build a town; industrious enough to flood Italy with its products; and civilized enough to cover its monuments and tombs with inscriptions.[3] But

---

[1] See L. Ranke, *History of the Popes*, ii. 198.

[2] 'Ομβρικοὶ ὅταν πρὸς ἀλλήλους ἔχωσιν ἀμφισβήτησιν, καθοπλισθέντες ὡς ἐν πολέμῳ μάχονται καὶ δοκοῦσι δικαιότερα λέγειν οἱ τοὺς ἐναντίους ἀποσφάξαντες (Nic. Damasc., *ap*. Stob. Flor., 10, 70). Here we have the judicial duel of the Middle Ages. They said, too: 'Ἀναγκαῖον ἢ νικᾶν ἢ ἀποθνήσκειν. (*Ibid.*, 7, 39.)

[3] M. de Longpérier says of one monument, which was found at Cervetri (Caere): "It is directly connected with the Corinthian art of the seventh century, so that this tomb may give us an exact idea of what that of Demaratus, the father of Tarquin the Elder, must have been." (*Musée Napoléon III.*, explanation of pl. LXXX.) Let us note that the Etruscans interred their dead, and did not burn them; the contrary was the case in the later times of the Republic and under the Empire [or rather, both customs prevailed. — *Ed.*].

ETRUSCAN TOMB.

	Aeolo-Dorian.	Etruscan.	Umbrian.	Sabellian.	Oscan.		Aeolo-Dorian.	Etruscan.	Umbrian.	Sabellian.	Oscan.
A	A	A	A	ᴀᴧᴧ	N	O	O	*	*	*	*
B	B	*	B	B	ꟼ	P	⌐	⌐	⌐	⌐	⊓
C G	⊂⊂	⊃	*	*	⋁	Q	ᑫ	*	*	*	*
D	D	*	*	R	ꟼᖯ	R	ᑫ	ᑯᑫᑫ	ᑯ=ᑯ	ᐃᐃ	ᗡ
E	ᕮ	ᕮ	ᕮ	ᕮ	ᕮ						
F	FᒪᏞ	ᑊᑊ	ᒐ	ᒪ	ᒐ	S			ᔗᔖᔖ	ᔗᔗ	ᔗ
Z	I	⧻⧻	⧻		H	S	ꟽ	ꟽ	ꟽ	ꟽ	ꟽ
Eta	B	B	⊘	⊂⬥	B	T	T	⧻⧻⧻			T
T H	⊕	⊗⊙	⊙		*	V	⋁ᵞ	⋁ᵞ	⋁	⋁	⋁
I	I	I	I	I	I	PH	⊕ᐧ	⊕	,	,	,
K	K	*	K	K	K	PS	↓ᵞ	↓ᵞ	,	⊠	V
L	↓	ᐯ	ᐯ	↓	ᐯ	Ō	8	8	8	,	,
M	ꟽ	ꟽꟽ	ꟽ	ꟽ	ꟽ						
N	Ν	ᴧᴧ	ᴧᴧ	ᴧ	ᴧ						
(ss) X	⊞	*	*	*	·						

ALPHABETS OF CENTRAL ITALY (FROM LENORMANT'S ART IN SAGLIO'S DICT. OF ANTIQ.).

A much earlier alphabet than any of these, consisting of the old Phoenician 16 letters, has lately been found, and will be shown in Mr. Isaac Taylor's forthcoming work on Early Writing.

all this is mute, and modern science, wholly baffled, has hitherto been unable to interpret more than twenty words or so of the Etruscan language.[1] Their portraits which they have left us on their tombs tell us nothing more of them. These obese and thick-set men, with aquiline noses and retreating foreheads, have nothing in common with the Hellenic or Italiote type, and are not of the same race as the thin-featured people represented on their vases.

Whence did they come? The ancients themselves did not know. Deceived by the name of the Tyrrhenians, who had preceded the Etruscans north of the Tiber, the Greeks took them for Pelasgians, and represented them as having travelled from Thessaly and Asia Minor into Tuscany. But, on the testimony of Dionysius of Halicarnassus, their language, their laws, their customs, and their religion had nothing in common with those of the Pelasgians. Niebuhr and Otf. Müller consider that the Etruscans, or Rasena, as they called themselves, came from the mountains of Rhaetia.[2] As a matter of fact, there is no reason why the Etruscans, who placed the abode of their gods in the north, and gave[3] them the Scandinavian name of Ases,[4] should not be regarded as an Asiatic tribe, which, after having penetrated into Europe by the defiles of the Caucasus, by which the Goths afterward passed, had left on the

[1] See the work of M. Noël des Vergers, *L'Étrurie et les Étrusques, ou dix ans de fouilles dans les Maremmes Toscanes.* Varro (*de Ling. Lat.*, iv. 9) speaks of Etruscan tragedies which are lost. We have nearly two thousand inscriptions; but we cannot understand them, and Max Müller, in his *Science of Language*, is obliged to pass over the Etruscan in silence. The interpretations of Corssen, who [thought the language Indo-European, and] was for a time called "the Oedipus of the Etruscan Sphinx," have been abandoned, and the Sphinx remains mute [till we find a bilingual text. — *Ed.*].

[2] Livy (v. 33), Pliny (iii. 20), and Justin (xx. 5) maintain, on the contrary, that the Rhaetians are Etruscans who took refuge in the Alps after the conquest of Lombardy by the Gauls. Niebuhr supposes that the singular language of Groeden, in Southern Tyrol, is a remnant of the Etruscan language. Many names of places there recall the Rasena, and the Museum of Trent preserves vases and small figures in bronze with Etruscan inscriptions discovered in that province. Quite recently, in 1877, there were found in the Valteline, not far from Como, some Etruscan objects of great antiquity (*Rev. arch.*, Sept. 1877, p. 204). Ogiuli tried to prove in the *Giornale Acadico* the relationship of the Germans and Etruscans. M. Noël des Vergers, who has sought for the solution of the problem especially in the study of figured monuments, is disposed to accept the tradition of Herodotus as to their Lydian origin. But the plastic arts may have been introduced into Etruria later than the arrival of the Etruscans, by commerce, or previously to it by the Tyrrhenians. In short, the problem will remain insoluble until we decipher the Etruscan language.

[3] Fest. s. v. "Sinistrae aves."

[4] "Aesar . . . Etrusca lingua Deus vocaretur" (Suet. *Oct.* 97).

Florentine Inscription.	Etruscan Minor.	Perugian Inscription.	Patera from Nola, No. 2.	Vase from Bomarzo.	Vase Galassi.	Patera from Nola, No. 1.
A	ΔA	A	A	AA	AAA	AAAA
⟩	C	)	)	⟩	⟩ C	) ⟩
Ǝ	E	Ǝ	Ǝ	Ǝ	Ǝ Ǝ Ɛ	Ǝ Ǝ Ǝ
˥	⌐	Ⅎ	ᒣ	⌐ ˥	] ˥ ⌐	˥]
⊥	I	Ɛ	⸸			⸸ Z
⊟	日	⊠	⊟	◻	日⊟H	日⊟Θ
⊗	⊕	O	O	⬦	O⊙⬦▫	O⊙
I	I	I	I	I	I	I
⌐		⌐	✓	⌐	⌐	⌐
M	M	M	M	M M	M M M	M M M M
И	M	Ч	Н	И H	Ч Ч И	Ч Ч H
⋀	P	⌐	1	1	7 7	7 1 7
⋈		M	M	M	M	M M
⊲	q	D	q	⊲	⊲	⊲ ⊲ D
⟨	⟨	⟨	⟨	⟨	⟩ ⟨	⟩ ⟨ ⟨
†	T	†	†	†	† † T † ⎱	† † T Y
V	V	V	V	Y V	V Y Y	V Y
⬨		⌀		⬨	⌀	⌀ ⬨ φ
↓	Y	↓	↓	Y	↓ ↓	↓ ↓
8	8	8	8		8 8 8	8 8

SOME ETRUSCAN ALPHABETS.

south the peninsula of the Balkans occupied by the Pelasgian races, and had ascended the Valley of the Danube as far as the Tyrolese Alps. Priestly rule, division into strictly separated classes, and the predominance of fatalism, are characteristics more and more marked in proportion as we trace back the course of centuries and approach more nearly to Asia. Etruscan civilization has also in common with Semitic literatures the omission of the short vowels,

ETRUSCAN FIGURES. (ATLAS OF MICALI, PL. XIV).[1]

the reduplication of the consonants, and the writing from right to left. The dwarf Tages reminds us of the clever dwarfs and magicians of Scandinavia; whilst the obese figures found at Cervetri; the gorgons, of which there are so many representations; the gods with four wings, two spread and two drooped towards the earth; the sphinxes, the monsters which guard the approaches to the

[1] We reluctantly reproduce these figures, to which we find none analogous in Grecian art. But the Etruscans, so clever in the manufacture of bronzes, jewels, and vases, preserve the taste of barbarous nations for monsters to serve as bugbears. When they thought to make them terrible they made them hideous. We must show this side of their plastic art. [Similarly, in old Irish illuminations and carvings, the animals introduced are simply grotesque, and the human figures as bad as possible, while both the feeling and execution of the geometrical ornament is the most beautiful which can possibly be found. — *Ed.*]

mansions of the dead; the animals unknown to Italy, lions and panthers, devouring one another; the Egyptian scarabaei, the good and evil genii, like the *devs* of Persia, which conduct souls to the lower world; finally, a quantity of details of ornamentation,—show either borrowing from the East, or memories of their early home.

We have above compared the two industrious and universally persecuted races of the Finns and Pelasgians; we might also compare the two peoples who have taken their place,—the enigmatical language of the Rasena with the Scandinavian Runes; Odin, the Ases, and royal families of the Goths, with the Tuscan Lucumons, who were at the same time nobles and priests. Like the Germans, the Etruscans united what the East separates,—religion and arms, the caste of priests and that of warriors.

If the Goths believed in the death of the gods, and dared to strive against them, the Etruscans predicted the renewal of the world, and imagined that they could by their magic formulae constrain the divine will. The grave, melancholy, and religious character of this people, their respect for women, their kindness towards slaves,[1] the length and abundance of their repasts, would also suggest Germanic manners, if it were not probable that these resemblances are purely accidental. The saying of one of the ancients has, in fact, remained the opinion of modern science: "By their language and manners the Etruscans are separated from all other nations."

ETRUSCAN GORGON (CAMPANA MUSEUM).

We will suppose, without firm conviction, that the Etruscans came down from the Alps into the Valley of the Po, bearing with them from Asia, which they had perhaps quitted for but a few centuries, their half-sacerdotal government, and from the mountains, where they had recently sojourned, that division into independent cantons which has existed in all time among the people

[1] Dionys. *Ant. Rom.*, ix. 5. The Veientines enrolled them in their troops.

FIGURE WITH FOUR WINGS.

of the Alps. They first stopped in Cisalpine Gaul, where they possessed as many as twelve large towns; then they crossed the Apennines, and established themselves between the Tiber and the Arno. There they found some Tyrrhenian Pelasgians in possession of Hellenic beliefs, traditions, and arts, and in commercial relations with the Greeks of Southern Italy and Ionia. These Pelasgians, protected by cities stronger than the open villages of the Umbrians, could not be expelled or exterminated, and formed a considerable portion of the new nation.[1] Is it going too far to attribute the works of drainage,[2] the Cyclopean construc-

CHIMAERA IN THE GALLERY OF FLORENCE (MICALI, ATLAS, PL. XLII.).

tions, the pretended knowledge of omens, and the industrious activity of the Etruscans, to the influence, counsels, and example of these

[1] Especially in the towns of Southern Etruria, which always display characteristics differing from those of the northern cities, and through which the Greek religion obtained an entry into Rome. At Caere there have been found inscriptions thought to be Pelasgian. Moreover Caere and Tarquinii had each its treasure-house at Delphi, like Sparta and Athens, and the painted vases of Tarquinii are exactly similar to those of Corinth. We might call to mind, too, the religious character of the people of Caere and the reputation they had of having always abstained from piracy.

[2] See Noël des Vergers, *Etruria and the Etruscans*, i. 96. The railway through the Maremma has led to the discovery of a quantity of subterranean conduits for draining the soil.

Pelasgians,[1] who are said to have excavated the tunnels from Lake Copaïs through a mountain, to have built the fortifications, still remaining, of Argos, Mycenae, and Tiryns, and who passed for magicians on account of their learning? Moreover this people never had the spirit of hostility towards strangers; the tradition of Demaratus, the mixture of Umbrian, Oscan, Ligurian, and Sabellian names in the Etruscan inscriptions, and finally the introduction of the gods and arts of Greece, show with what facility they admitted men and things of other countries.

One particular feature of Etruscan manners is, however, in absolute contradiction to the Greek manners. This sensual people loved to heighten pleasure by scenes of death. They were accustomed to human sacrifices; they decorated their tombs with scenes of blood;[2] and gave to their neighbors of the Seven Hills those gladiatorial games which the towns of half the Roman world imitated.[3]

The ruin of the Umbrians was accomplished, said the Etruscan annals,[4] 434 years before the foundation of Rome. The Rasena succeeded to their power, and increased it by four centuries of conquests. From Tuscany, the principal seat of their twelve tribes, they subdued Umbria itself, with a part of Picenum, where traces of their occupation are to be found.[5] Beyond the Tiber, Fidenae,

[1] [To account for the Etruscans by referring them to the Pelasgi, and that, too, by attributing to the latter all sorts of works without any conclusive evidence, is indeed to explain *obscurum per obscurius*, and gives new point to Niebuhr's remark already quoted by the author. — *Ed.*]

[2] This design (see p. 68), taken from pl. XXI. of the *Atlas* of Noël des Vergers, represents Achilles immolating captives to the *manes* of Patroclus. This is the reading of the names written over the head of each figure, and M. Bréal's rendering of them, going from left to right, — ACHMENRUN (Agamemnon); HINTHIAL PATRUCLES (Ghost of Patroclus); VVP (?); ACHLE (Achilles); TRUIALS (Trojanus); CHARN (Charon); AIVAS TLMUNUS (Ajax Telamonius); TRUIALS (Trojans); AIVAS VILATAS (Ajax Oïleus). This scene of murder corresponded so well with the manners of the Etruscans, that when they wished to represent an episode of the Iliad, they chose the only narrative of this nature which is found in Homer. Many testimonies of ancient authors, and those which the Etruscans themselves have left on their monuments, bear witness to this odious feature of Etruscan society. Macrobius (*Saturn.* i. 7) says that Tarquin caused children to be immolated to the goddess Mania, the mother of the Lares. As for the winged figure who is standing behind Achilles, I should be inclined to take it for the genius of the hero. For the Etruscan doctrine of genii see below.

[3] [If more conjectures are encouraged, we shall soon have the Mexican Aztecs, so like the Etruscans in these and other points, declared to be their descendants. — *Ed.*]

[4] Varr., *ap.* Censor., 17; Dionysius said five hundred years. It is useless to add that these chronological data are valueless.

[5] Pliny, *Nat. Hist.*, iii. 5.

Crustumeria, and Tusculum, colonized by them, open the road towards the country of the Volscians and Rutulians,[1] who were brought into subjection; and towards Campania, a new Etruria was founded eight hundred years before our era, of which the principal cities were Volturnum, afterward called Capua, Nola, Acerrae, Herculaneum, and Pompeii.[2] From the cliffs of Sorrento, which were crowned by the temple of the Etruscan Minerva, they watched any vessels hardy enough to venture into the gulfs of Naples or Salerno, and their long galleys cruised as far as the coasts of Corsica and Sardinia, where they had settlements. "Then almost the whole peninsula, from the Alps to the Straits of Messina, was under their sway,"[3] and the two seas which wash the shores of Italy took and still keep, the one the name of this people, *Tuscum Mare*, the sea of Tuscany, the other of its colony of *Adria*, the Adriatic.

Unhappily, there was no union in this vast dominion. The Etruscans were everywhere, — on the banks of the Po, the Arno, and the Tiber, at the foot of the Alps and in Campania, on the Adriatic and on the Tyrrhenian Sea; but where was Etruria? Like Attica under Cecrops, like the Aeolians and Ionians in Asia, the Achaeans in Greece, the Salentines and Lucanians in Italy, the Etruscans were divided, in each country occupied by them, into twelve independent tribes, which were united by a federal bond, without any general league for the whole nation. For instance, when any grave circumstances occurred in Etruria proper, the chiefs of each city assembled at the temple of Voltumna, in the territory of Volsinii, to treat there concerning the interests of the country, or to celebrate, under the presidency of a supreme pontiff, the national feasts.[4] In the days of their conquests the union was doubtless very close, and, the chief of one of the twelve tribes being proclaimed generalissimo, exercised an unlimited power, indicated by the twelve lictors furnished by the twelve cities, with their fasces surmounted by

---

[1] Some tombs have been discovered at Ardea, the capital of the Rutuli, which appear to belong to the Etruscans, and the citadel of that town, more imposing than those of Etruria, is built, like them, of enormous stones.

[2] Livy, iv. 37; Cato, *ap.* Vell. Paterc., i. 7; Polybius, ii. 17. Lanzi adds to these five towns, Nocera, Calatia, Teanum, Cales, Suessa, Acsernia, and Atella.

[3] Cato, *ap.* Serv. in *Aen.*, xi. 567. Livy repeats it in almost the same terms in different places (i. 2; v. 33).

[4] Livy, v. i.; and elsewhere, *principes Etruriae*.

HUMAN SACRIFICE REPRESENTED IN THE CATACOMB OF VULCI.

axes. But little by little this bond was relaxed, and the Etruscans, who had at first presented the appearance of a great nation, were unable to escape this political particularism, which has been too dear to the Italians even up to our own days. At the epoch when

TUSCAN PLOUGHMAN.[1]

Rome seriously menaced Etruria, all union had decayed, and they had gone so far as to declare solemnly in a general assembly that each city must settle its own quarrels, and were not ashamed to explain that it would be imprudent to engage the whole of Etruria in the defence of one of its tribes.[2]

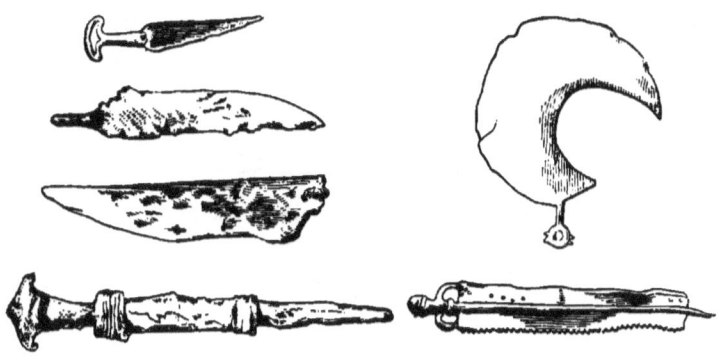

BRONZE ARMS AND TOOLS FOUND AT BOLOGNA.[3]

[1] This group in bronze, found at Arezzo, is thought to be connected with the legend of the birth of Tages.
[2] Livy, v. 17.
[3] In 1871 there were brought to light at the Chartreuse, near Bologna, 365 Etruscan tombs, and in the environs of Villanova numerous pre-historic objects, like

70   INTRODUCTION.

Each of these twelve tribes, represented by a capital which bore its name, possessed an extensive territory, and within it subject-towns were in dependence on the principal city, with inferior

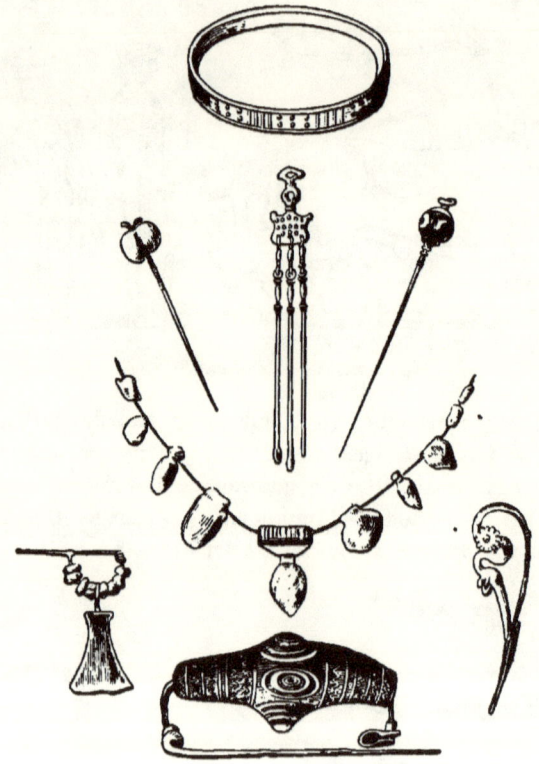

JEWELS FOUND AT BOLOGNA (SEE NOTE BELOW).

political rights; but in the capital itself the ruling power was the order of the Lucumons, the true patricians, who possessed, by

those of the lake-cities of Switzerland. In 1877 a single search at Bologna led to the discovery of an amphora 4½ feet high and 4 feet broad, buried doubtless at the moment of an invasion, and containing 14,000 bronze objects, utensils, arms, and ornaments. These bronzes were then precious and very expensive objects, spread through Italy and into the Transalpine countries by a commerce which was at once timorous and daring (*Rev. arch.* of June, 1877). Count Gozzadini places these bronzes as far back as the tenth century B. C.

hereditary right, power, religion, and learning. In some cases they governed the city in turn as annual magistrates, in others one of them governed as king,[1] but with a power limited by the privileges of that sacerdotal aristocracy which had united religion, agriculture, and the state by indissoluble bonds. The nymph Bygoïs had revealed to them the secrets of the augur's art, and the dwarf Tages the precepts of human wisdom with the science of the Aruspices. One day when a peasant was driving his plough in the fields of Tarquinii, a hideous dwarf, with the face of a child under his white

BRONZE VASES FOUND AT BOLOGNA.

hair, Tages, came out of a furrow.. All Etruria flocked thither. The dwarf spoke for a long time; the Etruscans collected his words, and the books of Tages, the basis of Etruscan discipline,[2] were for Etruria what the laws of Manu had been for India, and the Pentateuch for the Hebrews.

The common people, brought up by its superstitious fears to respect the great and to submit to the laws which they had dictated, did not dispute their dominion; and this docile obedience rendering violence superfluous, the aristocracy and the people were not separated by that implacable hatred which rends states asunder. Like the subjects of Venice, still so faithful, even in the last century,

[1] "Taedio annuae ambitionis regem creavere." (Livy, v. i.)
[2] Cic., de Div., ii. 23.

to the nobility of the Golden Book, the people fought for the maintenance of a social order wherein it held only the last place. But when the fortune of Etruria fell, the authority of the Lucumons was humbled. At Veii, at the commencement of the ten years' war, and at Arezzo, a century later, the plebeians dared to look their masters in the face and demand a reckoning.

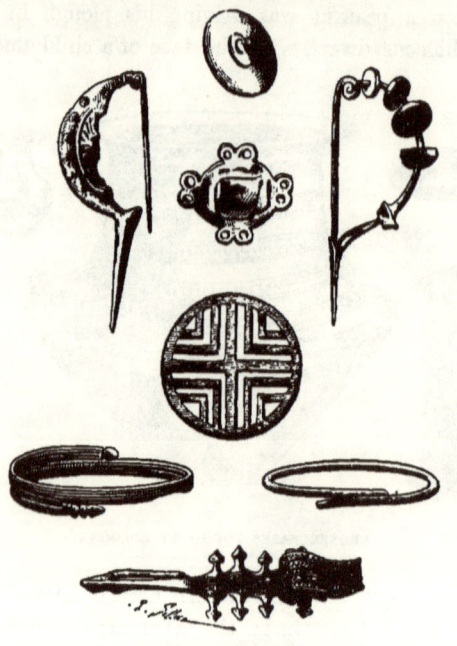

BRONZE JEWELS.[1]

The other Italian peoples lived scattered in straggling villages (*vicatim*). The Etruscans always had their towns walled, and generally placed on high hills, like so many fortresses dominating the country. Warriors, husbandmen, and merchants, they fought, drained the marshes, and dug harbors. India and Egypt, believing themselves eternal, spent centuries on majestic but idle monuments. Greece covered her promontories with temples, her roads with statues,

[1] For the description of these objects, see *Annales du Bull. archéol.* 1874, vol. xlvi. p. 249, *seq.*, and in the *Atlas*, vol. x. pl. x. *seq.*

the streets and open spaces of her towns with porticos. Here it was the disinterested genius for the arts, there a profoundly re-

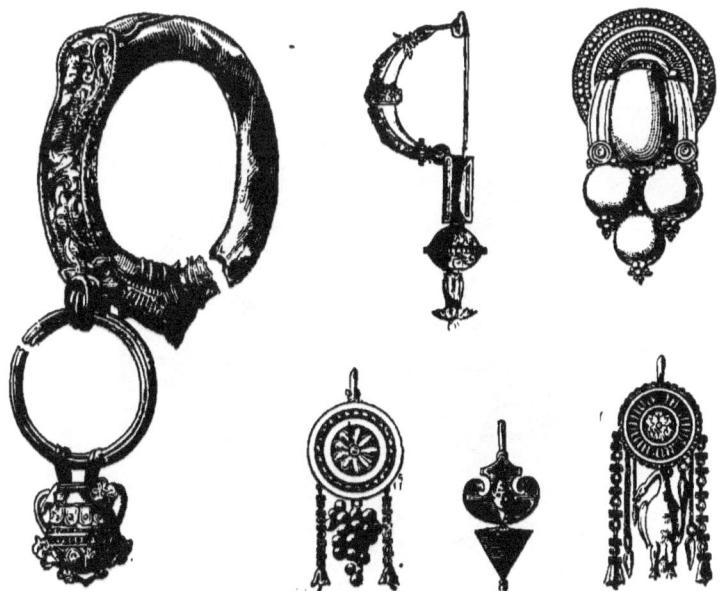

ETRUSCAN JEWELS AND EARRINGS.[1]

ligious sentiment and the hope of an endless existence. But Etruria knew that she and her gods must die; and anxious to live and

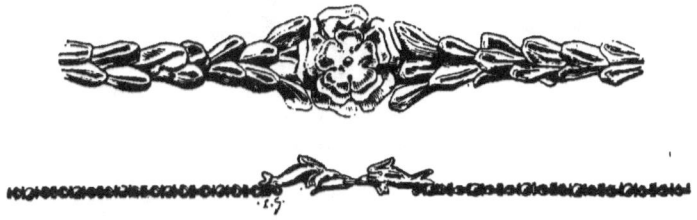

enjoy life before that anticipated end, she lavished time and men only on useful works, making roads, opening canals, turning aside rivers, surrounding towns with impregnable walls.

[1] These jewels are taken from Noël des Vergers' *Atlas*.

74 INTRODUCTION.

In Upper Italy, Mantua thus rose in the middle of a lake on the Mincio — a position to this day the strongest in the peninsula. Its metropolis, Felsina (Bologna), on the Reno, claims to have founded Perugia[1] also, and Pliny calls it the capital of Circumpa-

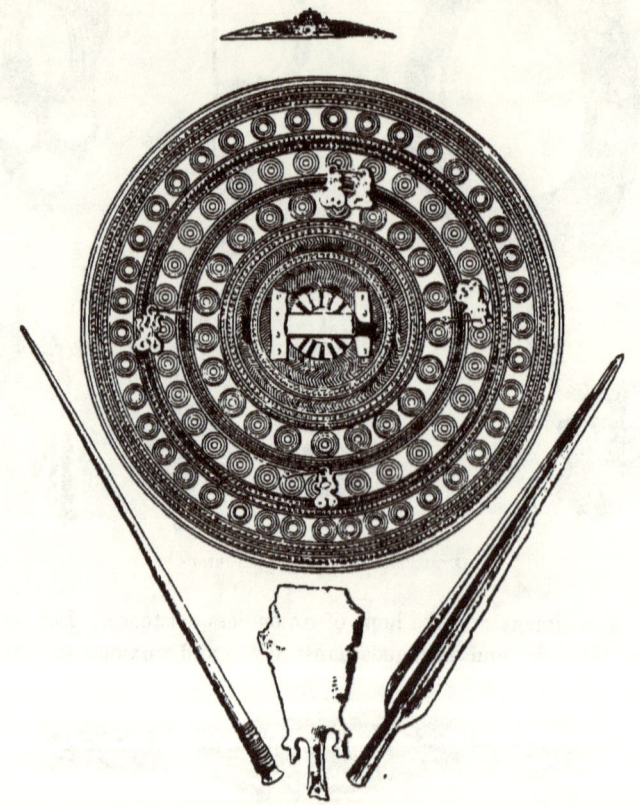

BRONZE ARMS.[2]

dane Etruria. Melpum, on the Adda, was able to stand against the Gauls for two centuries; and Adria, between the Po and the Adige, was surrounded by canals which, connecting the seven lakes of the Po, called the seven seas, rendered the delta of the river

[1] *Silius Ital.*, viii. 600.
[2] Bronze buckler and arms found in a tomb called that of the warrior at Corneto (Tarquinii): see *Atlas* of the *Bull. de l'Inst. archéol.*, vol. x. pl. x.

healthy. The waters, confined or let off, prepared the fertile lands for agriculture. Towns multiplied there; and from Piedmont to the Adige there are found Etruscan inscriptions, bronzes, painted vases, etc., relics of the rule of an industrious people.

In Tuscany the Valley of the Arno and that of the Chiana were drained, the Maremma made healthy, and six of the twelve capitals built upon that coast, now uninhabitable. While the towns carved marble, cast iron[1] and bronze, modelled clay into elegant vases, sculptured innumerable bas-reliefs, chased rich armor and precious jewels, and worked up linen for the priests, wool for the people, hemp for cordage, and wood for ships, a skilled agriculture — closely bound up with religion and an equitable division of land, which gave to each citizen his farm[2] — enriched the land, and covered it with a healthy population. Thus was realized that problem which antiquity was so seldom able to solve, — large towns in the midst of a fertile country, industry and agriculture, wealth and strength : *sic fortis Etruria crevit.*[3]

Meanwhile, from the numerous parts of the coast, from Luna, the town of the Marble Walls;[4] from Pisa, which was then nearer the sea than now; from Telamon, once a vast harbor, now only a swamp; from Graviscae; from Populonia; from Cosa; from Pyrgi; from the two Adrias;[5] from Herculaneum; from Pompeii, there sailed vessels destined for commerce, or cruising from the Pillars of Hercules to the coasts of Asia Minor and Egypt. More hardy adventurers went to Gaul to seek the tin of the Islands of the Cassiterides, necessary in the manufacture of bronze; farther still, to the shores of the Baltic, to seek the yellow amber, of which the women made their ornaments, and which was said by the Greeks to be formed of the tears of the daughters of the Sun weeping the death of Phaëthon. Silver coins of Populonia found in the Duchy of Posen show the route followed by the Etruscan

---

[1] The excellent ore of the Isle of Elba was brought to Populonia, where large foundries were established; the isle is only separated from the continent by a channel 10 kilom. wide (6 miles). [The mines are still worked, and give a good return. — *Ed.*]

[2] "Terra, culturae causa, particulatim hominibus attributa" (Varro, *ap.* Philarg. in *Georg.* ii. 169).

[3] Vergil, *Georg.* ii. 523.

[4] Near Carrara, *the Quarry*, where there is a mountain of white marble.

[5] The most famous between the Po and the Adige still bears the same name, but is more than 14 miles from the sea; the other, Atri, in Picenum, is 5 miles from the Adriatic.

merchants across the European continent. Carthage closed against them the Straits of Gades, beyond which they were desirous of leading a colony to a large island of the Atlantic, which she had just discovered;[1] but she gave up to them the Tyrrhenian Sea. Every strange vessel which they met westward of Italy was treated as a prize, unless some convention protected it.[2] When the Phocaeans came, in 536 B. C., to seek another country in these seas, the Etruscans united with the Carthaginians against those Greeks, whom the two nations met and fought everywhere.

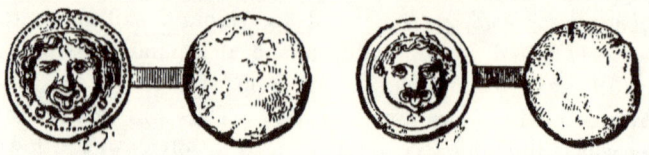

COINS OF POPULONIA WITH A GORGON'S HEAD, REVERSE SMOOTH.[3]

But this union could not last. The Carthaginians, who for their commerce with Gaul and Spain needed business settlements in Corsica and Sardinia, established themselves in those two islands in spite of treaties. Thence sprang up violent animosities, and an anxiety on the part of the Carthaginians to ally themselves with the Romans.[4] The hatred of Carthage was dangerous; yet less so than the rivalry of the Greeks, who occupied the most important commercial positions in Sicily, in Southern Italy, and as far as the centre of Campania, and who, through Cumae, menaced the Etruscan colony on the borders of the Volturno. As early as the middle of the sixth century some Cnidians established themselves in the Lipari Islands, whence they harassed the whole of the Tuscan commerce. Being attacked by a numerous fleet, they gained the victory, and in the joy of this unhoped-for triumph,

---

[1] Diod. v. 20. Ναυτικαῖς δυνάμεσιν ἰσχύσαντες καὶ πολλοὺς χρόνους θαλαττοκρατήσαντες.

[2] Aristotle, *Pol.* iii. 6.

[3] These medals give a full-face representation of the Etruscan Gorgon, which is seen on so great a number of vases and terra-cottas; but she no longer has the hideous head which the ancient monuments of Etruria gave her. The Greeks had the Gorgon too; but they disliked ugliness. When they had made her terrible, they made her beautiful; and Lucian ends by saying that it was by her beauty she exercised her fatal power of changing those who looked upon her to stone. [Lionardo's famous Medusa suggests the same idea. — *Ed.*]

[4] Shown by treaties of 509, 348, and 279 B.C.

THE ETRUSCANS.

they dedicated as many statues at Delphi as they had taken vessels.[1] Rhodes, too, showed among its trophies the iron-bound beaks of the Tyrrhenian vessels, and the tyrant of Rhegium, Anaxilaos, drove them from the Straits of Sicily by fortifying the entrance.[2] The Etruscans, therefore, sided with Athens against Syracuse. Hiero made them pay dearly for this alliance. In conjunction with Cumae, Syracuse inflicted on the Etruscans a defeat which marked the decline of their maritime power (474), and of which Pindar sung : —

"Son of Saturn, I conjure thee, cause the Phoenician and the soldier of Tyrrhenia to remain at their own hearths, taught

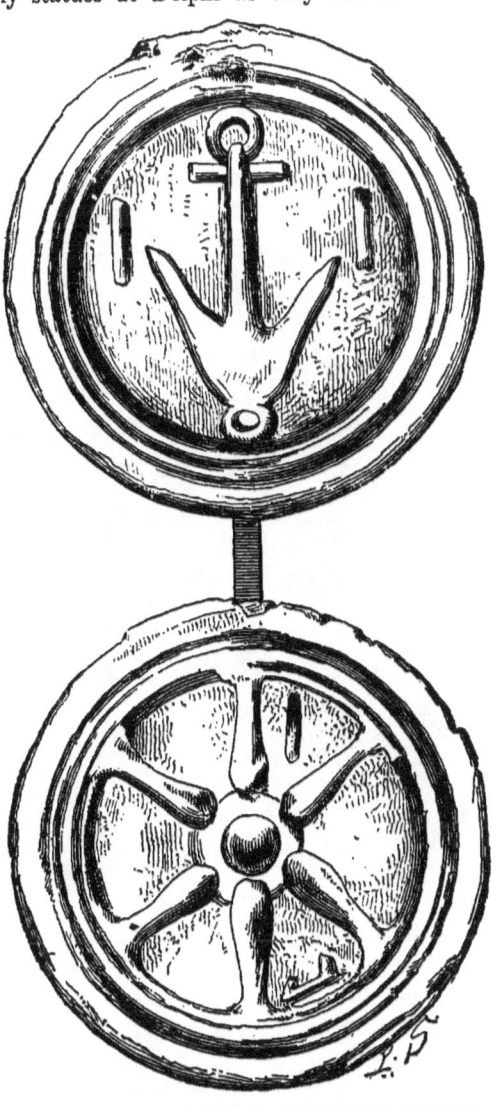

BRONZE COIN ATTRIBUTED TO THE ETRUSCO-UMBRIAN TOWN OF CAMERS.[3]

[1] Pausanias, x. 12 and 16. Thucyd., iii. 88.
[2] Strabo, VI. i. 5.
[3] This coin, with the sign of the wheel and the anchor, is a *dupondius*, or piece worth two asses, which are marked on the two sides of the anchor. Coins of even ten asses were made; but all these bronze multiples of the monetary unit are rare.

by the affront that their fleet received before Cumae, and by the evils that the lord of Syracuse wrought upon them, when victorious he cast all their brilliant youth headlong from the heights of the swift poops into the waves, and drew Greece from the yoke of slavery." Hiero made an offering to Zeus of Olympia of the

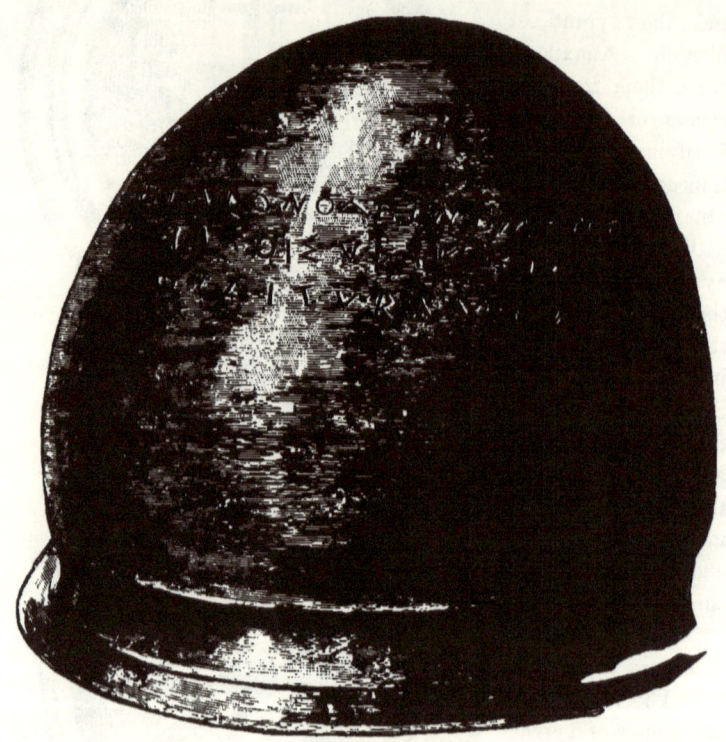

A LUCUMON'S HELMET.[1]

helmet of one of the Lucumons killed in this battle, with this inscription, which he had caused to be engraved on it: "Hiero, son of Deinomenes, and the Syracusans [have consecrated] to Zeus the Tyrrhenian [arms] from Cumae."[2]

[1] [This helmet was found in 1817 in the bed of the Alpheus, and is now in the British Museum.]
[2] Pindar, *Pyth.* i. 136, *seq.*; cf. plate above.

From all quarters enemies then rose up against the Etruscans. Threatened on the north by the Gauls, in the centre by Rome, and on the south by the Greeks and Samnites, they lost Lombardy, the left bank of the Tiber, and Campania, where the Samnites made themselves masters of Volturnum, slaying all the inhabitants in one night. At the end of the fifth century B. C. they retained only Tuscany. Moreover, divisions prevailed amongst them; in the midst of the public misfortune the league had been dissolved. Veii, attacked by the Romans, was left to herself, just as Clusium was abandoned when threatened by the Gauls. Such selfishness brought its own punishment. Veii succumbed, Caere became a Roman municipality, and Sutrium and Nepeta were occupied by Latin colonies. These disasters taught them no lesson, and Etruria viewed with indifference the earlier efforts of the Samnites. At last, however, she saw that it was a question of the liberty of Italy, and she roused herself fully. But she was crushed at Lake Vadimo; a second defeat completed the work. This was the last blood shed for the cause of independence. For some time longer the Etruscans, under the name of Italian allies, might think themselves free; but little by little the hand of Rome pressed more heavily on them, and at the end of a century, without any noticeable change, Etruria found herself a province of the Empire.

Calm under the yoke, and sadly resigned to a fate which had been long predicted,[1] this nation made no effort to strive against its destiny. They tried to forget, in luxury and the love of art, the loss of their liberty; and preserving amid their sensual pleasures the ever-present idea of death, they continued to decorate their tombs with paintings, and to bury in them thousands of objects, which in workmanship and material indicate extreme opulence. Etruria, in fact, was still rich; it will be seen what its towns gave to Scipio after sixteen years of the severest warfare.

[1] In the midst of the civil wars of Marius and Sylla, the Tuscan soothsayers declared that the great day of Etruria was drawing to a close. According to the calculations of their astronomical theology, the actual world would only last eight great days, or eight times 1,100 years, and one of these days of the world was accorded to each great people (Varr. *ap.* Censor, 17). Cicero, in the *Dream of Scipio*, also believes in the periodic renewal of the world: "Eluviones exustionesque terrarum quas accidere tempore certo necesse est" (*de Rep.* vi. 21). Virgil has clothed this grand idea with his magnificent poetry: "Aspice convexo nutantem pondere mundum," etc. (*Ecl.* iv. 50).

80   INTRODUCTION.

But the economical revolution which followed the great wars of Rome reacted on the provinces. As in Latium and Campania, the slave took by slow degrees the place of the free man, the shepherd that of the husbandman, and small properties were lost in great domains. When Tiberius Gracchus traversed Etruria, on his return from Numantia, he was alarmed at its depopulation. Sylla completed its ruin by abandoning it to his soldiers as the price of the civil war; the Triumvirs gave it another visitation. Thenceforward Etruria never recovered. Her social organization had perished; her language, too, was gone. From so much glory, art, and learning, one thing only survived; up to the last days of the ancient world the Tuscan augur retained his fame with the country people. None could better read signs in the entrails of victims, in the lightning flashes, or in ordinary phenomena.[1] It was a vain science, which rested on the enervating dogma of fatalism, and which infected the nation with a deathlike torpor.

The Etrurians played a considerable part, however, in the civilization of Italy, — not by their ideas, for they added nothing to human thought; nor by art, since as regards ideal work, theirs has little originality; but by their utilitarian conception of life, by their industry, and by the influence which they exercised upon Rome.

Livy calls the Etruscans the most religious of nations, the one which excelled in the practice of established ceremonies; the Fathers of the Church looked upon Etruria as the mother of superstitions. We shall see that she deserved this report. Their augurs' doctrine was famous among the ancients. They believed that the great events of the world were announced by signs; and they were right in believing it, if only, instead of observing the phenomena of physical nature, they had studied those of the moral order, — since the best policy is that which discovers the signs of the times. But the augur's art was only a collection of puerile rules, which held the mind in bondage, and made first them, and then the Romans, the greatest formalists in the world.

If we except the Greeks settled on the shores of the gulfs of Naples and Tarentum, they were the most civilized of the Italian

---

[1] Cicero, *de Divin.* ii. 12, 18. *Exta, fulgura,* et *ostenta* were the three parts of the science of divination.

nations. Their artisans were skilful, their nobles loved pomp in their ceremonies, and magnificence in their dress; and they gave Rome these tastes, together with their horse-races and athletic combats. They gave them, too, their massive architecture, which was a clumsy imitation of the Doric order. The temple of Jupiter

GATE OF VOLATERRA.

on the Capitol derived from them that flattened look which suited so well the dull Roman imagination, but so ill the God of the lofty heavens.[1] The gate of Volaterra and the Cloaca Maxima prove that they knew how to construct arches and vaults, which

[1] [This was mainly the result of the wide separation of the pillars, which give the Etruscan style a feeble and sprawling look, as compared with the Greek. The effect of widening these inter-columnar spaces is very marked. — *Ed.*]

the Greeks of the grand epoch had forgotten [or neglected]. The rude ogive of some Cyclopean gate had doubtless inspired them with the idea, and architecture was endowed by them with a new and precious future. They do not appear to have turned it to account for majestic constructions, as did the Romans of the Empire; but they employed the vault in their canals and tunnels to carry off the water and render the country healthy.

The senators of Rome, who lodged their gods in the Etruscan manner, lodged themselves like the Lucumons of Veii or Tarquinii: the *atrium*, which was the characteristic feature of patrician villas, is borrowed from the Etruscans; and from the Roman *atrium* came the *patio* of the Spaniards or Moors, and the Catholic cloister.[1] But whilst the Romans placed their tombs on the surface of the soil, as we do, the Etruscans dug funereal chambers underground, or in the rocky sides of their hills. Some of these, as, for instance, in the valley of Castel d'Asso, have a singular likeness to those which are seen at Thebes in Egypt. Sometimes they raised strange structures over the excavation which contained their dead, of which the fabulous tomb of Porsenna would be the most complete representation, if the description which the ancients have left us could be reduced to the conditions of probability.

Varro, if Pliny has copied him accurately, had made himself the echo of vague memories which tradition had preserved and embellished in its own fashion. "Porsenna," says he, "was buried beneath the town of Clusium, in the place where he had caused a square monument of hewn stone to be built. Each face is 300 feet long and 50 feet high. The base, which is square, enclosed an inextricable labyrinth. If any one entered it without a ball of thread, he could not regain the outlet. Above this square are five pyramids, four at the angles and one in the middle, each 75 feet broad at the base, and 150 feet high; so exactly equal that with their summits they all bear a globe of brass and a kind of cap, from which bells are suspended by chains, which when moved by the wind, emit a prolonged sound, such as was heard at Dodona. Above the globe are four pyramids, each 100 feet

---

[1] [More probably this method of house-building was common to all the Aryans of Southern Europe, certainly to the Homeric Greeks, as well as the Italians. It is the form now adopted all through the Mediterranean countries. — *Ed.*]

high. Above these last-mentioned pyramids, and on a single platform, were five pyramids, whose height Varro was ashamed to note. This height, according to Etruscan fables, was the same as that of the whole monument."[1] It has been attempted to explain this impossible construction by saying that the pyramids were not placed upon one another, but upon retreating surfaces.[2] This legend was, however, only half fabulous. Even at Chiusi, there have been discovered sepulchral chambers, forming a sort of labyrinth, through the narrow passages of which it is difficult to

THE CUCUMELLA.

make one's way, and the *Cucumella* of Vulci leads to the supposition that the glorious king of Clusium had a sumptuous tomb.

The Cucumella, situated in a plain, now an uninhabitable waste, is a *tumulus*, or conical mound of earth, from 45 to 50 feet high, probably higher in ancient times, and 650 feet in circumference. Though it has been searched several times, this tumulus has not given up its secret. Tombs have been met with, it is true, in the excavations; but only the obscure dead had their last abode there, and, like faithful servants, guarded the approaches to the place

---

[1] Pliny, *Nat. Hist.* xxxvi. 19.
[2] Quatremère de Quincy, *Recueil de Dissert. arch.*, 1836.

84   INTRODUCTION.

where their master reposed. The Lucumo and his kin were further in, in a central crypt, the access to which had been shut by a wall of such thickness that the workmen could not break through it. All efforts made to discover the entrance to this singular monument were useless: the pyramids of Egypt have not defended their sepulchral chambers so well. In the cuttings made round the outer wall were found animals in basalt, winged sphinxes, lions standing or couched, watching over this palace of the dead to drive away the audacious visitor who should attempt to pass the gate. On the summit were still seen the bases of partially crumbled

BRONZE VESSELS.[1]

towers. With the help of these remains it was possible to restore this mysterious tomb with some appearance of probability.[2] The edifice is utterly devoid of grace. But purely Etruscan art had not that gift which Greece received from Minerva; and strange as this construction appears, it is not more so than the *tumulus* of the Lydian king, Alyattes, on the banks of the Hermus.[3]

[1] For the description of these objects, see *Annales du Bull. arch.* for 1874, vol. xlvi. p. 249 *seq.*, and in the *Atlas*, vol. x. pl. 10–12.

[2] This restoration was made under the directions of the Prince of Canino, whose domain comprised the site of Vulci.

[3] Herodotus, i. 93; Stuart, *Mon. of Lydia*, p. 4; Texier, *Description de l'Asie min.* iii. 20.

VALLEY OF CASTEL D' ASSO.

THE ETRUSCANS.

To bury their chiefs under great *tumuli* was the custom of the Scythians, Germans, Celts, and Lydians, and consequently of the Pelasgians: it is therefore quite natural to find it again in Etruria, especially in the region where the Tyrrhenians had settled. The type of the Egyptian tombs shows itself, on the contrary, in the valley of Castel d'Asso, five miles from Viterbo.[1] The town has been destroyed, but its necropolis exists, excavated in the rock like the tombs of Medinet Abu. The façade is of the Doric order, — a general feature of Etruscan architecture, — and the gates, narrowing at the top, the decorations in relief, and the mouldings, recall the monuments on the banks of the Nile. Soana and Norchia, too, have their valley of tombs; those of Castel d'Asso were still unknown in 1808. In former days an immense nation moved in those solitudes, wherein the traveller dare no longer venture, as soon as he feels the close and deadly effluvia of the spring time in the Maremma.

BLACK VASES OF CLUSIUM (CHIUSI).[2]

The Etruscan excavations have yielded us an innumerable quantity of bronzes, terracottas, jewelry, and domestic utensils, all of excellent workmanship. Their *toreutic* was renowned even in Athens; the chasings, candelabras, mirrors of engraved bronze, gold cups and jewels from the land of the Tyrrhenians were sought for everywhere; and

---

[1] Castel d' Asso corresponds to the village of Axia, *Castellum Axiae*, which was situated "in agro Tarquiniensi" (Cic. *pro Caec.*, 20). See the description which Dennis gives of it, *Etruria*, i. 229–242; also the *Bull. arch.* for 1863, pp. 18–86. The cut is taken from the *Atlas* of the *Bulletin*, vol. i. pl. 60.

[2] Taken from Noël des Vergers' *Atlas*, pls. xvii., xviii., and xix; see the explanation of these cuts on pp 12–14 of the same work.

when, some years ago, the Campana Museum brought these marvels to our knowledge, the modern goldsmith was obliged to conform for a time to the Etruscan fashion.

Their figures have the rigidity of Egyptian statuary: the style had not reached even that of Aegina. Yet they furnished Italy with many bronze and terra-cotta statues of large dimensions. The Romans, who were niggardly even with their gods, thought that terra-cotta statues were a sufficient decoration for their temple of Jupiter Capitolinus, and they placed some of them upon the pediment.[1] They provided themselves yet more cheaply with statues of bronze, when they carried off two thousand at the sack of Volsinii.

BLACK VASE OF CLUSIUM.[2]

The ancients, who only learned very late to make wooden casks, were the best potters in the world: our museums contain more than fifteen thousand antique vases. The red pottery of Arezzo and the black pottery of Chiusi are purely Etruscan. The form is sometimes odd, but often very elegant. The ornaments in relief which decorate them, the fantastic animals seen upon them — sphinxes, winged horses, griffins, and sirens — recall subjects familiar to Oriental artists, and lead us to the conclusion already propounded on the diverse sources of Etruscan civilization. Some of these vases might even be taken for Egyptian *canopes*, those urns of which the cover is formed by a man's head. Among the specimens which we give is a ewer in the shape of a fish; the Campana Museum has another in the form of a bird. The learned are agreed to consider these black vases as very ancient, and Juvenal asserted that good King Numa had no others —

"... quis
Simpuvium ridere Numae, nigrumque catinum ...
Ausus erat?"[3]

As for the painted vases, they are copied from Greek vases, or

---

[1] [But it is not unlikely that the same fashion existed in Greece before they had learned to carve in deep relief or set up marble figures in the pediment itself. — *Ed.*]

[2] Taken from Noël des Vergers' *Atlas*, pls. xvii., xviii., and xix; see the explanation of these cuts on pp. 12-14 of the same work.

[3] *Sat.*, vi. 343.

else they were imported in the active commerce which Italy carried on with all the countries bordering on the eastern part of the Mediterranean — Egypt, Phoenicia, Cyprus, Rhodes, and, above all, both European and Asiatic Greece. The subjects most frequently represented on these vases are borrowed from the Epic cycle, from the mythology and heroic traditions of Hellas. Whenever they reproduce myths peculiar to Etruria, some reminiscence or imitation of the foreigner appears. Some vases of gilt bronze which were found at Volsinii have figures which remind us of the most beautiful coins of Syracuse.

We ought to give the Etruscans credit for having apprenticed themselves to those who, in the domain of art, have been the masters of the whole world, and for having preserved to us some of their masterpieces.

The most admirable of the antique vases come from the excavations at Chiusi;[1] and since an inhabitant of Vulci esteemed a Panathenaic vase precious enough to be buried with him, let us put in evidence what Etruria loved as well as what she manufactured.

[1] The François Vase at Florence, of which a representation will be found in the *Atlas* of the *Institut archéolog.*, vol. iv. pl. liv., lv., lvii.

IV.

OSCANS AND SABELLIANS.

IN their central parts, eastward of Rome and Latium, the Apennines have their highest peaks, their wildest valleys. There the Gran Sasso d'Italia, the Velino, the Majella, the Sibilla, and the Great Terminillo raise their snow-capped heads above all the Apennine chain, and from their summits afford a view of both the seas which wash the shores of Italy.[1] But their sides are not gently sloped; it seems as if they lacked space to extend themselves. Their lines meet and break each other; the valleys deepen into dark chasms, where the sun never reaches; the passes are narrow gorges; the watercourses torrents. Everywhere there is the image of chaos. "It is hell!" say the peasants.[2] In all ages this place has been the refuge of brave and intractable populations, and the most ancient traditions place there the abode of the Oscans and Sabellians, — the true Italian race.

Long driven back by foreign colonists, and, as it were, lost in the depths of the most sombre forests of the Apennines, these people at last claimed their share of the Italian sun. Whence did they originally come? It is not known; but historic probabilities, strengthened by the affinity of language and religion,[3] point to a common origin. The difference of the countries wherein they definitely settled down — the Sabellians in the mountains; the Oscans in the plain — established between them differences of customs and perpetual hostilities, which obscured their original kinship. Of these two sister nations, the one, profiting by the feebleness of the Siculi, must have descended, under the identical names of Oscans, Opici, Ausoni, and Aurunci, into the plains of

---

[1] [This wild Alpine country repeats itself twice again as you go southward; once along the boundaries of Apulia, where the Abruzzi, from Potenza down to the Monte Pollino, form a splendid chain, and again in Calabria, where the Sila Mountains embrace a large district of inaccessible Alpine country. — *Ed.*]

[2] They call one of these valleys *Inferno di S. Columba.*

[3] The Samnites spoke Oscan, the language of the Campanians, and the Atellan farces written in that language were understood at Rome. (Strabo, V. iii. 6.)

Latium and Campania, that ancient *land of the Opici*, which they had never, perhaps, entirely abandoned; the other must have in later times peopled with its colonies the summits of the Apennines and part of the Adriatic coasts: the latter led, in their warlike temper, by the animals sacred to Mars; the former by Janus and Saturn, who taught them agriculture, and of whom they made gods of the sun and the earth,—the sun which fertilizes, and the earth which produces.

In the time of their power the Siculi had possessed the land of the Opici; but the miseries which the invasion had inflicted on the Pelasgians of the banks of the Po gradually spread over the whole race, and a lively reaction brought the indigenous inhabitants out of their Apennine catacombs, and put them in possession of the plains which the Siculi had occupied. The Casci or Aborigines, that is to say, the oldest inhabitants of the land, began a movement which, though several times arrested by the conquests of the Etruscans, Gauls, and Greeks, finally resumed its course with Rome, and ended by substituting the indigenous race for all these foreign nations.

The latter, descending from the high land between Amiternum and Reate, established themselves south of the Tiber, where, by their union with the Umbrians, the Ausonians, and the Siculi, who remained in the country, was formed the nation of the *Prisci Latini*,[1] which occupied, between Tibur and the sea (33 miles), and from the Tiber to beyond the Alban Mount (19 miles), thirty villages, all independent.[3]

ALBA LONGA.[2]

In the first rank stood Alba Longa, which took the title of the Metropolis of Latium,[4]—a title which Rome, founded three hundred

---

[1] Dionys., *Ant. Rom.* i. 14; Nonius, xii. 3; Cic., *Tusc.* i. 12; Varro, *de Ling. Lat.* iv. 7; Fest. s. v.

[2] On the obverse, a helmeted head of Mercury; on the reverse, a Pegasus. But this Pegasus is neither the winged horse of the Muses nor that of Aurora, the legends of which are of comparatively recent origin; he bears the thunder and lightning of Jupiter, or rather, he is the lightning itself, traversing the heavens at a bound (Hesiod., *Theog.* 281; Apollod. ii. 3, § 2 and 4, § 2; Ovid, *Metam.* iv. 785 and vi. 119). This coin, of very clumsy workmanship, is very old, and may be assigned to the third or fourth century of Rome.

[3] Strabo, V. iii. 2: ὧν ἔνια κατὰ κώμας αὐτονομεῖσθαι συνέβαινεν ὑπ᾽ οὐδενὶ κοινῷ φύλῳ τεταγμένα.

[4] "Omnes Latini ab Alba oriundi."—LIVY: i. 52.

years later, claimed to have inherited. A religious bond, in the lack of any other, united these nations, and common sacrifices gathered them on the Alban Mount, at Lavinium, the sanctuary of the mysterious Penates and the native gods.[1]

Thus the nation from which Rome sprang was itself only a mixture of different tribes and races. Elsewhere successive races, instead of blending, drive out or overlay each other,— one ruling, the other enslaved. With the Oscans and Sabellians there is, on the contrary, a fusion of victors and vanquished. Greek traditions, which were always so intelligent, have faithfully echoed this origin of the Latin people; and it was by intermarriages and peaceful unions that Evander, Aeneas, Tibur, and the companions of Ulysses established themselves, just as at a later period intermarriages unite Rome and the Sabines. By its local traditions, as well as by its own origin, Rome was prepared for that spirit of facile association which gives her a distinctive character among ancient polities, and which was the cause of her greatness.

COIN ATTRIBUTED TO
THE RUTULIANS.[3]

In the eighth century the prosperity of the Latins was declining. The Etruscans had traversed their country, the Sabines had crossed the Anio, the Aequians and Volscians had invaded the plain and seized several Latin towns.[2] Alba herself, in tradition, seems feeble enough for a handful of men to have caused a revolution there. This weakness was of advantage to the growth of the Eternal City.

Ties of relationship and alliance united the Rutuli with the *Prisci Latini*. The Rutulian capital, Ardea,[4] was already enriched

---

[1] Janus, Saturn, Picus, Faunus, and Latinus were among these indigenous gods. Sacrifices were also offered in memory of Evander and of his mother, the prophetess Carmenta. One of the gates of Rome was called the Carmental.

[2] In the first centuries of Rome, Latin towns are assigned in turn to the Aequians, Sabines, Latins, and Volscians.

[3] On the obverse, a tortoise with two o's, the mark of the sextans; on the reverse, a wheel, — *rota*, the root of the word *Rutuli*.

[4] "Ardeam Rutuli habebant, gens ut in ea regione atque in ea aetate divitiis praepollens." — LIVY: i. 57.

by commerce and surrounded by high walls. Saguntum, in Spain, was said to be its colony.

Around this primitive Latium, which did not extend beyond the Numicius, and which nourished a stout population of husbandmen,[1] were settled the Aequians, Hernicans, Volscians, and Auruncans, all included by the Romans in the general term of Latin

WALL OF ALATRI.

people; further on, between the Liris and the Silarus, were the Ausonians.

The Aequians, a little nation of shepherds and hunters, insatiable plunderers,[2] had, instead of towns, only fortified villages, situated in inaccessible places. Quartered in the difficult region

" Et nunc magnum manet Ardea nomen;
Sed fortuna fuit."—VERGIL: *Aeneid*, vii. 412.
Dionys. (*Ant. Rom.*, iv. 64) is still more expressive.
[1] "Fortissimi viri et milites strenuissimi ex agricolis gignuntur."—PLINY: *Nat. Hist.* xviii. 5.
[2] "Convectare juvat praedas et vivere rapto."—VERGIL: *Aeneid*, vii. 749.

traversed by the upper Anio, they reached, by way of the mountains, as far as Algidus, a volcanic promontory, from which the Roman territory might be seen, and whose forests covered their march. Thence they suddenly poured into the plain, carrying off crops and herds; and before the people could take arms, they had disappeared. Faithful, however, to their plighted word, they had established the fetial right which the Romans had borrowed from them,[1] but which they seem no longer to have recognized at the time when, by their rapid incursions, they every year turned the attention of the people from their quarrels in the Forum. Notwithstanding their proximity to Rome, and two centuries and a half of wars, they were the last of the Italians to lay down arms.

Less given to war and plunder, because their country was

VOLSCIAN COIN.

richer, notwithstanding the rocks which covered it,[2] the Hernicans formed a confederation, the principal members of which were the cities of Ferentinum, Alatrium, and Anagnia.[3]

The imperishable walls of the two first-named towns, the linen books wherein Anagnia recorded her history, her reputation for wealth, the temples that Marcus Aurelius found there at every step, and the circus where the deputies of the whole league assembled, bear witness to their culture, their religious spirit, and their ancient might.[4] Placed between two nations of warlike temper, the Hernicans displayed a pacific spirit, and early associated

---

[1] Livy, i. 32.

[2] "Saxosis in montibus" (Serv. in Aen. vii. 684); he takes them for Sabines.

[3] "Dives Anagnia" (Verg., Aen. vii. 684). Strabo (V. iii. 10) calls it illustrious (πόλις ἀξιόλοχος).

[4] Ferentinum, on the Via Latina, between Anagnia and Frusino; Alatrium, a town of the same nation, is seven miles from the former.

themselves with the fortune of the Latins and Romans against the Aequians and Volscians.

The Volscians, who were more numerous, inhabited the country between the land of the Rutulians and the mountains which separate the upper valleys of the Liris and Sagrus. The Etruscans, who were for some time masters of a part of their country, had there executed great works for carrying off the water, as they had done in the valleys of the Arno, Chiana, and Po, and had brought under cultivation lands which yielded thirty and forty fold. These swamps, famous under the name of the Pontine Marshes, had been at first only a vast lagoon, separated from the sea, like that of Venice, by the long islands which afterward formed the coast from Astura to Circeii. They were bounded toward the south by the Island of Aea, which in later times was united to the continent under the name of the Promontory of Circeii.[2] The superstitious fears which always people deep forests and wave-beaten rocks with strange and threatening powers, placed the abode of Circe, the dread enchantress, on this promontory, as in Celtic tradition the nine virgins of the Island of Sein ruled the elements in the stormy seas of Armorica. This legend, which appears to be indigenous around the mountain, may be the remains

CIRCE, ULYSSES, ELPENOR.[1]

---

[1] This Etruscan mirror, taken from the *Etruskische Spiegel* of Gerhard (vol. iv. pl. cdiii.), was found at Tarquinii in 1863, and represents Ulysses, aided by Elpenor, forcing the enchantress to restore the human form to his companions, whom she had changed into swine. One of them still has a man's leg. The three names in Etruscan characters are: Cerca for Circe, Uthste for Ulysses, Felparun for Elpenor.

[2] Front., *Epist.* iv. 4.

of an ancient belief. Is not Circe, whom the Greeks connected with the ill-omened family of the King of Colchis, but who was said to be the daughter of the Sun, doubtless because in the morning, when the plain is still in shadow, her mountain is lighted by the first rays of the rising sun, — Circe, who changes forms, and compounds magic draughts of the herbs[1] her promontory still bears,[2] — may she not be some Pelasgian divinity, a goddess of medicine, like the Greek Aesculapius, who was also an offspring of the Sun, and who, fallen with the defeat of her nation, was degraded to a dread sorceress by the new comers?

The Volscians of the coast — with the Island of Pontia and the stretch of coast which they possessed; with the ports of Antium and Astura, and that of Terracina, which has a circumference of no less than nine miles;[3] with the lessons or example of the Etruscans, — could not fail to be skilful sailors; at all events they became formidable pirates. The whole Tyrrhenian Sea, as far as the lighthouse of Messina, was infested by their cruisers; and the injuries they inflicted on the Tarentine commerce nearly resulted in a war between the Romans and Alexander, the Molossian king of Epirus. Yet Rome had already conquered Antium and destroyed its fleet.

The Volscians of the interior were no less dreaded in the plains of Latium and Campania; and after two hundred years of war,[4] Rome only got rid of them by exterminating them. In the time of Pliny[5] thirty-three villages had already disappeared in the

---

[1] The *Crepis lacera* abounds there (Mic., i. 273); Strabo (V. iii. 6) was also aware that poisonous herbs grew there in great numbers; cf. Verg. *Aen.* vii. 10, *seq.* The memory of the dread enchantress still lives there; and not long ago no peasant could have been found who would dare for any money to penetrate into the grotto said to be Circe's. (De Bonstetten, *Voyage sur le théâtre des six derniers livres de l'Énéide*, p. 73.)

[2] Pliny, *Nat. Hist.* ii. 85 (87); iii. 11 (9) thought, as indeed the appearance of the region proves, that the promontory of Circeii had been once an island, which some were inclined to recognize as the problematic Island of Aea of Homer (*Odyss.* x. 135).

[3] De Prony, "Mém. sur les marais Pontins." "Anxur . . . oppidum vetere fortuna opulentum."—Livy, iv. 59. Cf. Pliny, *ibid.* iii. 9.

[4] Livy, vi. 21. "Volscos velut sorte quadam prope in aeternum exercendo Romano militi datos."

[5] Pliny, *Nat. Hist.* iii. 9: "A Circeiis palus Pomptina est quem locum xxxiii urbium fuisse Mucianus ter consul prodidit." In the whole of ancient Latium he mentions fifty-five ruined towns.

Pomptinum, since the reign of Augustus a region of pestilence and desolation.[1]

Between the Volscian country and the River Liris, in a mountainous region where but two narrow roads gave passage from Latium into Campania, dwelt the Aurunci. Inheriting the name of the great Italian race, they seem to have possessed also its unusual stature, its threatening aspect, and its bold character.[2] Accordingly, it is at Formiae, on their coast, that tradition placed the abode of the giant Laestrygones.[3] But since historic ages this race has remained obscure; Livy names the Aurunci only to relate the pitiless war that Rome made upon them, and the destruction of three of their towns.

Southward from the Liris lay the country known to the Romans as Campania, — a mild and enervating region, where no form of government outlasted more than a few generations, and the ground itself, with its constant changes, seemed to share in the vicissitudes of human affairs. The Lucrine Lake, once so celebrated, afterward became a muddy swamp; and the Avernus, "the mouth of hell," changed into a pellucid lake. At Caserna a tomb has been found ninety feet under ground; and the beds of lava upon which Herculaneum and Pompeii were built, themselves conceal a stratum of productive soil and traces of ancient culture. "There," says Pliny, "in that land of Bacchus and Ceres, where two spring-times bloom, the Oscans and Greeks, the Umbrians, Etruscans, and Campanians, rivalled one another in luxury and effeminacy;" and Strabo, marvelling that so many nations have been by turns dominant and enslaved in this land, lays the blame on its soft sky and fertile soil, — whence, says Cicero, come all vices.[4]

The Oscans in Campania have been, since historic times, only a race subject to foreign masters and blended with them, — Greeks being established along the coast, Etruscans in the interior, and Samnites coming down from the Apennines. A few Ausonian tribes, such as the Sidicini of Teanum and the Aurunci of Cales, alone

---

[1] Livy, vi. 12: "Innumerabilem multitudinem liberorum capitum in eis fuisse locis, quae nunc, vix seminario exiguo militum relicto, servitia Romana ab solitudine vindicant."
[2] Dionys., *Ant. Rom.* vi. 32, and Livy, ii. 26.
[3] Homer, *Odyss.* x. 80, 134.
[4] Pliny, *Nat. Hist.* iii. 9: ". . . summum Liberi Patris cum Cerere certamen." Cf. Florus, i. 16; Strabo, V. iv. 9; Cicero, *de Lege Agrar.* i. 6, 7.

preserved their liberty in the mountains which separate the Volturnus from the Liris. In Apulia, on the other side of the peninsula, the main stock of the population was also of Ausonian origin, as is proved by names of towns in the interior, and by the prevalence of the Oscan language through a great part of Southern Italy.

The Sabines, from whom nearly all the Sabellian peoples are descended,[1] originally occupied the high region of the Upper Abruzzi around the head-waters of the Velino, the Fronti, and the Pescara,

WALL OF AURUNCA.[2]

a country where the gradual melting of the snows keeps the pasturage good long after the sun has scorched the plains below. Here they had a city, Amiternum, and hence they came down upon the territory of Reate, driving out the Casci, while by way of Mount Lucretilis they stretched across to the Tiber. On the north they crowded the Umbrians back beyond the Nera; making predatory excursions southwards, they occupied part of the left bank of the Anio,

[1] "Paterque Sabinus" (Verg., *Aen.* vii. 178).
[2] Taken from the *Ann. du Bull.*, vol. iv. 1839.

and in the eighth century they were, after the Etruscans, the most powerful people in the peninsula.[1]

The Sabines, shepherds and husbandmen, like all the Sabellians, lived in villages; and notwithstanding the large population, which brought under culture and peopled the land up to the summits of the most rugged mountains, they had scarce any towns but Amiternum and Reate. Cures, the gathering-place of all the nation, was only a large village.

They were the Swiss of Italy: their habits were severe and religious; they were temperate, courageous, and honest; they had the unostentatious but solid virtues of the mountaineer, and they remained in the eyes of Italy a living picture of ancient times.[2] History, which recognizes in them one of the principal elements of the Roman population, will not hesitate to refer to them the frugal and laborious life, the austere gravity, the respect for the gods, and the strictly constituted family which are found at Rome in the early centuries, and which were long preserved there.[3] They resemble the ancient Romans, too, in their contempt for mental culture, — in all their land not a single Sabine inscription has been found.

When in these arid mountains famine seemed imminent or some war was unsuccessful, they devoted to the gods, by a sacred spring-time (*ver sacrum*), everything which was born in March or April. Even children were offered in sacrifice. In later times the gods grew milder, only cattle were immolated or redeemed; and the children, when they reached the age of twenty, were conducted with veiled heads out of the territory, like those Scandinavian hordes, which, at fixed epochs, the law drove from the land in order to prevent famine. Oftentimes the god himself protected these young colonies, *sacranae acies vel Mamertini*, and sent them divine guides. Thus of the animals sacred to Mars, a woodpecker (*picus*) led the Piceni; a wolf (*hirpus*) the Hirpini; and a wild bull the Samnites.[4]

---

[1] Livy, i. 30.

[2] "... Severissimorum hominum, Sabinorum" (Cic., *in Vat.* 15; *pro Lig.* 2). "Disciplina tetrica ac tristi veterum Sabinorum" (Livy, i. 18).

[3] Verg., *Georg.* ii. 532; Servius in *Aen.* viii. 638: "Sabinorum mores populum Romanum secutum Cato dicit."

[4] Fest. s. v. "ver sacrum;" Pliny, *Nat. Hist.* iii. 18. During the Second Punic War the

98   INTRODUCTION.

"From the Sabines," says Pliny,[1] "the Picentines are descended, by a sacred spring-time." But too many different races occupied this coast for an unmixed people to have resulted therefrom. In their fertile valleys the Picentines remained unaffected by all the Italian wars, and multiplied at leisure. Pliny asserts[2] that when they submitted to Rome, in 268, they were 360,000 in number. Among them were counted the Praetutians, who formed a distinct nation, settled in the high lands. By a singular chance, it was these poor mountaineers, scarce known to the historians of Rome, who gave their name to the centre of the peninsula, the Abruzzi.

COIN OF TEATE, CAPITAL OF THE MARRUCINI.[3]

The vast province commonly called by the name of the Samnium, and which includes all the mountains south of Picenum, and the Sabine land as far as Magna Graecia, was divided between two confederations, formed of what were held to be the bravest nations in Italy.

In the first league the Marsi and Peligni were most renowned for their courage. "Who shall triumph over the Marsi, or without the Marsi?"[4] said they. Next to the Etruscan aruspex there were no diviners more celebrated for their skill in reading signs, especially the flight of birds, than those of the Marsians. Among them we meet again with the *psylli* of Egypt and the physician-sorcerers of the natives of the New World, who

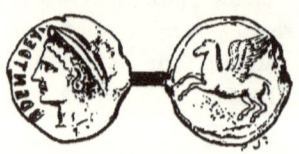

COIN OF THE FRENTANI.[5]

Romans made a similar vow, with the exception of the proscription of children (Livy, xxii. 9). Sabine traditions said, too, that Semo Sancus, also named Dius Fidius, the divine author of the Sabellian race, had substituted rites free from blood for human sacrifices (Dionysius, *Ant. Rom.* i. 38).

[1] *Hist. Nat.* iii. 13.
[2] Ibid.
[3] On the obverse, a head of Pallas, above, five o's, the sign of the quincunx; on the reverse, this same mark, a crescent, an owl standing on a capital, and the word TIATI.
[4] Appian, *Bellum civile*, i. 46. "Genus acre virum" (Verg., *Georg.* ii. 167). "Fortissimorum virorum, Marsorum et Paelignorum" (Cic., *in Vatin.* 15).
[5] A head of Mercury with the word FRENTREN in Oscan characters; on the reverse, Pegasus flying.

healed with the simples gathered in their mountains, and with their magic incantations, *neniae*.¹ One family, which never intermarried with the rest, had the gift of charming vipers, with which the country of the Marsians abounded, and of rendering their bites harmless.² In the time of Elagabalus the reputation of the Marsian sorcerers still remained; even to this day the jugglers who go to Rome and Naples to astonish the people by their tricks with serpents, whose poisonous fangs they have extracted, always come from what was once the Lake of Celano (*Fucinus*³). Now it is St. Dominic of Cullino who bestows this power; three thousand years ago it was a goddess held in great veneration in those same places, the enchantress Angitia, sister of Circe, or perhaps Medea herself, of the gloomy race of Aeetes. Names change, but superstition endures, when men remain under the influences of the same places and in the same state of ignorance.

The country of the Marsians and Pelignians, situated in the heart of the Apennines, was the coldest in the peninsula:⁴ thus the flocks, which in summer left the scorched plains of Apulia, went then, as they do now, to feed in the cool valleys of the Pelignians, who moreover produced excellent wax and the finest of flax.⁵ Their stronghold of Corfinium was chosen during the Social war to serve, under the significant name of *Italica*, as the capital of the Italians who had risen against Rome.

The other great Sabellian league consisted of the Samnite people, who had more brilliant destinies, great riches, a name dreaded as far as Sicily, as far even as Greece, but who paid for all this glory by fearful disasters Being led, according to their legends, from the country of the Sabines to the mountains of Beneventum by the wild bull whose image is found on the coins of the Social war, the Samnites mingled with the Ausonian tribes,

---

¹ Cf. Hor., *Epod.* xvii. 29.

² "Spargere qui somnos cantuque manuque solebat,
Mulcebatque iras et morsus arte levabat."
VERGIL: *Aeneid*, vii. 754.

³ Lake Fucinus, the area of which was 37,500 acres, and the depth 58 feet, was drained by Prince Torlonia between Aug. 9, 1862, and the end of June, 1875.

⁴ The ancients had a proverbial saying, *Peligna frigora* and *Marsae nives*; now they say *freddo d' Abruzzo*.

⁵ Pliny, *Nat. Hist.* xi. 14; xix. 2.

who remained in the Apennines, and spread from hill to hill as far as Apulia. While the Caudini and Hirpini[1] settled on the slopes of Mount Taburnus, the foot of which reached to a valley rendered famous by them under the name of the Caudine Forks, the Frentani established themselves near the upper sea, and irregular bands of them passed over the Silarus and formed on the further side the nation of the Lucanians, which early separated itself from the league. This was composed of four nations (*Caraceni, Pentri, Hirpini,* and *Caudini*), to whom belongs more particularly the glorious name of Samnites.

SAMNITE WARRIOR, AFTER A PAINTED VASE IN THE LOUVRE.

Their country, surrounded by the Sangro, Volturno, and Calore, is covered with rugged mountains (the Matese), which preserve the snow until May,[2] and of which the highest peak, Mount Miletto, rises to 6,500 feet. Thus the flocks found fresh pasturage and abundant springs among these high valleys during the scorching summer. These constituted the wealth of the country. Their produce sold in the Greek towns on the coast; the pay which they often received under the title of auxiliary troops; but, above all, the booty which they brought back from their raids into Magna Graecia, accumulated great wealth in the hands of these warlike shepherds. In the time of the war against Rome the abundance of bronze in Samnium was so great that the younger Papirius carried off more than two million pounds of it;[3] and his colleague Carvilius had made, with nothing but the armor taken from the Samnite foot-soldiers, a colossal statue of Jupiter, which he placed on the Capitol, and which could be seen from

---

[1] Festus, s. v. *Hirpinos;* cf. Strabo, V. iv. 12; Serv. *in Aen.* xi. 173.
[2] Keppel-Craven, *Excursion in the Abruzzi.*
[3] Livy, x. 46.

the summit of the Alban Mount.[1] Like all warrior-nations, the Samnites exhibited their luxury in their armor; bright colors shone on their war-dress, gold and silver on their bucklers. Each soldier of the higher classes, arming at his own cost, was anxious to prove his valor by the splendor of his arms. And yet the wealth of the army does not imply the wealth of the people.

Calculating according to the numbers furnished by the historians of Rome, the population of Samnium has been rated at two million souls.[2] This result is an evident exaggeration, like the premises on which it rests. If the Samnites were not able to arm against Rome more than 80,000 foot soldiers and 8,000 cavalry, their population must have amounted at the most to 600,000 inhabitants. But it was sufficient for these stout soldiers, sometimes united under the supreme command of an *embradur* (imperator), to spread their raids and conquests all around their mountains. Their principal wealth consisted in their flocks; but for six or seven months the snow covered the pasture in the mountains, so that it was necessary to descend into the plains.[4] Hence came continual wars with neighboring nations.

MEDAL OF SAMNIUM.[3]

Though united in the same league, the four Samnite nations each formed under its *meddix tuticus* a distinct and sovereign society, which often neglected the general interest to follow out particular enterprises. These sons of Mars, whose ancestors religion and policy had exiled, remained faithful to their origin. They preferred to the bonds which give strength, the isolation which first gives liberty, but presently promotes slavery.

[1] Pliny, *Nat. Hist.* xxxiv. 7 (18).
[2] Micali, *Storia*, etc. i. 287.
[3] Obverse, helmeted, the head of Mars, with the words *Mutii embradur*, in Oscan characters; reverse, two chiefs taking oath over a pig, which a kneeling soldier holds, and the legend C.ΡΛΑΡΙ for Papius, in Oscan characters. One C. Papius Mutilus was *embradur* of the Samnites in the Social War, 90—89 B. C.
[4] We know that the tribute levied on the cattle which passed from the plains to the mountains in summer and back again in winter was the principal revenue of the kingdom of Naples, in later times nearly £800,000 per annum. The kings of Arragon had forced the tenants of the crown in Apulia to let the flocks of the Abruzzi pasture in their fields in winter. In our own days the landlords of Apulia were obliged to keep two thirds of their land for grazing; see Keppel-Craven, *Excursion in the Abruzzi*, 1,267, and Symonds, p. 241.

If the thirteen Sabellian nations had been united, Italy was theirs. But the Lucanians were at enmity with the Samnites, the latter with the Marsic confederation, the Marsians with the Sabines, and the Picentines remained strangers to all the mountaineers' quarrels. Yet Rome, which represented, as no other ancient State had ever done, the opposite principle of political unity, only triumphed after the most painful efforts, and by exterminating this indomitable population.[1] She was, moreover, compelled to undertake the work of destruction twice over. The Samnite and Second Punic wars had already made many ruins and solitudes; but when the vengeance of Sulla had passed over that desolated land, Florus could say: "In Samnium itself it would be vain to seek for Samnium." The ruin was so complete that only a few monuments of those people are left us; and more than twenty of their towns have disappeared without leaving any trace behind.

On the south-east, Tarentum and the great towns of Apulia stayed the Samnites; but towards the west the Etruscans of Campania were unable to defend that rich territory against them. Tired of their continual expeditions, the Etruscans thought to buy peace by sharing with the Samnites their fields and towns. One night they were surprised and massacred (about 423); Vulturnum took the name of Capua, and that of Campanians distinguished the new masters of the country.[2] The great Greek city, Cumae, was then taken by assault, and a Campanian colony replaced a part of the massacred inhabitants; yet without making the Oscan language and Sabellian customs supersede the Greek.[3] These herdsmen, who in their mountains raised fine breeds of horses,[4] became in the Campanian plains the best horsemen of the peninsula; and the

MEDAL OF TERINA.[5]

---

[1] Livy, and after him all the historians of Rome, have exaggerated this depopulation of Samnium, since according to the census preserved by Polybius, that country could furnish 77,000 soldiers after the First Punic War.

[2] Diod. xii. 31: τὸ ἔθνος τῶν Καμπανῶν συνέστη.

[3] See Livy, xl. 42, where the Cumaeans demand the substitution of Latin for Greek in public records.

[4] Especially in those of the Hirpini, whose country still rears an excellent breed.

[5] Silver coin: obverse, a woman's head; reverse, the nymph Lygea seated.

renown which this conquest won for them led the way to more. To the north, east, and south they were surrounded by difficult countries and warlike nations, which blocked the road to fresh enterprises; but the sea remained open, and they knew that beyond the gulfs of Paestum and Terina there was booty to be obtained and adventures to be found in Sicily. Under the ancient and expressive name of *Mamertines*, the Campanian horsemen offered to serve any one who would pay them. The rivalry between the Greek cities, the ambition of the tyrants of Syracuse, the Carthaginian invasion, and the ceaseless war which desolated the whole island, always provided them with purchasers for their valor; and this trade of mercenaries became so lucrative that all the bravest of the Campanian youth passed over into the island, where the Mamertines were soon numerous enough to lay down the law and take their own way.

But whilst beyond the straits they were become a power against which Carthage, Syracuse, and Pyrrhus strove in vain, their towns on the banks of the Vulturnus were being enfeebled by the same migrations which increased the military colony in Sicily. As early as the middle of the fourth century, at Cumae, Nola, and Nuceria, the ancient inhabitants became masters again; and if Capua maintained its supremacy

COIN OF CAPUA.[1]

over the neighboring towns, it was only by losing all its Sabellian character. The effeminacy of the ancient manners reappeared, but stained with more cruelty. In funeral ceremonies there were combats of gladiators in honor of the dead; in the midst of the most sumptuous feasts, games of blood to enliven the guests,[2] and constant murder and treason in public life.

We havé seen how the Samnites possessed themselves of the town by the massacre of their entertainers; the first Roman soldiers who were placed there, wished, according to their example, to put the inhabitants to death. During the Second Punic War, Capua

---

[1] Laurel-crowned head of Jupiter; two soldiers joining swords, taking the oath over a pig.

[2] Athenaeus, iv. 39; Livy, ix. 40; Silius, xi. 51.

sealed her alliance with the Carthaginians by the blood of all the Romans settled within her walls, and Perolla wished at his father's table to stab Hannibal. When, finally, the legions re-entered it, all the senators of Capua celebrated their own funeral rites at a joyous feast, and drank poison in the last cup. No history is more bloody, and nowhere was life ever more effeminate.

COIN OF LUCANIA.[1]

The Lucanians had a destiny both less sad and less brilliant. Following the chain of the Apennines, this people entered ancient Oenotria, the coasts of which were occupied by Greek cities, and where Sybaris ruled from the Gulf of Paestum to that of Tarentum. After having slowly increased in the mountains, their population came down upon the cultivated territory of the Greek cities, and towards the middle of the fifth century, Pandosia, with the neighboring towns, fell into their power. Masters of the western shores, they turned towards those of the

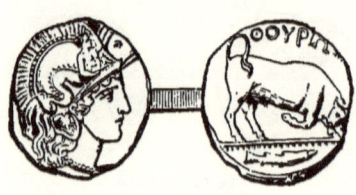

COIN OF THURII.[2]

Gulf of Tarentum, and placed the Greeks, already menaced on the south by the tyrants of Syracuse, between two dangers. Towards 430 B. C., they were already contending against Thurii; and such was their progress in the space of thirty-six years, notwithstanding their small number, which did not exceed 34,000 combatants,[3] that a great defensive league, the first that the Greeks of this coast had made, was formed against them and Dionysius of Syracuse. The penalty of death was pronounced against the chief of the city whose troops should not have assembled at the first news of the approach of the barbarians (394 B. C.).[4] These measures were fruitless; three years afterward, all the youth of Thurii, desirous of recapturing the city of Laus, were

---

[1] Helmeted head of Mars; reverse Bellona.
[2] Head of Minerva, and the bull so frequently found on the coins of Southern Italy.
[3] Diodorus, xiv. 101-102.
[4] Ibid. 91.

destroyed in a battle which gave almost the whole of Calabria into the hands of the Lucanians.[1] Dionysius the Younger, frightened in his turn, in spite of a treaty concluded with them in 360 B.C.,[2] traced from the Gulf of Scylacium to that of Hipponium a line of defence, intended to protect his Italian possessions against them.[3]

This period marked the greatest extension of the Lucanians. Thenceforth they did nothing but give way, enfeebled as they were by the lack of harmony between their different cantons, each of which had its peculiar laws and its chief (*meddix* or *praefucus*). Towards 356 B.C., the Bruttians make their appearance, whose revolt was countenanced by Dionysius; and little by little the frontier of Lucania receded as far as Laus and the Crathis. Shut in on the south by the Bruttians, who were as brave as themselves, they sought compensation at the expense of the Greeks on the shores of the Gulf of Tarentum; but this was only to call down upon them the arms of Archidamos, of Alexander the Molossian, and of the Spartan Cleonymus. Later, their attacks on Thurii brought on the war with Rome which cost them their independence.

Of all the Sabellian peoples, the Lucanians seem to have remained the most unpolished, and most eager for war and destruction. The civilization which surrounded them was not powerful enough to penetrate into those rugged mountains, into those deep forests, where they sent their sons to hunt the bear, the wild boar, and other game, in order to accustom them early to danger.[4] Not very numerous, and often divided, they nevertheless kept the conquered population rigorously enslaved, and extinguished in them even that Greek culture which had such vitality. "Having been barbarized," says Athenaeus[5] of the inhabitants of Posidonia, "having lost even their language, they had at least preserved a

---

[1] From Pandosia to Thurium, and even as far as Rhegium, Scylax, who wrote about 370 B.C., knows nothing but Lucanians all along the coast.

[2] Diod., xvi. 5.

[3] Strab., VI. i. 10.

[4] Justin, xxiii. 1. [The wild boar and the wolf are still found in these mountains, especially in the wild forests of the Sila. — *Ed.*]

[5] Justin, xiv. 31. [It is difficult to conceive any real forgetfulness of their Hellenic culture, with the splendid temples before them, and which now, even in their ruin, are among the finest and most suggestive remains which modern Hellenists can study. — *Ed.*]

Greek festival, during which they gathered together to re-awaken the ancient traditions, to recall the beloved names and their lost country; and then they parted weeping," — a sad and touching custom, which attests a hard slavery. At the extremity of Eastern Calabria (the land of Otranto), inscriptions have been found which cannot be assigned to any known dialect.[1] They had been left there by the Iapygians, one of the most ancient nations of the peninsula. They seem to have ruled as far as Apulia, but were early brought under Hellenic influence, and began early to lose their nationality among the Greek colonists.

V.

GREEKS AND GAULS.

WE have just spoken of truly Italian races, of those, at least, who, with the exception of the Etruscans, made use of a sister language to the Hellenic, and who gave to Rome its population, its manners, and its laws. There remain two nations to study, the Greeks and the Gauls, who established themselves later in the peninsula. The latter harassed it for a long time by their raids for plunder; the former opened it up to Hellenic civilization. A few years ago Greek was still spoken in the neighborhood of Locri;[2] in the Calabrias, a sort of sacred dance resembles that which is represented on antique vases; and at Cardeto the women have so well preserved the type of Hellenic beauty, that it is said of them, "They are Minervas." In the same way it has been thought that, from Turin to Bologna, the persistent traces of the Celtic invasion[3] are to be seen in the features and in the comparatively harsh and guttural accent of the Piedmontese, Lombards, and Romagnols.

[1] [These Messapian texts are being deciphered by Deecke, and are related to Italic dialects. — *Ed.*]

[2] [There are also five villages near Bari, where a Greek patois is still spoken; but Lenormant has lately proved, in his interesting work on Magna Graecia, that all these remains of Greek date from the repopulation of these parts of the Byzantine Empire in the ninth-eleventh centuries A. D., and not from old classical times. — *Ed.*]

[3] Dr. Edwards, in his letter to Am. Thierry.

The history of the Greek colonies in Italy is divided into two epochs. About the one, commencing in the eighth century before our era, there can be no doubt;[1] the other, ascribed to the fourteenth century, has all historical probabilities against it. It is of course possible that, in the times which followed the Trojan War, after that great disturbance of Greece, Hellenic troops, driven out of the mother country by revolutions, landed on the shores of Italy. But as to what is said of the settlement of Diomede in Daunia, or among the Veneti, who in the time of Strabo sacrificed a white horse to him every year; of the companions of Nestor at Pisa, of Idomeneus at Salentum, — although Gnossus in Crete held his tomb, — of Philoctetes at Petelia and Thurii, of Epeus

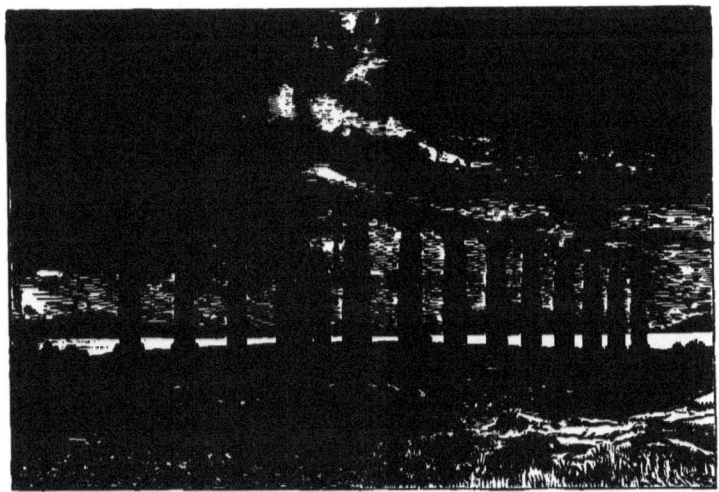

RUINS OF THE TEMPLE OF METAPONTUM (TAVOLA DEI PALADINI).

at Metapontum, of Ulysses at Scylacium, of Evander, of Tibur, of Telegonus, son of Ulysses, in Latium, at Tusculum, Tibur, Praeneste, Ardea, etc., — these legends, we may say, can only be regarded as poetical traditions invented by rhapsodists in order to give an illustrious origin to these towns.

[1] [On these eighth-century dates, and their invention, cf. my *History of Greek Literature*, vol. i., App. B. — *Ed.*]

Nothing was wanting to sanction these glorious genealogies: neither the songs of the poets, nor the blind or interested credulity of the historians, nor even the venerated relics of the heroes. On the banks of the Numicius the contemporaries of Augustus used to visit the tomb of Aeneas, who had become the Jupiter Indigetes, and every year the consuls and Roman pontiffs offered sacrifices there. Circeii exhibited the cup of Ulysses and the tomb of Elpenor, one of his companions;[1] Lavinium, the undecaying ships of Aeneas[2] and his Penates; Thurii, the bow and arrows of Hercules, given by Philoctetes; Macella, the tomb of this hero; Metapontum, the iron tools which Epeus used for making the Trojan horse;[3] Luceria, the armor of Diomede;[4] Maleventum, the boar's head of Calydon; Cumae, the tusks of the Erymanthian boar. Thus the inhabitants of a town of Armenia exhibited the remains of Noah's Ark.[5]

No one any longer holds to these fabulous origins, except those people of Rome who still say: *Siamo Romani*, and would willingly say like the Paduans: *Sangue Troiano*. Moreover, even if we considered as authentic the first settlements of the Greek race in Italy, we could not allow them any historical importance; for, left without intercourse with the mother-country, they lost the character of Hellenic cities; and when the Greeks arrived in the eighth century, they found no further trace of these uncertain colonies. To this class of legendary narratives belong the traditions of the Trojan Antenor, founder of Padua, and of Aeneas carrying into Latium the Palladium of Troy. The Roman nobles desired to date from the Trojan War, like the French from the Crusaders.

According to Herodotus, the first Greeks established in Iapygia were Cretans whom a tempest had cast there. Induced by the fertility of the soil, they had burned their ships and built Iria in the interior of the country. But the most ancient Grecian colony of which the establishment is beyond doubt, is that of the Chalcidians, founders of Cumae. Led by Hippocles and Megasthenes, they ventured, says tradition, across unknown seas, guided in the daytime by a dove, and at night by the sound of the mystic

---

[1] Strabo, V. iii. 6.
[2] Procopius, iv. 22.
[3] Justin, xx. 2.
[4] Pliny, *Hist. Nat.* iii. 26.
[5] Jos., *Ant. Jud.* xx. 2.

bronze.¹ They built Cumae on a promontory which commands the sea and the neighboring plains, opposite the Isle of Ischia. Its prosperity was so rapid, owing to a position in the middle of the Tyrrhenian coast, facing the best ports and in the most fertile country of Italy, that the colony was able to become in its turn a metropolis,² to assist Rome and the Latins, in the time of Porsenna, to shake off the yoke of the Etruscans of the north, and to contend on its own account with those of Campania. The battle of the year 474 B. C. resounded as far as Greece, where Pindar celebrated it. But in 420 B. C. the Samnites entered Cumae. Yet, notwithstanding the estrangement, and in spite of the barbarians, Cumae remained for a long time Greek in language, manners, and memories; and every time a danger menaced Greece, she thought in her grief that she saw her gods weeping.³ These tears repaid the songs of Pindar.⁴

In this volcanic land, near the Phlegraean Fields and the dark Avernus, the Greeks believed themselves to be at the gates of Hades. Cumae, where, according to some tradition, Ulysses had evoked the shades, became the abode of one of the Sibyls and of the cleverest necromancers of Italy; each year many awestruck pilgrims visited the holy place, to the great profit of the inhabitants.⁵ It was there, too, in this outpost of Greek civilization, in the midst of these Ionians full of the Homeric spirit, that the legends were elaborated which brought so many heroes from Greece into Italy.

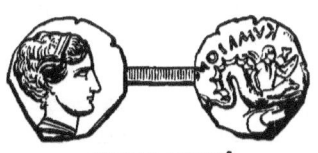

COIN OF CUMAE.⁶

¹ Strabo, V. iv. 4 : πασῶν ἐστι πρεσβυτάτη τῶν τε Σικελικῶν καὶ τῶν Ἰταλιωτίδων. With the Chalcidians were mingled colonists from Cyme, on the coasts of Asia Minor, where Homer sang. The father of Hesiod was born at Cyme, and Hesiod mentions Latinus as the son of Ulysses and Circe. Eusebius in his *Chronicle* places this event in 1050. It is a very remote date.

² Cumae founded *Dicaearchia* or *Puteoli*, which served as its port, *Parthenope*, and *Neapolis*, which eclipsed it. Naples reckoned also amongst its founders Athenians and Eretrians. These were first settled in the Island of Ischia, whence they had been driven by a volcanic eruption (Strab., V. iv. 9). Avernus and the Lucrine Lake abounded in fish: "vectigalia magna praebebant" (Serv. in *Georg.* ii. 16).

³ The miracle of the tears of Apollo of Cumae was renewed at the time of the war of Aristonicus and Antiochus.

⁴ [No one would have been less content with such remuneration than Pindar. — *Ed.*]

⁵ Cic., *Tusc.* i. 5.

⁶ A woman's head, and on the reverse the monster Scylla, which defended the entrance of the Strait of Messina. The Σκύλλαιον was the rock which bounds Bruttium on the West.

After Cumae and its direct colonies, the most famous of which is *the New City*, Naples, the other Chalcidian cities were Zancle, afterward called Messina, and Rhegium, both of which guarded the entrance to the Straits of Sicily, but whose military position was too important not to draw upon them numerous calamities. The Mamertines, who took Messina by surprise and massacred all its male population, only did what, some years later, a Roman legion repeated at Rhegium.

The Dorians, who ruled in Sicily. were less numerous in Italy; but they had Tarentum, which rivalled in power and wealth Sybaris and Croton, and which preserved its independence longer than these two towns.[1] Rich offerings, deposited at the temple of Delphi, still bore witness, in the time of Pausanias, to its victories over the Iapygians, Messapians, and Peucetians. It had also raised to its gods, as a token of its courage, statues of a colossal height, and all in fighting attitude; but these could not defend it against Rome, and the conqueror who razed its walls left in derision the images of its warlike divinities.

COIN OF ANCONA.[2]

Ancona, founded about 380 B. C., in Picenum, by Syracusans who fled from the tyranny of Dionysius the Elder, was also Dorian.

The most flourishing of the Achaean colonies was at first Sybaris, which had subdued the indigenous population of the countries of wine and oxen (*Oenotria* and *Italy*). At the end of a century, about 620 B. C., it possessed a territory covered by twenty-five towns, and could arm three hundred thousand fighting men. But a century later, in 510, it was taken and destroyed by the Crotoniates. All Ionia, which traded with it, lamented its downfall, and the Milesians went into mourning. Its land used to yield a hundredfold:[3] it is now only a deserted and marshy shore.

---

[1] Livy, xxvii. 16. Strabo says (VI. iii. 4): ἴσχυσαν δέ ποτε οἱ Ταραντῖνοι καθ' ὑπερβολήν. The wealth of Tarentum arose from its fisheries, from its manufacture [and dyeing] of the fine wool of the country, and from its harbor, which was the best on the south coast.

[2] Ancona in Greek signifies *elbow*, hence the half-bent arm on the reverse. The ancients often rendered a name by a figure which gave the meaning of it; thus certain coins of Sicily, the island with three promontories, have three legs pointed in different directions and united at the top. The modern Sicilians have kept this emblem, the *triquetra*.

[3] Varro, *de Re rust.* i. 44. [The site of the town is not yet accurately known, but

On the western coast of Lucania, Laus, which the Lucanians destroyed after a great victory over the confederate Greeks, and Posidonia, whose imposing ruins[1] have rendered famous the now deserted town of Paestum, were colonies of Sybaris. Other Achaeans, invited by them, had settled at Metapontum, which owed great wealth to its agriculture and to its harbor, now converted into a lagoon.[2] Crotona had as rapid a prosperity as Sybaris, its rival, but one which lasted longer. Its walls, double as great in extent (100 stadia) indicate a more numerous population, whose renown for pugilistic combats [for cookery and for medicine] would also lead

COIN OF LAUS.

us to consider the population more energetic. Milo of Crotona is a well-known name. The tyrants of Syracuse took it three times, and it had lost all importance when the Romans attacked it. Locri, of Aeolian origin, never attained to so much power. Its downfall, begun by Dionysius the Younger, was completed by Pyrrhus and Hannibal.

COIN OF CROTONA.[3]

The Ionians had only two towns in Magna Graecia: Elea, famous for its school of philosophy, and Thurii, the principal founders of which were the Athenians. Hostile to the Lucanians and to Tarentum, Thurii, like its metropolis, entered early into the alliance of Rome.

COIN OF ELEA.[4]

It is remarkable that all these towns had a rapid growth, and that a few years sufficed for them to become states, reckoning the number of their fighting men by

is somewhere under the Crathis, which was turned over it. The plain is really rich in grass and in cattle, but much visited by malaria. Excavations, accompanied by a change in the river's course, would probably bring to light the most interesting remains yet found in Italy. — *Ed.*]

[1] The two temples and stoa of Paestum.
[2] Now Lago di Santa Pelagina. When the water is low, remains of ancient constructions are seen there; it was destroyed by the bands of Spartacus.
[3] Head of Juno Lacinia; on the reverse, Hercules sitting.
[4] Helmeted Minerva; lion couchant.

the hundred thousand. It was not only the favorable climate of Magna Graecia, the fertility of the soil, which, in the valleys and plains of the two Calabrias, excelled that of Sicily,[1] nor even the wisdom of their legislators, Charondas, Zaleucus, Parmenides, and Pythagoras, that effected this marvel, but the clear-sighted policy which admitted all strangers into the city,[2] and for some centuries converted the Pelasgian populations of the south of Italy into a great Greek nation. Doubtless distinctions were established; and there were probably in the capitals plebeians and nobles, in the country serfs of the soil, and in the conquered towns subjects; but these differences prevented neither union nor strength. It was by this means, too, by this assimilation of conquered and conquerors, that Rome increased. But Rome preserved its discipline for a long time, whereas the towns of Magna Graecia, undermined within by intestine divisions and menaced without by Carthage and Syracuse, by the tyrants of Sicily and the King of Epirus, incessantly harassed by the Italian Gauls and the Samnites, especially by the Lucanians, were, moreover, enfeebled by rivalries which prepared for the Romans an easy conquest.

If Umbria owes its name to a Gallic tribe, our fathers must have crossed the Alps the first time in a large body at a very early epoch.[3] The invasion of the sixth century is more certain.

---

[1] Dolomieu, *Dissertation sur le tremblement de terre de 1783.* [In natural beauty Calabria far surpasses the greater part of Sicily. — *Ed.*]

[2] Polybius, ii. 39; Diod., xii. 9. Sybaris ruled four nations and twenty-five towns (Strab., VI. i. 13). There is doubtless a great exaggeration in the figure of 300,000 fighting men; but the number of inhabitants must have been much larger than that of the towns of Greece proper. At certain of its feasts, Sybaris assembled as many as 5,000 cavalry, four times more than Athens ever had (Athen., xii. 17 and 18; Diod., fragm. of bk. viii.; Seymn., 340). It was the same at Crotona. The Pelasgians of Lucania and Bruttium showed the same readiness as those of Greece in allowing themselves to be absorbed by the Hellenes and in adopting their language and manners, and for the same reasons, — identity of origin, or at least near relationship. This influence of the Hellenes was so strong, that notwithstanding the later Roman colonies, Calabria, like Sicily, remained for a long time a Greek country. It was only at the commencement of the fourteenth century that the Greek language [re-introduced in the eleventh] began to be lost there. As to the prosperity of these towns, it is connected, more than has been shown, with that of the Greek colonies in general. Masters of all the shores of the great basin of the Mediterranean, the Greeks had in their hands the commerce of the three worlds. Continued intercourse united their towns, and every point of this immense circle profited from the advantages of all the others. The prosperity of Tarentum, Sybaris, Crotona, and Syracuse, corresponded with that of Phocaea, Smyrna, Miletus, and Cyrene.

[3] Geographical names, dolmens, etc., reveal the presence, in the Valley of the Danube, from the Black Sea to the Schwarzwald, of numerous Gallic populations which may have come thence directly into Italy. In that case the Gauls of the banks of the Loire would only

HARBOR OF METAPONTUM.

It is said that the Gallic tribes of the northwest, driven back on the Cevennes and the Alps by invaders from beyond the Rhine, accumulated there, and, like waves long pent up, overflowed to the number of three hundred thousand across the Alps into the Valley of the Po. On the banks of the Ticino, the Biturigan Bellovesus overwhelmed an Etruscan army and established his people, the Insubrians, between this river, the Po, and the Adda.[1]

Bellovesus had shown the way; others followed it. In the space of sixty-six years, the Cenomani, under a chief surnamed the whirlwind (*Elitovius*), Ligurians, Boians, Lingones, Anamans and Senones,[2] drove the Etruscans from the banks of the Po and the

have been the western group of this great nation. Cf. *Revue archéolog.* for January, 1881, p. 50.

[1] Livy, v. 34, 35.

[2] With the Senones, Strabo unites (V. i. 6) the Gesates, "The two nations," says he, "who took Rome."

ALPHABETS OF NORTHERN ITALY.

Umbrians from the shores of the Adriatic as far as the River Esino (*Aesis*). Some remains of the Etruscan and Umbrian powers existed, however, in the midst of the Gallic populations, and formed small states which were free, but tributary and always exposed, from the fickleness of these barbarians, to sudden attacks. Thus Melpum was surprised by treachery, and destroyed on the same day, it is said, as the Romans entered Veii.[1]

As conquerors, the Gauls did not go beyond the limits where the invasions of the Senones had stopped. But this vigorous race, these men eager for tumult, plunder, and battle, long troubled the peninsula as they did all the ancient world, until the legions were able to reach them in the middle of their forests and to fix them to the soil. They inhabited unwalled villages, says Polybius, slept on grass or straw, and had no knowledge except of fighting and a little husbandry. Living chiefly on meat, they only valued flocks and gold, — ready wealth which does not impede the warrior, and which he carries everywhere along with him. Under their rule Cisalpine Gaul returned to the barbarism from which the Etruscans had saved it; the forests and marshes spread; the passes of the Alps especially remained open, and new bands continually descended from them, which claimed their share of the *country of the wine*. Their high stature, their savage shouts, their passionate and menacing gestures, and that parade of courage which, on days of battle, made them strip off all their clothing in order to fight naked, frightened the Italians so much that at their approach the whole population took up arms. When the young and fortunate Alexander threatened them, the Gauls of the Danube replied that they feared nothing but that the sky should fall; and the first Roman army that saw those of Italy fled terrified. Yet Rome was compelled to meet them everywhere, at Carthage, in Asia, with Hannibal, at her gates even, and up to the foot of the Capitol!

Italy in this early age has only a twilight of history, the uncertain rays of which with difficulty pierce the darkness in which the commencement of the nations is concealed. However, by this still doubtful light we can recognize some facts important to general history, and particularly to that of Rome.

---
[1] Pliny, *Nat. Hist.* iii. 17 (21).

Thus all, or nearly all, the Italiotes belonged to the Aryan race. They were more connected with the Hellenic tribes than the Germans are with the Celts and Slavs, which are also detached branches of this powerful stem. But if this relationship to the Greeks disposed them to yield to the influence of Hellenic civilization, they borrowed from their brothers of Hellas neither their language, nor their worship, nor their institutions of early days.

In what concerns Rome we note the following points: —

The preponderance, in the eighth century, on both banks of the Tiber, of the Sabines and Etruscans, and consequently their influence on the institutions and manners of the nation which arose beside them and which increased at their expense.

The feebleness of the Latins, which favored the beginnings of the Eternal City.

The power, but insubordinate spirit, of the Sabellians.

The political divisions of the Italian nations, sustained by the very division of the soil and the diversity of their origin.

Let us imagine in the midst of these tribes, rendered strangers to one another by long isolation, a small nation which made a necessity of war, a daily habit of the exercise of arms, a virtue of military discipline; and we shall understand that this nation, formed for conquest, must triumph over all these tribes, often related to it in origin, which, when attacked in succession, perceive too late that the downfall of each was the threat and the announcement of the coming downfall of the next.

VI.

POLITICAL ORGANIZATION OF THE ANCIENT NATIONS OF ITALY.

IN Italy, as in the rest of Europe, the most ancient civilization seems to retain something of the theocratic forms of Asia, whence it has come, — with this difference, however, that an order of priests is not found distinct from the rest of the citizens. The same men were heads of the people and ministers of the gods; so that according to the more *human* and more political spirit of the West, the relations were the reverse of what they had been in the East: the warrior took precedence of the priest; before being pontiff or augur, the noble was a patrician; he did not shut himself up in a sanctuary, but lived before the public gaze; he did not remain tied to unchangeable forms, but modified them, according to the wants of the state; religion, in fact, was for him not only an end, but a means and an instrument all the more formidable, because it was employed by believers, so that statecraft could bring fanaticism to its aid.

Among the Etruscans the two characters of the priest and warrior appear in equilibrium. Their lucumos, alone instructed in the augur's science, alone eligible by hereditary right for public functions, guardians of the mysteries and masters of everything divine and human, form a military theocracy founded on divine right and the antiquity of families. Among the Oscan and Sabellian nations the balance seems disturbed, to the advantage of the warrior. The chief is the man revered for the antiquity of his race and the grandeur of his house, powerful by the extent of his domains and the number of his relatives, slaves, and clients.

Agricultural and shepherd nations, for the very reason that they remain in contact with nature, follow it closely in their institutions; for them, Jews and Arabs, Celts of Scotland and Ireland, or natives of Latium and the Sabine country, the family is the first element of society, and the patriarchal authority of the chief who, like Abraham, fights and sacrifices in turn, is the earliest government. At Rome, all rights came from the family; the heads of the state were the fathers, *patres* and *patricii;* property was the *patrimonium;* the country, the common property of the fathers, *res patria.* Yet the right of primogeniture, which is found among so many nations, was unknown on the banks of the Tiber. With the family are connected the servants, devoted for life and death to him who nourishes and protects them, who leads them to battle, and enriches them with spoil, like the German *comites*, the Aquitanian *soldurii*, the members of the Scotch clans, — like, in fact, the Italian clients, as regards their patron. Patronage, *patrocinium*,[1] and the patriciate ought then to be raised from the rank of a particular institution, in which historians have long placed them, to that of a law of the very organization of primitive societies. When there are no institutions, it is very necessary for the nascent state that there should be, between the strong and the feeble, between the rich and the poor, an early association, — an association with varying obligations, granting here more, there less, to the liberty of the protected and to the rights of the protector. At Rome, this relation was called clientship; in the Middle Ages, feudalism.

Like the Etruscan lucumos, the Latin and Sabine patricians were the priests of their families and clients; they sacrificed to the domestic Penates; they fulfilled the public ceremonies, and held the magistracies, — in a word, they had both religious and political authority. But in Latium, religion, because it was more popular, protected their privileges less than in Etruria. So the great men of Rome lost no time in borrowing from the Etruscans their augural knowledge, and in buying, at a great price, the Sibylline books, in order to place by the side of the popular religion, accessible to all, a state religion, reserved for themselves alone.

From this union between statecraft and religion, from this

---

[1] Dionysius Hal. (ii. 10, 9) expressly regards Roman *patronage* as an old Italian custom. The Javan *tiatias* and Albanian *phars* rest upon the same principle; they are families composed of a head, relatives, and servants, all depending upon him. Clientship existed among the Sabines (Livy, ii. 16; Dion., v. 40, and x. 14); among the Etruscans (Livy. v. 1, ix. 36, and xxiii. 3, Dion. Hal., ix. 5). Cf. Livy, x. 5, the *gens Licinia* at Arrezo; at Capua (Livy, xxiii. 2, 7); among the Samnites, who have their *principes, primores, nobiles, equites, milites aurati et argentati.*

double character of the Italian aristocracy, especially in Etruria. it resulted that public and private rights were closely united with religious rights, that religion, as in the East, was the bond of every city and the principle of all jurisprudence, and that ancient legislations, placed under divine sanction, gained thereby a higher authority. Moreover, as it is the essence of all religions to love mystery, especially of those that are in possession of the heads of the state, the civil laws were wrapped up in secret and mysterious religious forms.[1] " Preserved in a dumb language, and only explaining themselves by holy ceremonies, whereof some rites remained in the *acta legitima,* they were long obeyed with scrupulous piety."[2] The aristocracy, who were its sole depositaries, found therein a power which for centuries the plebeians dared not dispute.

The greatest strength of this aristocracy was, however, the possession of the soil, even in Etruria, where industry and commerce had created the movable wealth of gold beside the inconvertible wealth of land. To possess land was, as in the Middle Ages, not only the sign of power but power itself; for vast domains furnished a whole army of servants and dependants. Originally these domains were equal,[3] and the aristocracies, by their number and the equality of their members, were truly democracies. In the Graeco-Italian states, generally formed by a few migrations, colonies, or *Sacred Springs,* society existed before property. There were citizens before there were landowners; and when a town rose, the soil could be divided geometrically: each citizen received an equal share. The principle of feudal and continental Europe, that political rights flow from possession of property, was inverted by antiquity. At Lacedaemon it was as Dorians, as citizens and founders of the state, that the Spartans received 9,000 shares; and no new right sprang from that concession of property. Before receiving their part of the promised land,

---

[1] The passage of Festus about the Etruscan ritual shows clearly the sacerdotal character of Etruscan legislation. It is religion rules all things; it was there written, said he, " quo ritu condantur urbes, arae, aedes sacrentur; qua sanctitate muri, quo jure portae, quo modo tribus, ceteraque ejusmodi ad bellum ac pacem pertinentia."

[2] Vico, ii. 283.

[3] As at Sparta; the 9,000 shares given to the Spartans were inalienable. [But this was probably a modern theory, devised in the time of Agis and Cleomenes, as Grote has conclusively shown, in spite of the arguments of recent German critics. — *Ed.*]

PLAIN OF SYBARIS

the Hebrews were all equal, all members of God's people; and after the division they remain as they were before. In Egypt, at Cyrene, in all the Greek colonies, similar divisions took place, without implying any political consequence.[1]

With us these agrarian laws would be a supremely iniquitous measure, because property now represents the accumulated fruits of the labor of many generations; in ancient times they only resulted in the increase of the number of citizens, in annulling unjust usurpations, and leading the state back to primitive equality. They were nevertheless violently rejected wherever there arose, as at Rome and in Etruria, a second people, poor and oppressed, which might have become too formidable if to the power of numbers they had joined that of fortune. To avoid these reforms even Religion was called to the aid of civil law, and made to imprint on landed property a sacred character. She it was who divided the land, who by prayers, libations, and sacrifices marked the boundaries that no one could remove without incurring the divine wrath.[2] *Numa . . . statuit eum qui terminum exarasset, et ipsum et boves sacros esse.* This religion of property had its god, *Terminus*, the immovable guardian of landmarks, who, in tradition, will not fall back even before the Master of heaven and earth. "Ill-luck," said an old prophecy, "to him who displaces Terminus, in order to increase his domain! His land shall be beaten with storms, his wheat

THE GOD TERMINUS, AFTER A STATUE IN THE LOUVRE.

---

[1] Joshua xx.; Plut., *Lyc.;* Herod., ii. 109; Arist., *Pol.* vii. 4.

[2] The land to be marked out was for the *agrimensor*, who was both priest and augur, an enclosure wherein a religious act was to take place. Like the sanctuary of the gods, it was a *templum*, whose limits were put in connection with the divisions which the augur established in aërial space, when he consulted the omens. An altar was raised at the limit, and the entrails of the victims were placed under the boundary stone, which by this consecration became itself a god; and the property, the *ager auspicatus vel limitatus*, could not be usurped. Cicero, in the Second Philippic (§ 40), denies that any one had the right to lead a new colony into the territory of an ancient one not yet destroyed. "Negavi in eam coloniam, quae esset auspicato deducta, dum esset incolumis, coloniam novam deduci posse."

eaten with mildew, his house overthrown, and all his race shall perish." Never has landed property been more energetically protected, and with it the hereditary power of riches. Thus it was that Roman society remained deeply aristocratic to its last day.

This consecration of property was especially the work of the Etruscans, whose conquests and influence extended the use of it into a great part of the peninsula; and no divinity, says Varro, was more honored in all Italy than the God of Limits.[1]

On this double basis of religion and property rose the old aristocracy of Italy, and in late times that of Rome. Uniting these two elements of strength, which each separately confer power, what might not be its duration and ascendency? As long indeed as the city did not assume the proportions of an empire, no families arose possessing power by hereditary right. The magistrates were almost always elected annually, like the lucumos of Etruria, the *meddix tuticus* of the Campanians,[2] and the praetor or dictator of the Latin cities. In grave circumstances a supreme chief was elected, such as the *embradur* (imperator) of the Sabellians, the king whom the twelve Etruscan cities named, each sending him a lictor in token of the power over the whole of the nation[3] which was committed to him,— such, in short, as that dictator of Tusculum, Egerius, who was recognized chief of the Latin confederation, in order to undertake the dedication of the common temple of Aricia. In the heroic age, legend tells of kings in Latium; but at the time of the foundation of Rome there were none left save in the little towns of the Sabine territory.[4] Even Alba no longer had aught but dictators; and in detestation of the royal name, popular stories were already repeated about the cruelties of Mezentius and of those tyrants who, struck by the divine anger, had been buried with their palaces at the bottom of Lake Albano. When the waters fell, it was thought that these guilty dwellings might be seen.[5]

On a hill, on the borders of a lake, or on the steep banks of some

---

[1] Ovid, *Fast.* ii. 639-684.
[2] Livy, xxiv. 19; Festus, s. v. *Tuticus*.
[3] Livy, i. 8.
[4] At a later epoch there were still kings among the Daunians, Peucetians, Messapians, and Lucanians. (Strabo, V. and VI. *passim*; Livy, i. 17; Paus., x. 13.) But they were perhaps only simple leaders in war, like the Samnite *embradur*.
[5] Verg., *Aen.* viii. 7 and 481; Dionys., i. 71.

river, but always in a position difficult of access,[1] rose the capital of each state, generally not very extensive, and fortified, especially in Etruria, with all the art of the times. Faesulae, Rusellae, Populonia, and Cosa, the walls of which may still be seen, were only three quarters of a league round, Volaterrae a league and a half, and Veii, the largest of all the Etruscan cities, less than two and a half leagues. The Latin cities were not nearly so large; yet they, according to the Etruscan ritual followed in Latium, preserved a free space between the nearest buildings and the walls, as well as between the wall and the cultivated fields. This was the *pomerium*, the sacred boundary of the city, within which dwelt none but true citizens,—that is to say, heads of families, the fathers or patricians, with their servants and clients (*gentes patriciae*). Plebeians and foreigners remained outside the pomerium, without the political city.

On a place set apart in the midst of the town the patricians assembled in arms,[2] like the Germans and Gauls, to deliberate on their common interest. According to the Etruscan usage,[3] they were divided into tribes, curies, and centuries, the number of which was determined by a sort of sacred arithmetic. The Eugubine tables show that this division took place in Umbria likewise; but the Oscans and Sabellians, freer from sacerdotal fetters than the Etruscans, do not appear to have recognized that mysterious authority of number which plays so great a part in Rome.

In states subjected to the authority of a powerful aristocracy, there is often found side by side with the docile population another population in revolt, which dwells in the depths of the forests and lives by pillage. These outlaws, the heroes of barbarous times, must have been very numerous in ancient Italy, where, moreover, amid so many rival cities, the military spirit

---

[1] Many towns of modern Italy are still in the place of the ancient cities. That of Capistrello commands the Valley of the Liris, above the point where the escape channel of Lake Fucinus, designed by Caesar and carried out by Claudius, opens.

[This peculiar character of Italian towns is still very striking to the traveller, especially in Southern or mountainous Italy. Owing to long injustice and weakness of home governments, and the raids of pirates up to the present century, isolated homesteads are a rare exception, and the population live in villages perched like eagles' nests on the top of the rocks, from which they come down to till the slopes and valleys, and return in the evening. — *Ed.*]

[2] *Quir*, lance; thence *quirites* and *curia*, the place where the quirites assembled.

[3] Fest., s. v. *Rituales*; Verg., *Aen.* x. 201.

sustained by continual warfare gave rise to bands of mercenaries who sold their services, like the condottieri of the Middle Ages, or made war on their own account.[1] We shall see how the Mamertines fared in Sicily. The fortune of a few Tuscan chiefs was no less brilliant,[2] and the Etruscan condottiere Mastarna, the son-in-law and heir of Tarquin the Elder, involuntarily calls to mind that other condottiere, Francesco Sforza, son-in-law and successor of a duke of Milan. Romulus himself, proscribed from the time of his birth, rejected by the patrician caste of Alba, associated in tradition[3] with other condottieri similarly repulsed by the Etruscan aristocracy, appears to have been nothing but one of these warrior chiefs, who knew how to choose with marvellous instinct the admirable position of Rome, and hide his eyrie between the river, the wooded hills, and the marshy plains which extend from their foot to the Tiber.

VII.

RELIGIOUS ORGANIZATION.

EXCEPT in Etruria, ancient Italy had few mysteries or profound dogmas. Its religion was simple; from the necessities of life and from the labors of the field[4] it derived the impressions of admiration or affright which that lovely and changeable nature produced. In this essentially rural religion all services took place in the open air. The first-fruits of the field and flock were offered to the god on the altar of sacrifice which stood before the temple; there were pious songs, prayers, religious dances, garlands of flowers and foliage suspended on the sacred walls; and when the faithful were rich enough for such an outlay, a few grains of incense were burned on the altar, and perfumes in the interior of

---

[1] Livy (iv. 55; vi. 6) speaks of the bands who issued from the country of the Volscians without leave from the national council, and Dionys. (*Ant. Rom.* vii. 3) of the mercenaries whom the Etruscans took into their pay.

[2] Tac., *Ann.* iv. 65.

[3] Dionys., *Ant. Rom.* iii. 37. There is also mention of Oppius of Tusculum, and of a Laevus Cispius of Anagnia, in the time of Tullus Hostilius. (Varro, ap. Fest. *Septimontium*.)

[4] The oldest Roman almanac (*Corp. Inscr. Lat.*, vol. i. p. 375) mentions none but rural festivals.

the sanctuary, where the actual presence of the god filled the soul with pious awe.

One of the features which distinguished these creeds of Central Italy is the moral superiority of their gods, — as, for instance, Vesta, the immaculate virgin, who protects both the private and public hearth (*focus publicus*);[1] the Penates, the protectors of human life and of the city; Jupiter, arbiter of the physical and moral world, the sustaining father and supreme preserver; the gods Terminus and Fidelity, who punish fraud and violence; the Bona Dea, who fertilized the earth and rendered unions fruitful, though she herself ever remained a virgin;[2] and that touching worship of the Manes, *dii manes*, which, restoring life to those who had been loved, showed ancestors watching beyond the tomb over those whom they had left among the living. Three times every year the Manes left the infernal regions, and the son who had imitated the virtues of his fathers could see their revered shades.

ENTRANCE OF A SHRINE.[3]

The gods of Greece are so near to man, that they have all his weaknesses; those of the East are so far from him, that they do not really enter into his life at all, notwithstanding their numerous incarnations. The Italian gods, the guardians of

---

[1] Vesta is the Agni of the *Véda*. The Pelasgians had brought the worship of this divinity of fire from Asia. There were Vestals at Lavinium (Serv. in *Aen.* iii. 21), at Tibur ('Tivoli'), and elsewhere. The temple represented on page 124, was dedicated, according to some, to Vesta, according to others, to the Sibyl Albunea, "Domus Albuneae resonantis" (Hor., *Odes*, I. vii. 12); others again see in it the temple of Hercules: it is *adhuc sub judice*. The main point is that the ruin is lovely. To the right of the round temple there is another square one about which the same uncertainty exists.

[2] It is Varro who says so, in Macrobius, *Saturn.* I. xii. 27. . . "nec virum unquam viderit vel a viro visa sit:" but others related her adventures, and her festivals. at least in the time of Caesar, were considered as licentious, though all men were rigidly excluded from them.

[3] After a miniature from the Vatican Vergil.

property, conjugal fidelity, and justice, the protectors of agriculture, the dispensers of all earthly good, preside over the actions of men without sharing their passions, but also without raising their mind above selfish interests. Art and science feel the loss, morality gains.[1] We shall not find the Roman Olympus either teeming with life, light, and beauty, like that of Greece, or profound, mysterious, and terrible, like those of Egypt and India. We shall find its gods inglorious and practical,[3] whom during long years, selfish worshippers dared only address with just prayers. Their service will be a means of preservation for a society devoid of enthusiasm, not an element of progress.

OPS, OR WEALTH.[2]

These modest divinities could not display the terrible requirements that are found in larger theogonies. They very rarely demanded human blood on their altars;[4] but they accepted a voluntary sacrifice, the redemption of the people by the devotion of a victim, — a Curtius, who closes the gulf in the heart of the city by leaping into it,[5] and a Decius, who by his death changes defeat into victory.

GOOD SUCCESS.[6]

Another characteristic of the Italian gods is their infinite multitude. Every town has its tutelar divinity. At Narnia it is Visidianus, at Ocriculum Valentia, at Casinum Delventius, at Minturnae Marica, among the Frentani Palina, at Satricum Matuta

---

[1] Saint Augustine (*de Civ. Dei*, vii. 4) remarks that Janus was the hero of no questionable adventure. Ovid, however, has compromised him somewhat (*Fast.* vi. 119, *seq.*); but in the time of Ovid the sense of the ancient rites was lost.

[2] She holds some ears of corn. Gold coin of Pertinax, struck at the close of 192 A.D.

[3] *Sator*, seed; *Ops*, work in the fields; *Flora*, flower; *Juventas*, youth; *Fides*, faith; *Concordia*, concord; *Fors*, fortune; *Bonus Eventus*, good success. [The reader will notice that among Greek authors Xenophon alone, following the homely side of the Socratic religion, exhibits this selfish and vulgar piety. Cf. my Social Life in Greece, p. 370. — *Ed.*]

[4] See page 139, note 1.

[5] This gulf was but ill closed by Curtius; at least as far as we are concerned; for in modern times alone it has re-opened three times, in 1702, 1715, and 1818 A. D. (Wey, *Rome*, p. 36).

[6] Success (*Bonus Eventus*) standing, holding a bowl and ears of corn; at his feet an altar burning. Bronze coin of Antoninus, struck by order of the Senate (S. C.) during his second consulship (*Cos.* II.) in 139 A. D.

TEMPLE OF VESTA, OF THE SYBIL, OR OF HERCULES, AT TIVOLI.

Mater; in the Sabine country Nerio, who was identified by the *gens Claudia* with the Roman Bellona, the wife or sister of Mars.[1] To these must be added the numerous *Semones* or *Indigetes*, the nymphs, heroes, and deified virtues: Concordia, Flora, Pomona, Juventas, Pollentia, Rumina, Mena, Numeria, and the swarm of local divinities which Tertullian calls *decuriones deos*, and the gods of the lower world, Larvae and Lemures, and those of the *indigitamenta*, those books which were both collections of prayers whereof the priests kept the secret, and lists of divine beings whom Tertullian compares to the angels of the Bible; one might add that they call to mind the saints of the popular beliefs of Roman Catholic countries.

CONCORD.[2]

Not only each town, but each family, each man, paid honor to special gods and to genii who protected his life and goods (Lares, Penates): there were gods for every act of man's life, from the cradle to the grave.[3] Thus at the close of the Republic Varro could count as many as thirty thousand gods. With nations in their infancy, imperfect language supplies, by the variety of particular names, the absence of the general terms which represent the unity of the species. The Italians possessed so many deities only because their minds were incapable of rising to the conception of one only God, — a defect which lasted a long time with them, and which, with others, lasts even till now.

YOUTH.[4]

This divine democracy necessarily escaped from the control of the greater gods and their priests. This is the reason why religious

---

[1] Nerio appears to have denoted strength; the inscription is known *Virtuti Bellonae* (Orelli, 4,983).

[2] Concord (*Concordia*), seated, leaning with her elbow on a horn of plenty, and holding a patera. Gold coin of the Emperor Aelius Hadrianus, struck in the second year of his tribunitian power, and during his second consulship, consequently in the year 118 A. D.

[3] See in Saint Augustine (*de Civ. Dei*, vi. 9) the manifold and very humble employments of these gods, after Varro, who himself had doubtless described them in the order of "indigitamenta, a conceptione . . . usque ad mortem . . . et dei qui pertinent ad ea quae sint hominis, sicuti est victus atque vestitus," etc.

[4] Youth (*Juventas*) standing near an altar, in the form of a candelabrum, into which she throws a grain of incense, and holding a patera in her left hand.

toleration was one of the necessities of Roman government; and if the patricians had not held the secret of the augur's science, of the symbolic formulae and ceremonies, they would not have been able to add the ascendency of religion to that of birth and fortune.

TWO WOMEN BURNING INCENSE AND PERFUMES UPON TWO PORTABLE ALTARS BEFORE AN IMAGE OF MARS.[1]

Some gods had more numerous worshippers than others, such as Jupiter, god of air and light; Janus, the Sun, who opened and closed the heavens and the year; Saturn, the protector of rustic labor, whose hollow statue was filled with the oil of the olives he had caused to grow; Mars, or Maspiter, the symbol of manly strength, also called Mavors, the god who slays; Bellona, the terrible sister of the god of war; Juno *Regina*, queen of heaven, and also the helpful, *Sospita*, in whom woman at all moments of her life found aid, but who favored only chaste love and inviolate unions.

The worship of these divinities was often the only bond which attached cities of the same origin to one another. Thus the Etruscans assembled at the temple of Voltumna, the Latins at the sacred wood of the goddess Ferentina, at the temple of Jupiter Latialis on the Alban Mount, and in those of Venus, at Lavinium and Laurentum;[2] the Aequi Rutuli and Volsci at the temple of Diana at Aricia. Similar gatherings took place among the Sabines, Samnites, Lucanians, Ligurians, etc. They were really Amphic-

---

[1] Taken from Marini, *Gli Atti e monum. de' fratelli Arvali*, after a painting found at Rome, which Winckelmann has also reproduced in his *Mon. inédits*, pl. 177.

[2] The worship of Venus at Lavinium and Laurentum only dates from the epoch at which the legend of Aeneas took form. There was no goddess bearing the name of Venus at Rome in the time of the kings. (Varro, in *Augurum libris*, fragm. of book vi.; Macrob., *Saturn.* I. xii. 8–15.)

RELIGIOUS ORGANIZATION.

tyonies, over which religion presided, and which the Romans abolished when they themselves had made use of the Latin feriae to insure their supremacy in Latium.

In religion, as in politics, the Etruscans were originally distinct from the rest of the Italian nations, from whom they afterward received gods or to whom they gave them. Their religious doctrines, a distant echo of the great Asiatic theogonies, proclaimed the existence of a supreme being, Tinia, the soul of the world, who had for counsellors the *dii consentes*, — impersonations of the forces of present Nature, and destined to perish with her; for the Scandinavian and Oriental belief in the destruction and renewal of the world is found also in Etruria.

HEAD OF JUPITER.[1]

These *dii consentes* could hurl thunderbolts, but not more than one at a time. Tinia alone, who was identified with Jupiter, manifested his will by three consecutive bolts. Thus he was represented holding a lightning flash with three points.

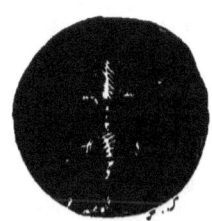

THUNDERBOLT WITH 12 FORKS.

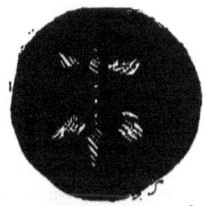

THUNDERBOLT WITH 8 FORKS.[2]

Beside him were seated Thalna, or Juno, and Menafru, or Minerva, his divine family. Vejovis was the

---

[1] The famous bust found at Otricoli, which is supposed to be the finest head of Jupiter that antiquity has left us (Winckelmann, History of Art, vi. 31 *seq.*)

[2] Large bronze medals of Antoninus, representing one a thunderbolt, of six or twelve flashes, the other of four or eight, with the words: *To divine Providence.* [Many of these bronzes are close imitations manufactured in North Italy in the last century.— *Ed.*]

baleful Sun; Summanus, god of night and nocturnal thunders; Sethlaus, or Vulcan, the great smith; Nortia, fate or fortune, etc. By an old contract, Nortia lent the inner walls of her temple for the reception of the sacred nail which marked the changeless order of time and the regular return of the years. Higher yet, hidden in the unfathomable depths of heaven, mysterious deities whose names were never uttered, the *dii involuti* (or veiled) played the part of the destiny to which even the gods were subject; they helped to explain the inexplicable mystery of life.

VULCAN OF ELBA.[1]

Man has in all ages been desirous of passing in thought over the threshold of death, and of looking into the great unknown beyond. The more uncertain and confused his view, the more his mind peopled it with vague phantoms. Believing that death separated two different but not absolutely distinct things, the body which falls lifeless, and the other self, that of dreams, memories, and hopes, which still exists,[2] — this other self was looked upon as formed of a corporeal substance. With the exception of Pythagoras and Plato, all the philosophies, all the

---

[1] It is thought that this bronze statuette, found in the Isle of Ilva (Elba), and now in the Museum of Naples, represents the god who must have been the protector of the island whence the smiths of Etruria got their iron.

[2] This was the most ancient belief of Egypt, and it is found everywhere. Although a philosopher had dared to say at the time of the construction of the pyramids: "Of those who have entered the coffin, was there ever any who came out again?" all Egypt thought that there existed a class of beings who were neither the living nor the dead. The dead who had been good during their lives could at will resume terrestrial existence in any place or form which suited them. (Chabas, *Les Maximes du Scribe Ani*, in *Mél. Égypt.* p. 171.) This in some belief was popular in Greece, where many Sarcophagi and funeral urns show souls in some way deified (Ravaisson, *Mon. de Myrrhine*); and it was still current in the world in the sixteenth century. "There are aërial beings," says Guicciardini (*Ricordi politici*, ccxi), "who hold converse with man: I know it by experience." It still exists in China. To send gold and silver to the manes of the dead in the other world, *sacrificial papers* are burned, which are gilded or silvered, and there are prepared at certain dates, as was done at Rome, repasts in which they are supposed to come and take part. But to prevent them from taking undue advantage thereof, petards are fired, to send them back to the place whence they came. For the Esquimaux the whole world is peopled with genii, and every object has its own. In our own days some people pretend even to converse with the spirits. In many points the difference between the barbarian and the civilized man is not so great as is thought. [The Christian doctrine of the resurrection of the body implied that the idea of a pure soul existing hereafter without its body was found inconceivable. — *Ed.*]

religions of classic antiquity, even some of the earliest Fathers of the Church, admitted the corporeal nature of the soul. Impalpable yet material shades, the genii were like a sacred humanity which peopled the invisible universe. One of them is seen in an Etruscan painting which represents two old men bewailing the dead, whose genius hovers above them under the form of a winged woman.

The Lares were the genii of the family; the Manes, those of the lost dead. Genii dwelt in woods, fountains, mysterious

DEMONS LEADING AWAY A SOUL.[1]

grottos; the Romans even assign them to everything which has a sort of collective life, — to the curia, the legion, and the cohort. Every man and every thing has one of its own.

When the gods issued from the obscurity which enveloped them in ancient days, and the theogonies settled order among the divine race, the genii became the ministers of their beneficent or terrible will. The sombre imagination of the Etruscans delighted in picturing, on vases and mural paintings, infernal genii armed with serpents, hideous monsters, a grimacing Charon, dragging the departed to the lower regions, or, armed with a heavy hammer, assisting at human sacrifices, to put an end to the victims whom the

[1] Conestabile, *Pitture murale*, pl. xvii.

knife might spare.[1] Something of this gloomy spirit appears to have survived in modern Tuscany. What are the gorgeous and hideous paintings of the Etruscans beside the dreadful pictures of Dante and Buonarotti?

One essential difference between this religion and the Asiatic cult, was the science of augury. The unknown fills the child with fear, and attracts the man who still dreads it, but who seeks therein, according to the age of the world, the marvellous or the scientific element. Now men of that time were in the age of the marvellous, and they demanded from physical phenomena, instead of a revelation of the laws of nature, the knowledge of the future.

The Assyrians imagined they could read in the stars those impenetrable secrets; the Etruscans sought them in terrestrial phenomena, in the flight of birds and the entrails of victims. The Greeks and Italians practised the latter two kinds of divination; but the Etruscans formulated their rules, and made of them a complicated system. They were especially skilled in interpreting the signs furnished by thunder and lightning.[2] When the echoes of the Apennines repeated the crashes of nocturnal thunder, it was the god Summanus speaking; and his voice must be understood.

This country, then, so often affrighted by earthquakes, and where, on account of its frequent storms, lightning still claims so many victims,—this land, so fertile and ever so menaced, was sure, more than any other, to nourish religious terror. Men had faith in an occult power which manifested its will in a manner outside the natural order of things, and the art of explaining prodigies, of gaining the favor of that dreaded power, became the supreme science.[3] The nobles alone knew it, and in their hands it became a weapon, long unfailing, against popular innovations. In these rituals everything was calculated; for the priest, the better to assure his power, was unwilling that there should be a single indifferent action; and a shameful superstition, weighing on the people, tied its

---

[1] See the engraving on p. 68. Charon and his club passed on to Rome; under the name of Pluto he put an end with his hammer-strokes to the wounded in the Games who were not worth the trouble of curing.

[2] This was the "maximum auspicium." (Serv. in *Aen.* ii. 693.)

[3] This science was afterward committed to the *libri fulgurales.*

tongue, its mind, and even its gestures. But the heavier the yoke, the more violent was the revolt; we shall see how in the last century of the Republic the most audacious infidelity succeeded the blindest faith. Men came to believe in naught but chance or fortune; still later in nothing at all, except perhaps unbridled pleasures, and then the repose of death,—nameless sensualities, and after satiety, suicide.

Thus among the Oscans and Sabellians we find a simple worship, with numberless gods; in Etruria, a religion which would fain account for life and death, for good and evil,—which, showing everywhere the arbitrary intervention of the gods, and in the natural phenomena a manifestation of their capricious will, required a class of men devoted, for the sake of public safety and the private interests of each citizen, to the interpretation and explanation of portents. All this was to find its way into Rome,—the Latin or Sabine sacrificer and the Tuscan augur, the popular worship and the sacerdotal religion.

But we do not find those oracles of Greece which were so often the voice of wisdom and patriotism, or those sacred poets of the East whose songs purified the national beliefs. In Italy religion, which was rather a contract with the gods than a prayer and an act of gratitude, never opened up those large heavens towards which the spirit soars; and the Latin genius was condemned by this shabby creed to an incurable sterility. High abilities were wanting, for invention at least; and it had neither philosophy — that deadly, but inevitable companion of great religions, for it is the search after the ideal in thought — nor art, which is the search after the ideal in sentiment and nature. Whereas the glorious artists of Greece pierced the depths of Olympus with their glance, to obtain thence the image of Zeus or Athene, the Roman veiled his head while accomplishing the sacred rites; he feared to look upon his gods, and he never held in esteem those who endeavored to place them before him in marble or in bronze.

We might even claim the religious institutions of Numa for the ancient populations of the peninsula, and look upon the Twelve Tables as a monument of old Italian customs. The laws concerning marriage, the power of the father and husband, and usury, certainly belong to the most remote times; and the atrocious nature of the punishments recalls the cold cruelty of the heroic age, as some other laws and customs appear to have been taken from a society of still nomadic shepherds.[1] Neither let us forget the fecial right established by the Aequi, the order of battle (*acies*) of the Etruscans, whose infantry, drawn up in deep lines, resembled a wall of iron (*murum ferreum*); the golden crowns in imitation of oak-leaves, as a military reward; the armor of the Samnite soldier, which became that of the legionary; and the simple worship, frugal life, and severe education of the shepherds and husbandmen of Latium and the Sabine country; the luxury and art of Etruria, — and, in short, a mass of customs which would show that Rome already existed in ancient Italy, were it not necessary to add something especially Roman, — the idea of the State overruling all, and that admirable discipline which of such diverse elements formed an original society and the most powerful empire that the world had hitherto known.

VIII.

SUMMARY.

THIS is a very deliberate excursion through ancient Italy; but, if we are not mistaken, the circuit will only have the effect of shortening our route. Although we have travelled this long journey illumined only by stray lights, we have been able to catch a glimpse of the very cradle of Rome, of the institutions from which hers were derived, of the nations who, after having formed her population, produced her greatest men. In the consular annals we find among the consuls of the years 510 to 460, B. C., Volscians, Auruncans, Siculians, Sabines, Rutulians, Etruscans, and Latins. Amongst the great families, —

The Julii, Servilii, Tullii, Geganii, Quinctii, Curatii, and Cloelii, come from Alba;

---

[1] Dornseiffen: "Vestigia vitae nomadicae tam in moribus quam in legibus Romanis conspicua."

SUMMARY.

The Appii, Postumii, and probably the Valerii, Fabii, and Calpurnii, who called themselves the descendants of Numa, from the Sabine country;

The Furii and Hostilii, from Medullia in Latium;

The Octavii, from Velitrae;

The Cilnii (Maecenas was of this family) and the Licinii, from Arezzo;

The Caecinae, from Volaterra;

The Vettii, from Clusium;

The Pomponii, Papii, and Coponii, from Etruria;

The Coruncanii and Sulpicii, from Camerium;

The Porcii and Mamilii, who claimed descent from Circe, from Tusculum, etc.

Amongst the great names of Roman literature, only two, those of Caesar and Lucretius, belong really to Rome; all the others are Italians: Horace is Apulian; Ennius, a Messapian; Plautus, from Umbria; Vergil, from Mantua; Statius, from Elea; Naevius, from Campania; Lucilius, from Suessa-Aurunca; Cicero, like Marius, is a Volscian; Ovid, a Pelignian; Cato, a Tusculan; Sallust, a Sabine; Livy, from Padua; the two Plinys, from Como; Catullus, from Verona; [Martial and Seneca were Spaniards]. Terence was even a Carthaginian. So much for men. Let us proceed to material marks.

ROMAN IN TOGA.[1]

---

[1] Bronze statuette in the Payne Knight Collection at the British Museum; in Mr. Payne Knight's collection it is described as Cicero.

Rome received from Etruria,—the division into tribes, curiae, and centuries, the order of battle, the dress of the magistrates, the laticlave, the praetexta, the toga, the apex,[1] the curule chair, the lictors, all the display of the triumphs and public games, the nundinae,[2] the sacred character of property, and the science of the augur,—that is to say, the state religion. From Latium, the names of dictator and praetor, the fecial right, a simple religion which placed all the works of rural life under the protection of the gods, the worship of Saturn, protector of agriculture, and that of Janus and Djana, the sun and the moon, united in the double Janus; in fact, agricultural customs and even language. From Samnium and the Sabine country, the title of *imperator*, the armor and weapons of the soldiers, severe and religious customs, and warrior gods. From all the nations which surrounded them, the patriciate or patronage, the division into *gentes*, clientship, paternal authority, the worship of the lares and fetich gods, such as bread or Ceres, the spear or Mars, the divinities of the rivers, lakes, and warm springs. In short, as a faithful representation of this formation of Roman society, Romulus and Tullus are Latins; Numa and Ancus, Sabines; Servius and the two Tarquins, Etruscans.

The following beautiful and expressive legend is found in Plutarch. Romulus, says he, called men from Etruria, who taught him the holy ceremonies and sacred formulae. They had a trench dug round the *Comitium*, and each of the citizens of the new city threw into it a handful of earth brought from his native country. Then they mixed the whole, and gave to the ditch, as to the universe, the name of the world (*mundus*).[3]

---

[1] *Laticlave*, a tunic, edged from top to bottom with a broad purple band, woven in the material, the mark of a senator; *praetexta*, a toga bordered with purple and worn by magistrates (or noble children); *apex*, a headdress of the flamens and the Salii. The apex is seen on a quantity of coins and monuments; the laticlave in very rare paintings.

[2] *Nundinus* (*novena dies*), the ninth day, or market-day.

[3] The *mundus* of Romulus was the world of the manes and the subterranean deities. Every time that a city was founded, a *mundus* was opened, into which were thrown the firstfruits of all the crops, with objects of good omen. It was a religious custom, which existed even in Assyria, where, in the foundations of monuments, were placed the idols which should protect them. When we fix coins in the first stone of an edifice, we do something analogous with totally different ideas; and this custom, which only serves to mark the date of the erection of the monument, is perhaps a very remote souvenir of a religious usage which has been secularized.

SUMMARY. 135

Thus all the Italian nationalities, all the powers, all the civilizations of the ancient world were destined to fall into the bosom of Rome and mingle there.

JANUS AS, COIN FOUND AT VOLTERRA.

HISTORY OF ROME.

FIRST PERIOD.

ROME UNDER THE KINGS (753–510 B. C.).

FORMATION OF THE ROMAN PEOPLE.

CHAPTER I.

TRADITIONAL HISTORY OF THE KINGS.[1]

> Ὡς ἐν τοῖς πατρίοις ὕμνοις ὑπὸ
> Ῥωμαίων ἔτι καὶ νῦν ᾄδεται.
> DIONYSIUS: *Ant. Rom.* I. 79.

I. ROMULUS (753–716).

ROME, the city of strength[2] and war and bloodshed, was pleased to place an idyl at the beginning of her formidable history; Nero's city, ascribing to her first days the virtues of the age of

---

[1] We do not propose to discuss the legends of the royal period. The reader curious in intellectual diversions of this kind will do well to consult the first volume of Niebuhr, in which all these traditions are collected and critically considered; also Schwegler's History, in which they are also taken up and discussed. For ourselves, to any hypotheses, however ingenious and erudite, — which must still be as incapable of proof as are the legends they combat, — we prefer Livy's admirable narrative, if not as actual truth, at least as picture. Details more or less authentic in respect to the biographies of certain personages are, after all, of little consequence. One thing only is really important, since it is what men of all times desire to understand, and that is the question how this singular state was formed, which grew to be a nation, a world. This problem will occupy us far more than the idle or insoluble questions which, since Niebuhr's time, have been so much agitated in Germany. [The course here adopted is that of Arnold, who tells the old legends as legends, without any attempt to sift history from them. Mommsen contemptuously ignores them altogether. Ihne's little book on the earliest epoch of Roman history is the best discussion of the problem in English. — *Ed.*]

[2] The Greek word for Rome means strength; and the city's secret name was perhaps *Valentia*, from the verb *valere*, which has the same meaning. See p. 142, n. 2.

gold, began her legendary annals with a reign of Saturn, — a period of innocence, peace, and equality, of rustic labors and simple pleasures.

In the beginning, says tradition, a stranger king reigned over the people of Latium, Janus, the sun-god, whose dwelling was upon the Janiculum. His subjects had the innocent and simple, but rude and uncultured, manners of primeval man. From this king, Saturnus, who had been driven out of heaven by Jupiter, obtained the gift of the Capitoline Hill;[1] and in return for this hospitality, taught the Latins how to cultivate corn and the vine. This is the age of agriculture, succeeding the pastoral age, when men lived by the fruits of the chase and upon the acorns which they gathered under the great oaks of the Latin forest. Saturnus, "the good sower,"[2] was also the good harvester, and was long represented with a sickle, which later ages, perverting the original myth, converted into the scythe of Time.

SATURNUS.[3]

SATURNUS.[4]

To him succeeded Picus, his son, a famous soothsayer having the gift of oracles, and "the good" Faunus, the founder of important religious institutions, who was worshipped in later times in his twofold character as the god of fields and shepherds, and as an oracular and prophetic divinity. Faunus also

---

[1] This hill was called at first the Mount of Saturn. (Varro, *de Ling. lat.* v. 42; *Aen.* viii. 358.)

[2] *Sator* means sower.

[3] Taken from the *Monuments of Ancient Art* of Müller-Wisler.

[4] The cross placed under the chin indicates that the piece is a silver denarius. Behind there is the sickle of the divine husbandman.

TRADITIONAL HISTORY OF THE KINGS.   139

welcomed the Arcadian Evander, son of Mercury and the nymph Carmenta. Evander built a town on the *Palatine*, then covered with woods and meadows, and diffused among the natives the use of the Greek alphabet and more refined manners. Hercules also came unto Latium, where he abolished human sacrifices;[1] he married the daughter of Evander, killed the brigand Cacus on the Aventine, in the middle of a thick forest, and pastured the oxen of Geryon in a place where, afterward, an ox of bronze, set up in his honor in the *Forum boarium*, consecrated the memory of this circumstance. Thus the gods, the demi-gods, and the heroes sojourned on the banks of the Tiber. This was an omen of the future grandeur of the City of the Seven Hills; or rather, legend brought them thither when Rome, having become powerful, was desirous that immortals should have surrounded her cradle.[3]

AENEAS CARRYING ANCHISES.[2]

---

[1] Professor Capellini thinks that he has found traces of cannibalism in the Island of Palmaria. Many facts lead one to the belief that this practice, which still exists in certain islands of Oceania, was universal in the first ages of humanity. Certain Roman customs recalled the memory of it. Every year, says Varro (*de Ling. lat.* vii. 44), the Vestals threw into the Tiber, from the top of the Sublician Bridge, twenty-four osier figures, to replace the human victims that they no longer threw in after the time of Hercules. The *oscillae*, small dolls which were placed over the door of the house or hung on the neighboring trees, also recalled to memory the heads of men which were formerly offered to Saturn as a redemption. (Macr., *Sat.* I. vii. 31, and xi. 48.) At the feast of the Luperci, the priest with a bloody knife touched the foreheads of two young men, and until the time of the Empire, at the Latin Feriae, a criminal was slain whose blood sprinkled the altar of Jupiter. [All this points only to human sacrifices, not to cannibalism.—*Ed.*]

[2] Painting on a vase of Nola, at the Munich Museum.

[3] On the legend of Hercules and Cacus, see the learned memoir of M. Bréal (*Mél. de Myth.*), in which he follows, from the banks of the Ganges to the shores of the Tiber, a similar history, that of the contest of Indra and Vitra, of Ormuzd and Ahriman, of Hercules and Cacus. "Vergil," says he (p. 159), "has related this history as a poet of the Vedic times might have done; and the verses which he puts into the mouth of the Salian priests would not be out of place in the most ancient of the hymns of the Aryan race."

Through Saturn, the father of the gods, Rome was connected with what was greatest in heaven; through Aeneas, the son of Venus and ancestor of Romulus, with that which Greek poetry had made the greatest upon earth,— the city of Priam. Having escaped from the burning Troy with his father Anchises, his son Ascanius, and his wife Creüsa, who carried the sacred objects and the Palladium, he crossed the Hellespont; and after having wandered for a long time on land and sea, he was led by the star of his mother, which guided his ship by day as well as by night, to the shores of Latium.[1] Latinus, king of the country, welcomed the stranger, gave him his daughter Lavinia to wife, and to his companions seven hundred acres of land, seven for each. But in a battle against the Rutulians, Aeneas, conqueror of Turnus, disappeared in the midst of the waters of the Numicius, the sacred water of which was afterward used in the worship of Vesta. The gods had received the hero. He was worshipped under the name of Jupiter Indigetes. The war, however, continued, and in single combat Ascanius killed Mezentius, the ally of Turnus. Then, leaving the arid and unhealthy coast where his father had founded Lavinium, he came to build Alba Longa, in the heart of the country, on the Alban mountain, the summit of which commands all Latium, and affords a view of the Tiber, the sea, and the storm-beaten crests of the Apennines. Twelve kings of the race of Aeneas succeeded him; one of them, Procas, had two sons, Numitor and Amulius. The former, by right of age, ought to have inherited the kingdom; but Amulius took possession of it, killed the son of Numitor, placed his daughter Sylvia among the Vestals, and only allowed his brother a portion of the private domains of their father. Now one day when Sylvia had gone to the fountain of the sacred

AENEAS.[2]

---

[1] Serv. in *Aen.* i. 382. As early as the sixth century B. C., Stesichorus asserted the arrival of Aeneas in Italy. Aristotle, in the fourth, adopted this tradition, and the historian Timaeus, in the third, popularized it. We shall see later on that at the time of the First Punic War it was accepted at Rome.

[2] P P. TR. POT. COS. III. SC., that is to say, Father of the country, third year of the tribunitian power, and third consulate (A. D. 140); a piece struck by order of the Senate. It is the reverse of a large bronze of Antonine representing Aeneas, who is carrying Anchises and holding his son Ascanius by the hand.

wood, to draw the water necessary for the temple, Mars appeared to her, and promised divine children to the frightened maiden. Having become a mother, Sylvia was condemned to death, according to the rigorous laws of the worship of Vesta, and her twin sons were exposed on the Tiber. The river had then overflowed its banks; the cradle was gently carried by the waters as far as the Palatine Hill, where it stopped at the foot of a wild fig-tree.[1] Mars

RHEA SYLVIA.[2]   ROME AND THE SHE-WOLF.[3]   FAUSTULUS.[4]

did not abandon the two children. A she-wolf, attracted by their cries, or rather, sent by the god whose symbol was the wolf, nourished them with her milk. Afterward a sparrow-hawk brought them stronger nourishment, while birds sacred to the augurs hovered over their cradle to keep off the insects. Struck by these miracles, Faustulus, a shepherd of the King's flocks, took the two children and gave them to his wife, Acca Larentia, who called them Romulus and Remus.[5]

[1] The *ficus Ruminalis*, religiously preserved through centuries. *Ruma*, or *rumis*, has the meaning of *mamma* (Varr., *de Re rust.* II. i. 20), and the Tiber itself was called *Rumon*, that is, the river with fertilizing waters. (Serv. in *Aen.* viii. 63.) Hence came the names of Rome, Romulus, and Remus. (Philargyr. in Verg., *Ecl.* i. 20.) The bed of the Tiber formerly reached from the Pincio to the Janiculum. Although this river has now a width of only 185 feet, it still frequently overflows into the streets; a rising of 32 feet has been marked on the church of Minerva. That of the 29th of December, 1870, was 18 yards, 2 feet.

[2] The Aemilii pretended that Rhea Sylvia belonged to the Aemilian gens, and they put her image on some of their medals. That which we give is taken from a die of Antoninus, who was fond of recalling on his coins, facts or monuments of the primitive history of Rome.

[3] A didrachme of Campanian make, in silver. Pieces of two drachmae are rare. The drachme was almost equivalent to a franc.

[4] SEX . POM . FOSTLVS ROMA. Faustulus standing on the left; before him the wolf suckling the twins; in the background the Ruminal fig-tree with three crows. Reverse of a silver coin of the Pompeian family.

[5] Livy (i. 4) alludes to other accounts, in which Acca Larentia, on account of her loose morals, was given a name for courtesan, *lupa*, the she-wolf. Nothing more would be required for forming the famous legend on this name. It was already popular in 296, a time when the wolf and the twins were officially consecrated on the Palatine; but it was not very ancient, since the coins of Rome bore the impress of the sow before that of the wolf, which does not appear till the *quadrantes* of the fifth century. Acca Larentia was a telluric goddess, who personified the earth in which we place the dead, and seeds, whence life springs;

Brought up on the Palatine in huts of straw, like the hardy children of the shepherd, they grew in strength and courage, fearlessly attacking wild beasts and brigands, and asserting their rights by force. The companions of Romulus were called the Quintilii: those of Remus, the Fabii; and already division broke out between them. One day, however, the two brothers had a quarrel with the shepherds of the rich Numitor, whose flocks fed on the Aventine, and Remus, surprised in an ambush, was taken by them to Alba before their master. The prisoner's features, his age, the twin birth, struck Numitor: he caused Romulus to be brought before him; and Faustulus disclosed to the two young men the secret of their birth. Aided by their companions, they killed Amulius, and Alba returned to the sway of its lawful king. In return, Numitor permitted them to build a town on the banks of the river, and gave up to them all the country which extended from the Tiber on the road to Alba as far as a place called *Festi*, about five or six miles distant.[1]

Equal in power and authority, the two brothers soon disputed the honor of choosing the site and the name[2] of the new city. It was left to the gods, whose will they consulted by the Sabellian augury through the flight of birds. Remus, on the Aventine, first saw six vultures; but almost at the same time twelve appeared to Romulus, on the Palatine; and their companions, won over by this happy omen, pronounced in his favor. So the plebeian hill, already sullied in the most ancient

so her festival was celebrated at the winter solstice. At the sixth hour, at the moment when the year passed away, the Quirinal flamen offered a sacrifice to the manes in honor of the "Mother of the Lares,"— this is the meaning of her name; and the rest of the day was consecrated to Jupiter, the god of light and regenerated life. [The curious analogies in the stories of the birth and education of Cyrus, preserved by Herodotus, show that we probably have before us an old Aryan legend, however late it may appear at Rome. — *Ed.*]

[1] This is the *ager Romanus*. Under Tiberius expiatory sacrifices were still offered there, intended to purify the primitive frontier. The Roman mile, or thousand paces of five feet, is equivalent to about 1,620 yards.

[2] The profane name was *Roma* (see p. 137, n. 2); the sacerdotal name, *Flora*. There was a third secret name, possibly *Amor*, an anagram of *Roma*, which it was forbidden to pronounce, under pain of death. (Munter, *De occulto urbis Romae nomine*.) Others think it *Valentia*, or *Angeroma*. (Cf. Maury, memoir on *Servius Tullius*.) Great care was taken to conceal this name, says Pliny (*Hist. Nat.*, xxviii. 4), because it belonged at the same time to the tutelar deity of the city. As long as it remained unknown, the hostile priests could not induce this god to abandon his people, by promising in their city greater honors, *ampliorem cultum*, which, according to the idea of the ancients, was the determining reason of the favor of the gods.

TRADITIONAL HISTORY OF THE KINGS. 143

traditions as the abode of the brigand Cacus, remained so by the unlucky omen of Remus. It seems always doomed: at the present day it is a waste, where a few monks dwell about deserted churches.[1]

Following Etruscan rites[2] Romulus yoked a bull and a heifer without spot to a plough, and with a bronze ploughshare he traced around the Palatine a furrow which represented the circuit of the walls, the *pomerium*, or sacred enclosure,[3] beyond which began the secular town, the city of strangers and plebeians, devoid of auspices (April 21, 754[5]).

Already the rampart was rising, when Remus in derision jumped over it; but Celer, or Romulus himself, killed him, crying out: "Thus perish every one who shall cross these walls." Legend placed blood in the foundations of this city, which was destined to shed more than any city of the world has done.[6]

ROMULUS.[4]

The Palatine, the highest of the seven hills of Rome (168

---

[1] M. Maury sees in this legend the opposition of two *oppida* existing on the two rival hills, one of which, the Aventine, bore the name of *Remuria*, — whence the name of Remus.

[2] Varro, *de Ling. lat.* v. 32; Plut., *Rom.* 11.

[3] Aulus Gellius, xiii., xiv.: . . . *qui facit finem urbani auspicii.* Under Servius six hills were enclosed in the pomerium; up to the time of Claudius, the Aventine remained outside this enclosure. Fest., s. v. *Posimerium;* Dionys., iv. 13; Tac., *Ann.* xii. 24.

[4] We give this figure as we give the legendary history of Rome. Neither the one nor the other is authentic. The statues of the Seven Kings were certainly preserved on the Capitol, but they were conventional images. It is, however, as interesting to know how the Romans represented their great personages as to know how they conceived the history of their first days. [Nevertheless, these imaginary portraits are only of interest if really ancient, and not the conscious invention of a late and sceptical age. The portraits of these kings look more like Renaissance fancies, than old Roman work. They are apparently enlarged from heads found on coins with the legend of the names. — *Ed.*]

[5] This ancient wall of *Roma quadrata* was found in the excavations undertaken on the site of the Palace of the Caesars. It is a wall evidently built under the influence of the architectural ideas of Etruria. The same is the case with the wall of Servius.

[6] The difficulties of Roman chronology are as inextricable as the legends of its history:—
1st. Until the time of Augustus they reckoned by the consuls and from the expulsion of the kings; but some consulships were omitted. Livy himself, by his own calculations, may be convicted of having omitted several. On account of city troubles, or by the fraud of the pontiff, some were made to last longer, others less, than the year. The intercalations of interregnums and dictatorships, the variations of the date of entering on their duties, fixed sometimes on the 31st of December, sometimes (after the Second Punic War) on the 19th of March or on the Ides of May, finally, after the year 153, on the 1st of January, led to such confusion, that, when

144 ROME UNDER THE KINGS.

feet), was nearly 2,000 yards in circumference, so that access to it was easy.

But, at a little distance, the Capitoline Hill (145 feet) descended by steep declivities into the marshes; this position, then, was already strong in itself. Romulus there carried out works of defence, which made it the citadel of Rome.

In order to increase the population of the new city, he opened

Caesar reformed the calendar, it was necessary to make a year of fifteen months, in order to put the civil year in accord with the course of the sun.

2d. The Roman year is four months behind the Christian year, and three months in advance of the Greek year; so that the year of Rome 300 corresponds to eight months of the year 454 B. C., and four months of the year 453 B. C.; and for the Olympiads, to three months of Ol. 81, 3, and nine months of Ol. 81, 4. Consequently, even if this chronology were certain, there must be continual rectifications in reckoning the years before Christ.

3d. Livy avows that great confusion still existed concerning the period which followed the expulsion of the kings, — *tanti errores implicant temporum* . . . (ii. 21); and there is, in truth, no certainty in Roman chronology until after taking of Rome by the Gauls, because the Greeks knew this event and connected it with their own chronology, in Ol. 98, 1 or 2, or even, according to Varro, Ol. 97, 2. When they began at a rather late date to establish a chronology for Roman history, it was a traditional belief (see Serv. in *Aen*. i. 268) that Rome had been founded 360 years after the downfall of Troy, and that between its foundation and destruction by the Gauls the same number of years had elapsed. Of this period of 360 years, a third, or 120, was allowed for the consuls; the other two thirds, or 240, with four intercalary years, 244, formed the period of the kings. Now 390 B. C., the date of the taking of Rome by the Gauls, plus 364, give 754. But as there was a variation of some years in the same fundamental date, some took 754, others 753, or 752 (Fabius, Ol. 8, 1; Polybius and Corn. Nep., Ol. 7, 2; Cato, Ol. 7, 1; Varro, Ol. 6, 3; and *the Capitoline Annals*, Ol. 6, 4). They went as far as to fix the day (April 21st), and even the hour, when Romulus had traced out the pomerium. The value of such a chronology will be easily appreciated.

[The early Roman, like the Greek, chronology, reasoned down from remote mythical dates, not up from known historical facts. The use of 60-year cycles is just as clear in the legends of the birth of Homer. Cf. the criticism in my *Greek Literature*, vol. i. Appendix B., and in my Essay on the Olympiads in the *Journal of Hellenic Studies*, ii. 164, *seq*. — *Ed.*]

4th. As regards the three last kings in particular, Cicero and Livy represented Tarquin the Proud, who died in 495 B. C., as the son of Tarquin the Elder, who had come to Rome with his wife 135 years before, — hence chronological impossibilities of which the legend had never dreamed.

5th. Finally, the 244 years of the royal period give on an average 35 years for each reign. Now Rome was an elective monarchy, in which the throne was only reached at the age of experience and maturity; moreover, of seven kings, two only finished their life and their reign in peace. So Newton, only allowing 17 years as an average for each reign, reduced these 244 years to 119, and placed the founding of Rome about 630 B. C. Niebuhr has remarked that Venice, a republic which also had elective chiefs, reckoned, from 805 to 1311, 40 doges; which gives an average of 12½ years for each. We can infer nothing from these calculations, for, in Spain, from 1516 to 1759 (243 years), there were only seven kings, but not elective; as many in France, from 987 to 1223 (236 years), and from 1589 to 1830, 240 years, there would have been, reckoning as the Restoration did, seven kings, two of whom died a violent death, a third finished his life in exile, and a fourth died at the age of ten.

This chronology of the early times of Rome must therefore be suspicious, like the history of its first kings. We will follow it, however, in default of a better one.

REMAINS OF THE WALL OF ROMULUS.

an asylum in the midst of the oaks which grew in the *intermontium*, between the two summits of the Capitoline, and he made it a sacred wood;[1] then he asked those in the neighboring cities to unite themselves by marriages to his people. Everywhere they refused with contempt. "Open," said they, "an asylum for women too." He dissembled; but at the festival of the god Consus,[2] he caused all the young girls to be carried off who had come to the games with their fathers. There was no concerted action to punish this outrage. The Coeninates, the first ready, were beaten; Romulus killed their king, Acron, and consecrated his arms, as *spolia opima*, to Jupiter Feretrius. The Crustuminians and the Antemnates met with the same fate and lost their lands. But the Sabines from Cures, led by their king, Tatius, penetrated as far as the Capitoline Hill, and took possession, through the treachery of Tarpeia, of the citadel, which Romulus had built on one of the peaks; the other summit bore later on the temple of Jupiter. For opening the gates to the Sabines, Tarpeia had asked from them what they carried on the left arm, — namely, golden bracelets. But on this arm they also carried their bucklers; on entering, they threw them at her, and she was smothered under their weight. The people long believed that at the end of the gloomy tunnels excavated in the Cápitoline, the beautiful Tarpeia lived, seated in the midst of her treasures; but that he who attempted to penetrate to her, must infallibly perish.[4] The Romans were already fleeing, when Romulus, vowing a temple to Jupiter Stator,[5] renewed the combat, which was stayed by the Sabine women throwing themselves

TARPEIA.[3]

---

[1] Not only were certain woods sacred, but also certain trees, notably those which had been struck by lightning. Pliny (*Hist. Nat.* xii. 1, 2) calls trees the first temples of the gods. This worship was, in fact, very ancient, since it commences among the Greeks with the oak of Dodona, and is continued by the laurel of Apollo, the olive of Minerva, the myrtle of Venus, the poplar of Hercules, etc., and it was still in active existence at the time of Apuleius.

[2] This god, whose name it has been attempted to derive from the adjective *conditus*, which signifies hidden, appears to have been a subterranean deity. (Hartung, *Die Religion der Röm.*, ii. 87.)

[3] TVRPILIANVS III. VIR., that is to say, monetary triumvir. Tarpeia crushed by the shields and raising her hands to heaven. Silver coin of the Petronian family.

[4] This is the only ancient legend which still exists amongst the people of Rome, said Niebuhr; but since his time it has been forgotten.

[5] This temple, at first very unpretending, was several times reconstructed. The engraving on p. 146 gives its restored form according to the works of Canina and M. Dutert, the author of a very fine memoir of the Roman Forum.

between their fathers and their husbands. Peace was concluded, and the first basis of the greatness of Rome established by the union of the two armies. The double-headed Janus became the symbol of the new nation.[1]

ROMAN BRACELET.[2]

At the end of five years Tatius was killed by the Laurentines, to whom he refused justice for a murder, and the Sabines consented to recognize Romulus as sole king. Victories over the Fidenates and Veientines justified this choice. But one day, when he was reviewing his troops near the Capraean marsh, a storm dispersed the assembly; when the people returned, the King had disappeared. A senator, Proculus, swore that he had seen him ascend to heaven on the chariot of Mars, amid thunder and lightning, and he was worshipped under the name of Quirinus. The Senate had sacrificed him to their fears, or the Sabines to their resentment.

TRADITIONAL FIGURE OF TATIUS.[3]

II. NUMA (715–673).

THE two nations could not agree as to the appointment of his successor, and for a year the senators governed by turns as *interreges*. At length it was settled that the Romans should make the selection, on condition that they chose a Sabine. A voice named

---

[1] In memory of this peace Roman ladies celebrated on the Calends of March (March 1st) the festival of the *matronalia*. In the morning they ascended in pomp to the temple of Juno, on the Esquiline Hill, and placed at the foot of the goddess the flowers with which their heads were crowned. (Ovid, *Fast.* iii. 205.) In the evening, in order to commemorate the marks of tenderness which the Sabine women had received from their husbands, they remained at home richly adorned, waiting for the gifts of their husbands and relatives. Tibullus chose this day, on which custom allowed presents to be offered to women, to send his books to his beloved Neaera. (Tib., *Carm.* iii. 1.)

[2] In gold and open work, with coins set in : it is reduced to almost half size, which proves that it was worn on the upper part of the arm. The medals are of the third century of our era. (Cf. *Dictionary of Antiquities*, p. 437.)

[3] Visconti's *Iconographie Romaine*. (See p. 143, note 4.)

TEMPLE OF JUPITER STATOR (RESTORATION BY CANINA AND DUTERT).

TRADITIONAL HISTORY OF THE KINGS. 147

Numa Pompilius. All proclaimed him king; but he did not accept till he had obtained favorable signs from Heaven. "Led by the augur to the summit of the Tarpeian Mount, he seated himself on a stone and turned towards the south. The augur, with his head covered, and holding in his hand the *lituus*, a curved stick without a knot in it, cast his eyes over town and country, praying to the gods meanwhile; then he marked out a space in the heavens from east to west, declared the region of the south to be the right, that of the north the left, and determined the extreme point of the horizon to which his sight could reach. Then he took the lituus in his left hand, laid his right on the head of Numa, and said: "O Jupiter, O father! If it be good that this Numa Pompilius, whose head I hold, reign in Rome, show me certain signs in the space that I have marked out." He announced the omens he required, and when they had been manifested, Numa, declared king, descended from the *templum*.[2]

TRADITIONAL PORTRAIT OF NUMA POMPILIUS.[1]

Numa was the most just and wise of men, the disciple of Pythagoras,[3] and the favorite of the gods. Inspired by the Nymph Egeria, whom he went to consult by night in the solitude of the wood of the Camenae or Muses,[4] he arranged the religious ceremonies, the functions of the four pontiffs, the guardians of worship; of the flamens, the ministers of the greater gods; of the augurs, the interpreters of divine will; of the fetiales, who prevented unjust wars; of the vestals chosen by the high priest from the

---

[1] Visconti's *Iconographie Romaine*.
[2] *Templum* was the name given to sacred enclosures, afterward to religious edifices. I have borrowed these details from Livy (i. 18), who has certainly furnished us with an extract from the ritual, and shown us an augur at his duties. The aruspices were simply diviners who examined the entrails of victims; they had no religious character, and did not form a college. They never arrived at the authority and consideration that the augurs enjoyed.
[3] Tradition says so; but chronology and probability are opposed to the idea. Pythagoras lived a century later [than the *traditional* date of Numa].
[4] In proof of this the Romans still show, not far from the Capena Gate, the grotto wherein the goddess gave sage counsel to the new king. This grotto was, in fact, a *nymphaeum* consecrated to some water divinity; but Egeria never dwelt there, even according to the legend. The abode assigned to her by the ancients was in the wood of the Camenae, on the Caelius, where from a dark cave came a fountain that never dried up.

most noble families to keep up the perpetual fire, the Palladium, and the Penates; and lastly of the Salii, who guarded the shield that had fallen from heaven (*ancile*) and celebrated the festival of

THE EIGHT COLUMNS OF THE TEMPLE OF SATURN.[1]

the God of War by songs and armed dances. He forbade bloody sacrifices, the representation of the God by images of wood, bronze, or stone, and paid special honors to Saturn, the father of Italian civilization, the king of the golden age, of the times of virtue,

[1] Remains of a temple of Saturn, rebuilt by the Emperor Maxentius.

plenty, and equality, whose festival, a day of mad joy and liberty even for the slave, suspended hostilities on the frontiers

HEADS OF THE DII PENATES.[1]

SALIAN PRIEST.[2]

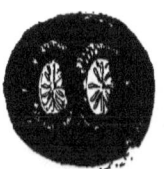
ANCILIA.[3]

and the execution of criminals in the city.[4] In later times the temple of this god was a kind of state sanctuary. The public treasure was preserved there, with the official documents and the ensigns of the legions.

That each might live in peace on his farm, Numa distributed among the people the lands conquered by Romulus, raised a temple to Good Faith on the Capitol, and consecrated the limits of property (festival of the *Terminalia*) by devoting to the gods of the infernal regions those who should remove the boundaries of the fields. He moreover divided the poor into guilds of craftsmen, and built the temple of Janus, the open gates of which announced war, the closing of them peace. It was needful that during war time the god should leave his temple to protect the young warriors of Rome; peace rendered this aid useless. Under Numa "the neighboring towns seem to have breathed the healthful breath of a soft, pure wind, that blew from the side where Rome lay," and the temple of Janus always remained closed.[6]

JANUS.[5]

[1] DEI PENATES. Coupled heads of the Penates. Silver coin of Antian family.
[2] AVGVST. DIVI F. LVDOS SAE. Salian priest. Silver coin of the family Sanquinia, commemorative of the secular games.
[3] The *ancilia*; reverse of a bronze of Antoninus.
[4] The Saturnalia legally lasted one day in ancient times, three in last centuries of the Republic, and five under the Empire; but seven were often taken. During these feasts, which in certain customs recall our old carnival, official life was suspended and the tribunals closed. Cf. Macr., *Sat.* I. *passim*.
[5] *Jano Patri.* Janus standing, holding a patera and a sceptre. Aureus, or gold piece of Gallienus.
[6] With the worship of Janus was perhaps connected the vague notion of a supreme god, who was both sun and moon, the beginning and end of all things, the creator of the world and arbiter of battles. The old deity was successively despoiled of his warlike attributes in favor

150 ROME UNDER THE KINGS.

Beyond these works of peace, tradition knows nothing of the second King of Rome, and remains silent on the subject of this long reign of forty-three years. He himself had recommended the worship of silence, the goddess *Tacita*. At his death Diana changed Egeria into a fountain, and the spring still flows at the place which was the sacred wood of the Camenae. Near the tomb of Numa, dug at the foot of the Janiculum, were buried his books, which contained all the prescriptions to be followed to ensure the accomplishment of the rites so as to gain certain favor from the gods. Being recovered at an epoch when Greek idolatry had replaced the old religion, these books were judged dangerous, and were burned by order of the Senate.[2]

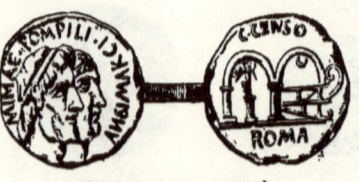

COIN OF THE MARCII.[1]

III. — TULLUS HOSTILIUS (673-640).

To the pious and pacific prince there succeeds the sacrilegious warrior king; after Numa, Tullus Hostilius. The Sabines, in consequence of the agreement made between the two nations about the election of Numa, chose him among the Romans, as the latter, after Tullus, name the Sabine Ancus. Romulus was the son of a god, Numa, the husband of a goddess; with Tullus begins the reign of men. He was grandson of a Latin of

---

of Mars, an old god of the field (Cato, *de Re rust.* 141, and Saint Augustine, *de Civ. Dei*, ii. 17), and of his supreme majesty in favor of Jupiter. In the *Fasti* (i. 101, 117 *seq.*) Ovid makes him say: —

"Me Chaos antiqui, nam sum res prisca, vocabant . . .
Quidquid ubique vides, caelum, mare, nubila, terras,
Omnia sunt nostra clausa patentque manu."

[1] This coin of the Marcii, who asserted their descent from the fourth King of Rome, himself said to be the grandson of Numa, gives the traditional features of these princes. On the reverse are two arcades: under the first stands victory on a column, under the second the crescent moon and the prow of a vessel, another souvenir of the port of Ostia built by Ancus and of his success over the Latins. We see the custom the Romans had of recalling on their coins the facts of their annals, and the interest that these coins offer from the double point of view of history and art.

[2] The fact is reported by Dionysius, Livy, and Cicero. We shall see at the right place what to believe about this pretended discovery of the books of Numa made in the year 181 B.C., which was a pious fraud.

NYMPHAEUM OF EGERIA.

Medullia, who had fought valiantly under Romulus against the Sabines. Tullus loved the poor, distributed lands among them, and went to live among them himself on Mount Caelius, where he established the conquered Albans.

Let us hear Livy relating the ancient legend; although no translation can convey the brilliancy of his narrative. Alba, the mother of Rome, had by slow degrees become a stranger to her colony, and mutual incursions brought on a war. Long the two armies remained face to face, without daring to commence the sacrilegious strife. "As there were found in each of the two nations three twin brothers, of nearly the same strength and age, the Horatii and Curiatii, Tullus and the dictator of Alba charged them to fight for their country; the supremacy should belong to the victors. The convention that was made was this. The fetialis, addressing Tullus, said: 'King, dost thou bid me conclude a treaty with the *pater patratus* of the Alban people?' And on an affirmative answer being given, he added: 'I demand of thee the sacred herb.' 'Take it pure,' replied Tullus. Then the fetialis brought the pure herb from the citadel, and addressing Tullus anew: 'King, dost thou name me interpreter of thy royal will and that of the Roman people, descended from Quirinus? Dost thou approve of the sacred vessels, and the men who accompany me?' 'Yes,' replied the King, 'without prejudice to my right and that of the Roman people.' The fetialis was M. Valerius; he made Sp. Fusius *pater patratus* of the Albans, by touching him on the head and hair with vervain. The *pater patratus* took the oath, and sanctioned the treaty by pronouncing the necessary formulae. When the conditions had been read, the fetialis continued: 'Hear, Jupiter, hear, father patratus of the Alban people; hear, too, Alban people. The Roman people will never be the first to violate the conditions inscribed on these tablets, which have just been read to you,—from the first line to the last without fraud or falsehood. From this day they are clearly understood by all. If it should happen that by public deliberation or unworthy subterfuge the Roman people infringe them first, then, great Jupiter, strike it as I strike this swine, and strike with more severity, as thy power is greater.' When the imprecation was ended, he broke the skull of the pig with a stone. The Albans, by the mouth of the Dictator and priests, repeated the same formulae and pronounced the same oath.

"When the treaty was concluded, the three brothers on each side take their arms. The cheers of their fellow citizens animate them; the Gods of their country, and even, so it seems to them, their country itself, have their eyes fixed upon them. Burning with courage, intoxicated with the sound of so many voices exhorting them, they advance between the two armies, who, though exempt from peril, were not so from fear; for it was a matter of empire depending on the valor and fortune of so small a number of champions.

"The signal being given, the six champions spring forward sword in hand, and bearing in their hearts the courage of two great nations. Heedless of their own danger, they only keep before their eyes triumph or slavery, and the future of their country, whose destiny depends upon their acts. At the first shock, when the clash of arms was heard and the swords were seen flashing, a deep horror seized the spectators. Anxious expectation froze their utterance and suspended their breath. Still the combatants fight on; the blows are no longer uncertain, there are wounds and blood. Of the three Romans two fall dead. The Alban army utters shouts of joy, and the Romans fix looks of despair on the last of the Horatii, whom the Curiatii are already surrounding. But these are all three wounded, and the Roman is unhurt. Not strong enough for his enemies united, yet more than a match for each separately, he takes to flight, sure that each will follow him according to the degree of strength he has left. When he had gone some distance from the scene of combat, he turned, and saw his adversaries following him at unequal distances, one alone pressing rather close upon him.

"Quickly he turns, darts on him with fury, and while the Albans are calling on the Curiatii to help their brother, Horatius, already victorious, hastens to his second combat. Then arose from the midst of the Roman army a cry of unexpected joy; the warrior gathers strength from the voice of his people, and without giving the last Curiatius time to approach, he puts an end to the second. There remained only two; but having neither the same confidence nor the same strength: the one unwounded, proud of a double victory, and advancing with confidence to a third combat; the other exhausted by the blood he had lost and by the distance he had run, hardly able to drag himself along, and conquered beforehand by the death of his brothers. There was hardly a struggle. The Roman, transported with joy, cries out: 'I have just sacrificed two to the manes of my brothers; I sacrifice this one that Rome may have rule over the Albans.' Curiatius could scarcely support his arms; Horatius plunged his sword into his throat, threw him to the ground, and despoiled him of his arms. The Romans surround the victor and cover him with praises, all the more delighted because they had at first trembled. Each of the two peoples then turned to burying its dead, but with very different feelings. The one had won empire, the other had passed under foreign rule. The tombs of these warriors[1] are still seen at the spot where they each fell; the two Romans together and nearer Alba; the three Albans on the side next Rome, at some distance from one another, according as they had fought.

"Then by the terms of the treaty, Mettius asked Tullus what is his will. 'That thou hold the Alban youth under arms,' answered the King, 'and I will employ them against the Veientines if I make war on them.' The two armies returned home, and Horatius, loaded with his triple trophy, marched at the head of the legions, when near the Porta Capena he met his sister, who was betrothed to one of the Curiatii. She recognized on her brother's shoulders her lover's tunic, which she herself had woven, and her sobs burst forth; she asks for her husband, she utters his name in a voice choked with tears. Angry at seeing a sister's tears insult his triumph and the joy of Rome, Horatius draws his sword and stabs the girl, overwhelming her with imprecations. 'Go with thy mad love,' says he, 'go and rejoin thy betrothed, thou who forgottest thy dead brothers, and him who remains, and thy country. So perish every Roman woman who shall dare to weep the death of an enemy.' This murder caused a profound sensation in the Senate

---

[1] If this combat ever did take place, the Horatii must have fallen at that spot; and the *tumuli* seen there, which recall the sepulchral buildings of Etruria, perhaps covered their bones. The Romans at least thought so.

and among the people, though the brilliant exploit of the murderer took from the horror of his crime. He is led before the King, that justice may be done. Tullus, fearing to become responsible for a sentence, the severity of which would raise in revolt the multitude, calls the people together and says: 'I name duumvirs,[1] according to the law, to judge the crime of Horatius.' The law was fearfully severe. 'Let the duumvirs (it ran) judge the crime; if the judgment is appealed from, let the appeal be pronounced upon; if the sentence is confirmed, let the head of the condemned be covered, let him be hanged on the fatal tree and beaten with rods within or without the circuit of the walls.' The duumvirs immediately take their seats; 'P. Horatius,' says one of them, 'I declare that thou hast merited death. Go, lictor, bind his hands!' The lictor approaches; already he was passing the cord round him, when by the advice of Tullus, a merciful interpreter of the law, Horatius cries, 'I appeal!' and the case was referred to the people. Then the elder Horatius was heard crying that the death of his daughter was just; otherwise he himself, in virtue of his paternal authority, would have been the first to punish his son; and he besought the Romans, who on the preceding day had seen him father of so fine a family, not to deprive him of all his children. Then, embracing his son, and showing the people the spoils of Curiatii, hung up in the place called to this day the Pillar of Horatius: 'Romans,' said he, 'the man whom you saw with admiration so lately marching in the midst of you, triumphant, and bearing illustrious spoils, will you see him tied to the degrading post, beaten with rods, and put to death? The Albans themselves could not endure such a spectacle. Go, lictor, bind those hands which have just given us empire! Go, cover with a veil the head of the liberator of Rome; hang him on the fatal tree; strike him within the town, if thou wilt, but in presence of these trophies and spoils; without the town, but in the midst of the tombs of the Curiatii. Into what place can you lead him where the monuments of his glory do not protest against the horror of his punishment?' The citizens, conquered by the tears of the father and the intrepidity of the son, pronounced the absolution of the guilty; and this grace was accorded

---

[1] *Duumviri perduellionis* (Livy, i. 26; cf. Lange, *Römische Alterthümer*, i. 328, *seq.*).

TOMB OF THE HORATII.

him rather for their admiration of his courage than for the goodness of his cause. In order, however, that so glaring a crime should not remain without expiation, they obliged the father to redeem his son by paying a fine. After some expiatory sacrifices, whereof the family of the Horatii since preserved the tradition, the old man placed a post across the middle of the street, a kind of yoke, under which he made his son pass with veiled head. This post, preserved and kept in perpetuity by the care of the Republic, exists to this day. It is called the Sister's Post." [1]

Did this combat, twice consecrated, once by the great historian of Rome, again by the masculine genius of Corneille, ever take place? We may doubt it; but at Rome every one believed it, and for centuries there existed proofs of it which appeared irrefutable: the Sister's Post, the Cluilian ditch,[2] the tombs of the Horatii, the expiatory sacrifices renewed every year by their House to appease the manes of a beloved victim. All this compels us to admit that there is at least hidden under the ornament of epic narration, embellished by popular poetry and by the pride of the *gens Horatia*, some actual fact. Legend is often wrong as regards the exploits which it relates: it is nearly always right about the manners and institutions which it reveals; and it is in order to show this portion of truth that we have given this long narration.

Alba had submitted; but in a battle against the Fidenates, whom the Veientines aided, the dictator of the Albans, Mettius Fuffetius, stood aloof with his troops, awaiting the issue of the combat. Tullus invoked Pallor and Terror, promising them a temple if they spread fear among the enemy's ranks; then, being victorious, he said to the traitor: "Thy heart is divided between me and my enemies: so shall it be with thy body;" and they bound him to two chariots, which were driven in opposite directions. Then Alba was destroyed, its population transferred to Rome on Mount Caelius, its patricians admitted to the Senate, and its rich men among the knights.[3] Rome inherited the ancient legends of

---

[1] Livy, i. 24–26.
[2] The *fossa Cluilia* was supposed to be the trench of the camp in which Cluilius, king of Alba, had entrenched himself in the war against Tullus. He must have died there, and have been replaced by the dictator, Mettius Fuffetius.
[3] Livy, i. 30. *Equitum decem turmas ex Albanis legit*. Each *turma* consisted of thirty men. Cf. Fest. s. v.

Alba, the family of Julii, whence Caesar sprang, and its rights as metropolis of several Latin towns. Six centuries later, the Hostilii, who claimed descent from the third King of Rome, had represented on their coins the two dread divinities, whom their ancestor, said they, had invoked. Tullus again fought successfully against the Sabines and the Veientines, whose town he besieged. But he neglected the service of the gods, and their anger brought on Rome a contagious disease which attacked the King himself. Like Romulus, he came to a mysterious and tragic end. He thought he had found in Numa's books a means of expiation, and the secret of forcing revelations from Jupiter Elicius.[2] A mistake made in these dread adjurations drew down lightning upon him, and the flame devoured his body and his palace (640 B. C.).[3] "He," says Livy, "who had hitherto considered it unworthy of a king to occupy himself with sacred things, became the prey of every superstition, and filled the city with religious practices." An old story, ever new! A more prosaic account says he was slain by Ancus.[4]

TERROR.[1]

PALLOR.[1]

IV. ANCUS MARCIUS (640–616).

THE reign of Ancus, who was said to be the grandson of Numa, has not the poetic brilliancy of that of Tullus. After the example of his ancestor, he encouraged agriculture, re-established neglected religion, caused the laws regulating ceremonial to be inscribed on tables[5] and exposed in the Forum; but he could not, like Numa, keep the temple of Janus shut, and he was obliged to lay aside the service of the gods in order to take up arms. The Latins had just broken the alliance concluded with Tullus. Four of their towns were taken; their inhabitants settled upon

---

[1] Silver coin of L. Hostilius Saserna.
[2] The priests of Jupiter Elicius claimed the power of making the thunder fall; and they were thought to be able to do so. (Pliny, *Nat. Hist.* ii. 4, and xxvii. 4.) They kept this secret so well, that the world had to wait for Franklin to discover it again.
[3] Livy, i. 31.
[4] Dionys. iii. 35.
[5] Livy, i. 32; Dionys. iii. 36.

the Aventine,[1] and the territory of Rome extended as far as the sea. Ancus found brine-pits, which are still there, and forests, which are gone; he appropriated the revenue of them for the royal treasury.[2] At the mouth of the Tiber there was a favorable site for a port; he there founded Ostia (the mouths), which is now a league from the sea. He built the first bridge over the Tiber (*pons Sublicius*),[3] making it of wood, that it might be easily broken down if the enemy wished to make use of it; and he defended the approach by a fortress over the Janiculum. To protect the dwellings of the new colonists on the left bank of the river, he traced the ditch of the Quirites; and in order to deter from crimes, which had become numerous with the increase of population, he dug in the tufo of the Capitoline the famous Mamertine prison, which may still be seen, and which was led up to by the steps of the *Gemoniae*, or "Stair of Sighs." His reign of twenty-four years, according to Livy, of twenty-three by Cicero's account, finished tranquilly, like that of Numa; and the Romans always honored the memory of the prince, wise and just in peace, brave and victorious in war.[4]

TRADITIONAL PORTRAIT OF ANCUS MARCIUS.

V. TARQUIN THE ELDER (616–578).

IN the reign of Ancus, a stranger had come to settle at Rome.[5] He was said to be the son of the Corinthian Demaratus, a rich merchant of the family of the Bacchiads, who, fleeing from the tyranny of Cypselus, had retreated to Tarquinii. In Etruria, all hope of power was forbidden to the stranger. But Tanaquil[6]

[1] Cicero, *de Rep.* ii. 18; Livy, i. 33.
[2] Aurel. Vict. *de Vir. ill.* 5.
[3] From *sublica*, a pile. Festus. s. v. *Sublicium*.
[4] He is said to have carried on seven wars, against the Latins, Fidenates, Sabines, Veientines, and Volscians.
[5] Schwegler (*Röm. Gesch.* i. 677) makes the Tarquins an ancient Roman *gens*.
[6] Others say his wife was Gaia Caecilia, the good spinner and beneficent enchantress, to whom the young brides paid honor. (Pliny, *Hist. Nat.* viii. 74.)

had read in the future the fortunes of her husband. He came to Rome with his wealth and numerous attendants. On the road the forecasts of his future greatness were renewed. The Romans were not particular in the matter of omens; they admitted all that were told to them, and Livy gravely repeats the nursery tales which tradition transmitted to him. We must repeat them after him, because they show us the mental condition of the nation, which had no imagination except for this kind of things, and because they teach us how the aruspices analyzed a sign. "As Tarquin approaches the Janiculum, an eagle slowly descends from the high heavens and carries off his cap; then hovers about the car with loud screeching, swoops down afresh, and replaces it on the traveller's head. At this sight Tanaquil, versed in the art of augury, embraces her husband with delight. She tells him to consider well the kind of bird, the part of heaven whence it came, and the god who sends it. Another manifest sign was that the prodigy was accomplished on the highest part of the body; the ornament which covered his head was only raised an instant, to be replaced on it immediately. The gods, then, promise him the highest fortune." Tarquin accepted the omen; but at the same time helped himself. At Rome he gained by his wisdom the confidence of Ancus, who left to him the guardianship of his sons; and by his worth and his kindness towards them he won the affection of the people, who proclaimed him king, to the exclusion of the sons of the old prince.

The new King embellished Rome, enlarged its territory, and undertook the encircling of the town with a wall, which was finished by Servius. The Forum, drained and surrounded by porticos, was used for the gatherings and pleasures of the people. The Capitol was begun, and the Circus levelled, for the shows and Great Games brought from Etruria. But the most considerable of these works were the subterranean sewers, which to the present day support a great part of Rome, notwithstanding earthquakes, and in spite of the weight of edifices a hundred times rebuilt over their vaulting.[1] For such works, which have not the majestic uselessness

---

[1] In consequence of the raising of the bed of the Tiber, perhaps also of the height of waters at the time when the drawing was taken, only the top of the sewer is seen in our engraving on page 160. This construction astonished the contemporaries of Augustus by its size and the amount

of the Egyptian constructions, it must have been necessary to subject the people to wearisome drudgery, and the treasury to heavy expense. For the latter, however, Tarquin was able to provide, with the spoils taken from the Latins and Sabines in his successful wars which made him master of the lands lying between the Tiber, the Anio, and the Sabine mountains, known as the territory of Collatia. Livy, in relating the story of this conquest, has preserved to us the formula employed by the Romans in all capitulations of cities: "Tarquin, addressing the deputies, asked them: 'Are you the deputies sent by the Collatian people to put yourselves and the people of Collatia in my power?' 'We are.' — 'Are the people of Collatia free to dispose of themselves?' 'They are.' — 'Do you surrender, to me and to the Roman people, yourselves, the people of Collatia, the city and the fields, the waters, the boundaries, the temples, the movable property, and all things divine and human therein contained?' 'We do.' — 'I accept them, in my own name and in that of the Roman people.'"

Livy makes no mention of wars carried on by Tarquin against the Etruscans; but his contemporary, Dionysius of Halicarnassus, has much to say upon that subject. This rhetorician, who endeavored to be a historian, lends a ready ear, in his Roman *Archæology*, to all the fables tradition offers him; and tradition was eager to make out that this Etruscan king, to justify his Roman royalty, had carried on victorious wars against his former countrymen. According to Dionysius, the conquered Etruscans sent Tarquin, in token of their submission, the twelve fasces, the crown, the sceptre surmounted by the royal eagle, the curule chair, and the purple robe. This victory is more than doubtful; and the gift, if it was ever made, does not at all indicate the submission of those offering it. Rome, in later days, gave things like these to the kings entering into alliance with her, — compensating them thus at small expense for their aid in war, or for their splendid presents made to her.

Tarquin was the first to celebrate the Roman triumph, displaying a pomp till then unknown; his robe being embroidered with

that it had cost. "Three things," said Dionysius of Halicarnassus, "reveal the magnificence of Rome, — " the aqueducts, the roads, and the sewers." Nearly over the mouth of the Cloaca stands the little rotunda known as the temple of the Sun, disfigured by an abominable roof, with which it has been covered for the purpose of protecting its nineteen fluted Corinthian columns of Carrara marble, — a construction probably belonging to the period of the Antonines.

golden flowers, and his chariot drawn by four white horses. From his reign dates the introduction into Rome of Etruscan costumes, the royal robe, the war-mantle, the toga praetexta, and the tunica palmata, worn by the victorious general at his triumph; and to his time belong the twelve lictors and the curule chair,—an ivory seat whose material the Etruscans obtained from Asia or Africa. Tarquin made an attempt to change the constitution; but, notwithstanding his popularity, he did not succeed in re-arranging the tribes. The patricians who opposed him made religion speak by the mouth of the augur, Attus Navius. This personage maintained his opposition to the King by aid of a miracle. "Augur," said Tarquin, hoping to bring him to confusion, "can the thing be done which I now have in mind?" The augur consulted the heavens, and declared that it could. Tarquin presented him with a razor and a whetstone, saying: "Cut this stone, then, with this knife." Attus cut the stone through with the knife; and to keep the event fresh in the minds of the people, the razor and the stone were preserved under an altar, and a statue of Navius erected beside it,—a figure with veiled head in the attitude assumed by the augurs when awaiting the revelation of the divine will. The popular faith had no difficulty in accepting a legend which grew up about the cut stone, and the college of augurs, naturally considering it historic truth, erected the statue to consecrate it.

MIRACLE OF NAVIUS.[1]

Tarquin had reigned for thirty or forty years with great renown in peace and war, when one day two shepherds, suborned by the sons of Ancus, presented themselves before the King, praying him to settle a dispute which had arisen between them. The King listened to them; and while one was engrossing his attention, the other suddenly struck him a mortal blow on the head with an axe. Upon this, Tanaquil at once closed the palace doors, and gave out word to the people that the King was not dead, but merely wounded, and that meantime he had deputed his son-in-law Servius

---

[1] The augur Navius, on his knees, cutting a stone; Tarquin standing before him; behind the King another stone. Bronze of Antoninus.

THE CLOACA MAXIMA.

TRADITIONAL HISTORY OF THE KINGS. 161

to reign in his stead. For several days she concealed his death, and when it was known, Servius became king without being accepted by the assembly of the Curiae, but with the consent of the Senate (578 B. C.).

VI. — SERVIUS TULLIUS (578–534).

His origin was surrounded with mystery. Some said he was the son of a female slave[1] or of the prince of Corniculum, who was killed in a war against the Romans; others related how a

AGGER OR RAMPART OF SERVIUS.

genius had appeared in the flame of the hearth to Ocrisia, a servant of Queen Tanaquil, and that at the same instant she had conceived. After his birth the gods continued their favors to

[1] Independently of the Saturnalia, slaves were granted a day of liberty on the Ides of the month of August, in memory of the servile birth of Servius Tullius (Plut., *Quaest. Rom.* 100; Festus, s. v. *Servorum*). This festival proves that we ought carefully to examine the customs which, though themselves often sprung from a legend, would appear to give to the latter the character of a historic fact. This observation applies to many Roman usages.

VOL. I. 11

him, and he grew up in the King's palace in the midst of prodigies and manifest signs of his future greatness. We shall see later on what history and archaeology make of these traditions, which concealed a totally different fate.

Having become king, Servius made great changes in the city and in its laws. He gave Rome the dimensions which it

FRAGMENT OF THE WALL OF SERVIUS TULLIUS.

had under the Republic, by uniting the Viminal, the Esquiline, and the Quirinal to the city, by a wall and a mighty bank of earth (*agger*), with a ditch in front, 100 Roman feet wide, and 30 deep.[1]

[1] This is a little less than 100 feet one way, and 30 the other. The Roman foot is equivalent to 11.6 inches. This wall was not continuous. It did not exist by the side of the Tiber, which appeared a sufficient defence in itself, since the fortress of the Janiculum defended its approaches, and certain sides of the Capitol were steep enough to appear inaccessible. "There exist between the Esquiline and Colline gates considerable remains of the great *agger* of Servius, which Tarquin the Proud enlarged. In the section represented in the engraving there is shown a wall, now visible, of a height of 26 feet. Built in regular courses, this wall has a foundation of blocks averaging 10 feet in length. In order the better to resist the pressure of

Rome was then the size of Athens, two leagues and a half in circumference. He divided it into four quarters or city tribes,

SECTION OF THE AGGER OR RAMPART OF SERVIUS TULLIUS.

the Palatine, the Suburan, the Colline, and the Esquiline, each quarter having its tribune, who drew up the lists for conscriptions and military service. At the birth of each boy a piece of silver had to be deposited in the treasury of *Juno Lucina*, the protectress of women in travail. The territory was divided into twenty-six cantons, also called tribes, and all the people, patricians and plebeians, according to the census — that is to say, according to their fortune — into five classes and a hundred and eighty-three centuries, the last of which was formed by the Proletariate. The last named were excluded from military service; Servius was unwilling to intrust arms to citizens who, possessing nothing, could not take an interest in public affairs, nor give the state a guarantee of their fidelity.[2]

JUNO LUCINA.[1]

Moreover, Servius concluded with the thirty Latin towns a treaty, the text of which Dionysius claims to have seen preserved in the temple of Diana on the Aventine.[3] In order to draw closer the bonds of this alliance, a temple, in which was seen the first statue erected at Rome, had been built at the common expense.

Some Sabine tribes also came to sacrifice. These leagues, which

the earth which forms the rampart, the wall is flanked at intervals of 17 feet by buttresses 7 feet square. The ditch runs along this wall. . . . In the time of Augustus the *agger* was converted by Maecenas into a walk." *Dict. des Ant.* p. 140, *seq.*

[1] IVNONI LVCINAE s. c. Juno seated, holds in one hand the flower which precedes the fruit, and with the other a child in swaddling-clothes. The reverse of a large bronze of Lucilla, wife of the Emperor Lucius Verus.

[2] See below, Chap. vi.

[3] iv. 26. But if Dionysius saw this treaty, he could not understand it; for Polybius found it very difficult to read a document which was not so old by two centuries.

had their centre in the sanctuary of a divinity, were common among the Italiote nations, and recall the Amphictyonies of Greece.

We must keep them in mind, for we shall find these religious confederations under the Empire; and we shall have to reproach the Emperors with not having known how to utilize, in the interest of provincial liberties, an institution which might have saved the provinces and themselves.

But let us return to the legend. Livy relates how the ruse of one of the Roman priests, attached to the temple of Diana, gave Rome its hegemony over Latium. "A heifer of extraordinary beauty was born at the house of a Sabine mountaineer. The divines announced that he who should sacrifice it to the Diana of the Aventine would secure the empire to his country. The Sabine led his heifer to the temple, and was going to perform the sacrifice, when the priest, versed in prophecy, stopped him: 'What art thou about to do? Offer a sacrifice to Diana without having purified thyself? It is sacrilege! The Tiber flows at the foot of this hill; run and make ceremonial ablutions there.' The peasant went down to the river. When he returned, the priest had sacrificed the victim." And Livy adds: "This pious knavery was very agreeable to the King and to the people." Moreover, the immense horns of the predestined heifer were preserved for ages in the vestibule of the temple. Popular imagination loves to make the greatest results proceed from the smallest trifles, and some historians do likewise. If the Latins had already accepted the supremacy of Rome, it was because her arms had established it.

Tradition also spoke of a war of Servius against Veii, Tarquinii, and the inhabitants of Caere. The latter had united their arms with those of the Etruscans, notwithstanding their Pelasgian origin, which connected them with Rome (whose allies they became later on) and with Greece, which gave them so many of the vases now found in their tombs.[1] This war must have resulted for the Romans in an increase of territory; but the distribution of these lands which Servius made to the poor augmented still more the

---

[1] Two small black vases, found in these tombs, and very insignificant in form, have acquired a great importance, because it is believed that the inscriptions on them were Pelasgian.

TRADITIONAL HISTORY OF THE KINGS. 165

hatred of the patricians, whose power he had, by his laws, considerably limited. Thus they favored the conspiracy which was formed against the popular King.

The two daughters of Servius had married the two sons of Tarquin the Elder, Lucius and Aruns. But the ambitious Tullia

VASE OF CAERE.[1]

had been united to Aruns, the more gentle of the two brothers, and her sister to Lucius, who merited, by his pride and cruelty, the surname of Superbus. Tullia and Lucius were not slow in

---

[1] Corinthian vase found at Caere in 1856. It represents: on the lower band horsemen galloping, and on the upper band "Hercules (HEPAKΛEΣ) taking part in the banquet which the King of Oechalia offers him. The young Iole (EIOΛΛ) is standing between the table of the god and that of her brother Iphitus (EIΦITOΣ). The two other couches bear Eurytius (EYPYTIOΣ) and his three sons, Didaeon (ΔIΔAIEON), Clytius (KΛYTIOΣ), and Toxus (TOΞOΣ). All these names are in ancient Corinthian characters, and traced alternately from right to left and from left to right, so as to form, if they were arranged in a column, a *boustrophedon* text (like the turn of an ox ploughing)." (De Longpérier, *Musée Nap.* iii. pl. lxxi.) [For the benefit of readers not versed in palaeography, it should be noted that the old Corinthian E and H were written like the B of other inscriptions; the I has a zigzag form; the Σ is turned over, as in almost all older Greek writing. — *Ed.*]

understanding each other and in conferring about their criminal hopes. Tullia got rid of her husband and of her sister by poison, in order to marry Lucius. Overwhelmed with grief, Servius wished to abdicate, and establish consular government. This was the pretext which Lucius made to the patricians for overthrowing the King. One day, when the people were in the fields for harvest, he appeared in the Senate clothed with the insignia of royalty, threw the old prince headlong from the top of the stone steps which led to the Senate House, and caused him to be put to death by his confederates; Tullia, hastening to hail her husband as king, drove her chariot over the bleeding body of her father. The street retained the name of *Via Scelerata*;[1] but the people did not forget the man who had intended to establish plebeian liberties, and on the nones they celebrated the birth of the good King Servius (534).

VII. Tarquinius Superbus (534–510).

The king was succeeded by the tyrant. Surrounded by a guard of mercenaries and seconded by a party of the senators whom he had gained over, Tarquin governed without the aid of laws, depriving some of their goods, banishing others, and punishing with death all those of whom he was afraid. In order to strengthen his power, he allied himself with strangers and gave his daughter to Octavius Mamilius, dictator of Tusculum. Rome had its voice in the Latin *feriae*, in which the heads of forty-seven towns, assembled in the temple of Jupiter Latiaris,[2] on the summit of the Alban mount, which so majestically commands all Latium, offered a common sacrifice and celebrated their alliance by festivals. Tarquin changed this relationship of equality into an actual dominion, by what means we do not know, but certainly by now-forgotten struggles. Legend substituted the tragic adventure of Herdonius of Aricia for these tales of battle. "Tarquin," says Livy, "proposed one day to the chiefs of Latium to assemble at the wood of the goddess Ferentina, in order to deliberate on their common

---

[1] Livy, i. 41–48; Dionys. iv. 33–40, and Ovid (*Fast.* vi. 599) speak of a combat between the two parties, — *Hinc cruor, hinc caedes*, etc.

[2] The ruins of the temple, which still existed in the eighteenth century, were destroyed by the last of the Stuarts [the Duke of Albany].

interests. They arrived at sunrise, but Tarquin kept them waiting. 'What insolence!' cried Herdonius of Aricia at last. 'Is all the Latin nation to be thus mocked?' And he was persuading each of them to return to his home. At this moment the King appeared. He had been chosen, said he, as mediator between a father and son; this was the cause of the delay, for which he apologized, and proposed to postpone the deliberation to the morrow. 'It was very easy,' replied Herdonius, 'to put an end to this difference. Two words were sufficient: that the son should obey or be punished.' Tarquin, hurt by these outspoken words, caused arms to be concealed during the night in the house of Herdonius, and on the morrow accused him of wishing to usurp the empire over all Latium by the massacre of the chiefs. The Assembly condemned the alleged traitor to be drowned in the water of Ferentina, under a hurdle loaded with stones; and Tarquin, being rid of this citizen who had so little respect for kings, had the treaty renewed, but introduced into it a clause that the Latins, instead of fighting under their national chiefs, should be, in all expeditions, united with the legions and officered by Roman centurions."[1] This narrative is only the feeble echo of a violent rivalry between Rome and the town of which Herdonius was chief, Aricia, a powerful city, against which the empire of Porsenna was presently shattered.

Having become the actual leader of the Latin confederation, to which there also belonged the Hernici and the Volscian towns of Ecetra and Antium, Tarquin laid siege to and took the rich city of Suessa Pometia, which, doubtless, refused to enter into the league. He was at first less fortunate against Gabii. A check which he endured in an assault compelled him even to give up a regular siege. But his son Sextus presented himself to the Gabians. "Tarquin," said he, "is as cruel to his family as to his people; he wishes to depopulate his house as he has done the Senate. I, Sextus, have only escaped by flight from my father's sword." He was received, his counsels were followed, and successful inroads into the *ager Romanus* increased the confidence which was

---

[1] Livy, i, 50–52. The spring called *aqua Ferentina*, which was, perhaps, a natural outlet of the Alban Lake, burst forth in a sacred wood, in which, until the year 340 B.C., the Latins held their assemblies. Festus, s. v. *Praetor*. It is now the Marrana del Pantano, which flows in a deep valley near Marino.

placed in him. Soon no one had more credit in the city. Then he despatched to Rome a secret emissary, commissioned to ask the old King what Sextus ought to do in order to give the city into his hands. Tarquin, without speaking a word, passed into his garden, and, walking up and down, cut down with a stick the poppies which were highest; then he sent back the messenger, quite surprised at such a strange answer.

The Roman logographers took this story from Herodotus [who tells it about Periander, tyrant of Corinth]; but the submission of Gabii to Tarquin is none the less certain. Dionysius of Halicarnassus saw the treaty concluded between the King and this city: it was preserved on a wooden shield in the temple of Jupiter Fidius, — a place singularly chosen for a monument of treason, if the narrative of Livy was as true as it is celebrated.[2] On the lands taken from the Volscians Tarquin founded two colonies: the one enclosed behind the walls of the Pelasgian Signia, the other on the promontory of Circe. They were composed of Roman and Latin citizens, who had to furnish their contingent to the army of the league. This was the first example of those military colonies, which, multiplied by the Senate at all points of Italy, extended there the laws and language of Latium. At the same time they were permanent garrisons, advanced outposts, which would stop an enemy far from the capital, and whence valiant soldiers could be drawn at need.

COIN OF THE GENS ANTISTIA.[1]

Like his father, Tarquin loved pomp and magnificence. He hired skilful Etruscan workmen, and with the spoil obtained from the Volscians he finished the sewers and the Capitol, — that favorite residence of the god who holds the thunder, and whence "he so often shook his black shield and summoned the storm-clouds to him."[3] In digging up the soil for laying the foundations of this new sanctuary of Rome, they had found a human head which seemed freshly cut off. "It is a sign," said the augurs, "that this temple

---

[1] It bears the words FOEDVS CVM GABINIS, or treaty with the Gabians, and represents two persons offering a pig in sacrifice, in order to consecrate the convention.

[2] Hor., *Ep.* II. i. 25, and Fest. s. v. *Clypeus.* Gabii had obtained the isopolity with Rome. . . . σὺν τούτοις τὴν 'Ρωμαίων ἰσοπολιτείαν ἅπασι χαρίζεσθαι. (Dionys. of Hal., *Ant. Rom.* iv. 58.)

[3] Vergil., *Aen.* viii. 353.

will be the head of the world." The Sibylline books were shut up in a stone coffer under the Capitol. A prophetess, the Sibyl of Cumae, had come, disguised as an old woman, to offer to sell the King nine books. On his refusal she burned three of them, and returned to ask the same sum for the six others. A second refusal made her burn three more. Tarquin, astonished, bought

GATE OF SIGNIA.[1]

those which remained, and intrusted them to the keeping of two patricians. In times of great danger these books were opened at random, as it seems, and the first passage which was presented to the eyes served as an answer.[2] In the Middle Ages, too, they cast lots on the Gospels.

[1] We give a variety of these views, for the reasons given above.
[2] Dionys., iv. 62; Cic., *Divin.* ii. 54; Tac., *Ann.* vi. 12. Justin (i. 6) attributes this story to Tarquin the Elder. Athens appears to have had similar books. Cf. the discourse of Deinarchus against Demosthenes: ἐν αἷς τὰ τῆς πόλεως σωτηρία κεῖται. Many other towns had some: χρησμοὶ σιβυλλιακοί. The Dorians said σιώς for θεός and βολλά for βουλή. Σιοβυλή, whence Sibyl, signifies, then, *the counsel of God*. The most ancient that we now have were drawn up about the middle of the second century before our era, by Jews from Egypt. [The habit of opening the Bible at random for advice in difficult circumstances is

These menacing signs, however, frightened the royal family. In order to know the means of appeasing the gods, Tarquin sent his two sons to consult the oracle of Delphi, the reputation of which had penetrated as far as Italy. Brutus, a nephew of the King, who feigned madness[1] in order to escape his suspicious fears, accompanied them. When the God had replied, the young

WALL OF CIRCEI.[2]

men asked which of them would replace the King on the throne: "He," said the Pythia, "who embraces his mother first." Brutus understood the concealed meaning of the oracle: he fell down and kissed the earth, our common mother.

not yet extinct among ultra-Protestants in this kingdom; and there are men still living who have "cut for premium" in Trinity College, Dublin, when two equal competitors used to open the Bible at random, and priority of the second letter in the second line on the left-hand page determined the victor. — *Ed.*]

[1] He was made, however, tribune of the Celeres, who was, next to the King, the first magistrate of the state. His name, which in the ancient Latin signifies the grave and strong man (Fest. s. v. *Brutum*), but which also had the meaning of idiot, gave rise to the legend of his madness.

[2] See Dodwell, *Pelasgic Remains*, ¡ l. 104.

TRADITIONAL HISTORY OF THE KINGS.   171

The journey to Delphi was then for the Romans a very great journey, and the King had no motive for sending such an embassy.

But the Greeks wished that this homage should be rendered

THE CAVE OF THE SIBYL OF CUMAE.[1]

to their favorite oracle; and in order to complete the picture of the tyranny of Tarquin, they took a pleasure in showing the nephew of the King constrained to conceal his deep mind under the appearance of madness, as he had concealed a golden ingot in his travelling staff, in order to offer it to the god.

In a play of Attius, represented in the time of Caesar, the poet related that Tarquin, troubled by a dream, had called his diviners about him. "I saw in a vision," said he, "in the midst of a flock, two magnificent rams. I sacrificed one; but the other,

---

[1] Taken from an engraving of the Bibliothèque Nationale. The mountain seen to the right is the hill on which Cumae had been built. The summit bore its acropolis, and grottos had been excavated in it. One of these grottos, the entrance of which is seen, is supposed to have been the cave where the Sibyl gave her oracles. (See Vergil, *Aen.* vi. 41.)

dashing upon me, threw me to the ground, and severely wounded me with his horns. At this moment I perceived in the heavens a wonderful prodigy: the sun changed his course, and his flaming orb moved towards the right." "O King!" replied the augurs, "the thoughts which occupy us in the day-time are reproduced in our visions; there is no need, then, to be troubled. However, take care that he, whom thou dost not count higher than a beast, have not in him a great soul, full of wisdom. The prodigy which thou hast seen announces a revolution near at hand. May it be a happy one for the people! But the majestic star took its course from left to right; it is a sure omen. Rome will attain to the pinnacle of glory."[1] Was it the Greek fiction that the friend of Caesar's murderer took up in his *Brutus?* or did he recall a tradition preserved in the house of the founder of the Republic? Around great events there always gather a cycle of stories of adventure from which poetry and legendary history can draw.

When the embassy returned from Greece, Tarquin besieged Ardea, which was the capital of the Rutili, and had been that of Turnus, the rival of Aeneas.[2] It was a powerful city, in which the Etruscans had long ruled; Pliny there saw pictures which were thought more ancient than Rome;[3] and although its decay commenced as early as the third century, some statues have been found there which, in spite of their mutilations, suggest the inspiration of Greek art. What remains of its walls and citadel is more imposing than any of the ruins found in Etruria. The operations commenced against it by Tarquin were protracted and wearisome, so that the young princes sought to drive away by feasts and games the ennui of the siege; when one day there arose between them that fatal dispute concerning the merits of their wives. "Let us take horse," said Tarquinius Collatinus; "they do not expect us, and we will judge them according to the occupations in which we surprise them." At Collatia they found the King's daughters-in-law engaged in the delights of a sumptuous feast. Lucretia, on the contrary, in the retirement of her house, was spinning among her women

---

[1] This passage is all that remains of the *Brutus* and even of any Roman tragedy of the class called *praetextata*, or national.

[2] In the treaty concluded with Carthage, in the first year of the Republic, Ardea is called the subject of Rome.

[3] Pliny, *Hist. Nat.* xxxv. 6.

REMAINS FOUND AT ARDEA.

far into the night. She was proclaimed the best. But her discretion and her beauty excited criminal passion in the heart of Sextus. Some time afterward he returned one night to Collatia, entered the room of Lucretia, urged her to yield to his desires, and combined threats with promises. If she resists, he will kill her, place beside her the dead body of a murdered slave, and go and tell Collatinus and all Rome that he has punished the culprits. Lucretia is overcome by this infamous perfidy, which exposes her to dishonor; but no sooner was the outrage accomplished, than she sends a swift messenger to her father and her husband to come to her, each with a trusty friend. Brutus accompanies Collatinus. They found her plunged in deep grief. She informs them of the outrage, and her desire not to survive it; but demands of them the punishment of the criminal. In vain they try to shake her resolution; they urge that she is not guilty, since her heart is innocent; it is the intention which constitutes the crime.[1] But she says: "It is for you to decide the fate of Sextus; for myself, I absolve myself of the crime, but I do not exempt myself from the penalty; no woman, to survive her shame, shall ever invoke the example of Lucretia." And she stabs herself with a dagger which she had concealed under her dress.

Brutus drew the weapon from the wound, and, holding it up, cried: "Ye gods! I call you to witness. By this blood, so pure before the outrage of this King's son, I swear to pursue with fire and sword, with all the means in my power, Tarquin, his infamous family, and his cursed race. I swear no longer to suffer a King in Rome." He hands the weapon to Collatinus, Lucretius, and Valerius, who repeat the same oath; and together they repair to Rome. They show the bleeding body of the victim, and incite to vengeance the Senate, whom Tarquin had decimated, and the people, whom he had oppressed with forced labor on his buildings. A *senatus-consultum*, confirmed by the Curiae, proclaimed the dethronement of the King, his exile, and that of all

---

[1] [The Greeks and Romans, who were familiar with these misfortunes in the case of the noblest captives taken in war, and were accustomed to receive them back into their homes, felt the justice of this excuse far more thoroughly than we should do, among whom the stain is indelible. — *Ed.*]

his kin. Then Brutus hastened to the camp before Ardea, which he moved to insurrection; while Tarquin, having returned to Rome in all haste, found its gates shut, and was reduced to take refuge with his sons Titus and Aruns in the Etruscan town of Caere. The third, Sextus, having retreated to Gabii, was killed there by the relatives of his victims.[1]

This same year Athens was delivered from the tyranny of the Pisistratidae.

As a reward for their aid, the people claimed the restoration

BRUTUS (BUST IN THE CAPITOL).

of the laws of the good King Servius and the establishment of consular government; the Senate consented to it, and the *comitia centuriata* proclaimed as consuls Junius Brutus and Tarquinius

[1] Livy, i. 57-60.

TRADITIONAL HISTORY OF THE KINGS. 175

Collatinus, and afterward Valerius, when Collatinus, having incurred suspicion on account of his name, was exiled to Lavinium. Many others fared as he did; for " the people, intoxicated with their new liberty, exacted reprisals," says Cicero; " and a great number of innocent people were exiled or despoiled of their goods." [1]

Caere only offered a refuge to Tarquin. But Tarquinii and

THE GRINDER.[2]

Veii sent to Rome to demand the restoration of the King, or at least the restitution of the goods of his house and of those who had followed him.[3] During the negotiations the deputies planned a conspiracy with some young patricians who preferred the brilliant service of a prince to the reign of law, order, and liberty; the slave Vindicius discovered the plot; the culprits were seized, and amongst them the sons and some relatives of

---

[1] *De Rep.* i. 40.
[2] This beautiful statue is supposed to represent the slave listening to the conspiracy of the sons of Brutus, or to that of Brutus and Cassius against Caesar.
[3] Dionys., v. 4–6, and Plut., *Popl.* 3.

Brutus, who ordered and calmly looked on at their execution. Twenty days were granted to the refugees to return to the city.[1] In order to gain the people over to the cause of the revolution, they were allowed the pillage of Tarquin's goods, and each plebeian received seven acres of the royal lands; the fields which extended between the city and the river were consecrated to Mars, and the sheaves of wheat which they bore, seized and thrown into the Tiber, were stopped on the shallows which became afterward the Island of Aesculapius.[3]

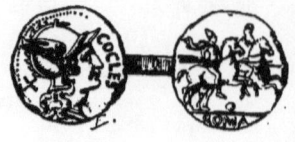

COIN OF THE GENS HORATIA.[2]

An army of Veientines and Tarquinians, however, marched on Rome. The legions went out to meet them; and in a single combat Brutus and Aruns fell mortally wounded. Night separated the combatants without decided victory. But at midnight a great voice, as it were, was heard proceeding from the Arsian wood and pronouncing these words: "Rome has lost one warrior less than the Etruscan army." The latter fled away in a panic. Valerius reentered Rome in triumph and pronounced the funeral panegyric of Brutus; the matrons honored by a year's mourning the avenger of outraged modesty, and the people placed his statue, sword in hand, on the Capitol, near those of the kings, which were still protected by a superstitious fear.

HORATIUS COCLES.[4]

[1] Dionys., v. 13.
[2] A coin bearing the name of Cocles and struck at an uncertain date by some member of the *gens Horatia*. In front, a head of Pallas; on the reverse, the Dioscuri.
[3] Dionys., *ibid.*, and Plin., xviii. 4. This *insula Tiberina* (di San Bartolomeo) was afterward joined to the left bank of the river by the *pons Fabricius* (Ponte Quattro Capi, on account of the figures of *Janus quadrifons* placed at its extremities), and to the right bank by the *pons Cestius*, which bears the modern name of the island. In memory of a miracle, which we shall have to relate later on, they gave to the *insula Tiberina*, by solid constructions, the form of the keel of a ship floating on the water, and its extremity represented a prow, the remains of which are still seen. To this island, very subject before these works to the inundations of the Tiber, they carried the slaves, old, sick, or infirm, and there abandoned them. Aesculapius afterward had his first temple there. Notwithstanding the neighborhood of the god "healer," the desperate who wished to quit life, without caring about their burial, generally chose the *pons Fabricius* in order to pass into eternity through the Tiber. (Hor., *Sat.* II. iii. 36.)
[4] Bronze medallion of Antonine. Cocles crosses the Tiber swimming; an enemy is trying to pierce him with his javelin, and a Roman finishes breaking down the bridge.

THE INSULA TIBERINA (PRESENT STATE).

Devotion to public affairs, piety towards the gods, and heroic exploits distinguished this nascent liberty: it was Valerius who, being suspected on account of his stone house built on the Velian, above the Forum, had it demolished in one night, and earned, by his popular laws, the surname of Poplicola; it was Horatius to whom the death of his son was announced during the dedication of the Capitol, and who would hear nothing of this domestic calamity because he was praying to the gods for Rome; and, lastly, when Tarquin armed Porsenna against his ancient people, it was Horatius Cocles who defended the *pons Sublicius* alone against an army; Mucius Scaevola, who, standing before the wondering Porsenna, put his hand into a brazier in order to punish it for making a mistake in killing, instead of the King, one of his officers; it was Cloelia, who, having been given as a hostage to the Etruscan prince, escaped from his camp and crossed the Tiber by swimming.[1] Then comes the war-song of the battle of Lake Regillus,[2] the last effort of Tarquin, who, abandoned by Porsenna, had again stirred up Latium to revolt. All the chiefs met there in single combat, and perished or were wounded. The gods even, as in Homeric times, took part in this last strife. During the action two young warriors of high stature, mounted on white horses, fought at the head of the legions, and were the first to cross the enemy's entrenchments; when the dictator, Aulus Postumius, wished to give them the siege crown, the collars of gold and rich presents promised to those who should first have entered the enemies' camp, they had disappeared; but on the same evening two heroes were seen at Rome, covered with blood and dust, who washed their arms at the fountain of Juturna,[3] and announced the victory to the people; they were the Dioscuri, Castor and Pollux. In order that their presence in the midst of the Roman army might not be doubted, for centuries the gigantic

---

[1] Between the Etruscan and Latin wars tradition places a war against the Sabines, which must have lasted four years, from 505 to 501, and during which the Sabine Attus Clausus (Appius Claudius), a rich citizen of Regillus, who had been adverse to the hostilities, had emigrated to Rome, where he was received into the Senate, and his family took a place amongst the new patrician *gentes*.

[2] M. Pietro thinks he has found Lake Regillus in a dried-up marsh, *il Pantano*, 15 or 16 miles on the way to Palestrina, south of the hill occupied by the village *la Colonna*.

[3] This fountain never dries, but at present it flows underground. It was this which fed what was called Lake Curtius. The temple of Castor was close by.

impression of the foot of a horse was shown in the rock on the field of battle, and Rome, which took pride in representing itself as the object of the constant solicitude of the gods, consecrated

THE THREE COLUMNS OF THE TEMPLE OF CASTOR.[1]

this legend by raising a temple to the divine sons of Zeus and Leda, which became one of the most celebrated in the city.

The victory was a bloody one. On the side of the Romans, three Valerii, Herminius, the companion of Cocles, Aebutius, the master of the horse, were left on the field of battle or quitted it wounded. On the side of the Latins, Oct. Mamilius, the dictator

[1] The temple of Castor and Pollux, in which the Senate often assembled, *in aede Castoris, celeberrimo clarissimoque monumento* (Cic., *in Verr.* II. i. 49) begun by Postumius and finished by his son, was rebuilt on the same spot under Augustus and Tiberius. The three magnificent columns which remain of it date from this latter epoch.

TRADITIONAL HISTORY OF THE KINGS. 179

of Alba, and Titus, the last son of Tarquin, fell. The old King

THE DIOSCURI WATER-ING THEIR HORSES AT THE FOUNTAIN OF JU-TURNA.[1]
AULUS POSTUMIUS, THE CONQUEROR OF THE LATINS.[2]
COIN COMMEMORATIVE OF THE BATTLE OF LAKE REGILLUS.[3]
COIN OF THE GENS MAMILIA.[4]

himself, struck with a blow of a lance, only survived all his

SUPPOSED TOMB OF THE TARQUINS.[5]

race and his hopes, to finish his miserable old age at the court of the tyrant of Cumae, Aristodemus (496 B. C.).

[1] Silver coin of the Albini, descendants of Postumius.

[2] It was a descendant of A. Postumius who had this silver medal struck. The portrait is certainly no true likeness; but all the patricians kept the images of their ancestors in the atrium of their house, and the coin may have been fairly accurate. Besides, we ought to do for figured Roman antiquity what we have done for its history; I mean that we cannot ignore the way in which the Romans represented their ancestors, any more than omit the legends which were all, great and small, considered as historic truth.

[3] The descendants of the Dictator caused a coin to be struck in remembrance of his victory, representing the head of Diana on the obverse; on the reverse three knights trampling a hostile soldier under the feet of their horses.

[4] This *gens* claimed to be descended from Ulysses, and put the likeness of this prince on their coins.

[5] The sepulchral cave of the Tarquins has perhaps been found in our days at Caere. Their Etruscan name, Tarchnas, is inscribed thirty-five times on the walls of this tomb, — a fact

180 ROME UNDER THE KINGS.

The Tarquins are dead; the founders of the Republic have one after the other disappeared; the time of heroes and legends is past: that of the people and of history begins.

which, however, is not sufficient for us to be able to affirm that this sepulchral chamber is that of the Tarquins of Rome.

[1] Large bronze of Antonine; the wolf on the left, the Tiber on the right.

ROME SEATED UPON THE SEVEN HILLS.

CHAPTER II.

CONSTITUTION OF ROME DURING THE REGAL PERIOD.
PRIMITIVE ORGANIZATION.

I. — SOURCES OF ROMAN HISTORY.

THE influence which Greek exercised over Latin literature extended to the history of Rome: we have already seen some proofs of it, and we shall see many more. The use of writing, however, was not so rare in ancient Italy as has been asserted. If we reject, as we are bound, the discovery of the books of Numa, it is nevertheless true that the treaty with Carthage in 509, B. C., the original of which Polybius read, the treaty with Gabii,[2] that of Spurius Cassius with the Latins, which Cicero[3] saw, the royal laws collected after the departure of the Gauls,[4] show that writing was employed, during the regal period, at least for public acts and to preserve the memory of important events.

COIN COMMEMORATIVE OF THE TREATY WITH THE GABII.[1]

All around Rome, the nations had also monuments of their national life. At the time of Varro there still existed Etruscan histories written about the middle of the fourth century before our era. Cumae had its historians,[5] and each city its annals engraved on sheets of lead, tables of brass, planks of oak, or written on linen, as at Anagnia and Praeneste. There is no doubt that the nation of the Volscians, so long powerful,

---

[1] Coin of Antistius Vetus. On the obverse, head of Augustus with the indication of his 8th *tribunitia potestas*; on the reverse, two fetials sacrificing a pig on a burning altar, and the words: FOED (us) CVM GABINIS, Treaty with the Gabini. [2] Dionys., iv. 58. [3] *Pro. C. Balbo*, 23; cf. Dionys., iv. 26. [4] Livy, vi. 1. [5] Festus, s. v. *Romam*.

possessed written monuments, as well as the Hernici and the Latins; Dionysius makes mention of their war-songs, Silius of those of the Sabines, and Vergil, who was as erudite as the learned Varro in the affairs of ancient Italy, speaks of the national songs of the *prisci Latini*.

Inscriptions on bronze and on stone, memorials, names attached to monuments and places, as the Sister's Post, the *via Scelerata*, and oral traditions which lived in families, might aid researches into their primitive history. But the most ancient of Roman annalists lived at the time when Rome, the mistress of Italy, entered into relations with Greece; they were dazzled by the brilliancy of Hellenic literature, and, misunderstanding the importance of native documents, which were extremely meagre, they became the pupils of those whom they had just subdued. There was then, as it were, a double conquest made, in different directions. The Greeks became subjects of Rome, the Romans the disciples of Greece; and the Etruscan education of young patricians was replaced by Greek education, — the journey to Caere by the journey to Athens.[2] Even

EARLY ROMAN (LATIN) ALPHABETS.[1]

[1] [These alphabets are taken (by F. Lenormant) from the *Priscae Latinitatis Mon. Epigrapha*, and represent the writing of the latter 5th, the 6th, and the 7th (Augustan) centuries A. U. C. — *Ed.*]

[2] Livy, ix. 36: *Habeo auctores vulgo tum* (in the fifth century of Rome) *Romanos pueros sicut nunc Graecis, ita Etruscis litteris erudiri solitos.*

long before the Romans thought of Athens, the influence of Greece had made itself felt in the centre of Italy, among the Etruscans, and even in Rome. The Sibylline books were written in Greek, and the ambassador from Rome to the Tarentines spoke to them in that language.

By a singular freak it was from the Greeks that the Romans learned their history : I mean that history which the Greeks made for them. The epic character which the influence of Homer and Hesiod had given to the narrative prose of the Hellenes, passed into the writings of the annalists of Rome. Two of her first historians, Ennius and Naevius, were epic poets; Dionysius said of their works: "They resemble those of the Greek annalists;" and he added concerning Cato, C. Sempronius, etc.: "They followed Greek story." Tacitus and Strabo reproached them with the same thing.[1] Thus the nations of Western Europe forgot in the Middle Ages their true origin for the pedantic reminiscences of ancient literature: the Franks said they were descended from a son of Hector; the Bretons, from Brutus; and Rheims had been founded by Remus.

On the origin of Rome and of Romulus, there are in Plutarch no less than twelve different traditions, almost all of which bear the stamp of Greek imagination; and the one which he preferred as being the most widespread was only the story of a Greek, Diocles of Peparethos, followed by a soldier from the Second Punic War, Fabius Pictor, the oldest of Roman annalists and the first ambassador from Rome into Greece.

The organization, however, being altogether religious, and as the priests were at every moment interfering in public affairs, the pontiffs were concerned in keeping up the memory of events as accurately as possible. Thus the Romans had the *Annals of the Pontiffs*,[2] or *Annales Maximi*, the *Fasti Magistratuum*, the *Fasti Triumphales*, the rolls of the censors, etc. But these annals were so laconic that they opened a wide field to interpretations and fables. Moreover, being written down from day to day, in order to preserve

---

[1] Strabo, III. vi. 19 : Οἱ δὲ τῶν 'Ρωμαίων συγγραφεῖς μιμοῦνται μὲν τοὺς Ἕλληνας. Dionys. i. 11 : Ἑλληνικῷ τε μύθῳ χρησάμενοι. [This agrees with Mommsen's view of the antiquity of writing in Italy, — a theory strongly corroborated by the recent discovery of the old Phoenician alphabet, with its *samech* and *tsadde* on vases at Caere and elsewhere. — *Ed.*]

[2] Cicero, *de Orat.* ii. 12, and Fest., s. v. *Maximus* and Servius *ad Aen.* i. 373.

the memory of treaties, the names of magistrates and of important events, they only went back to the period when established Roman society felt the simple need of rendering an account to itself of its acts and of its engagements with its neighbors. Beyond, there is nothing but mythological darkness; and this was the open field in which the imagination of the Greeks was exercised. They laid hold of this period and filled it up to suit their interests. Now in their own history they had preserved hardly any great record of ancient times, except that of the contest against Troy. With this event they connected the first history of Italy. It was towards Italy that they led the Trojan chiefs, escaped from the sack of the city, or the Greek heroes driven away from their homes by tempest, and each Italian town of any importance had as founder a hero of one of the two races. Let us note that the Greeks also found an advantage in this double manner of connecting Italy and Rome with their history, by their own colonies, and by the Trojan settlements, by Evander and Aeneas, by Ulysses and Antenor. To go back to Troy, was, for the Greeks, to go back to an epoch of glory and power; and, moreover, in ennobling through these legends the beginnings of Rome and of the Latins, the Greeks avenged themselves indirectly in exhibiting this city and nation formed by fugitives escaped from the victorious sword of the Hellenes. It was not derogatory for Rome to accept this origin. Troy was the greatest name of antiquity, the most powerful state of the ancient world; her reputation was immense, and at the same time it could not wound their pride, for Troy was long since destroyed. Moreover, she was the enemy of Greece. Rome would not so willingly have allowed it to be said that she sprang from Macedonia, Sparta, or Athens, which were of recent celebrity. We are not jealous of the glorious dead; to be their heirs is a new title to fame.

From the time of the First Punic War the belief in the Trojan descent of the Romans was current, as is seen in the inscription of Duillius, in which the Egestans, who were considered as a Trojan colony, are called *cognati populi Romani*. After Cynoscephalae, one of the first cares of Flamininus, who was anxious not to pass for a barbarian, was to set up at Delphi an inscription which called the Romans the race of Aeneas. When the Julian house had seized the Empire, this belief became an article of political faith; and, following the example of the Romans, the Italians eagerly laid claim to this origin; Trojan genealogies were bought, just as, in the last century, our fathers bought marquisates; and in the time of Dionysius[1] fifty Roman families, the *Trojugenae*, claimed descent from the companions of Aeneas. Moreover, even if Aeneas should truly have settled in Latium, as he came there, according to the most ancient tradition, with only a single vessel and a small number of Trojans, this fact would be of importance only to the vanity of certain families, of none to the civilization of the country.

II. Probable Origin of Rome.

ALL great nations have surrounded their cradle with marvellous tales. In Egypt the reign of gods and demi-gods preceded that of man. In Persia, Dschemschid opens the bosom of the earth with a golden sickle and drives away the Djinns. At Troy, Apollo and Neptune built the walls of the city of Priam with their own hands. Rome desired to have a no less noble origin; her obscure birth was hidden under brilliant fictions, and the head of a band of adventurers became the son of the god Mars, a grandson of the King of Alba, a descendant of Aeneas. If this is objected to in the name of historic truth, Livy replies by right of victory. "Such," says he with a proud majesty of style, "such is the glory of the Roman people in war, that when they choose to proclaim the god Mars as their father, as the father of their founder, other nations must suffer it with the same resignation as they suffer our sway."[2] From this strange idea of the rights of the historian, it followed that facts were to

---

[1] *Ant. Rom.* i. 85.
[2] In his preface Cicero (*de Rep.* ii. 2) also says: *Concedamus famae hominum;* and further on: *Ut a fabulis ad facta veniamus.* "We must not blame," says he, "those who, recognizing a divine genius in the benefactors of the nation, wished to attribute to them a divine origin." These are singular rules of criticism. Let us add, in order to show the difficulties which render the work of moderns so arduous, that we have lost the most ancient historians of Rome, Diocles of Peparethos, Fabius Pictor, the *Annales* of Ennius, the *Origines* of Cato, the history of Cassius Hemina; and let us add that Livy, Dionysius of Halicarnassus, and Plutarch, who had these works before them, rarely agree.

the great annalist of Rome like the subjects which in school are proposed for recitations and essays, and which savor far more of rhetoric than of the battle-field or the Forum. It is a veil covered with charming embroidery, which must be respectfully raised in order to find the fragments of truth hidden behind it.

Of these traditions the least improbable is the rape of the Sabine women, — a practice very common in the heroic age. This violence agrees well with the history of the place of refuge: according as the outlaws of the Palatine Hill carried off women, unions were arranged. Abduction was, moreover, the primitive form of marriage, and the recollection of it was preserved in the nuptial ceremonies until the last days of Pagan Rome.[2] But the fact of the rape of the Sabines cannot be reconciled with the legend that Rome was an Alban colony; for according to this it would have had the *connubium*, or right of marriage, with its mother city, and no one would have dared to reject the alliance of the dominant race. Moreover, the violent character of ancient Rome has been exaggerated, by making it a sort of intrenched camp, from which pillage and warfare ever issued. This was one consequence of the idea that the town had been founded by a troop of bandits. The severity of the first Roman institutions, the patriciate, and the political and religious privileges of the nobility, do not agree with this tradition of a mob collected at random, and long given up to all kinds of disorder.

RAPE OF THE SABINE WOMEN.[1]

We do not wish to reject the idea of the existence of Romulus; though the hymns, still sung in the time of Augustus, which preserved the poetic history of the first king of Rome, appear to us nothing but a legend, such as all ancient nations have had, and the counterpart of which it would be easy to find in other national traditions. Thus Semiramis, like Romulus, is the child of a goddess; like him, and like Cyrus, who was exposed in a

---

[1] L. TITVRI. Silver coin of one Sabinus Titurius.

[2] The bride was carried, as it were, by force from her father's house, and it was customary to lift her over the threshold of her husband's house. The latter practice still exists in a few villages in England, where it may have been introduced by the Romans; but it is usual in China (Dennis, *The Folk-lore of China*) and with the Esquimaux, which weakens the proof that might be thence adduced in favor of the legend of the Sabines.

forest and suckled by a bitch,[1] she is abandoned in the desert, fed by doves, and picked up by a shepherd of the king. Her history, too, is bloody. As Romulus kills his brother, she causes the death of her husband, and after a long reign she disappears; but some saw her ascend to heaven, and her people paid her divine honors. Nearer Rome, in Latium itself, Caeculus, son of Vulcan and founder of Praeneste, is abandoned after his birth, and brought up by wild beasts. In order to people his city, which remained empty, he called together the neighboring nations to solemn games; and when they came together from all parts, flames surrounded the assembly. In the Sabine country, Medius Fidius, or Sancus, who became the national god of the Sabines, was also born of a virgin who was surprised by Mars Enyalius in a temple of Reate; and, like Romulus, he had founded a town, Cures, which in tradition is the second metropolis of Rome. These legends, which are found as far as the banks of the Ganges, in the story of Chandragupta, were, with many others, the common inheritance of the Aryan race.

We may regard Romulus, who may be connected with the royal house of Alba,[2] to have been only one of those warlike chiefs such as both ancient and modern Italy have produced, and who became the king of a people to whom the position of Rome,[3] fortunate circumstances, and the ability of its aristocracy gave the empire of the world.

Numerous testimonies[4] prove that, long before Romulus traced a furrow round the Palatine, that hill was inhabited. There was, therefore, a Latin city there, the town on the Tiber, *Ruma*, having the manners and laws of Latium and of the Sabine country, the patriciate, paternal authority, patronage, clientship,

---

[1] Paris by a she-bear, Telephus by a hind, etc. This kind of legend was extremely widespread in ancient times, and sprang up again in the Middle Ages: Geneviève of Brabant, etc.

[2] In the legend, he is the grandson and sole heir of Numitor. He does not, however, succeed him, and the family of Sylvius is replaced on the throne of Alba by a new family, by Cluilius, king or dictator. Rome is called a colony of Alba, and yet there is no alliance between the two towns, and the modern city does not defend its colony against the Sabines, etc.

[3] "Place Rome at another point of Italy," says Cicero (*de Rep.* ii. 5), "and her rule becomes almost impossible."

[4] *Roma ante Romulum fuit et ab ea sibi Romulum nomen adquisivisse Marianus Lupercaliorum poeta ostendit.* (Philargyr., *ad* Verg., *Ecl.* i. 20.) None but towns founded in entirety and on a precise day by a *colony* have a certain date. The others have been at first hamlets, villages, and burghs. With London or Paris, when did the hamlet begin?

a senate, and perhaps a king, — in short, a truly political and religious organization, already ancient, and which Romulus, himself a Latin, only adopted. He may have come to establish himself victoriously there with his band,[1] the *Celsi Ramnenses*, giving the ancient town a new appearance and more warlike manners. On this ground he may have passed for its founder, and his companions for the heads of patrician houses. Is not the nobility

ANCIENT SUBSTRUCTIONS OF THE PALATINE.[2]

of England, so powerful and so proud, [in great part] descended from the adventurers who followed William of Normandy?

In spite of Niebuhr's disdain, sometimes so harshly expressed, for those who seek historic facts in these ancient legends, we may allow the abduction of certain Sabine women by the *Celsi Ramnenses*,[3] and the occupation, effected by a convention, of the

---

[1] Festus (s. v. *Ver sacrum* and *Mamertini*) attributes the origin of Rome to a *sacred spring-time*. There is always the idea of an occupation of the Palatine by an armed troop.
[2] Atlas of the *Bull. archéol.*, vol. v. pl. 39.
[3] In the most ancient of the Roman historians, Fabius, the number of the Sabine women

PRIMITIVE ORGANIZATION. 189

Capitoline and Quirinal by the Sabines of Cures.[1] The two towns remained separate, but the people met in the plain between the three hills. Circumstances, which legend explains to suit itself, led to the union, under a single chief, of the two *burghs* established on the Palatine and Capitol. In whatever manner this alliance was produced, history must yield to the Sabines a considerable and probably preponderant part in the formation of the Roman people.

But if we cannot pierce this veil of poetry which hides the real facts, let us study the institutions which ancient manners and circumstances produced. This we can do, for these customs lasted into the historic age; and as Cuvier from a few broken bones reconstructed extinct creatures, we may reconstruct, with the help of ancient remains, that society of which legends give us only interesting but deceptive pictures.

III. PATRICIANS AND CLIENTS.

ROME had no single legislator, as the Greek cities had. Its constitution was the work of time, circumstances, and many men. Hence arise numberless uncertainties. The most ancient traditions show the people divided into three TRIBUS, the *Ramnenses*,[2] or companions of Romulus, the *Titienses*, or Sabines of Tatius, and the *Luceres*, whose origin is referred to an Etruscan chief, Lucumo,[3] who may have come with a numerous band to aid Romulus in building his city and in gaining his first victories. But the political inferiority of this last tribe, which at first had neither senators nor vestals, would imply a conquered population, perhaps the ancient inhabit-

carried off is only thirty. Valerius Antias counts as many as five hundred and twenty-seven, and Juba six hundred and three.

[1] The lance (*quir*) was the national weapon of the Sabines, and the symbol of their principal divinity; hence the names of *Cures*, *Quirites*, *Quirinal*, and *Quirinus*, and perhaps of *Curia*. The two tribes together were called *Populus Romanus Quirites*, omitting, according to the use of the old Latin tongue, the conjunction *et*. This became afterward *Populus Romanus Quiritium*.

[2] *Celsi Ramnenses* (for *Romanenses*), or, as Dionys. says (ix. 44), καθαρωτάτη φυλή.

[3] Cic., *de Rep.* ii. 8; Fest., s. v. *Lucerenses*, from Lucerus, king of Ardea; according to others from *lucus*, the wood of refuge. In that case the Luceres would be those who had taken refuge.

ants of the town may have remained until the time of Tarquin under the yoke of conquest.

The tribe was divided into ten CURIAE, each curia into ten DECURIAE; and these divisions, which were also territorial and military,[1] had their chiefs, — tribunes, curiones, and decuriones.

In each tribe were included a certain number of political families, or GENTES, which were not composed of men only of the same blood, but also of men connected by mutual obligations, by the worship of a hero venerated as a common ancestor (*sacra gentilitia*), or by the right of inheriting one from another in the absence of a will or of natural heirs,[2] — a right which reminds us that, in the beginning, property had been common. Thus they were enabled to reduce to a small figure the number of these political families, — 200 at first, afterward 300, — and to allow only 3,000 citizens to the city of Romulus; but we must admit that these figures, like the English words *hundred*, *tithing*, were not a strictly exact arithmetical expression. Moreover by these 3,000 citizens of original Rome the patricians alone are understood.

COIN OF THE GENS FABIA.

Now to these heads of the *gentes* were attached numerous clients. In tradition the *gens* Appia numbers 5,000, the *gens* Fabia 4,000, and Coriolanus could form a complete army of his tribe. Let us accept 300 as the number of patrician houses, allowing for each house an average of 100 clients, and we shall have a population of more than 30,000. Even were these numbers purely imaginary, the *gens* would none the less be the basis of the primitive organization of Rome, as it has been among many nations. However far we trace back the course of history, we find in the family, natural or fictitious, the primordial elements of society. The Greek γένη, the Scottish clans, the Irish septs, answer to the Roman *gentes*; and the same organization

---

[1] Varro (*de Ling. Lat.* v. 35) speaks of a threefold division of territory for the three tribes; Dionys. (ii. 7) of a division into thirty allotments for the thirty curiae.

[2] Instead of *gens*, *genus* is sometimes found, which clearly explains the word *gens*. Thus *Cilnium genus* (Livy, x. 3–5). Cf. Aulus Gellius, xv. 27; Pollux, viii. 9; Harpocration, s. v. Γεννῆται. Paul Diac. (p. 94) also says: *Gentilis dicitur et ex eodem genere ortus et is qui simili nomine appellatur*. *Cliens* or *cluens*, from *clueo*, means he who hears and who obeys.

is met in Friesland, among the Ditmarses, the Albanians, Slavs, etc.

In Algeria the Arab *douar* and the Kabyl *dechera* resemble the Roman *gens*, the *sheikh* or *amin* represents the *paterfamilias*, and the chiefs of the douars and decheras, like the *patres* at the curia, discuss at their *jemâa* the interests of the families they represent. Studied more closely, history shows that customs long looked upon as peculiar to certain peoples and certain epochs have been general institutions, and represent the stages humanity has travelled.

Thus the *gens* united all its members by a bond of relationship, real or fictitious. The curia was this same family enlarged, and the tribe was a similar one, only more complete. Each curia had its days of feasts and sacrifices, its priests and tutelary gods. Religion united still more closely those whom ties of blood or social position already connected. The whole Roman state rested on this basis of family, and had the same strict discipline.

The members of a *gens* were divided, we said, into two classes, — those who belonged to it by right of blood, and those who had become associated with it by certain engagements.

The former, the patroni or PATRICIANS,[1] were the sovereign people, to whom everything belonged, and who had the two great outward signs which marked the nobility of the Middle Ages, family names and armorial bearings, — I mean the *jus imaginum*, speaking devices, which were far more proud and imposing than all the feudal coats of arms, since it seemed as though the ancestors themselves, clad in their insignia of office, guarded the entrances of patrician houses. In funeral ceremonies, individuals recalling in features[2] and form the persons whom it was desired to represent, assumed the costume and "honors" that these latter had worn, thus surrounding the dead patrician with a living escort of his ancestors. In later times they had another form of *escutcheons*, the representation upon coins of the objects that their name recalled. Thus Aquillius Florus, a

---

[1] *Patricios Cincius ait, in libro de Comitiis, eos appellari solitos qui nunc ingenui vocentur.* (Fest., s. v. *Patricios.*)

[2] [Rather, they wore the wax masks taken from the images in the atrium. — *Ed.*]

flower; Quinctius Mus, a *mouse;* Voconius Vitulus, a *calf;* Pomponius Musa, the nine muses on nine different coins, etc., — a custom infinitely more modest, which ended by being merely a play of wit, but which had at first served to recall heroic acts, — as, for instance, the collar of the Manlii, and doubtless the hammer of the Publicii and the axe of the Valerii.

FLOWER.[1]   CALF.[2]
MUSES.[3]
RAT.[4]   PICKAXE.[5]
MALLET.[6]
COLLAR.[7]   BULL.[8]
WOMEN CHANGED INTO TREES.[9]

The second class of the members of the *gens* comprised strangers domiciled in the town, the prisoners brought to Rome, the ancient inhabitants of the land, the poor, freed slaves, — in short, all who preferred dependence on the great and strong, with their protection, to isolation and an insecure liberty. These were the CLIENTS, or we might say vassals.

[1] Coin of *L. Aquillius Florus III. Vir* (monetary triumvir), representing on the reverse a large full-blown flower; an *aureus* of Augustus.

[2] *Q. Voconius Vitulus.* Vitulus means a calf; reverse of a denarius of Caesar's time.

[3] *Pomponius Musa.* Laurel-crowned head of Muse; behind, a buskin; on the reverse, Thalia standing, holding a comic mask. Denarius of the Pomponian family.

[4] *Ti. Q.* Tiberius Quinctius Mus, an unknown member of the family Quinctia. Silver coin representing a rat, in Latin *mus*, beneath some horses which the rider is restraining; in the exergue, D. S. S., that is, *de Senatus sententia*, struck by order of the Senate.

[5] *Acisculus*, hammer in a crown of laurel. The *acisculum* was a tool *quo utuntur lapicidae ad excavandos lapides* (Forcellini, s. v.). Reverse of a silver coin of the Valerian family.

[6] Head of Pallas, above, a mallet, *malleolus;* on the reverse *C. Mall.* (Caius Malleolus). Naked man with his foot on some armor; in front, an anchor; behind, the prow of a vessel. Denarius of the Poblician family.

[7] *L. Torquat. III. vir.* Tripod enclosed in a collar, *torques;* denarius of the Manlii.

[8] *L. Thorius Balbus*, denarius of the Thorian family. Taurus means a bull.

[9] *P. Accoleius Lariscolus.* Bust of Clymene, the mother of Phaeton; on the reverse, the three sisters of Phaeton changed into larches (*larix*).

The patrician, or PATRON, — for the words are synonymous, — gave a small farm to his client, or, in default of land, a *sportula*, that is to say, a certain amount of provisions;[1] he must watch over all his interests, follow his suits, aid him in law-courts, — do for him, in a word, what the father does for his children, the patron for his freedmen. The law allowed the client no appeal from his patron; but religion consigned the patron to the gods, if he did any wrong to him whose necessary protector he was.[2] The client, on his part, took the family name of his patron, *nomen gentilicium*, and when he died received shelter in his tomb;[3] he helped him to pay his ransom, his fines, his law expenses, his daughter's dowry, and even the expenses necessary to fulfil his functions and maintain the dignity of his rank. It was forbidden them to summon one another into a court of justice, to bear witness or to vote against one another; and it would have been a crime on the part of the client to maintain a suit against his patron. Clientship was then a considerable diminution of the liberty of the client, and for him a semi-slavery. Such was, in fact, the strength of this bond in ancient times, that if the patron was exiled or quitted his country, his clients followed him into foreign lands. But in 390, B. C., Camillus set out alone; the bond had slackened; some years later it was on the point of breaking, when Manlius thought that his words would be obeyed if he proposed to the clients to take arms against their patrons.[4] At this period some of them were already on the road to fortune; a century later we shall see them advancing to power: the Marcelli, for instance, had been in the clientship of the *gens Claudia*. The *gens* then loses its social and religious character; but considerable traces of it exist up to the time of Constantine. With the conquests of the Republic, patronage extends to whole towns and nations; so that in the civil wars the strength of the chiefs was thereby greatly increased. Under the Empire it was the precious

---

[1] *Agrorum partes attribuebant tenuioribus* (Fest., s. v. *patres*), probably on the same conditions that the state imposed upon farmers of the domain. See Appian, *Bell. Civ.* i. 7. Dionys., ii. 10: ἐξηγεῖσθαι τὰ δίκαια . . . This is the principal passage on clientship. The nomination to a curule magistracy in later times broke the bond of clientship.
[2] Serv., *ad Aen.* vi. 609.
[3] *Jus sepulcri.* (Cic., *de Leg.* ii. 22)
[4] Livy, vi. 18.

bond between the senators of Rome and the provincial cities, between the rich and poor; it freed the society of this age from the necessity of having these charitable institutions which Christianity multiplied when clientship had disappeared.

IV. SENATE AND KING; PLEBEIANS.

THE members of the *gentes*, of absolutely free condition (*ingenui*), or the comrades in arms (*comites*), that is to say, the patricians, mustered at the *Comitium*,[1] divided into thirty curiae, the COMITIA CURIATA, and there, by the majority of votes, but without discussion, they made laws, decided on peace or war, heard appeals, and appointed to public or religious offices. Here, also, they approved or rejected wills which modified the property of the citizens, and adoptions which changed their civil condition.

The chiefs of these *gentes*, or elders (*seniores*, whence SENATORS), to the number of at first a hundred, two hundred after the union with the Sabines, and three hundred after the admission of the *gentes minores* under Tarquin, were the guardians of the national customs.[2] By refusing permission to present a bill to the assembly of curiae, they rendered the latter powerless; and as the council of the supreme magistrate, they assisted him with their advice in his government as well as in the propositions which he made to the people.

Chosen for life by the comitia curiata, the KING fulfilled the triple functions of generalissimo, high priest, and supreme judge. Every nine days, according to Etruscan custom, he dispensed justice, or appointed judges to dispense it in his name. During war and outside the walls his authority was absolute for discipline,

---

[1] The *Comitium* was the part of the Forum nearest the Capitol. At first distinct from the Forum, or public place, it was confounded with it when the two nations became one. The Comitium was crowned by a platform, on which was an altar sacred to Vulcan, the *Vulcanal;* the kings, and afterward the consuls and praetors, dispensed justice there.

[2] Usually they sat in the curia Hostilia, built opposite the Comitium, at the foot of the Capitol (Livy, i. 30); later on they met in one of the temples of the city, and always in a place consecrated by auspices. They deliberated with open doors. This semi-publicity of the sittings was better insured when the tribunes of the people had been admitted to seats on benches at the doors of the curia.

PRIMITIVE ORGANIZATION. 195

as well as for the division of booty and conquered land, of which he himself kept a part; so that he possessed, under the name of state property, considerable domains. Strangers, that is, plebeians, were subject to him at all times and in all places. He convoked the Senate and the Sovereign Assembly, he named senators, watched over the maintenance of laws and customs, and took the census. Six centuries later we find these rights reappearing in the prerogatives of the Emperors. But appeal might be made to the people, that is to say, to the comitia curiata, or patrician assembly, from the King's judgments, which was not allowed from the sentence of the Emperors, — a difference which suffices to mark the limited power of the one and the absolute authority of the other.[1] There was another all-powerful restraint which does not exist under the Empire, — the augurs and priests, being appointed for life, had nothing to fear from the King, and they could arrest his proceedings by making the gods intervene.

He had for his guard, it is said, three hundred KNIGHTS, or *celeres*. But these knights, chosen from among the richest citizens, were probably only a military division of the tribes: in time of war they formed the cavalry of the legions.[2] Their chief, the *tribune of the celeres*, was, after the King, the first magistrate of the city, as under the Republic the *magister equitum*, the dictator's lieutenant, is the second person in the state. When the King quitted Rome, a senator, whom he had chosen from among the ten first of the assembly, governed the town, under the name of guardian.[3] In case of a vacancy in the royal power, the Senate named an interrex every five days. Finally, the quaestors charged with the institution of criminal proceedings watched over the distribution of public charges, *munia*, and the levy of certain taxes and dues;[4] and the *duumviri perduellionis*

---

[1] 'ἱερῶν καὶ θυσιῶν ἡγεμονίαν ἔχειν (Dionys., ii. 14). [The Emperors monopolized the right of appeal under the *tribunicia potestas*.— *Ed.*]

[2] Niebuhr's school include all the patricians in the three centuries of knights, without reflecting that in Italy, especially at Rome, all the military forces consisted of infantry, and that in a Roman army there were never more than a small number of cavalry, as the nature of the country required.

[3] *Custos urbis*. The appellation of *praefectus urbi* is more modern. See Joan. Lyd., *de Magist.* i. 34, 38; Tac., *Ann.* vi. 11.

[4] Tacitus (*Ann.* xi. 22) places the institution of the financial quaestorship as far back as the kings; but it is not mentioned before 509.

judged such cases of high treason as the King did not reserve for his own decision.

By the side of this people of patrician houses,[1] which alone forms the state, makes laws, furnishes the Senate with members and the Republic with kings and priests, which possesses everything, — religion, the auspices by which it holds communication with the gods, political and private rights, lands, and, in the multitude of its clients, a devoted army, — below this sovereign class are found men who are neither clients, nor vassals, nor members of the *gentes*, who may not enter the patrician houses by legal marriage, who have neither the paternal authority,[2] nor the right of testamentary disposition or of adoption, — who do not interpose in any affair of public interest, and remain outside the political, as they dwell outside the actual, city, beyond the pomerium, on the hills which surround the Palatine. These men are the PLEBEIANS. Ancient inhabitants of the seven hills, or captives carried to Rome,

MERCURY FOUND AT PALESTRINA.[3]

---

[1] The three tribes, τὰς τρεῖς φυλὰς τὰς γενικάς (Dionys., vi. 14).

[2] *Patria potestas* is derived from patrician marriage by *confarreatio*, and the plebeians cannot contract such. Wills and adoptions, to be valid, must be accepted by the curiae, and they cannot enter these.   [3] *Mus. Pio Clem.*, Pl. 6.

foreigners attracted to the place of refuge, clients who have lost their patrons, they are, as Appius afterward says of them, without auspices, without families,[1] and without ancestors. But they are free, they hold property,[2] they practise crafts, and already pay honor to Mercury, the plebeian god of commerce, who in time will enrich some among them;[3] they settle their disputes by judges chosen from their midst, they receive no order but from the King, and they fight in the ranks of the Roman army to defend the fields they cultivate and the walls beneath whose shelter they have built their huts. Soon we shall find them become, by the laws of Servius, citizens of Rome.

In antiquity, as in the Middle Ages, victory assigned to the conqueror the person and lands of the conquered. Romulus having become in some way or other, by conquest or voluntary cession, master of the *Ager Romanus*, was then enabled to divide it equally among the families of the victors. This primitive division, attested by all writers, established among the citizens an equality of fortune, the restoration of which was several times attempted by the agrarian laws. Each *gens* received, perhaps, an allotment of twenty *jugera*, on the condition of supplying ten fighting men or one horse-soldier for the army; the legion was then formed of three thousand infantry and three hundred cavalry. I fear this explanation may seem like an idea copied from the organization of the feudal armies, as clientship recalled to our minds vassalage. The same system, however, is found in Greece. Sparta also had three tribes (φυλαί) and thirty curiae (ὠβαί), to each of which were given three hundred lots of lands, and the members of which formed the army and the sovereign people. At Rome itself the possession of the soil entailed, like that of a fief, the obligation of military service; and the landless citizen, *aerarius*, was no more admitted into the legions than the Frank without a

---

[1] That is to say, they do not form *gentes*, and they have not the *jus imaginum*.

[2] Either those which they had reserved on the territory of conquered cities, or the *assignations* of the kings. Two words express this separation of the two people, — the plebeians had neither the *connubium*, or marriage right, with the patricians, nor the *commercium*, or right of buying and selling.

[3] At least Livy says (ii. 27) that a little before the establishment of the tribuneship, the dedication of a temple to Mercury took place at Rome, and that a college of merchants was established under the patronage of the god.

domain or the Lombard without a war-horse[1] into the King's host. Under different aspects, many ages of the world are alike. In nature a small number of essential elements produces an infinite variety of creatures; just so in the political world the most diverse social forms often hide similar principles. Still it need not be concluded from this that humanity surges to and fro like the waves of the ocean, in continual ebb and flow; in that eternal evolution of beings and empires, principles do not remain immutable; they are modified and developed. The world seems to roll in the same circle; but this circle is a spiral which at times returns on itself, and always ends on a higher level.

What we have now been relating was, according to tradition, the work of the first king, — that is to say, of ancient times; for popular imagination, which sees only gods in the phenomena of nature, sees only men in the great phases of history, and attributes to heroes, whose names it invents or receives, the work of many generations. For the Romans, it was Romulus who had divided the people into tribes and curiae, who had created the knights and the Senate, established patronage and paternal and conjugal power, and forbidden nocturnal sacrifices, the murder of prisoners, and the exposure of children, unless they were deformed.[2] It was he again who, by offering an asylum and by setting the great example of inviting conquered people to the city, had prevented Rome remaining, like Sparta and Athens, a city with only a few citizens, or, to adopt the expression of Machiavelli, an immense tree without roots, ready to fall at the least wind.[3]

[1] *Luitpr. Leg.* v. cap. 29.
[2] Dionys., ii. 15.
[3] "Sparta and Athens were exceedingly warlike; they had the best of laws; yet they never increased as much as Rome, which seemed to be less well administered, and governed by less perfect laws. This difference can only come from the reasons explained above [the introduction into Rome of the conquered populations, or the concession of the citizenship]. Rome, anxious to increase its population, could put 280,000 men under arms; Sparta and Athens were never able to exceed the number of 20,000 each. All our institutions are imitations of nature, and it is neither possible nor natural that a slight and feeble trunk should support heavy branches . . . The tree loaded with branches thicker than the trunk grows weary of supporting them, and breaks in the least wind." — MACHIAVELLI.

CHAPTER III.

RELIGION AND RELIGIOUS INSTITUTIONS.

I. — THE PUBLIC GODS.

JUST as those civil institutions which had belonged to Central Italy, whence the Romans sprang, were attributed to Romulus, so Numa has been looked upon as the author of the religious customs brought from Latium and the Sabine country. We know their gods. The most honored were first Janus, the great national divinity, whose name stands at the head of all solemn invocations — the god with two faces: for he it is who opens and shuts, and begins and ends;[1] Jovis, or Jupiter, the god of light, who is called father and preserver of all things; Saturn, who protects the grain sown in the earth; Minerva, who warns the husbandman in time of the works to be undertaken;[2] Mars, the symbol of life renewed in the spring-time, and of manly force, against which no obstacle can stand;[3] Quirinus, the Sabine god, who, later on, being confounded with Romulus, descends to the rank of a demigod; Vesta, whose altar marked the centre of domestic life in the house and of political life in the city; Vulcan, another god of fire, — of the

MARS.

---

[1] According to Dionys. (fr. 18), Janus is represented with two faces because he knows the past and the future. This interpretation is relatively modern. In fact Janus must have been a solar deity, a symbol of the eternal revolution of things.

[2] Minerva, or rather Menerva, is a name belonging to the same family of words as *mens, monere, meminisse;* hence the transformation of this agricultural deity into the goddess of science and art, and the confounding of her with the Greek Athene. (Bréal, *Mél. de mythol.* p. 35.)

[3] Coins sometimes represent him by the figure of a young man with a helmet on his head, sometimes mounted on a chariot, brandishing a lance and bearing spoils. With the legend of Mars is connected the much less clear one of *Anna Perenna,* whose festival, as Ovid describes it, recalls certain features of the popular *fêtes* of modern Rome.

fire which devours and destroys, of the fire which conquers iron and constrains the hardest metals to bend to the wants of men. He early had an altar, the *Vulcanal*, below the *Comitium*. It was there, according to tradition, that Romulus and Tatius met to conclude peace.

Diana and Jovino were the feminine forms of Janus and Jovis: the one, goddess of the night and of gloomy woods; the other, Juno, of the day and of life, queen of heaven, *mater regina*, and *Juno Sospita*, protector of matrons who preserved their conjugal fidelity. Her sanctuary at Lanuvium was famous; the priests there kept a serpent, to which every year a virgin offered a sacred cake, — a dreadful ordeal. If he refused it, the maiden had not kept her virgin purity. Diana, who was afterward joined with the Hellenic Artemis, was also a kind of Lucina, whom women called to their aid in childbirth. Men paid her honor, as the goddess of mysterious forests; and as Latium was covered therewith, she was one of the great divinities of the Latins.

JUNO NURSING HERCULES (STATUE IN THE VATICAN).[1]

We have seen how Servius raised a temple to her on the

---

[1] We need hardly observe that the Ancient Romans long had, as representations of their gods, nothing but the trunks of trees roughly hewn into shape, or coarse symbols, and that consequently the busts and statues here given are of a period when Greek art reigned at Rome, and when the town was encumbered with statues taken by the proconsuls from the cities of Hellas and Asia Minor.

Aventine, when he wished to unite the destinies of Rome to those of the Latin cities.

At a period of refined philosophy Plutarch explained that the worship of Fortune complemented that of Destiny; that the goddess of the swift wings ruled over accidental events, whereas the "Son of Necessity"[1] watched over the maintenance of the unchangeable laws of the universe and the execution of the sovereign decrees pronounced by the supreme God; it was the opposition of the contingent and the necessary, of the domain wherein human liberty can be exercised, and that wherein divine providence rules. The Romans did not philosophize so deeply; but they had a confused idea that everything in life did not obey inevitable laws, and according to their custom they had created a divinity corresponding to this feeling, — *Fortuna*, an old Italian deity, whom Servius was supposed to have introduced into Rome, and who had certainly come there in an isolated way. She was held in great honor at Praeneste and at Antium,[2] and in time she counts more worshippers than the great gods of the Capitol.[3] The common people and slaves held a yearly festival, on the 24th of June, in honor of her who could bestow liberty and riches; and in their prayers they joined the name of Servius with that of the good goddess who from an

FORTUNA (STATUE IN THE VATICAN).

---

[1] Plutarch (*de Fato*), says that in Plato's *Republic* Destiny is the work of the Virgin Lachesis, daughter of 'Ανάγκη, Necessity.

[2] The *sortes* of Praeneste, so famous throughout Italy, were little sticks, which were drawn by a child, as the numbers of a lottery are still drawn at Rome.

[3] According to Pliny (*Nat. Hist.* ii. 5) Fortune was the great divinity of his time.

adventurer had made him a king. "When she entered Rome," says Plutarch,[1] "she folded her wings as a sign that she wished to remain there." And in fact she is still there; the Roman of the present day believes as firmly in chance as the Roman of bygone ages.

Innumerable were her titles, and consequently her temples; for as every epithet bestowed on her expressed a special kind of

TETRASTYLE TEMPLE OF FORTUNA (VIRILIS).[2]

favor expected from her, there seemed to be as many goddesses of fortune as there were motives for making supplication to Chance. The Romans thus divided the deity according to the functions which they meant it to fulfil; and all their gods had several different phases, as though this people were incapable of contemplating a divine being in its grandeur and serenity.

Women even desired to have their goddess of Fortune, *Fortuna muliebris*, to whom the matrons whose tears overcame Coriolanus erected a temple. They consecrated another to *Fortuna virilis*,

---

[1] *De Fort. Rom.* 4.

[2] A tetrastyle temple of the last days of the Republic, the base of which is still surrounded by the ancient pavement of the Palatine Way. It is situated near the Temple of the Sun (p. 160) and a house made entirely of the ancient ruins. See Wey, *Rome*, p. 162.

which had at first a very moral function, that of preserving to wives the affection of their husbands, but which ends by being only the goddess of every kind of feminine coquetry. This temple still exists, — and with good reason, since the goddess has not ceased to reign.

The gods of the lower world, — Tellus, Terra-Mater, Ceres, Dis-Pater, etc., — caused the seed to germinate in the bosom of the silent earth, and kept guard over the dead. Those of the sea, — so numerous among the Greeks, who passed half their lives upon the waters, — could not possess much credit with a people who had no fleet. But in the middle region dwelt the deities of the earth, *Medioxumi*,[1] gods of the field and forests, of the harvest and vintage, of the springs and rivers, — gods more popular and more honored than the great gods who lived far away. There Bona Dea reigned, or Maia, the earth which produces all things necessary to life, and who was

FAUN OF PRAXITELES.[3]

therefore called the Great Mother, *Mater Magna;*[2] Saturn, "the Good Sower," Faunus, Sylvanus, and Pales, gods of the woods and meadows, who protected the farm, the poultry-yard, and the garden established in some forest clearing, and who drove away the wolf and fatal diseases.

[1] Plautus, *Cistellaria*, II. i. 45.   [2] Macrobius, *Sat.* I. xii. 20.
[3] Ancient copy of the Faun of Praxiteles, in the Capitoline Museum.

204 ROME UNDER THE KINGS.

In ancient times Italy was, as it is now, the country of great pastures; and the Roman Campagna still keeps the race of wild shepherds whose sports Vergil depicts. Their great festival, the *Palilia*, was celebrated on the anniversary of the founding of Rome, April 21, and the royal hill of Romulus bears the name of their divinity.[1] Rumina, the foster-mother, watched over the nourishment of the young cattle; hence the name of the Ruminal fig-tree, under whose shade the she-wolf suckled the twins. Rubigo preserved the wheat from mildew, Vertumnus and Pomona caused the fruit to ripen in the orchard. Feronia, the goddess of flowers, of joy, and of all natural pleasures, seems to have been less lavish of useful favors; yet she was held in so great honor that Hannibal found a rich treasure to carry off from her temple at the foot of Soracte. Besides this temple she had others at Terracina, at Trebula in the country of the Sabines, and at Luna in Etruria. In later times Flora and Venus became formidable rivals to this goddess.

MATRI MAGNAE.

FERONIA.[2]

THE TIBER.

Liber, the genius whose modest duty it was to secure abundance on the tables of his worshippers, later fell heir to the rich legend of the Theban Dionysos and the Indian Bacchus; in the same way Hercules, the herdsman, became the glorious son of Jupiter and Alcmena [Herakles] when a wave of Greek poetry had fertilized the soil of Italian mythology.[3]

Above the naïads, and nymphs, and all the water genii, rose Father Tiberinus, the mighty river, who scorned to be fettered with a bridge of stone, and for many centuries permitted to span his

---

[1] Palatine, from *pales*, a word which is itself derived from the root *pâ*, which formed the verbs signifying "to pasture" in Greek, Latin, and French.

[2] This coin was struck in the time of Augustus by the monetary tribune Petronius Turpilianus, who has not bestowed beauty on the Goddess Feronia. But Roman artists, even in the time when they were most under the influence of Greek art, did not seek their goddesses in heaven, they took them from the Roman Campagna. The Minerva of the magnificent chest of Praeneste, called the Ficorini, looks like a *contadina*.

[3] The first mention of the worship of Herakles, or Hercules, at Rome, is made by Livy (v. 13) in connection with the *lectisternium* of the year 418 B. C.

waves naught but the *Pons Sublicius*, built of wood, without a single piece of iron. Moreover, in order to avert the anger of the gods, the pontiffs had undertaken the construction of it themselves; and they directed all repairs, which were only executed amid religious ceremonies. In the distant ages the Tiber had exacted human victims; he was now content with twenty-four mannikins of osier, which the Vestals yearly (on the 13th of May) cast from the top of the Sublician Bridge into his stream.

To all these gods the name of father was given, which would have made a friend of Horace smile, but which in ancient Latium was the most august title for men and gods. Eros, who plays so high a part in the *Theogony* of Hesiod as the harmonious arranger of the elements of chaos, and excites sweet feelings in men and gods, has no place in the Roman religion of the early ages. These gods are united in pairs, Saturn and Lua, Quirinus and Hora, Mars and Nerio; but the son of Aphrodite is not yet among them. These loveless and childless couples represent in their severity the Latino-Sabine family, which granted no place at the hearth but to the matron and her rough husband.

The innumerable gods of the *Indigitamenta*, that is, whose names were written on the registers of the pontiffs, formed a class apart. They had the singular character of presiding over every action of life, even the very lowest, from birth to death, — over all the needs of mankind, food, clothing, lodging; over all his works, etc.; but in such wise that each of them supplied only one of these needs. They are only known by the epithet which designates their duty.[1] The need satisfied or the act accomplished, no further prayer is addressed to them, and they seem as if they no longer existed. Some busy themselves about conception or pregnancy; others about childbirth; some watch over the suckling of the child; some make it utter its first cry,— and so on for the whole of life. Strange illusion of man, to adore the conceptions

---

[1] See in Saint Augustine (*De Civ. Dei*, vi. 9, and 10) all the employments of these gods, the enumeration of which he concludes with these eloquent words: *omnem istam ignobilem deorum turbam quam longo aevo superstitio congessit.* Cf. Maury, *Réligions de l'antiquité* vol. ii. p. 1236. [The same sort of feeling is seen in those curious early Latin hymns, chiefly of Celtic origin, which are called *Loricae*, and consist in invocations to protect every spot in the body, even the most minute and ignoble. There are several specimens in Mone's *Hymni Lat. Med Aevi.*— *Ed.*]

of his own mind! But this people, possessed of such terrible energy, who knew nought of dreamy contemplations or mystic ardors, — these men of action and of perseverance could do nothing by themselves. Whether his private interests or the affairs of the state were in question, the Roman must have a god at hand. Another characteristic trait we notice: the Greeks held their political assemblies in the theatre; the Roman Senate met to deliberate in the temples of the gods.

II. THE DOMESTIC GODS.

CERTAIN of the Roman divinities — who may be called official, having temples, priests, and a public ritual, with the homage of the crowd — were besides honored in a special manner in the *gentes*, by the *sacra gentilitia*. Each of the great families had its protecting deity, — as the mediæval corporations were wont to make choice of a heavenly patron; and this cult closely united all the members of the *gens*. To abandon it was to perish; the *gens* not surviving the desertion of its ancient altar. Livy relates that the Potitii, having given up to the state the worship of Hercules, peculiar to their race, all died within the year.[1]

DOMESTIC ALTAR.[2]

Each household, even the poorest, had also its domestic gods, modest and humble, some unseen, the Genii and Manes; others, the Lares and Penates, represented by small rude earthen figures, coarsely moulded and baked in an oven, but held in as much honor as are the holy pictures of the Russian peasants in our time. All these are with difficulty distinguished from one another, representing more or less clearly the idea of a supernatural protection exercised by departed spirits over the house which had once been their home. This faith appears to have existed in Greece; we also find it in Etruria; and it would seem to be one of the earliest manifestations of the religious instinct.

[1] ix. 29.
[2] The domestic altars were sometimes very small, like the Penates themselves. The one we give is only reduced to a quarter of its real size.

Let us first dispose of the numberless crowd of Genii. That strange doctrine is well known which makes men, and even gods, of a double nature, and gives each in his lifetime two existences, one of which continues after death.[1] The Genii pre-

THE LARES.[2]

sided over all the phenomena of physical and moral life. Nothing took place without them, and the favor or enmity reached the individual, the family, the city, even the whole nation.

[1] See p. 128.—*Sub terra censebant reliquam vitam agi mortuorum.* (Cic. Tusc. i. 16.)

[2] Lares taken from the Campana Museum, and comparatively modern. These statuettes, so full of pretentious affectation, were certainly not honored with the same strong faith accorded to the shapeless fetiches of ancient days. The Penates, who insured joy and abundance to the house, were in late days represented in a joyous attitude, holding in one hand a drinking-horn, and in the other a dish.

The Penates, or gods of the interior, whom Vergil calls paternal gods,[1] were the spirits of the house, in which they provided abundance, *penus*. With the Lares or Lords, the spirits of ancestors, were connected all endearing and sweet memories. The Lares shared the joys and griefs of the family, and were associated with its good or evil fortune. In every festival they took part, on all happy occasions they were crowned with flowers or foliage, and the young man, when he took the *toga virilis*, consecrated to them the *bulla* which he had worn. No meal was eaten without a portion being set apart for them, a kind of communion with the gods which in grave circumstances was performed by the whole city, when she invited all her guardian deities to the solemn feast of the *lectisternium*.

At an epoch already sceptical Plautus introduces on the stage a family Lar, who explains to the spectators the plot of one of his plays. "I am the Lar of this house. For many a year I have had the keeping of it, and I watch over it from father to son. The grandfather of the present holder confided a treasure to me with many supplications, and secretly hid it under the hearth, asking me to preserve it. He was a miser, and he departed without speaking to his son about it. When he was dead, I carefully observed his son, to see if I should receive more honor from him than from his father. I soon found that he diminished still more the expenses which concerned me. I punished him for it, and he never knew of the secret hoard. His son resembles him; but his daughter never misses a day in offering me incense, wine, and prayers; so I will lead her to discover the treasure."[2]

Take away the disrespectful handling of the poet, who makes the familiar Lar a piece of theatrical machinery, and you will find the god whose worship was the consolation and hope of many a generation.

With the worship of the Lares was associated that of the domestic fire; and it may be said that the two corner-stones which

---

[1] Macrobius (*Sat.* III. iv. 6 and 8) calls the Penates the peculiar gods of the Romans: *dis Romanorum propriis . . . per quos penitus spiramus, per quos habemus corpus, per quos rationem animi possidemus.*

[2] Prologue of the *Aulularia*.

upheld Roman society were the hearthstone and the tombstone. The family was formed around the one, and, in spite of the sad separation, it continued around the other. He who had no Penates wandered about in life as he who had no tomb wandered in death; and the hearth is a sacred place. On the kalends, the ides, the nones, on all feast-days, a crown of flowers is hung there,[1] and on entering the house the father salutes, first of all, the Lares of the hearth.[2]

Great Vesta reigns over the public hearth, "a living flame that neither gives nor receives any germ of life,"[4] consequently an eternal virgin, who can have none but virgins for companions. Each house also possesses a domestic Vesta. The hearth is her altar, and the fire which burns there is a god,—the god who sustains life in the house, as the sun does in nature, who bakes the bread, makes the tools, and aids in all kinds of work; but the god who purifies too; who is never soiled; who receives sacrifices and bears to the other deities the prayers of mortals, when the flame, quickened by oil, incense, and the fat of victims, blazes up and darts towards heaven.

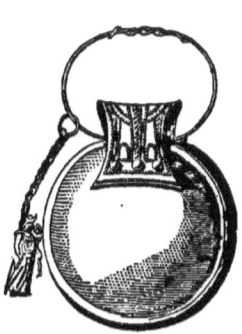 

1. BULLA.[3] 2. YOUNG ROMAN WEARING THE BULLA.[3]

"O Hearth," says an Orphic hymn, "thou who art ever young and beauteous, make us always happy! Thou who dost nourish, receive in good part our offerings, and give us in return happiness and health." With less of religious fervor, but with

---

[1] Cato, de Re rust. 143.
[2] Ibid. 2.
[3] No. 1 represents the golden *bulla*, without ornamentation, except on the clapper-ring. No. 2 shows a statue from the Louvre representing a young Roman clad in the *praetexta* and wearing the *bulla*. The poor wore leather ones; but all had them, for the *bulla* was supposed to possess the power of averting evil.
[4] ... *Vivam flammam ... quae semina nulla remittit nec capit.*
OVID: *Fast.* vi. 291-294.

an emotion which gives an idea of this eternal worship of the hearth, Cicero says, later on: "Here is my religion, here my race and the traces of my fathers. I find in this place an indefinable charm, which penetrates my heart and enthralls my senses." And we of modern times still say similar things when we return to our paternal hearth.

III. The Manes.

The souls of the dead, or *Lemures*, were of two kinds, — those of the wicked, the *Larvae*, and those of the good, the *Manes*.

The *Manes*, "the pure beings," were the dead purified by funeral ceremonies, and become the protectors of those whom they had left behind them in life. At Rome, as everywhere, the dead was not thought to be altogether dead. He had his place of abode like the living; *his* hearth was in the tomb. There he began a second life, sad, but calm, if the funeral rites had been accomplished; fretful and unhappy when funeral honors had not been paid him. Separated from his mortal remains, the human being did not quit the earth to ascend into ethereal spheres or to descend into the lower regions. Invisible, but ever present, he remained near those he had loved, inspiring them with wise thoughts, protecting their abode and their fortune, — on the condition, however, that the living should render to the dead the worship due to ancestors. Originally these rites were cruel, — at least on the day of the funeral ceremonies; for it was thought that the Manes loved blood. On the tomb of a king or hero they immolated his wife, his slaves, his war-horse or captives; and from this custom came the combats of gladiators, which were at first, as was the Spanish *auto-da-fé*, an act of devotion. But on anniversaries the Manes were satisfied if the relations came to deck the tomb with wreaths of foliage, as we place flowers thereon, and to deposit cakes of honey and meal, to make libations of wine, milk,[1] and the blood of some unpretending victim. They were present in invisible form at these pious ceremonies,

---

[1] Ovid, *Fast.* ii. 537, *seq.*

and took their part of the offerings.¹ A great number of bas-reliefs and paintings represent the dead engaged in their "Elysian repasts." Lucian, who laughs at everything, ridicules this appetite of the dead;² and in fact, in his time, nay, even long before him, there were miserable wretches, the *bustirapi*,³ who played the part of the dead, by carrying away in the night the food deposited on the tombs. But pious people believed that the benevolence of the Manes was secured by these offerings, and that to forget them was to expose oneself to their anger. Wandering then in the silent night, they came to terrify the living, or to cast disease on the flock, barrenness on the land.⁴ Thus even at a time when the credit of Jupiter had fallen very low Cicero wrote: "Render to the Manes what is due to them, and hold them for divine beings; for our ancestors would that those who had quitted this life should be of the number of the gods!"⁶ We make the sign of the cross on passing near a tomb. The Roman said to the dead, "Sleep in peace!" or else, "Be propitious to us!" and he saluted with the same gesture of adoration that he used in worshipping the gods. Even when a family was obliged to sell the field in which its funeral vault was placed, the law reserved a right of passage, that they might go to perform the sacred rites there.⁷ On the return of

ADORATION BEFORE A TOMB.⁵

---

¹ Varro, *de Ling. Lat.* vi. 13. The custom of the funeral feast on the day of the obsequies is preserved in our provinces. In my childhood it still existed, even in Paris; but it is no longer more than an act of politeness towards the guests, and none of the religious idea which the ancients attached to it now remains.

² *De Luctu*, 9.

³ Plautus, *Pseud.* I. iii., 127.

⁴ ... *Tacitae* ... *tempore noctis*
Perque vias urbis, Latiosque ululasse per agros
Deformes animas.
OVID: *Fast.* ii. 552.

⁵ Taken from a painted vase, on which Orestes is represented approaching the tomb of Agamemnon.

⁶ Cic., *de Leg.* ii. 9 and 22 ... *Majores eos, qui ex hac vita migrassent, in deorum numero esse voluissent.* We must call to mind this belief, so persistent among the Romans, when we see the Emperors declared *divi*.

⁷ *Dig.* xviii. 1, 6. These rites of the tomb are found as far as the extreme East. Among the Annamites, children inherit the property of their father in equal portions, except the eldest,

the *Feralia*, the last day of the festival of the dead, there was celebrated in each house the *Caristiae*, a feast in which all the relatives took part. Then they recalled the glorious memories of the family; together they worshipped the Lares, the protectors of the paternal roof, and they separated with mutual wishes for prosperity. "At this fraternal banquet," says Ovid, "Concord always came to take a seat."[1]

This religion of death is at once the most ancient and the most touching; it established a bond between the past generations

GESTURE OF ADORATION.[2]

GESTURE OF ADORATION.[3]

and those which survived them. The soul of the ancestors was the soul of the family, and there was in this firm belief a great principle of social conservatism.

But let us take notice that this festival of the dead differed essentially from ours, which is a beautiful idea of universal charity continued beyond the tomb, — a prayer offered by all for all. Among the Romans the worship of the dead was essentially domestic; near relatives alone were entitled to make the offerings, and no stranger had the right to be present at the funeral repast, the pious representation of the banquets of the Elysian life, which

who holds an extra portion, in order to keep up the tombs of his ancestors. (Ch. Lemire, *Cochinchine franc.*, 1877.)

[1] *Concordia fertur . . . adesse.* (*Fast.* ii. 631.)

[2] Bas-relief from the Louvre.

[3] Taken from a painting on a Greek vase. A young Greek woman and young man saluting a Hermes. To put the right hand up to the mouth is still a mode of salutation in the East, and sometimes even with us.

AN ELYSIAN REPAST.

were the only joy the Roman and Greek could imagine for their dead.[1] The man, then, who died without leaving a family behind him, lacked those honors which were necessary to the repose and consolation of the dead. In order to avoid this misfortune, the childless Roman, in default of a natural family, created for himself a legal family; and to religious belief must be attributed the importance of that civil custom of adoption, as frequent at Rome as it is rare with us. The funeral colleges under the Empire are another means of providing oneself with relatives, who may accomplish the rites necessary to this second life in the tomb.

The *Larvae*, the messengers of the gloomy abode, brought the living unlucky dreams, threatening visions, and terrible apparitions; they were the phantoms that peopled the night, and whose anger people sought to deprecate by throwing black beans over the shoulder, or by striking a bronze vessel. All were not so easy to exorcise, and about some of them there circulated dreadful stories, which strengthened the belief in evil Genii. "Ulysses," say Pausanias and Strabo, "having stopped at Temesa, on the coast of Bruttium, one of his companions, Polites, outraged a maiden, and was stoned by the inhabitants. Ulysses did nothing to avenge this murder and appease the manes of the hero, so the spectre of Polites returned every night to spread terror and death among the people of Temesa. In order to escape his anger, they were about to abandon their town, when the Pythoness revealed to them that they would appease the hero if they built a sanctuary to him, and yearly offered to him the most beautiful among their daughters. The shrine was raised in the thickest part of a wood of wild olives, and the fearful sacrifice was performed, till the day when a

TEMESA OF BRUTTIUM.[2]

---

[1] The engraving on page 213 represents the paintings on a tomb at Tarquinii (Corneto). In the foreground an Elysian repast; on the two side-pieces, persons dancing, doubtless the initiated celebrating some rite of Bacchus in the midst of a sacred wood. On the two sides of the door of the tomb, two horsemen and some tigers or panthers, probably in memory of the funeral games. (*Atlas du Bull. arch.*, 1831, Pl. xxxii. For the description, see *Annales*, vol. iii. p. 325, *seq.*)

[2] The first three letters of the name of the town, and a helmet; on the reverse a tripod, two greaves; silver coin.

famous athlete of Locri, named Euthymos, entered the temple, saw the maiden, and, touched with compassion and love, resolved to fight the demon on the following night. He conquered, drove him out of the territory, and obliged him to cast himself into the waves of the Ionian Sea. After that time never did the fatal spectre re-appear; but there long existed the proverb, 'Beware the hero!'"[1]

IV. NATURALISM OF THE ROMAN RELIGION AND FORMAL DEVOTION.

THERE is a poetry in the pious ceremonies performed near the hearth and around the tombs. Poetry of another kind, too, is found in the worship of the sacred groves. The Apennines were then covered with those immense forests, whose silence and mystery long inspired a religious terror. To find protection amid these unknown, and, consequently, so much the more dreaded, dangers, men consecrated in some glade a group of trees, which henceforth became an inviolable sanctuary. Sometimes a single tree, which had been struck by a thunderbolt, or whose crest topped the whole forest, and which allowed nothing to grow beneath the depths of its shadow, became a divine being. In 456 B. C., three ambassadors from Rome came to demand of the Aequi the fulfilment of a treaty. The chief, seated under

SACRED TREE.[2]

---

[1] Pausanias, VI. vi. 7–11; Strabo, vi. p. 255; Suidas, s. v. Εὔθυμος; Aelianus, *Hist. Var.* viii. 18. See, in the reign of Tiberius, the story of the matron delivered by the priests of Isis to the god Anubis.

[2] Bas-relief in the Louvre. Cymbals are hung on the branches of the sacred tree; behind it stands the altar, on which a ram, which a child leads, is about to be sacrificed; behind, a veiled priestess and the flute-player, necessary in all sacrifices. Behind the altar a second woman, bearing offerings on her head. The worship of sacred trees still exists in many places.

an immense oak, answered them derisively: "Address yourselves to this tree; I have other business than listening to you." "Good," cried one of the Romans; "let this sacred oak, and the god, whosoever he be, who dwells therein, know that you have violated your promised faith; may they lend a favorable ear to our complaint and aid us in the fight."[1]

Vergil and Lucan saw the remains of this old naturalism still in existence. They speak of trees held in veneration, of the olive-tree of Faunus, whereon sailors, when they came back from a dangerous voyage, suspended their *ex-voto*, and of the ancient oak that stretches towards heaven its withered arms, yet ever bears the remains of victims offered by the people, and the sacred gifts of the chiefs. Though around it there spreads the sturdy green forest, it alone is honored.

> "Exuvias populi . . . sacrataque gestans
> Dona ducum . . .
> Sola tamen colitur."

Animals naturally played a part in this religion of nature. In the temple of *Juno Sospita* at Lavinia a serpent received offerings. The woodpecker, which, with its strong beak, seems to attack the largest trees in search of food, and the wolf, king of the Italian forests, were the symbols of Mars. When under the leafy cover, in the silence and shade, the woodpecker was heard afar, striking his short, sharp blows, it was the rustic god who spoke, and the augur gave a meaning to his words.

In substance, the religion of the early Romans was not far removed from fetichism. Quirinus, represented by a spear; Jupiter Lapis by a stone;[2] Vesta by fire; Mars by his shield; and the gods and goddesses of fallow lands, of weeding, of manure, of rust, of the grindstone, of the oven, of fear, of fever, and all that represented the physical agencies which man loves or dreads, — are scarce above the level of those good or evil beings which barbarous nations worship. For the magistrate as well as for the private person, the song or flight of a bird, an unusual noise, a sudden

---

[1] Livy, iii. 25.
[2] According to Varro (St. Aug., *de Civ. Dei*, iv. 31), the Romans remained 170 years without possessing any statues. I do not know whether the date is exact, but the fact must have good foundation.

or involuntary sadness, a false step, the flickering of a flame, the groans of the victim, the prolongation or speedy termination of its death-pangs, the color and form of the entrails, — everything, in fact, was an omen, and the appetite of the sacred chickens or the size of a victim's liver often carried grave decisions.

The Roman knew nothing of divine love; on the contrary, he trembled before the innumerable deities,[1] capricious and vindictive, whom he pictured to himself lying in wait everywhere along the path of life; and in the words of the most religious of pagans,[2] "Full of affright, he entered their sanctuary, as though their temple were the cave of a bear or dragon." Should he by mischance cross the threshold of his house with his left foot first, should he hear the squeak of a mouse or his glance fall on any object held to be unlucky, immediately he re-entered his house distracted, and could not feel re-assured till he had offered an expiatory sacrifice. He believed in the evil eye,[3] like the Italian of the present day, and like him too he thought to guard against it by a *fascinum*[4] which he hung round the necks of his children, in his garden and over his hearth. Hence came the god Fascinus, whose worship was intrusted to the vestals, and who was placed on the chariot of generals at their triumph, to turn aside envy and to avert evil fortune.[5] There was, however, a sure preservative against spells, which was to spit into one's right shoe before putting it on.[6]

Cato the Elder died in 149 B. C. He lived, then, at a period in which the grand age of Roman civilization began; yet how superstitious is this cool-headed and calculating man! He believes in charms and in magic words for healing sickness. Here is his prescription, for instance, against dislocations. "Take a green rush, four or five feet long, cut it in two in the middle, and let

---

[1] Varro said 30,000, which was also Hesiod's reckoning (*Works and Days*, 252); but Maximus Tyrius (*Dissert.* i.) thought this figure far too small.

[2] Plutarch, *de Superst.* 25; Cic., *de Divin.* ii. 72.

[3] *Nescio quis teneros oculus mihi fascinat agnos.* (Verg., *Ecl.* iii. 103.)

[4] This *fascinum* was commonly a *satyricum signum* (Pliny, *Nat. Hist.* xix. 19), or a little bell suspended on a branch of coral. Almost all young Chinese wear this latter kind of amulet. This does not imply that the superstition travelled from Pekin to Rome. The human mind, in all races, passes through similar stages, which lead to unexpected results.

[5] *Fortuna gloriae carnifex.* (Pliny, *Nat. Hist.* xxviii. 7.)

[6] *Ibid.*

two men hold it on your thighs. Begin to sing: *daries dardaries astataries dissunapiter*, and continue to do so until the two pieces are joined together again. Wave a blade over them when the two pieces are joined and touch one another, seize hold of them, and cut them across lengthways. Make a bandage therewith on the broken or dislocated member, and it will heal. Sing, however, over the dislocation daily: *huat hanat huat, ista pista sista, domiabo damnaustra*, or else *huat haut haut ista sis tar sisordaunabon dannaustra.*" And he introduced into his *de Re rustica* many similar receipts. Yet Cato is one of the greatest personages of Rome. It is evident that this people was, on certain points, very small indeed.

Superstitions quite as gross and credulity as blind have been seen in later, and even in highly civilized ages, and in many places there exist others worthy of them. Even the Genii of ancient Rome are not all dead; they live again under other names, to people that infinity of heavens whereof the void and silence frighten us. But what belongs more particularly to the Roman religion is its formalism. There is no fervor or divine aspiration, still less philosophic reflection, in its piety. The words, attitudes, and gestures are ordered by the ritual. To leave the established rule, even to be generous to the gods, was to go beyond what was proper, and to fall into superstition. In the temple, the most religious state of the soul was absolute calm; silence on the lips, silence in the mind.[1] For the ceremonies, all was settled beforehand, even to the prayer, which should only rise from the heart; and soon they begin to pray in forms which are no longer understood. In the time of the Antonines the brotherhood of Arvales chanted songs which dated perhaps from Numa. It was needful, too, to repeat these ancient compositions with religious care, for a peculiar virtue attached to the very expressions. By the omission of one word a sacrifice became useless, a prayer vain. The lawyers say at a later period: *quia virgula cadit, causa cadit,*—through a comma, one loses his suit. The same was thought to be the case with the gods. When a consul had a religious formula to pronounce, he read it from the

---

[1] *Templum in quo verbis parcimus, in quo animos componimus, in quo tacitam etiam mentem nostram custodimus.* (Quintil., *Declam.* 265.)

ritual, for fear of omitting or transposing a word. A priest followed the reading in a second book, in order to be sure that all the sacramental phrases were said aright; another saw that absolute silence was observed among the bystanders; lastly, a musician drowned with the modulations of his flute every sound which could have broken the charm attached to the words that the officiating person recited.[1]

The feeling of religion has submitted to much slavery, but never has it been enchained in such strict bonds. It might be thought that Rome, like a certain famous institution, was afraid of religious excitement, if we did not know that in this institution the regulation of piety is the result of policy, whereas with the Romans it was the spontaneous production of the national character. But if this childish credulity lowers the spirit of the people, it yet renders them very easy to govern; and the vigorous devotional discipline, which has nothing to do with religious feeling, produced citizens in whom respect for the rules of the temple long inspired respect for the law in the Forum.

We may make another remark: these divinities of Rome appear less beautiful, but more moral, than those of Greek polytheism;[2] and the Fathers of the Church consider the religion

---

[1] Pliny, *Nat. Hist.* xxviii. 3. Here is the longest passage left us of the old historian Fabius Pictor. At the same time may be seen the poverty of this ancient literature, the miserable state of men's minds, and how grievous was that sacerdotal slavery in which there is nowhere felt beating a truly religious heart. "It is a crime for the flamen of Jupiter to ride on horseback or to see the centuries under arms; thus he rarely has been named consul. He is not permitted to take an oath; the ring he wears must be hollow and of open work. No fire must be carried from his house but the sacred fire. If a man enters that house bound, he must be unbound, and the bonds must be carried through the inner court up the roof and thrown into the street. The flamen has no knot about him, either on his cap, his girdle, or any other part. If a man who is going to be beaten with rods falls at his feet as a suppliant, the guilty one cannot be beaten without sacrilege that day. None but a freeman can cut a flamen's hair. He never touches or names a she-goat, raw flesh, hare, or beans. He must not clip the tendrils of the vine that climb too high. The feet of the bed he sleeps in must be plastered with mud. He never quits it three consecutive nights, and no one else has the right to sleep therein. There must not be near the woodwork of his bed a box with sacred cakes in it. The parings of his nails and the cuttings of his hair are covered with earth at the foot of a fruit-tree. For him all days are holy days. He is not allowed to go into the open air without the *apex*; and even as to remaining bareheaded under his own roof, the pontiffs have only quite recently decided that he may do so." (Aulus Gellius, *Noct. Att.* x. 15.) Another example of this minute and childish formalism is furnished by Table xli. of Marini. (*Atti e monumenti de' Fratelli Arvali.*) [One might imagine this page of old Fabius taken out of the Zend-avesta or from the laws of Manu. — *Ed.*]

[2] See page 124.

RELIGION AND RELIGIOUS INSTITUTIONS.

of Numa to have been a decent religion.[1] Yet the Roman gods do not require their believers to practise justice. The purity they exact is bodily purity, *castitas*.[2] They may be approached without repentance, but not with unwashed face or hands, or stained raiment. Thus a clean toga is necessary for festivals; and ablutions and baths were an act of piety before they were a matter of health. It might even be said that the *thermae*, the architectural glory of Rome, are derived, like her theatres and circuses, from a religious idea. Between these gods and mankind there was but a bond of interest. They wished to be honored, and, like a patron proud of the great number of his clients, they required that the crowd should surround their altars; they demanded sacrifices and libations, songs and sacred dances, wreaths of flowers and foliage round their temples and altars, and a numerous attendance, that their dignity might be raised among the gods, and their credit among men. In return they promised protection, and as they were feared, men sought to appease them. As it was thought they could give health, fortune, and victory, men performed all the acts which could constrain them to grant prosperity.

GARLANDS OF LEAVES ROUND A TEMPLE.[3]

The Roman did not love his gods, and they did not live in him, did not purify his heart or elevate his soul. Religion was a bargain, and worship a contract in due form; a *quid pro quo*. Plautus bluntly says so: "He who has made the gods propitious always gains large profits."[5] This piety, which calculates so exactly, shows us that the people

VESTA HOLDING THE PALLADIUM AND A SCEPTRE.[4]

---

[1] Tertull., *Apol.* 25.
[2] *Casta placent superis: pura cum veste venite.* (Tibullus, II. i. 13.) Aulus Gellius (ii. xxviii.) says: *Veteres Romani . . . in constituendis religionibus . . . castissimi, cautissimique.* The *lustratio*, one of the greatest religious acts of Rome, and one of the oldest, was at first a purification by water. This word comes from the verb *luo*, to wash, wipe out.
[3] DIVO AVG. S. C. Sacrifice before the temple. Large bronze coin of Caligula.
[4] Large bronze of Sabina, wife of Hadrian.
[5] *Curculio*, IV. ii. 45.

lacked certain high qualities of mind; having no religious spirit, they had in later times no philosophic spirit.

Vesta, however, had brought virgin purity into honor; Juno and all the other goddesses of marriage or nurture had done the same for the wisdom and devotion of matrons; the Lares loved domestic virtues; the Manes concord in families; Fides, good faith in contracts; Terminus, respect for all rights; and with the exception of certain rustic divinities, who delighted in gayety and laughter — who allowed even far more — all the gods had the Roman gravity. Still we should not go as far as to repeat what is said of this religion, "that, like the philosophy of Socrates, it brought divinity down to earth, and obliged it to regulate the life and manners of men." The Socratic philosophy was a mighty effort of reflection; the Roman religion, on the contrary, sprang spontaneously from customs; and in primitive ages customs precede belief, which in their turn preserves them. The Latino-Sabine populations, among whom the family tie was so strong, created domestic gods who never can be immoral, and their agricultural life compelled them to have gods who protected property and agreements. Before he was carried to the ends of the field to serve as the sacred boundary, Terminus had risen from the furrow opened by the Latin plough.

FIDES, OR GOOD FAITH.[1]

V. Sacerdotal Colleges.

Thus the Roman religion is twofold in its nature. There is that of the state, or of society as a whole, and that of individual persons; but there exists a very good understanding between the two, because in the main it is the same thing answering to two different needs. The family has its Penates, which the state respects; the city its gods, which private indi-

---

[1] FIDES AVGVST. S. C. Good Faith, standing, holding some ears of corn and a basket of fruit. Large bronze of Plotina.

viduals honor not only by associating themselves with the public ceremonies of their worship, but by particular devotions to such and such a divinity, by sacrifices at such and such a temple. In

1. *Lituus*, or augur's baton. 2. *Secespita*, or sacrificial knife. 3. *Patera*. 4. Sacrificial vase, wrongly confounded with the *praefericulum*, which had no handle. 5. *Simpulum*, small cup employed in libations. 6. Sprinkler. 7. *Apex*, or flamen's cap. 8. Tripod surmounted by the *cortina*. 9. Axe with wolf's head, for killing great victims.

INSTRUMENTS OF SACRIFICE; TAKEN FROM VARIOUS COINS IN THE CABINET DE FRANCE.

addressing one of the gods of the city, there is no need of a mediator. "The Aruspicium," says Varro,[1] "enjoins that each should sacrifice according to his own custom, — *suo quisque ritu sacrificium faciat;*" and this principle constituted the religious tolerance of the Romans, so long as they did not believe that the state was threatened by particular religions. When the father of the family, who

---

[1] *De Ling. Lat.* vii. 38. Cicero also says, *ritus familiae patrumque* . . . that must be preserved, *adis quasi traditam religionem*. (*De Leg.* ii. 11.)

was sovereign pontiff in his own house, had recourse to the priest, it was to assure himself that he properly carried out all the rites, and employed the forms necessary to constrain the divine will in his favor.[1] Hence it resulted that all the priests, though appointed for life[2] and forming particular colleges, remained, as senators and magistrates, active members of society, and as citizens subject to the law and its representatives.[3]

If then religion and its ministers were, at Rome, closely connected with political matters, it was not by ruling them, but in remaining subordinate to them. This dependence lasted as long as pagan Rome; thence came her superiority in government and her inferiority in art and poetry, which in Greece were born in the precincts of the temples.

Neither special knowledge nor peculiar vocation was required of those who desired to be priests. If Rome had a clergy, she had no sacerdotal class possessing great wealth or receiving tithes; and no religious interest was recognized apart from state interest. The augurs could only consult auspices on the order of the magistrates; and it was forbidden to reveal an oracle to the people unless the Senate had authorized it.[5]

ANCILIA, OR SHIELDS OF MARS.[4]

"Our ancestors," says Cicero, "were never wiser or better inspired by the gods than when they settled that the same persons should preside over religion and the government of the Republic.

---

[1] M. Bouché-Leclercq (*Les Pontifes de l'ancienne Rome*) very justly remarks that at Rome the priest only figures in religious solemnities as the master of ceremonies.

[2] Pliny, *Ep.* iv. 8.

[3] Only the *duumviri sacris faciundis*, afterward the decemvirs, the interpreters of the Sibylline Books, the flamen of Jupiter, and, after the commencement of the Republic, the *rex sacrorum*, could fulfil no other public charge. The Vestals were also devoted to the altar; yet they could, after thirty years of duty, re-enter civil life. The pontiff and augurs once claimed to be exempt from the taxes imposed on other citizens; but the quaestors forced them to pay. (Livy, xxxiii. 42.)

[4] Taken from a gem in the collection of Florence.

[5] Dionys., xxxix. 5.

By this means magistrates and pontiffs unite to save the state."[1] There was, then, no dependence of either of these two powers upon the other. The state and religion were one, and as later the different functions of these innumerable gods could quite logically become simple attributes of one divinity, the state did not feel itself threatened by the elastic interpretation of creeds; and there existed at Rome, when philosophic thought was brought thither from Greece, that religious liberty which churches with precise dogmas will not and cannot recognize.

The most highly honored of these priests were the three flamens, or *lighters* of the altars of Jupiter, Mars, and Quirinus, who could not appear in public or in the open air, even in the courtyard of their houses, without the *apex*, the sign of their priesthood;[2] the three augurs,[3] the sacred interpreters of omens; the Vestals, guardians of the public hearth, the fire whereof must never die; the twelve Salii, or leapers,[5] keepers of the *Ancilia*, who every year in the month of March danced the war-dance, and as soon as war was declared, entered the temple of the "God who slays," to strike his bronze shield with their pikes, crying, "Mars, awake!" the twelve Fratres Arvales, or brothers of the fields, priests of Dea-Dia, a Telluric divinity; and finally the four pontiffs,[6] who, free from all control, and rendering no

FRATER ARVALIS.[4]

---

[1] *Pro domo*, i.

[2] The same obligation was imposed on the Salii. Cf. the fragment of Fabius Pictor, above quoted (page 220).

[3] Afterward four, then nine, in the year 300 B. C.; finally fifteen under Sulla and sixteen under Caesar. I do not speak of the aruspices, who did not form a college in the state. They were diviners, whom generals took with them, and whom private individuals consulted.

[4] For the ceremonies of their worship, the Arvales surrounded their heads with a crown of ears of corn, held together by fillets of white wool. The head of their college was called *magister*, and under the Empire the Emperors took the office. The figure given above represents Marcus Aurelius as a Frater Arvalis.

[5] On the first day of the month, which bore the name of their god, the Salii passed through the quarters of Rome, stopping before the aedicula, or resting places, to perform their rites. This procession, which lasted several days, was interspersed with dances and songs in honor of the gods; perhaps, too, in honor of some great citizens. In the time of Varro (*de Ling. Lat.* vii. 3) no one any longer understood the *Saliaria carmina* and *axementa*.

[6] Four at first, then eight; fifteen under Sulla, and an indefinite number under the Empire.

account to either Senate or people, watched, under the presidency of the high pontiff, over the maintenance of the laws and religious institutions; they also settled the calendar, and which days were lucky or unlucky, — thus rendering the administration of justice and the holding of the comitia to a certain extent dependent upon them. On the day that the new moon showed her golden sickle in the heavens, one of the pontiffs, called (*calare*) the people together on the Capitol, and taught them how many days to reckon from the kalends to the nones.[1] On the day of the nones another pontiff announced the festivals to be celebrated during the month, — an announcement which is made on Sundays in our churches. Finally, the pontiffs kept the record of sacred acts, phenomena, and all events which appeared to have a religious character; hence came the *Great Annals*.

The Vestals were at first four in number, two for each tribe; after the addition of the *Luceres* there were six. When a vacancy occurred in the college, the King, as chief pontiff, chose twenty young patrician maidens of from six to ten years of age, without any blemish, and who seemed to promise beauty. The lot, as representing the divine will, designated which of them was to be consecrated priestess. When the selection was made, the head pontiff took the hand of the chosen one: "I take thee," he said; "thou shalt be priestess of Vesta, and shalt perform the sacred rites for the safety of the Roman people." Then he led her to the *regia*, the sacerdotal dwelling, where her locks fell beneath the shears,[2] and where her sisters clad her in white. It was our modern taking of the veil.

The virgins of Vesta watched by turns over the maintenance of the fire which burned night and day on her altar. If it should

---

[1] The Roman year seems to have at first counted only ten months, — March, April, May, June, the v., vi., viii., ix., and xth months. Those latter, from the seventh to the tenth, have not changed their name; we still say September, October, November, and December. Livy (i. 19) attributes to Numa the division of the year of 355 days into twelve lunar months, with the insertion of complementary months, which at the end of nineteen years put the lunar year in agreement with the solar. Each month was divided into three parts, the kalends, which marked the first day, the nones (*nonus*, ninth), which comprised the nine days preceding the *ides*, and these (*iduare*, to divide) which began in the middle of the month, the last day of which was called the eve of the kalends.

[2] Pliny, *Nat. Hist.* xvi. 85. The *regia*, which was asserted to be the house of Numa, was the head pontiff's residence; behind it were the *atrium* and temple of Vesta.

happen to go out, it was a terrible omen for Rome; she who had been guilty of the neglect was beaten with rods in a dark place by the chief pontiff, who afterward re-lighted the fire by rubbing together two pieces of wood taken from a tree of good fortune, *felix arbos;* in later times, by concentrating in a metal vase the rays of the sun.[1] They had to make libations, offer sacrifices, and perform a strange ceremony, which doubtless had some connection with their vow of virginity. When, on the 15th of April, the pontiffs immolated thirty pregnant cows, the embryos were taken and committed to the Chief Vestal, who burned them and carefully kept the cinders, which she distributed among the people on the day of the Palilia, that they might make expiatory offerings of them.[3] Every morning they cleansed the temple with water drawn from the fountain of Egeria in a vessel with a large mouth and ending in a point, *futile,* so that it could not be set down on the ground without the water being spilled. They had the protection of Fascinus, the god who averts evil spells, and that of the holy relics, pledges of the duration of empire, *fatale pignus imperii.*[5] These relics, preserved in the most secret place of the sanctuary, were the Palladium, a shapeless statuette of Pallas, and the fetiches which were said to have been brought from Samothrace to Troy by Dardanus, and from Troy to Italy by Aeneas. The Chief Vestal, *maxima virgo,* alone penetrated this holy of holies.

VESTAL.[2]

FUTILE, VASE OF THE VESTALS.[4]

Their functions lasted thirty years, at the end of which the Vestals could re-enter the world, and even marry; but very few took advantage of this right; they ended their lives near the goddess to whom they had vowed their virginity. As a compen-

---

[1] Dionys. ii. 67; Plut., *Numa,* 10; Festus, s. v. *Penus Vestae.* The *arbores felices* were, however, rather numerous,—the oak, the holm-oak, the beech, the mountain-ash.

[2] Taken from the *Cabinet de France.*

[3] Ovid, *Fast.* iv. 629, *seq.* Mention has been made (page 189) of the twenty *argei,* or figures of men in wicker-work, which were thrown by the Vestals into the Tiber every year.

[4] Servius (*ad Aen.* xi. 339) asserts that hence comes the word *futilis,* designating a man incapable of keeping what is confided to him. Taken from the *Catalogue Durand* by M. de Witte.

[5] Livy, xxvi. 27.

sation for this sacrifice, they received the greatest respect and enjoyed great honors. Free from all ties of relationship, that is, released from paternal restraint, *patria potestas*, and from the guardianship of their kin, they could receive legacies and dispose of their goods by testament. In courts of justice they made depositions without being obliged to take the oath. On meeting them, the magistrate had the fasces lowered; and the criminal being led to punishment was set free, provided they declared they had accidentally crossed his path.

THE PALLADIUM.[1]

But, on the other hand, what a horrible death if they broke their vow! At the extremity of the Quirinal, between the Colline gate and the place where afterward stood the famous gardens of Sallust, was the "accursed field," *campus sceleratus*. There was dug an underground chamber, wherein the guilty priestess was to be buried alive. Placed on the bier, which was surrounded with thick coverings to stifle her cries, she was borne with mournful pomp across the Forum, through the silent crowd, to the vault, wherein were placed a bed, a lighted lamp, some bread, a little water, milk, and oil, provisions for one day, in an eternal prison, the mocking help of a piety unwilling to have to give an account to Vesta of the murder of one of her virgins! When the funeral train had arrived at the place of torture the high priest uttered secret prayers; then the bier was opened, and, wrapped in her white veils as in a shroud, the victim descended by a ladder into her tomb, the opening of which was speedily covered by the slaves. The earth was studiously levelled, in order that nothing might reveal the place where, in the dark night and cold of the grave, the Vestal expiated a sacrilege which perchance she had never committed. No one came there to make those libations which the poorest offered to the Manes.[2] She was cut off at once from the world of the living and of the dead.

When the sentence was accomplished, the crowd slowly melted

[1] After a silver coin of the Julian family.
[2] In the time of Plutarch, however (*Quaest. Rom.* 96), the priests came thither to perform expiations.

away, some deeply moved by the terrible end of a beautiful and noble girl, devoted from infancy to a dread office; the greater number convinced that evils which had threatened Rome had been averted by a necessary sacrifice.

Vesta did not always abandon her priestesses. Aemilia was about to be condemned to death for having intrusted the duty of keeping up the sacred fire to a novice who had let it go out. After having implored the goddess, the Vestal tore a strip from her robe and threw it on the cold cinders, when the fire blazed up again.[1] Another, Tuccia, accused of incest, cried out: "O Vesta! if I have ever approached thy altar with clean hands, grant me a sign to prove my innocence;" and taking a sieve, she went down to the Tiber, filled it with water, and came back again to pour it at the feet of the pontiffs.[2] An engraved gem has preserved the remembrance of this miracle, for each college of priests made a point of having one of its own; and these legends, by attesting divine intervention, freed the conscience of the Romans from the remorse of having condemned the innocent to a frightful death, when their merciless policy demanded a victim to calm popular terror.

THE VESTAL TUCCIA.[3]

The honors paid to the Vestal virgins corresponded with the religious importance of the worship which took place round this public hearth, whereon the fire must never go out.[4] But to the religious idea which had at first determined the conditions imposed on the priestesses was added, as a natural consequence, a moral idea, — only virgins could keep it up. This eternal flame, which symbolized the very life of the Roman people, and the institution of the College of Vestals, was an involuntary glorification of chastity; and in the days of faith this belief must have had a happy influence on manners.

---

[1] Dionys., ii. 68; Val. Max., I. i. 7. [2] Val. Max., VIII. i. 5; Pliny, *Nat. Hist.* xxviii. 2.
[3] Montfaucon, *Ant. Expl.* i. pl. xxviii., *Supplem.* i. pl. xxiii.
[4] Cic., *De Leg.* ii. 8 : *ignem foci publici sempiternum*.

The twenty *fetiales*, elected for life, and taken from the most noble families, formed a college at once political and religious, which presided over international acts. When Rome thought she had a right to complain of some nation, a fetialis — called, for the occasion, the *pater patratus* of the Roman people — was sent out. He set forth, on his head a fillet of white wool and a crown of vervain, which he had culled on the Capitol. When he arrived at the enemy's frontier he cried: "Hear me, Jupiter! Hear me, God of boundaries! And thou, sacred oracle of right (*fas*), hear. I am the messenger of the Roman people; I come in all justice, and my words deserve all trust." Then he enumerated the grievances of the Romans, bearing witness by solemn imprecations that they were well founded. "If it is against right and my conscience that I demand these persons and these things to be delivered up to me, the messenger of the Roman people, may Jupiter never permit me to return into my country." Advancing into the enemy's country, he addressed the same words to the first inhabitant whom he met, then to those whom he found at the gates of the principal city, and finally in the forum to the magistrates. If, at the end of thirty-three days, satisfaction had not been accorded him, he cried: "Hearken, Jupiter, and thou, Janus Quirinus, and all ye gods of heaven, earth, and the lower regions, I take you to witness that this nation is unjust and violates right. How shall we avenge outraged right? Our old men will decide." And he returned to Rome. If the Senate and people decided to have recourse to arms, the fetialis went back to the enemy's frontier bearing a javelin, the end of which had been burned and reddened in blood, and there cast this threat of fire and carnage, announcing at the same time the opening of hostilities. At a later period, and until the time of the Empire, when the enemy was on the Elbe and Euphrates, the fetialis performed the same ceremonies, but without going out of Rome. On the Field of Mars, near the Temple of Bellona, rose the *column of war*, which represented the limit of the Roman frontier. There the fetialis cast his

VESTALS ROUND THE ALTAR.[1]

---

[1] Gold coin from the *Cabinet de France*.

bloody javelin, and Rome thought she had conscientiously performed all the rites which obliged the gods to grant her victory.

At the sacrifice offered on the conclusion of a treaty, the fetialis killed the victim with a flint stone, — the stone whence sparks flashed, and which, on account of this property, was often placed in the hand of Jupiter, instead of the darts which represented lightning-flashes.[1]

The greater number of sacerdotal colleges filled up vacancies by co-option, that is to say, the survivors made the election.[2] This was one means of preserving secret the traditions of the corporation. The flamens were designated, like the Vestals, by the chief pontiff.

To aid the priests in the holy ceremonies there were associated with them children of noble family and perfect beauty, to whom was given the name of *camilli*, borne by Mercury, the messenger of the gods.[4] The divinities of Greece, especially also those of Rome, were thought to be much impressed by beauty, which was one of their gifts. They exacted it in their priests, and were offended if they were not served by the most perfect attendance; *e. g.* Juno, who, "in the belief of many," says Valerius Maximus,[5] "made Varro lose the battle of Cannae because he had given the care of the temple of Jupiter Capitolinus to a most beautiful young man, whom she wished to see attached to her own altar." We have preserved somewhat of this respect for the work of God in those who consecrate themselves to his service; certain bodily defects are an obstacle to ordination.

CAMILLUS.[3]

The expenses of worship and the maintenance of the priests

---

[1] Arnobius, vi. 25.
[2] Cicero, *Phil.* xiii. 5, and *Brut.* 1.
[3] This Camillus, or servitor of the pontiffs, seems to carry the sprinkler in his left hand, and in his right the *situla*, or pail, containing the water necessary for the ceremony.
[4] *Pueri seu puellae, ingenui, felicissimi, patrimi matrimique.* Cf. Fest., s. v. *Flaminius*.
[5] I. i. 16.

were provided for by a certain tract of land assigned to each temple.[1] In later times the state even allowed a subsidy.[2]

The domestic worship of certain families also made part of the public worship of the city; as, for instance, the *Lupercalia*, of which the *gentes* Fabia and Quinctia held the hereditary priesthood, and the sacrifices in honor of Hercules,[3] which must be performed by Pinarians or Potitians.

V. Public Festivals.

The festivals, like the gods, were innumerable; for in all ages the Italian has loved religious services, as being a break in the monotony of ordinary life, an occasion for pious ceremonies, noisy games, and meals in which the poor spent the savings of a whole week. It will here suffice to point out a few which display in a distinctive manner the customs of ancient times.

Certain festivals, still celebrated in the time of Caesar,[4] and long after, recalled the rural life, coarse manners, and selfish devotion of the Romans. From Pales they asked what their descendants asked of Saint Antony, the health of their flocks; of Lupercus, the god-wolf who protected the farm against the terrible beast whose name he bore, they asked their increase; of Dea-Dia, an abundant harvest. On the day of the Lupercalia, the priests ran half-naked through the town, armed with whips, the thongs of which were made with the skin of the deer and of dogs offered in sacrifice to the god of fertility, and with them they struck all whom they met, especially the women, who, by submitting, thought to escape the opprobrium of sterility, or to insure themselves a happy delivery. On the Palilia, the shepherds jumped thrice over a burning haycock, and made their animals go through the pungent smoke.

---

[1] Dionys., ii. 7; Festus, s. v. *Oscum*; Siculus Flacc., *de Cond. Agror.* p. 23, ed. Goes.

[2] To the Vestals (Livy, i. 20); to the augurs (Dionys., ii. 6); and probably to other colleges. The Vestals, the *pontifex maximus*, and the *rex sacrorum* had moreover a *domus publica*, or residence granted by the state.

[3] The Roman Hercules, who was identical with the Sabine Sancus, and was also the God of Good Faith (*mehercule*), because he was the strong god, took the name of Recaranus, or Garanus. (Aur. Vic., *Orig.* 6; Serv., *ad Aen.* vi. 203.)

[4] Plut., *Caes.* 61.

RELIGION AND RELIGIOUS INSTITUTIONS.

These were the fires of purification. The *Ambarvalia*, or lustrations of the fields, were performed in the name of the state by the Fratres Arvales before the wheat fell under the sickle, and the festival was renewed around each property. The proprietor, with his head bound round with an oak branch and followed by his kindred and slaves, passed three times round his estate, dancing and singing hymns to the Italian Ceres.

"God of our fathers, we purify our fields and those who till them. Drive away evil from our lands; let not the evil weed choke the promised harvest; let not the slow sheep be in fear of

ANIMALS BEING LED TO THE SACRIFICE OF THE SUOVETAURILIUM.[2] BAS-RELIEF FOUND NEAR THE COLUMN OF PHOCAS.

the swift wolf."[1] Libations of milk and honeyed wine, — a sacrifice and a feast at which the victim was eaten, — terminated these pagan supplications.

The *Amburbalia* were the purification of the town. Along the walls, led by the priests and preceded by the victims, rolled the long procession of citizens, who in honor of the solemn day were clad in spotless togas and crowned with leaves. When the hymns had ceased, when the victims had fallen under the sacred knife, and the portion set apart for the gods had been burned on the altar, these latter owed protection to the gates and walls.

The people themselves, at the end of the lustrum, were purified

---

[1] Tibullus, II. i. 17, *seq.*; cf. Verg., *Georg.* i. 336-350.
[2] This word is formed from the name of the three victims, — the hog, *sus*; the sheep, *ovis*; and the bull, *taurus*.

by an expiatory sacrifice. Being convoked by the herald, they assembled in the Field of Mars, whither the King, "scented with myrrh and sweet-smelling plants," had resorted at daybreak with the servitors, who led a hog, a sheep, and a bull. Three times he made the round of the assembly, repeating hymns and prayers; then he immolated the victims, and the *suovetaurile*[1] was performed. Songs, prayers, offerings, were all these good-natured gods demanded to keep them at peace with their people.

In grave circumstances, during a pestilence or amidst some public misfortune, they admitted their people to communion with them. Their statues were carried to a table ready spread; the gods were laid upon couches, as at the Roman meals, the goddesses were placed sitting; and the popular imagination, highly excited by danger, saw them accept the feast, or sometimes turn away their heads from it in anger.[1] Is it to some memory of these stony guests, still preserved in Spain, that the terrible legend of the commendatore (in Don Juan), *el Convidado de piedra*,[3] is due?

STATE BED FOR THE FESTIVAL OF LECTISTERNIUM.[2]

Such Gods and such festivals show the Roman revelling, like the Greek, in that intoxication with nature which the great enchantress had offered to all the Aryan race, — an intoxication delightful and fruitful for the sons of Homer and Plato, oppressive and barren for the sons of Romulus; for the former found therein a lovely and sublime ideal, which the latter never knew, and of which they only caught a glimpse on the days when they ceased to be Romans.

[1] Livy, xl. 59.
[2] Silver coin of the family of Caelia, with the names of L. Caldus, *septemvir epulonum*, and C. Caldus, monetary *triumvir*.
[3] Magnien, *Les Origines du Théâtre*, i. 252.

REVERSE OF A BRONZE PIECE OF FAUSTINA THE YOUNGER. VESTA HOLDING THE PALLADIUM AND THE CUP FOR LIBATIONS.

CHAPTER IV.

CHANGES IN RELIGION AND CONSTITUTION UNDER THE THREE LAST KINGS.

I. THE GODS OF ETRURIA AT ROME; REFORMS OF TARQUIN THE ELDER.

THE third and fourth kings of Rome are repetitions of the two first: Tullus is a new Romulus, Ancus a second Numa, — a suspicious symmetry which is repugnant to history, but in which legend delights. Legend, however, attributes a special characteristic to Tullus: he completes the city, by giving it its military institutions, — *militaris rei institutor*.[1]

The reign of the three last kings marks, on the other hand, a new era. Whatever may be the cause, — be it the peaceful or forcible settlement of some Etruscan chief, or a long period, unknown to us, which prepared the transformation, — it is certain that the city, whose territory was only six miles long by two broad, has become a great town, which covers the seven hills, and erects monumental buildings, which counts its inhabitants by the hundred thousand, and extends its power afar; and finally, which replaces ancient simplicity by the splendor of its feasts, its fetich gods by the great Etruscan divinities, and their modest altars by the Capitol with its hundred steps.

Whether it was a heritage of the Pelasgi, or, more probably, borrowed from the Greek colonies of Italy through the medium of the Campanian Etruscans, the gods of Greece were greatly honored in the southern cities of Etruria. Thence they came to Rome. Tarquin the Elder, it is said, drove all the gods

---

[1] Orosius, ii. 4. Florus, i. 3, also says: *hic omnem militarem disciplinam artemque bellandi condidit.*

236   ROME UNDER THE KINGS.

of Numa from the Tarpeian, in order to raise a temple there to the great celestial family, Jupiter, Juno, and Minerva. Youth alone and the god Terminus opposed it; for the Roman people was never to grow old, nor its frontiers to recede. Ceres, who was identified with Pales, and whose priestess was always a Greek, called from Naples or from Velia (Elea)[1] to do the duties of the sanctuary which was raised to her after the famine of 496 B.C.; Diana, who was confounded with Feronia,

JUNO.   JUPITER.   MINERVA.[3]

the protectress of the common people,[2] to whom Servius built a temple; Vulcan, whom Tatius already honored; Mercury, the plebeian god of the commerce which had arisen, and the eloquence which was to increase, offered a dangerous competition to the native gods. Apollo, Neptune, Cybele, and Venus did not

[1] Cic., *pro Balbo*, 24.
[2] Dionys., iii. 32.
[3] These three bronze statues, found in the excavations of Herculaneum, are of a comparatively recent date.

come till a later period. The first of these was destined to high fortunes. The Sibyl of Cumae, from whom Tarquinius Superbus bought the books, was a priestess of Apollo, the Redeemer, so called because he knew the necessary expiations. Under Augustus, he took his place by the side of the Capitoline Jupiter.

Thus the sphere of religious life goes on enlarging, and it becomes so wide that these innumerable divinities end by being effaced, to make way for the one God of whom they were only the obscure manifestations; but then, too, there comes a new society, new ideas, new laws; in fact, another world.

As if the gods of Greece carried art with them, their entrance into Rome was marked by the first effort to give to the immortals dwellings less modest and an appearance less rude. Tuscan workmen built the great temple of the Capitol, and the Etruscan Turrianus modelled in clay the statue of Jupiter which Tarquin placed there.[1]

AUGUR.[2]

Etruria moreover gave something else which properly belonged to her. The miracle of the Tuscan Navius diffused respect for the augurs through the city. No doubt the epoch when Rome adopted so many Etruscan customs, was that also of the introduction of the science of augury as the religion of the state. It was a surer means of government, inasmuch as both governors and governed put sincere faith in it. In order to study this mysterious art, some young patricians were sent to Etruria, and for a long time the augurs were only taken from the noblest families, from those whose members filled the Senate and the magistracy. The augur, in fact, was to be at once a sincere[3] priest and a shrewd politician: the latter

---

[1] Legendary history explains all these Etruscan importations by the conquest which Tarquin the Elder made of Etruria. Otf. Müller reverses this proposition, and makes the Etruscans conquer Rome and Latium; but what is not contested is, that the epoch of the Tarquins was marked by the preponderating influence in Rome of Etruscan civilization,—so much so that the greater part of the Greek historians, says Dionysius of Halicarnassus (i. 29), regarded Rome as a Tyrrhenian town, Τυρρηνίδα πόλιν εἶναι ὑπέλαβον.

[2] At the feet of the priest who holds the augur's rod is seen the sacred chicken, whose more or less keen appetite served as an augury.

[3] At an epoch when faith was much shaken, Tiberius Gracchus reading, in the depths of

inspiring the former and making him unconsciously report from heaven the divine decree most conformable to the interests of the state.[1]

This belief in signs ended by making the Romans the most religious people in the universe. "It was," said Polybius, "one of the causes of her greatness." And the friend of Scipio is right; for this blind piety, if it did not gain the favor of the gods, at least assured the power of the aristocracy, by keeping the people dependent on the most experienced and the wisest class. Besides, in spite of their belief in the augurs, the Roman nobility and its Senate never abandoned earthly things for religion till human prudence had nothing left to do. In case of need, they altered fatal presages by the freest interpretations, without their faith being alarmed thereat. A consul was about to engage in battle, and the diviner announced happy omens; he was mistaken, the signs were contrary. "That concerns him," said the consul, "and not me or my army, to whom favorable auspices have been promised;" and he engaged in action. At the first encounter the diviner fell; but the consul was victorious.

It was Tarquin the Elder, too, who first laid hands on the old constitution, not to change it, but to broaden its foundations. In spite of the opposition of the patricians and of the augur Navius, he formed a hundred new patrician families, whose chiefs entered the Senate (*patres minorum gentium*). Were these the richest and noblest of the plebeians, or only the chiefs of the Luceres,

---

Spain, the books which treated of sacred things, discovered that, as president of the consular comitia, he had omitted one of the rites. He hastened to make known this mistake to the college of augurs, who immediately informed the Senate of it, and the two consuls were obliged to abdicate. (Val. Max., I. i. 3 ; Plut., *Marc.* 5.)

[1] *Auguriis sacerdotioque augurum tantus honos accessit, ut nihil belli domique postea nisi auspicato gereretur.* (Livy, i. 36.) The augurs had the right of declaring the auspices to be contrary. *Comitiatus et concilia, vel instituta, dimittere, vel habita rescindere ... decernere ut magistratu se abdicent consules.* ... (Cic., *de Leg.* ii. 12.) The magistrates had to consult them for all their enterprises, and *quique non paruerit, capital esto.* (Id., *de Leg.* ii. 8.) But prodigies were only referred to the augurs by the order of the Senate, *si Senatus jussit, deferunto.* (*Ibid.* ii. 9.) "The science of augury," says Cicero elsewhere, "has been preserved for state reasons": *Jus augurum etsi divinationis opinione principio constitutum sit, tamen postea rei publicae causa conservatum ac retentum.* (*De Divin.* ii. 35.) In *De Republica*, ii. 10 and 9, he says of Romulus: *Quum haec egregia duo firmamenta rei publicae peperisset, auspicia et Senatum ... id quod retinemus hodie magna cum salute rei publicae.* ... The necessary information about the augurs will be found in Saglio's *Dict. des Antiq. Gr. et Rom.*, pp. 550-560, and about the auspices, *Ibid.*, pp. 580-583.

until this time kept out of the Senate, and now admitted to it by Tarquin, the foreign king? The increase in the number of Vestals, from four to six, would seem to confirm the opinion that he sought to raise the third tribe to an equality with the original two. Cicero, however, affirms that the patriciate was doubled;[1] and Livy, narrating the creation of three new centuries of knights, calls them *Ramnenses, Titienses,* and *Luceres posteriores*. Thus we have the first and second rank of Ramnenses, Titienses, and Luceres;[2] as later there was a division in the Senate, which is not very clearly understood, of *patres majorum* and *patres minorum gentium,* the latter voting after the former. The method of change is not important, the main fact being undoubted that the patriciate was radically modified by Tarquin; and we may consider this as a preparatory step towards the great reforms introduced by Servius.

II. Reforms of Servius Tullius.

WE have seen[3] that the Romans represented their sixth king as specially under protection of the gods. The Emperor Claudius, who composed a history of the Etruscans, said on one occasion in the Senate: "Our writers maintain that Servius was the son of a slave named Ocrisia, while Etruscan annals represent him as the companion-in-arms of Caeles Vibenna, and sharing all the latter's adventures. Driven out of Etruria by some unfortunate turn of events, these two chiefs established themselves, with what remained of their army, upon the Caelian hill, which took its name from Caeles Vibenna. Servius, who in Etruria had borne the name of Mastarna, now adopted the one by which he is known to us. Eventually he became King of Rome, occupying the throne with renown and for the good of the state."[4] A tomb at Vulci,

---

[1] *Duplicavit illum pristinum patrum numerum.* (*De Rep.* ii. 20.) Cf. Livy, i. 36; Val. Max., III. iv. 2.

[2] Livy, i. 36, *aa finem.* — *Civitas Romana in sex erat distributa partes,* in *primos secundosque Titienses, Ramnenses, et Luceres.* (Festus, s. v. *Sex suffragia.*) Hence six Vestals, *Ut populus pro sua quaque parte haberet et ministram sacrorum.* (Fest., s. v. *Sex Vestae Sacerdotes.*) This number was never changed again. Cf. Cic., *de Div.* i. 17; Dionys., iii. 71.

[3] Page 161.

[4] This discourse of Claudius, of which Tacitus has given the substance, is engraved on two

discovered about twenty years since,[1] confirms the recital of the imperial historian, or proves, at least, that this was a national legend in Etruria. Upon a wall of the tomb are represented two figures: one, who extends his bound hands, the other, who cuts the thong, and holds under his arm the sword with which he is about to arm his friend. Their names are written above their heads; Caeles Vibenna is the captive, and his deliverer is Mastarna. Here are the two

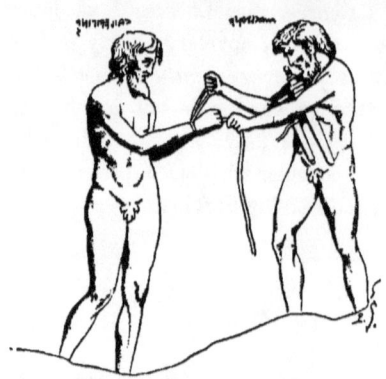

CAELES VIBENNA AND MASTARNA.

companions-in-arms, who after manifold adventures, sometimes perilous like that represented in the picture, arrived in Rome, where one becomes chief of the people of Mars, the other gives his name to the Caelian hill. It is easy to understand that Roman pride would greatly prefer the favorite of their great gods to this Etruscan adventurer, seeking fortune at the point of his sword.

This adventurer was, however, a man of peace. But one war is ascribed to him, a not very well authenticated campaign against the people of Veii,[2] which Dionysius of Halicarnassus transforms into a victory over the whole Etruscan nation. Servius is, above all, the legislator. But shall we say that the constitution which bears his name was really his own, or that it was the work of the time? This reformation, which still lasted as long as Roman liberty endured, must have sprung, not from the mind of one man, but from social and public needs. The patricians, or original

tables of bronze found at Lyons in 1524 by a peasant who was trenching his vineyard. [It is now to be found appended to most good editions of Tacitus' *Annals.—Ed.*]

[1] In 1857, in the same funeral chamber at Vulci in which Achilles was represented sacrificing some Trojan captives (see p. 68). The lucumo who had been laid there had without doubt some similar brother-in-arms; for the two pictures express the same idea, — the devotion of a warrior towards the friend who followed him in battle: Achilles avenges Patroclus, and Mastarna delivers Caeles. These followships in war must be an Etruscan custom. (Cf. Noël des Vergers, *Revue archéol.*, 1863, p. 462.) [They were, as we know, an old Greek custom, especially in Sparta and among the Abantes of Euboea. — *Ed.*]

[2] Livy, i. 42. [This does not agree with the researches of V. Gardthausen (*Mastarna*, p. 44), who shows that his rule was a military revolt against Etruria by an Etrurian leader of the Latins. — *Ed.*]

people who at first alone formed the army, must have been constrained, for safety's sake, to call in the plebeians gradually to serve with them in the legions. Servius doubtless did nothing but regulate the new state of things which insensibly sprang up; he does not the less merit that his name should remain attached to this great institution.

We will speak, then, of this prince as the ancients spoke of him, conceding to him, with the preceding reservation, the honor of having been the legislator of royal and republican Rome.

We know that the plebeians had neither the right of voting (*jus suffragii*), nor the right of intermarriage or exchange (*jus connubii et commercii*) with the patrician families, but that they enjoyed personal liberty. Since Romulus, their number had constantly increased;[1] for his successors had remained faithful to the policy of drawing the vanquished to Rome, to augment its military population. Until Servius, the plebeians remained without direction and without unity. These men of different origins might, however, combine, and some day become dangerous. The prince, himself of foreign birth, who feared the enmity of the patricians, understood what help this numerous and oppressed people would be to him. He took away from the patricians a part of the land that they had usurped from the public domain, and distributed to each chief of a plebeian family *seven jugera* (4⅝ acres) with full Roman rights; and he forced the aristocracy, already shaken by the innovations of Tarquin, to receive plebeians as members of the same city.

He used two means to attain this end: the *tribes* and the *centuries*, that is to say, the administrative and military organization of the state. He divided the Roman territory[2] into 26 regions, and the town into 4 quarters; in all, 30 tribes. This entirely geographical division was also religious, for he instituted festivals for each district, — the *Compitalia* for the plebs of the city tribes, the *Paganalia* for the country tribes. It was

---

[1] Romulus was said to have established at Rome the inhabitants of Caenina, Antemnae, Crustumerium (Dionys., ii. 35); Tullus, the Albans (Livy, i. 29); Ancus, the Latins of Politorium, Ficana, Tellenae, Medullia, etc. (Livy, i. 33.)

[2] Livy, i. 43.

administrative, for each district had its judges for civil matters,[1] its tribune (*curator tribus*) to keep account of the fortunes, and to assess the taxes; and lastly, it was military, for these tribunes also regulated the military service of their tribesmen, and in case of sudden invasion collected them in a fort built in the centre of the canton.[2] The state was composed, then, of 30 *communes* (parishes), having their chiefs, their judges, their particular gods, but no political rights, these rights being only exercised in the capital. Without touching the privileges of the patricians, Servius secured to the plebeians that municipal organization which must precede, and which introduces, political liberty. As the patricians gave their name to all the tribes except one, we have the right to conclude that they preserved their influence in the cantons where their estates were, and that they probably filled all the offices of judges and municipal tribunes. But for the first time they found themselves confounded with the plebeians in a territorial division in which birth and traditions were omitted. That alone was enough to cause a revolution. A time will come when these tribes desire and obtain political rights. That will be the victory of numbers; the centuries secured that of wealth.

Servius had made the census, or numbering, which was for the future to be renewed every five years (*lustrum*). Each citizen came to declare under oath his name, his age, his family, the number of his slaves, and the value of his possessions.[3] A false declaration would have led to the loss of property, liberty, and even of life.[4] Knowing thus all men's fortunes, he divided citizens, in proportion to their property, into five classes, and each class into a different number of centuries. Dionysius speaks of six classes, and assigns to the first 98 centuries, whilst the five others together had only 95. In each class there were the *juniores*, from 17 to 45 years of age, who composed the active army, and the

---

[1] Ἰδιώτας δικαστάς. (Dionys., iv. 25.) These judges doubtless formed the tribunal of the centumvirs, as the curators of the tribes formed the college of the tribunes of the treasury.

[2] Varro, *de Ling. Lat.* vi. 36.

[3] The census gave (Livy, i. 44) 80,000 citizens fit to bear arms, or, according to Dionysius (iv. 22), 85,300: ὡς ἐν τοῖς τιμητικοῖς φέρεται γράμμασιν.

[4] Some critics think that the valuation of cattle, slaves, and ready money was not required for the *census* until after the censorship of Appius, in 312. The ancient declaration would in that case have been more favorable to the aristocracy, since, for the division into classes, account would only have been taken of landed property.

CHANGES UNDER THE THREE LAST KINGS.   243

seniores, from 46 to 60, who formed the reserve. The first class thus contained 40 centuries of *seniores*, 40 of *juniores*, and, besides, 18 centuries of knights; that is to say, the 6 equestrian centuries of Tarquin (*sex suffragia*), and 12 new ones, formed by Servius of the richest and most influential plebeians. The state gave to each of these 1,800 knights a horse, and allowed for his maintenance an annual stipend (*aes hordearium*), which the orphans and unmarried women paid.[1] To the second class were attached two centuries of workmen (*fabri*), and to the fourth two of musicians (*tubicines*).[2] The poor, *capite censi*, formed the sixth class, and a single century, which did not serve in the legions.[3]

The total of the army was 170 centuries of foot-soldiers, 18 of horse-soldiers, 4 of musicians and workmen.[4]

Cicero, in the much-discussed passage in the second book of the *Republic*, only speaks of five classes, formed of *assidui* (*assesdare*, tax-payers[5]). To the first he assigns 89 centuries; to the four others, 104: in all, 193, as in the calculation of Dionysius, and one less than in that of Livy. The proletariate, whose census did not amount to 12,500 asses, *accensi* and *velati*,[6] followed the legions unarmed, to replace the dead, to skirmish, or to do orderly service. The poorest, *capite censi*, who were only counted on the register of

---

[1] This custom existed at Corinth. (Cic., *de Rep.* ii. 20.) *Orba* signified both widow and unmarried woman.

[2] Dionysius (iv. 16–19) gives the census of the first class at 100 minae (about £380). Pliny (xxxiii. 3) assigns to it 110,000 asses; Aulus Gellius (vii. 13), 125,000; Festus, 120,000; Livy (i. 43), 100,000. These figures are of a date posterior to the sixth century of Rome. From the time of Servius, the *aes grave*, or the *as libral*, was a pound weight of bronze, and there was then in Rome no one whose goods would represent 100,000 pounds of bronze, whether the value of 1,000 oxen, or of 100 war-horses, or 10,000 sheep. (Festus, s. v. *Peculatus*.) The basis of the census was doubtless the *jugerum* (2 roods, 19 poles), or what a pair of oxen could plough in a day. The *jugerum* was estimated later at 5,000 asses, which supposes 20 *jugera* for the first class, 15, 10, 5, and 2 or 2½ for the others. As for the *as libral* of 12 ounces, it was successively reduced, about 268 B. C., to 4 ounces; about 241, to 2; in 217, by the Flaminian law, to 1; in 89, by the law Plautia Papiria, to ½.

[3] In grave danger they were armed at the expense of the State:
Proletarius publicitus scutisque feroque
Ornatur ferro. (ENNIUS, in Aulus Gellius, xvi. 10.)
Cf. Fest., s. v. *Accensi*.

[4] It is impossible to admit that the centuries of workmen and musicians, added to the first classes, voted with them. But the constitution of Servius being at first a military organization, there is nothing astonishing in the presence of workmen in the train of the *hoplites*.

[5] In the *mancipatio* there were witnesses representing the five classes of the Roman people.

[6] *Minimae fiduciae*. (Livy, viii. 8.)

the census by the head, like slaves and cattle, did not serve. Marius was the first who called them to the standards; and from that day the army lost its national character.

LIST OF LIVY.[1]		LIST OF DIONYSIUS.	
Centuries of Knights	18	Centuries of Knights	18
First Class. — 100,000 Asses.		**First Class. — 100 Minae.**	
Centuries of Seniors	40	Centuries of Seniors	40
Centuries of Juniors	40	Centuries of Juniors	40
Centuries of Workmen	2		
Second Class. — 75,000 Asses.		**Second Class. — 75 Minae.**	
Centuries of Seniors	10	Centuries of Seniors	10
Centuries of Juniors	10	Centuries of Juniors	10
		Centuries of Workmen	2
Third Class. — 50,000 Asses.		**Third Class. — 50 Minae.**	
Centuries of Seniors	10	Centuries of Seniors	10
Centuries of Juniors	10	Centuries of Juniors	10
Fourth Class. — 25,000 Asses.		**Fourth Class. — 25 Minae.**	
Centuries of Seniors	10	Centuries of Seniors	10
Centuries of Juniors	10	Centuries of Juniors	10
		Centuries of *Cornicines* and *Tubicines*	2
Fifth Class. — 11,000 Asses.		**Fifth Class. — 12½ Minae.**	
Centuries of Seniors	15	Centuries of Seniors	15
Centuries of Juniors	15	Centuries of Juniors	15
Centuries of *Cornicines* and *Tubicines*	3		
Centuries of *Accensi*		**Sixth Class.**	
Centuries of *Capite Censi*	1	Centuries of *Capite Censi*	1
Total	194	Total	193

The uncertainty of the number of the centuries and of the basis on which the assessment was made, does not prevent us from appreciating the political importance of this military reform. It is no longer birth which divides the citizens into patricians and plebeians; it is by fortune that are now regulated both their distribution into classes, their place in the legions, the nature of their arms, which they must procure for themselves, and the quota of the tax which each of them must pay. All the centuries must

---

[1] The text of Cicero (*de Rep.*, ii. 22), unfortunately mutilated in this place, as in so many others of the *Republic*, does not help us to make Livy's numbers agree with those of Dionysius.

contribute to the treasury according to their census, and later on they exercise, in the Field of Mars, beyond the patrician town, the same political rights. But the first class reckons 98 centuries, although it is much the least numerous, since it only contains the wealthy; it furnishes, then, more than half the tax, and its legionaries, by reason of their small number, are more often called into service. It is also by centuries that, after 510 B. C., votes are taken to decide on peace or war, to appoint to public offices and make the laws. The rich, divided in 98 centuries, have 98 voices out of 193, or the majority, — that is to say, a decisive influence in the government. Their unanimity, secured beforehand on every proposition affecting their interests, must render the rights of the other classes illusory. Sometimes, in case of disagreement between the centuries of the first class, those of the second may be called upon to vote; very rarely those of the third; never those of the last; although each of them contains perhaps more citizens than the three first together. "Servius," said Cicero, "did not desire to give power to mere number; it was by the votes of the rich, not by those of the people, that all was decided."[1] He might have added that the preponderance did not belong to wealth alone, it was given also to wisdom and experience; since the seniors or citizens above 45 years of age — only half as numerous as the juniors, from 17 to 45 years old — possessed as many votes.[2] Finally each had the duty which he could fulfil, and rights in the state were in proportion to duties.

In the new laws rank was as clearly marked as in the old constitution; but this inequality was effaced in the eyes of the poor by the honor of being counted among the number of the citizens and by the material advances made in their condition. If the rich kept political power, on them also weighed the consequent responsibilities: in the city the heaviest share of the tax; in the army the costliest equipment and the most frequent and dangerous service. But, at this time there was at Rome little wealth except landed property. Accordingly, as almost all the *Ager Romanus*

---

[1] Dionys. (iv. 20) also says: πάσης τῆς πολιτείας κύριοι (οἱ πλούσιοι). Livy, i. 43 : *vis omnis penes primores civiatis.* Cf. Dionys., x. 17.

[2] This preponderance of age was found again in the Senate, where the young only spoke after the old.

and the greatest part of conquered lands were in the hands of the patricians, they remained, as before, the masters of the state. These new laws, which recognized the plebeians as free citizens of Rome, and which, as a natural consequence, must some day call them to vote on public affairs, did not, therefore, in reality change the existing condition of the two orders. An immense step, however, was gained; in placing the aristocracy of wealth, — a variable power, accessible to all, — by the side of the aristocracy of birth, — an unalterable power, — these laws were preparing for the revolutions which established in republican Rome union and invincible strength.

This constitution struck another blow at the aristocracy by indirectly attacking clientship. It did not abolish patronage, which gave to the nobles material strength, without which privileges cannot long be defended, but it assured a place in the state to the clients who until then had lived under the protection of the Quirites. It separated them from their patrons on the day of the comitia, to mix them, according to their fortune, with the rich or the poor; it opened the road to the Forum for those who had never followed any but that to the patrician *Atrium*. Another law of Servius authorized the freedmen to return to their country, or, if they remained at Rome, to be inscribed in the city tribes. This law would have equally recognized in plebeians the right of patronage, so that the rich plebeian could from that time show himself in the town, surrounded like a Fabius, by a noisy and devoted band. But clientship becomes weaker by diffusion; and in the course of centuries, Rome, the seat of the empire, is peopled, to the ruin of its institutions, with freed slaves.

This constitution, which was to unite two people hitherto separated, had only been conceived with a view to the army; and the centuries were called the city army, *urbanus exercitus*.[1] The *seniores* guarded the town whilst the *juniores*, or the active army, went to meet the enemy. On the field of battle the legion drew up in serried lines which recalled the Macedonian phalanx.[2] In front

---

[1] The patricians could accept this reform under the title of a military regulation; they were too strong to allow it to be imposed as a political constitution. Nothing short of a revolution which rendered the help of the plebeians necessary to them, could wring this concession from them as payment. (Livy, i. 47.)

[2] Livy, viii. 8. [It may originally have been intended to reward Mastarna's mercenaries. — *Ed.*]

of the enemy, and exposed to the first onset, were the legionaries of the first class, fully clad in defensive armor; behind them, and in a degree shielded by them, were the second, third, and fourth classes (following Livy's list), while those of the fifth class served as skirmishers; and 300 horsemen formed the cavalry attached to each legion.

DIANA WITH THE HIND.

We have seen that the friend of the Roman plebeians was also favorable to the Latin cities, and that he invited them to offer common sacrifices to Diana upon the Aventine.[1] The temple built by the popular king upon this hill, regarded as unlucky in memory of the omens seen there by Remus, was adopted by the slaves as their sanctuary;

---

[1] Dionysius (iv. 26) says that he saw the decree containing the clauses of the alliance engraved on a bronze column in ancient Greek characters.

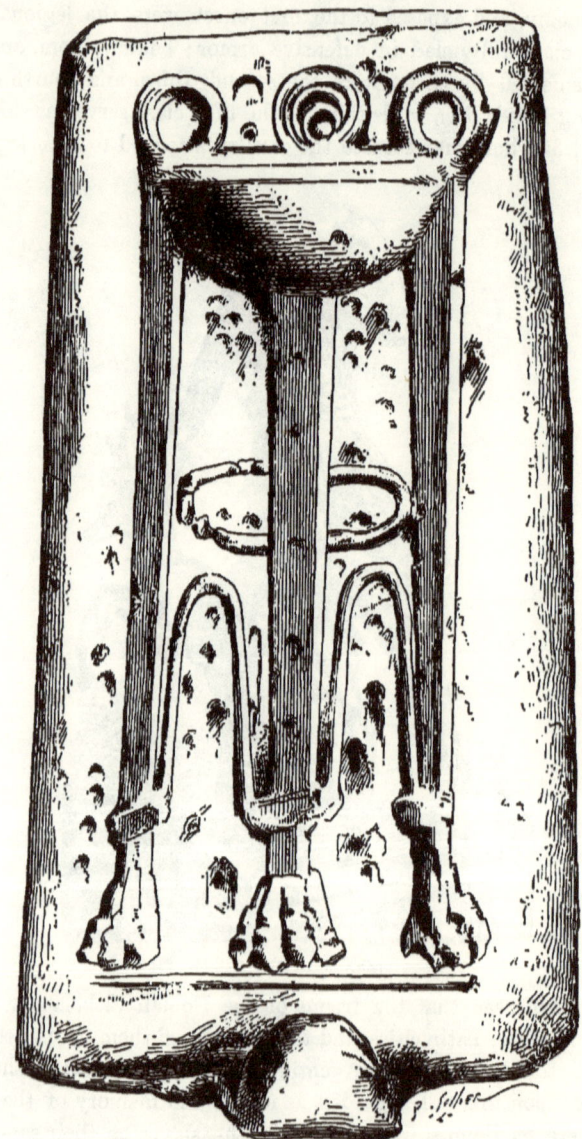

AES SIGNATUM. (ACTUAL SIZE.)

and they offered sacrifices there,[1] but the patricians do not seem to have

[1] Fest., s. v. *Servorum dies*.

admitted this goddess into the national worship, and no public festival was marked with her name in the book of the pontiffs. Of course no vestige of this temple or of the image which it contained, remains. When the Romans were Hellenized, they confounded their Diana, a fierce and eternal virgin, with the Greek Artemis, and gave her the attributes of the latter; their palaces and villas have preserved for us some statues of this goddess, which are among the most beautiful that Greek art ever produced.

Dionysius[1] assures us that besides his constitution Servius promulgated more than fifty laws on contracts, crimes, enfranchisement, the forms of acquiring property, weights and measures, coinage, which he was the first to mark with an impression, — *primus signavit aes*, etc.[2] If Servius is indeed the author of this last novelty, which was not new for the Greeks of Campania and of Southern Italy, it was a great service which he rendered his country, for money is to commerce what writing is to thought, — a powerful means of production.

The laws attributed to the great reformer of Rome seem to have had the same liberal character as his constitution, — that, for example, which Tarquin abolished, and which the people took nearly two centuries to recover, ordering the property only of the debtor, and not his person, to be responsible for his debt. Popular gratitude protected the memory of the plebeian King, born in slavery or on foreign soil; and they went so far as to believe that he had wished to lay down the crown in order to establish consular government.

Some years before, the Athenian Solon had divided rights in proportion to property. Thus at the same time the two greatest cities of the ancient world were desirous of renouncing the

[1] Dionys., iv. 13.
[2] Originally the Romans only had as a means of exchange the *aes rude*, bars of metal in bronze or mere copper, without any stamped impression and without any settled weight. The buyer put into the scales as many pieces as were necessary to make the weight equivalent to the price of the goods bought. This was barter,— a means of exchange which indicates a still ruder state of society. The *aes signatum* appears to have been coined under Servius; it was a flat piece of bronze, with the picture of an ox, a sheep, or a pig, or, like that which we give, with the impression of a tripod. Later on, more portable pieces were coined of circular shape, on which the value was marked by a distinguishing sign; we have already given some of them on pages 29, 57, 77. The bar represented on page 248, and taken from the *Cabinet de France*, weighs 1,495 grammes (3 lbs. 4 ozs.). At the base is seen the opening through which they ran the molten metal.

government of the families consecrated by the gods, and of adopting the principle which is still applied in many modern societies,—that power depends upon wealth. But at Athens customs had paved the way for the reform of Solon, and it was immediately applied; at Rome, that of Servius was in advance of his time, he could not establish it; but in the next generation it came about of its own accord.

III. Tarquin the Proud; Power of Rome at this Epoch.

It was, in fact, the democratic laws of Servius which helped Tarquin the Proud, posing to the patricians as the defender of their threatened privileges, to dethrone his father-in-law. Having become king by a murder, he destroyed the tables on which were inscribed the results of the census, abolished the system of the classes, and forbade the religious gatherings of the plebeians;[1] then, supported by his numerous mercenaries, he obliged the people to finish the Circus, the Capitol, and the great Cloaca. But counting too much on his Latin and Hernican allies, he did not spare the patricians more than the plebeians, and to escape death, many senators went into exile. This oppression was likely to unite the two orders by a common hatred. It lasted however, until the outrage upon Lucretia had given the multitude one of those exciting proofs of slavery which, even more than bloodshed, bring about revolutions, because the injury done to the individual is felt by all.

"If the constitution of Servius had been maintained," says Niebuhr, "Rome would have attained, two hundred years sooner, and without sacrifices, to a happiness . . . which she could recover only at the cost of fierce combats and great sufferings." Happily in the history of a nation, as in the life of a man, good often results from evil. This difficult struggle trained the youth of Rome and retarded its decline; but "woe to him from whom the offence came, and curses on those who destroyed plebeian liberty to the utmost of their power!"

[1] Dionys., iv. 43.

ROCK OF TERRACINA.

The Tarquins, however, had extended their reputation far and wide. Under her last kings Rome is no longer the obscure city whose territory extends a few miles from her walls. The treaty with Carthage, concluded in 509 B.C., the grandeur of the

THE CAPITOLINE HILL (RESTORATION OF CANINA).[1]

city, the importance of her edifices, and her 150,000 fighting men [2] (whatever reduction we make from this figure), testify that she then formed one of the most powerful states of Italy. The Tiber was already bounded by quays, and some of the foundations laid to support the Capitol still exist.[3] This temple, which was worthy of Rome at the time of its grandeur, formed an almost exact square of 200 feet on each side.[4] A double colonnade surrounded it on three sides. But the peristyle of the south, which faced the Palatine, had a triple row of six columns. It stood on one of the two summits of the Tarpeian Hill, that on the northeast, at the place where now stands the church of the Ara-Coeli; the God who held the thunderbolt has given place to the Child who holds the cross, — *il Bambino.* But the church is turned the opposite way from

TEMPLE OF JUPITER CAPITOLINUS.

---

[1] On the position of the temple of Jupiter, which some place on the west, others at the opposite extremity of the Capitoline Hill, see the discussion of Ampère, *L'Histoire Romaine à Rome,* vol. ii. p. 59, *seqq.*

[2] This is the census of the year 496; but these figures are most probably exaggerated. The census of 509 had only given 130,000 men, and that of 491 gave only 110,000. (Cf. Dionys., v. 20, 75; vi. 65, 96.) These numbers, if they were exact, would certainly imply a population of at least 600,000 souls.

[3] It may be that those which are still seen only date from the war with Samnium.

[4] Vitruvius, iv. 7.

the temple, which faced the Forum, and rose majestically above it. Grace, however, was wanting to this majesty. With its short columns and quadrangular form, without a corresponding elevation, the temple of Jupiter had a heavy and stunted appearance. This sanctuary well suited a nation of soldiers which laid so great a burden upon the world.

Of all Tarquin's works, the most important was the *Cloaca Maxima*. Its foundations were sunk deep under the earth, and its numerous branches brought the water and mud from the low districts of the city and led them into the Tiber. It was only when this immense work had been finished that the marshy plain [1] which extended between the Seven Hills was rendered healthy and dry. Such was the height of the triple vault [2] of the main channel, which was built with long stones of peperino, laid without cement, that Agrippa entered it in a boat, and Pliny asserts that a cart-load of hay could have passed through it. Tradition also speaks, as in the case of the great constructions of the Egyptian kings, of the misery of the people condemned to such tasks.

CLOACA MAXIMA.

The rule of Rome, however, was then extensive enough for the greatness of the state to be shown by the magnificence of its buildings. In the treaty concluded with Carthage in the very year of the expulsion of Tarquin, which Polybius [3] translated

---

[1] This plain formed the quarters of the *Velabrum*, the *Subura*, the *Forum Romanum*, and the *Circus Maximus*. This circus, which was 3½ stadia in length by 1 in width, could hold 150,000, or according to others, 380,000 spectators.

[2] The vaulting is formed by three concentric arches, and the diameter of it is 20 ft. It may be remarked that the Greeks only began to use the vaulted arch at the time of Alexander, although M. Heuzey saw many more ancient in Epirus and Acarnania. [Pausanias speaks as if the ancient Minyan treasure-house at Orchomenus had been really arched with a keystone: but according to Schliemann's researches he must have been mistaken. — *Ed.*]

[3] III. 22. The authenticity of this treaty would, if necessary, be confirmed by the account of Livy, which represents Tarquin as the recognized chief of the league of forty-seven

from the original, preserved in the archives of the aediles in the Capitol, all the towns of the coast of Latium, Ardea, Antium, Circei, Terracina, are mentioned as subjects of Rome. In the interior of the country, Aricia obeyed her under the same title. Suessa Pometia had been captured, and Signia colonized. Between the Tiber and the Anio, all the low Sabine country belonged to her, and the stories about Porsenna prove that on the north of the Tiber her frontier extended so far that ten of her thirty tribes had their territory in Etruria. Even her navy, especially that of her allies, was not without importance, since we can conclude from the terms of the treaty that merchant vessels, which started from the Tiber or the ports of Latium, traded as far as Sicily, Sardinia, and Africa. It was doubtless the road to Egypt which the Carthaginians wished to close against them, by forbidding to Rome and her allies all navigation to the east of the *Fair Promontory*. The republican revolution cost her this dominion, which it cost more than a century and a half to recover.

The Greeks, who represented Romulus to be a descendant of Aeneas, Numa a contemporary of Pythagoras, and the successor of Ancus to be the son of a Corinthian, illustrated the history of the last Tarquin by stories copied from Herodotus. Thus Sextus enters into Gabii like Zopyrus into Babylon, and the silent but singularly expressive advice of Tarquin to his son is that of Thrasybulus to Periander. Servius, they said, had honored the Grecian Artemis by raising a temple to her on the Aventine; Tarquin honored the Hellenic Apollo by sending to Delphi an embassy, which in the legend only serves to show the feigned madness of Brutus, — an echo, perhaps, of that of Solon. In fact this King's character has been drawn after those of numerous tyrants whom Greece experienced. Even his fall remains a problem. Was it Lucretia, who, by her generous death, overturned the powerful monarch whose sway so many cities obeyed, or was it not the whole Roman people who revolted against a foreign master?

It is difficult not to consider the time of the royalty of the

---

Latin towns. See Livy, i. 52; Dionys., iv. 48–49. [Mommsen, *Rom. Hist.* i. 145, while proving from the Latin forms of Phoenician names the early date of the direct intercourse of Rome and Carthage, disputes the date of this treaty, which he believes to have been much later. But his opinion is much disputed by other scholars. — *Ed.*]

Tarquin as the period of an Etruscan rule, accepted or endured on the shores of the Tiber, and the Rome of Tarquinius Superbus as the capital of the most famous of the lucumonies. Being, as they were, masters of Tuscany and of Campania, they must also have been masters of Latium. Their influence at Rome is matter of history only as concerns the arts and religious beliefs which they carried thither; it was probably by a conquest which Roman pride was unwilling to remember, that this influence made itself felt.[1] Sufficiently strong and numerous to impose their authority and some of their customs, they had not the power to change the language, the civil institutions, and the population, which remained Latino-Sabine.[1] The story of the greatness and of the fall of the last of the Tarquins, and of the wars undertaken by the Etruscans to re-establish him on the throne, leads to the idea that the revolution of the year 510 was a national uprising, called out by some act of insolence like the outrage upon Lucretia. The fortune of the Rasena was everywhere on the wane. They had already lost the plains of the Po, and were losing, or about to lose, those of Campania. This reaction of the native races reached Latium and the city which was its most flourishing capital. In the exile of Tarquin, therefore, we may see the fall of the great Tiberine lucumony and the revival of the old Roman people.

[1] [Cf. the interesting arguments of Gardthausen (*Mastarna*, p. 5, *seq.*) to show the domination of the Etruscans about 600 B.C., and the remains of Etruscan names among the Latin towns. — *Ed.*]

ETRUSCAN SIDEBOARD.

CHAPTER V.

MANNERS AND CUSTOMS.

I. CHARACTER OF ANCIENT ROMAN SOCIETY.

NOTHING can be said of science, art, or literature in this period. When Tarquin fell, Greek literature had finished half its career, perhaps the most brilliant part. The best days of at least the higher kind of poetry had passed, and the works of Solon, Simonides, and Anacreon were an early decadence; but Pindar, Aeschylus, Herodotus, and Thucydides were born or were presently to appear. Thus, on one of the shores of the Adriatic Greece had for centuries listened to her immortal singers, while on the other literary genius was yet asleep. And it must be so, because, if the Romans had a worship, they had not a religion, in the sense of a mythology. Instead of the magnificent development of the Greek theodicy and of those great [philosophical] systems which explained the world, we only find at Rome dry rituals. Those living and passionate divinities which, around the Aegean Sea, shared human love and hate, were replaced about the Apennines by sober gods, without adventures, without history, who never cross the azure of the sky to betake themselves to the mountain, bathed in dazzling light, where the Olympians of Homer drink their nectar.

Rome doubtless had songs in honor of gods, kings, and heroes. But these rude and short songs, and careless expression of passions and recollections, were far beneath the clearly defined form which individual genius stamps upon its work. Formerly the value of popular songs was overlooked; now it is exaggerated. For the Romans especially, whose cold and severe character had neither the natural enthusiasm of the Greeks nor their brilliant and lively imagination, popular songs never could have been as rich in details and color as the school of Niebuhr [or Macaulay's lays] would make us believe. The language, moreover, was too poor to be adapted to varied requirements: the fragment which remains to us of a hymn of the Fratres Arvales shows of what little use this rude instrument had hitherto been.

CARMEN ARVALE.

Enos, Lases, iuvate.
Neve lue rue, Marmar, sins [*v.* sers] incurrere in pleores.
Satur fu, fere Mars. Limen sali. Sta. Berber.
Semunis alternei advocapit conctos.
Enos, Marmor, iuvato.
Triumpe.[1]

In royal Rome they merely knew how to engrave laws and treaties on wood or bronze; and the only works which are mentioned for that time are the collection of laws which Papirius is believed to have made after the expulsion of Tarquin the Proud (*jus Papirianum*), and of the Commentaries of King Servius, said to have contained his constitution.[2] It is characteristic that Latin was compelled to borrow from the Greek the words

---

[1] [.... "The hymn, though it has suffered in transliteration, is a good specimen of early Roman worship, the rubrical directions to the brethren being inseparably united with invocation to the Lares and Mars. .... The most probable rendering is as follows: 'Help us, O Lares! and thou, Marmar, suffer not plague and ruin to attack our folk. Be satiate, O fierce Mars! Leap over the threshold. Halt. Now beat the ground. Call in alternate strain upon all the heroes. Help us, Marmor! Bound high in solemn measure.' Each line was repeated thrice, the last word five times. As regards the separate words, *enos* — which should, perhaps, be written *e nos* — contains the interjectional *e*, which elsewhere coalesces with vocatives. *Lases* is the older form of *Lares*. *Lue rue* = *luem ruem;* the last an old word for *ruinam*, with the case-ending lost, as frequently, and the copula omitted, as in *Patres Conscripti*, etc. *Marmar, Marmor*, or *Mamor*, is the reduplicated form of Mars seen in the Sabine *Mamers*. *Sins* is for *sines*, as *advocapit* for *advocabitis*. *Pleores* is an ancient form of *plures*, answering to the Greek πλείονας in form, and to τοὺς πολλούς, "the mass of the people," in meaning. *Fu* is a shortened imperative. *Berber* is for *verbere*, imperative of the old verb *verbero, is*, as *triumpe* from *triumpere* = *triumphare*. *Semunes* from *Semo* (*se-homo*, apart from man), an inferior deity. .... Much of this interpretation is conjectural, and other views have been advanced with regard to nearly every word; but the above given is the most probable." — CRUTTWELL: *History of Roman Literature*, pp. 14, 15.]

[2] Pomponius, *Dig.* i. 2, 2, § 2; Dionysius, iii. 36; Cicero, *pro Rabir*, 5; Livy, i. 31, 32, 60.

MANNERS AND CUSTOMS.

for poet and poetry; but it possessed those which have to do with rustic life or with hardy and warlike manners. The common treasury was at first a basket of wicker-work (*fiscus*); their contract, a straw broken by the two contractors (*stipula*); their money, a herd (*pecus*); a fine, as much milk as a cow gives (*mulcta*, from *mulgeo*, to milk); war was a duel (*bellum*, from *duellum*); victory, the action of binding the conquered (*vincio*, to bind); and an enemy, the victim reserved for sacrifice (*victima*) and *hostia*.

The arts were no better cultivated. If the walls of Rome and the foundations of the Palatine were formed of squared blocks which marked an advance on the polygonal structure of the preceding age, huts covered the slopes about the seven hills, and we can reconstruct their clumsy form when we see the cinerary urns recently found under the lava of the Alban

CINERARY URNS,[1] REPRODUCING THE FORM OF THE COTTAGES CONSTRUCTED BY THE ANCIENT INHABITANTS OF LATIUM.

Mount. Montesquieu well observes: "We must not form the idea of the city of Rome at its beginning from the towns of the present day, unless it be those of the Crimea, made to contain plunder, cattle, and the fruits of the soil." The town had not even streets, unless we give this name to the continuation of the roads which terminated therein. The houses were very small or placed irregularly. Until the war with Pyrrhus these

[1] Cinerary urns in terra-cotta, containing calcined bones, recently found under the deepest lava of the Alban Mount, consequently of great antiquity, and reproducing the form of the cottages constructed by the most ancient inhabitants of Latium. (*Revue archéolog.*, May, 1876, p. 338.)

houses were only covered with planks,[1] which would give credence to the tradition that after the burning of Rome by the Gauls one year sufficed for its reconstruction.[2]

Athens converted her feasts into great national solemnities, during which the highest pleasures of the mind were found associated with the most imposing shows of religious processions, of the most perfect art and of the fairest nature. Those of Rome were the games of rude shepherds, or shouts of the delighted crowd, when the soldiers entered the city with some captives, sheaves of wheat, and the cattle taken from the enemy,— a rustic festival, which time and the fortune of Rome will change into that triumphal ceremony which is the continual ambition of her generals and one of the causes of her greatness.

ETRUSCAN CUPS, AFTER MICALI'S MONUMENTS INÉDITS.

To the north and south of the Tiber, however, among the Etruscans, Rutulians, and Volscians, the arts had already begun to make way. Pliny saw at Caere and Ardea some paintings still preserving all the freshness of their colors, which he regarded as anterior in date to Rome. The numerous objects found in the second of these towns prove that it had a regular school of artists. Praeneste was also a city fond of works of art; every day some

---

[1] Pliny, *Hist. Nat.* xvi. 15. [2] Plut., *Cam.* 32.

are discovered in its ruins. A tomb which is believed to have belonged to the *gens* Sylvia, from which Romulus was said to be descended, has just yielded a treasure which dates perhaps from seven or eight centuries before our era.

The Romans, who adopted everything from their neighbors, adopted from them even the statues of their divinities; but they themselves made none. For a long time they represented the gods by a naked sword, a lance, or an unhewn stone. For them, the place where a thunderbolt had fallen became a temple, *puteal*;[2] the tree struck by lightning a sacred object; and from a handful of baked earth they made their Lares and Penates, whom they thought they saw dancing in the flame on the hearth. Strange fortune of religious conceptions! Art, one of the elements of the human trinity,[4] was born of the religions of India, Egypt, and Greece,

GROUP IN BRONZE RECENTLY FOUND AT PALESTRINA (PRAENESTE).[1]

PUTEAL OF LIBO (SILVER COIN).[3]

---

[1] Of course this group, like the Mercury on page 196, is of a relatively modern period. We shall see later on a very curious cup, also found at Praeneste.

[2] *Puteal* means the brink of a well. It was a stone enclosure surrounding a well or consecrated place. The puteal of Libo is often represented on the medals of the *gens* Scribonia; it protected, according to some, a place in the Forum which had been struck by a thunderbolt; according to others, the place where Navius had performed his miracle. Scribonius Libo having repaired it, gave his name to it.

[3] See Cohen, *Med. Consul Aemilia*, No. 10.

[4] The Good, the Beautiful, and the True.

where it grew and developed; but it could not proceed from the temple of Jehovah, and on the soil of ancient Rome it always remained a foreign importation.[1] Even after the Tarquins, the images of the gods, the work of Etruscan artists, were still made only in wood or clay, like that of Jupiter in the Capitol, and like the quadriga placed on the top of the temple. Etruria also furnished the architects[2] who built the *Roma quadrata* of the Palatine and constructed the first temples; she provided even the flute-players necessary for the performance of certain rites.

II. PRIVATE MANNERS.

ALL the activity of the Roman tended to a practical end, — public affairs, agriculture, and domestic cares. Two words signified

THE PLOUGHMAN.[3]

for him all good qualities, all virtues,[4] — *virtus et pietas* ; that is to say, courage, force, an immovable firmness, patience in work, and respect for the gods, his ancestors, his fatherland, and his family, for the established laws and discipline. Cicero well remarks,[5]

---

[1] This sterility of Judaea and Rome is, of course, only shown in plastic arts.
[2] *Fabris undique ex Etruria accitis.* (Livy, i. 56 ; cf. Pliny, *Hist. Nat.* xxxv. 12.)
[3] After an engraved stone in the collection of Florence.
[4] *Appellata est ex viro virtus.* (Cic., *Tusc.* ii. 18.) [The peculiar Roman *gravitas* should have been added. — *Ed.*]
[5] *Tusc.* i. 1. Properly speaking, the originality of the Greeks exists especially in political constitutions; that of Rome in civil laws. Cicero says (*de Orat.* i. 44), *Incredible*

without unduly flattering the national pride: "In sciences and letters, the Greeks surpass us; but there is more order and dignity in our customs and conduct. Where else is there to be found that severity of manners, that firmness, that greatness of soul, that uprightness, that good faith, and all the virtues of our fathers?"

Their domestic life, in fact, was simple and austere: no luxury, no idleness; the master ploughs with his slaves, the mistress spins in the midst of her women.[1] Royalty, even wealth, does not exempt from labor; like Bertha the Spinner, Queen Tanaquil[2] and Lucretia set the example to the Roman matrons. "When our fathers," says Cato, "desired to praise a man of property, they called him a good ploughman and a good farmer; this was the highest of eulogiums[3] [and on many epitaphs noble women were praised for chastity and diligent spinning]. Then men lived on their lands, in the rustic tribes, which were the most honorable of all, and they only came to Rome on market days[5] or assembly days. In the villa — a miserable cabin made of mud, rafters, and branches — not a day, not a moment, was lost. If bad weather prevented work in the fields, there was plenty to do at home in cleaning the stables and the yard, in mending old ropes and old

A WOMAN SPINNING.[4]

est enim quam sit omne jus civile, praeter hoc nostrum, inconditum ac paene ridiculum. He went too far in this contempt for the civil laws of Greece, as is proved in numerous works recently written upon the jurisprudence of Athens. We even find in the Digest the text of the Athenian laws which were copied by the Romans.

[1] Colum., de Re rust. xii. praef.

[2] At the time of Varro, they showed in the temple of Sancus her distaff and spindle, still full, they said, of the wool which she spun. (Pliny, Hist. Nat. viii. 48.)

[3] Cato, de Re rust., praefat., and Pl., ib. xviii. 3. The persons of most consideration in the city were the locupletes loci, hoc est agri plenos, and the anniversary of the foundation of Rome was celebrated on the 21st of April, the day of the feast of Pales, the guardian deity of flocks.

[4] Taken from a bas-relief at Rome, representing the arts of Minerva.

[5] Nundinae, every nine days. After the year 287 the comitia could be convoked on market-days. Nundinarum etiam conventus manifestum est propterea usurpatos, ut nonis tantummodo diebus urbanae res agerentur, reliquis administrarentur rusticae. (Colum., praef., and Macr., Sat. i. 16.)

clothes; even on feast days one can cut brambles, trim hedges, wash the flock, go to the city to sell oil and fruits."[1] In order to regulate the order of these country labors, calendars were afterward drawn up, which we have found, and which are the predecessors of our almanacs.

Here follow the indications given by one of them for the month of May:—

MENSIS	The Month
MAIVS	of May
DIES. XXXI	XXXI days.
NON. SEPTIM	The nones fall on the 7th day.
DIES. HOR. XIIII S	The day has 14½ hours.
NOX. HOR. VIIII S	The night has 9½ hours.
SOL TAVRO	The sun is in the sign of Taurus.
TUTEL APOLLIN	The month is under the protection of Apollo.
SEGET RVNCANT	The corn is weeded.
OVES TONDVNT	The sheep are shorn.
LANA LAVATVR	The wool is washed.
IVVENCI. DOMANT	Young steers are put under the yoke.
VICEA. PABVLAR SECATVR	The vetch of the meadows is cut.
SEGETES LVSTRANTVR	The lustration of the crops is made
SACRVM. MERCVR ET FLORAE.[2]	Sacrifices to Mercury and Flora.

Horace does not draw a more agreeable picture of ancient city manners. "At Rome," he says, "for a long time a man knew no other pleasure and no other festival than to open his door at dawn, to explain the law to his clients, and to lay out his money on good security. They asked from their elders, and taught beginners, the art of increasing their savings and escaping ruinous follies."[3] In this Italy, so full of superstitions, Cato will not have the farmer lose his time in consulting the aruspices, augurs,

SYLVANUS.[4]

---

[1] Verg., *Georg.* i. 273; Colum., *de Re rust.* ii. 21, and Cato, *de Re rust.* 39.

[2] This inscription (*Corpus inscr. Lat.* vol. vi. p. 637) is taken from the *Calendarium rusticum Farnesianum*, also called *Menologium rusticum Colotianum*; it is a marble cube, bearing on its four sides the indication of the works and festivals for each month.

[3] *Ep.* ii. 1, 103–107.

[4] This bronze of Hadrian represents Sylvanus, the guardian of the rural domain, who for this reason was associated with the Lares, dragging a ram and holding the *pedum*, or crooked

and soothsayers; he forbids him religious practices which would take him away from his home. His gods are on the hearth and at the nearest cross-roads. The Lares, Manes, and Sylvani are sufficient for the protection of the farm; there is no need of other gods.[1]

These laborious and economical habits, which introduced usury, one of the plagues of Roman society, have been those of all agricultural nations; but everywhere men forgot them to welcome the guest who was sent by the gods, and hospitality was, even for the poorest, a religious duty. Among the Romans, avarice and mistrust closed against the stranger the doors of the *villa*, which was always surrounded with broad ditches and thick hedges, for useless expenses must not be incurred; nor was it ever right to give or lend without gain,[2] except on the great day of the festival of Janus, the 1st of January, when everybody exchanged good wishes and presents, *strenae*. The French have kept both the word and the thing, *étrennes*. "The father of the family," said Cato, "must make money of everything, and lose nothing. If he gives new brooms to his slaves, they must return the old ones; they will do for pieces. He must sell the oil if it is worth anything, and what remains of the wine and wheat; he must sell old oxen, calves, old carriages, old iron, old slaves and sick ones; he must sell always. The father of the family must be a seller, not a buyer."[3] *Durum genus!*

The father of the family! It is always he who is mentioned, for there is no one else in the house; wife, children, clients, slaves, — all are only chattels,[4] instruments of labor, persons without will and without name, subjected to the omnipotence of the father. At once priest and judge, his authority is absolute; he alone is in communication with the gods, for he alone performs the *sacra privata*,

---

staff of the shepherds. In front, there are a temple, a burning altar, and a bird; behind, a tree, which recalls the god of the woods. As the god cannot offer sacrifices to himself, and we see neither the sacred knife nor the cup of libations, I should be inclined to think that they wished to signify by this representation, that, thanks to Sylvanus, the altar would not lack the necessary victims.

[1] *De Re rust.: Rem divinam nisi compitalibus, in compito aut in foco faciat.*
[2] *Satin semen, cibaria, far, vinum, oleum, mutuum, dederet nemini.* (Cato, *de Re rust.* 5.)
[3] Ibid. 2.
[4] *Mancipia*, hence *emancipatio*; they are not *sui*, but *alieni, juris*, and cannot enter an action. It is the father who answers for them or judges them.

and as master, he disposes of the powers and life of his slaves. As husband, he condemns his wife to death[1] if she forges false keys or violates her vow, and he is exempt, in her case, from the religion of mourning, the piety of remembrance.[2] As father, he kills the child that is born deformed, and sells the others, as many as three times, before losing his claims upon them. Neither age nor dignities emancipate them. Though consuls or senators, they may be dragged from the platform or the senate-house, or put to death like that senator, an accomplice of Catiline, who was killed by his father. If he is rich, he will lend at 12, 15, or 20 per cent., for the father of the family must turn his money as well as his lands to account, and the law grants to him the liberty and even the life of his insolvent debtor. Finally, at his death, neither his children nor his wife can claim any of his goods, if he has bequeathed them to a stranger; for he has the right to dispose of his *res* as he chooses.[3] Nevertheless the city includes and rules the family. For the wish of the father to be carried out, it is necessary for his will to be accepted by the Curiae, and they do not like the patrimony to depart from the family.

It is through women especially that manners change, that families, classes, and fortunes mingle; but in this society, so severely disciplined, the woman, the changing element, remains under guardianship[4] all her life. She belongs to the house, not to the city, and in the house she always has a master, — her father when she is a girl; her husband when she is married; her nearest male agnate when she is a widow. One of the causes of the ruin of Sparta was the right which Lycurgus had left to women of inheriting and disposing of their goods.[5] At Rome, if the woman

---

[1] Dionys., ii. 25; Pl., *Hist. Nat.* xiv. 13; Suet., *Tib.* 35; Tac., *Ann.* xiii. 32; Plut., *Rom.* 22; κλειδῶν ὑποβολῇ *Egnatius Mecenius uxorem, quod vinum bibisset, fusti percussam interemit.* (Val. Max., VI. iii. 9.) [But not, I fancy, without a family council. — *Ed.*]

[2] *Uxores viri lugere non compellentur.* — *Sponsi nullus luctus est* (Dig. iii. 2, 9); and elsewhere, *Vir non luget uxorem, nullam debet uxori religionem luctus.*

[3] *Uti legasset super pecunia, tutelave suae rei, ita jus esto.* (*Fr.* XII. Tab.) Wills had to be presented for the sanction of the Curiae or at the moment of setting out for an expedition in *procinctu (exercitus, expeditus, et armatus)*. (Ulp., *Fr.* xx. 2; Gaius, ii. 101.)

[4] *Nullam ne privatam quidem, rem agere feminas sine tutore auctore . . . in manu esse parentium, fratrum virorum. . . .* (Cato, ap. Livy, xxxiv. 2.) The guardian had over the ward the rights of the *patria potestas*. (Fest., s. v. *Remancipata*.)

[5] Arist., *Polit.* ii. 6.

obtained any share[1] in the heritage of her father or husband, she could not, except in the case of the Vestals, *in honorem sacerdotii*, either transfer or bequeath it without the consent of her guardians, that is to say, of her husband, brothers, or her nearest male relatives on the paternal side, all interested, as her heirs, in preventing a sale or a legacy. They had also the right of opposing ordinary marriage (*coemptio vel cohabitatio*). The father only, by refusing his consent, could prevent solemn marriage (*confarreatio*),[2] which, in any case, did not take place between a plebeian and a patrician. Placed under perpetual tutelage, she could confer no right, and the relationship established by her had no civil effects; the child followed the father. In short, when she passed into another house, the woman did not take the lares of the paternal hearth, for these domestic gods never went to dwell under a strange roof. For her there was another family, and other gods. "Marriage," said the lawyers later, "is an association based on the community of the same things, divine and human."[3]

But, whether maid or matron, the woman was treated with reverence. Marriage was a holy thing, consecrated by religion; and the mother of a family reigned alone by the side of her husband in the conjugal dwelling, in which polygamy was proscribed. Like him, she performed the sacred rites at the altar of the Penates; if he was a flamen, she became a priestess, *flaminica;* she alone had the right of wearing in the streets the *stola*, which caused a matron to be recognized at a distance, and assured her public respect.

The right of life and death given to the husband over his wife was originally only applied in the case of patrician marriage by *confarreatio*, the law not yet concerning itself with plebeian unions. As soon as the betrothed had tasted of a symbolical cake (*far*), passed under a cart-yoke, put the *as* in the balance, on the Penates, on the threshold of the conjugal house, and pronounced the formula, *Ubi tu Gaius, ego Gaia*, she fell, according

---

[1] The share of a child, τελευτήσαντος τοῦ ἀνδρὸς κληρονόμος ἐγένετο τῶν χρημάτων ὡς θυγάτηρ πατρός. (Dionys., ii. 25.)

[2] Dionysius says of this sort of union that it took place κατὰ νόμους ἱερούς.

[3] *Nuptiae sunt conjunctio maris et feminae consortium omnis vitae, divini et humani juris communicatio.* (Dig. xxiii. 2, 1.) *Uxor socia humanae rei atque divinae.* (Cod. ix. 32, 4.)

to the hard expression of the law, into the hand of her husband (*in manum viri*), and her dowry became, like her person, the property (*res*) of her husband.[1] The XII. Tables grant the same rights to the plebeian marriage when it has lasted a year without interruption, *usu anni continui in manum conveniebat*.

In case of divorce, the husband kept the dowry. But in this age of harsh and austere manners, divorce was unknown,[3] and the matrons had not yet raised that temple to Modesty whose doors were closed against the woman who had twice offered the sacrifices of betrothal.

Customs and beliefs, on the contrary, made almost a necessity of divorce, when the marriage remained barren. For it was not the union of two hearts, but the accomplishment of a civil and religious obligation,— to give new defenders to the city and perpetuate for the domestic gods the rites of the hearth — for the ancestors, the honors of the tomb. When a family disappeared, they said, "It is a hearth extinguished."

STOLA.[2]

Aristocratic associations insured to the future head of the family — the eldest son — greater advantages than to his brothers.

---

[1] *Omnia quae mulieris fuerunt, vira fiunt, dotis nomine.* (Cic., *pro Caecina*.)

[2] Distinctive garment of Roman matrons. Taken from the *Mus. Borbon.* iii. pl. 37.

[3] The first divorce mentioned by the Annals, that of Sp. Carvilius, is in the year of Rome 520 (233). "He separated from his wife," says Aulus Gellius (IV. iii. 2), "although he loved her much, because he could not have children by her."

Roman law did not go so far as proclaiming the right of primogeniture, which proceeds from a principle unknown to antiquity, — the indivisibility of the fief, — for it was too much preoccupied with the absolute power of the father to limit his rights in anything; but in leaving him the free disposition of his goods, it permitted him, in the interest of his house, to settle a greater portion on the eldest of his children.[1] These rights of the father, however, being once reserved, Roman law ordained, in case of decease *without will*, equal division among all the children. This entirely democratic clause, after having enfeebled the patrician aristocracy, enabled the lawyers of the Middle Ages to make a breach in the feudal system.

Such is the law of the Quirites, *jus Quiritium*, and we find here the triple basis on which rests this society, so profoundly aristocratic, — the inviolability of property, of land, or of money; the unlimited rights, and the religious character of the head of the family.[2]

III. PUBLIC MANNERS.

THE rights of parental authority were likely to produce docile subjects. Having become a citizen, the son transferred from his father to the state the same respect and the same obedience. It is a characteristic of small societies that patriotism varies inversely with the extent of territory, and is stronger in proportion as the enemy's frontier is nearer. For then the man belongs more to the state than to his family. He is rather a citizen than husband or father, and domestic affections are postponed to love of the native soil and its laws. To serve the state was the first law of the Romans; and in the *Dream of Scipio*, that half-Christian essay, immortality is promised only to great citizens. By these causes is explained

---

[1] Thus, in Greek mythology, Hercules is submissive to Eurystheus.

[2] Dionysius (ii. 26) contrasts the prodigious extension at Rome of the *patria potestas* with the narrow limits in which Solon, Pittakos, Charondas, and all the Greek legislators had confined it. At Rome the father was everything in the family, as the state was everything in the city. This severe organization proves that at first the most rigorous discipline had been necessary to insure its safety, and that some trace of it was left in the *gentes*.

the respect of the plebeians for institutions, even when they were opposed to them, and those *secessions*, unaccompanied by pillage, those bloodless revolutions, that pacific progress which took place gradually in constitutional ways. Hence come, too, in ordinary life, the submission to old customs and to the letter of the law, on which it would be sacrilege to put a new construction, — that blind faith in the incomprehensible formulae of worship and jurisprudence, and the authority, so long recognized, of the *acta legitima*.

The word religion signifies bond [or obligation]. In no other country, in no other times, has this bond been so strong as at Rome; it united the citizens to one another and to the state. As the Romans saw gods everywhere; as all nature, sky, earth, and water was to them full of divinities who watched over human beings with benevolent or jealous eyes, there was no act of life which did not require a prayer or an offering, a sacrifice or a purification, according to the rites prescribed by the ministers of religion. This piety, being the offspring of fear, was all the more attentive in observing signs considered favorable or the reverse; so that everything depended on religion, — private life, from the cradle to the tomb, public life, from the comitia to the field of battle; even business and pleasure.[1] Games and races were celebrated in honor of the gods; the people's songs were hymns, their dances a prayer, their music, uncouth but sacred harmonies; and, as in the Middle Ages, the earliest dramas were pious mysteries. By the continual intervention of the pontiffs, who knew the necessary rites and sacred formulae, by that of the augurs, aruspices, and all the interpreters of omens, this religion, devoid of dogmas and of clergy, of ideal and of love — made up of silly superstitions, like that of some of their descendants — was yet a great force of cohesion for the state and a powerful discipline for the citizens.

No people — some famous examples notwithstanding — ever pushed so far the religion of the oath. Nothing could take place — raising of troops, division of booty, lawsuits, judgments, public affairs, private affairs, sales, contracts, or anything else — without the swearing

[1] Livy well says (vi. 41): *Auspiciis hanc urbem conditam esse, auspiciis bello ac pace domi militiaeque omnia geri, quis est qui ignoret?*

of either fidelity and obedience or of justice and good faith, the gods being called upon to bear witness to the sincerity of the parties. At sales the purchaser, in the presence of five citizens of full age, put the bronze, the price of the purchase, into a balance held by the *libripens*, and touching with his hand the land, the slave, or the ox which he was buying, said: "This is mine, according to the law of the Quirites; I have paid for it in copper duly weighed." This right of selling or buying by *mancipation*[1] (*manu capere*, to take with the hand), without the intervention of a magistrate and without written receipt, was one of the privileges of the Quirites, and doubtless one of their most ancient customs. It explains the importance of that law, — *Uti lingua nuncupassit, ita jus esto*, such as the word is, so is the right, — which penetrated so far into the Roman habits that it made them the most faithful of all nations to their word, but to the literal word, to the actual sense, even should good faith be impaired thereby. Thus for a loan it was necessary to say: *Dari spondes?* Dost thou promise the gift? And the lender must reply: *Spondeo*, I undertake to do so. Should either of the two change one of these words, there was no longer any contract, no creditor or debtor; and if the money had been delivered it was lost. A man brings into court a neighbor who has cut his vines, and produces against him the terms of the law; but the law speaks of trees, he says vine — the suit cannot proceed. The leaders of a sedition, seeing that the soldiers are hindered from joining by the oath they have sworn to the consuls, propose to kill the latter. "When they are dead," say they, "the soldiers will be free from their oath." At the Caudine Forks the generals give the Samnites a verbal promise; but there is not, as is necessary to bind two nations, any treaty concluded by the fetiales with the sacred herb, and consecrated by the sacrifice of a victim, therefore the agreement is, as regards religion, invalid, and the Senate annuls it.[2]

This servile attachment to legal forms came from the religious

---

[1] All objects of property were divided into *res mancipi* (lands, houses, slaves, oxen, horses, mules, asses), and *res nec mancipi*. The possession of the latter was transmitted by the simple delivery to the purchaser. For the others, the formalities just described were necessary.

[2] Livy, ii. 32.

character of the law and from the belief imposed by the doctrine of augury, that the least inadvertence in the accomplishment of rites was sufficient to alienate the good will of the gods. Consuls were often obliged to resign on account of some negligence committed in the consultation of omens.[1] How often did religion itself suffer thereby, when by clever evasions the Romans deceived their gods with an easy conscience!

The principal occupation of the Romans was agriculture; for the small amount of manufacture then at Rome, save a few trades necessary to the army, was abandoned to the poor citizens and strangers.[2] But agriculture did not enrich the small proprietor; it was well when it yielded him a livelihood, and he was not forced, in order to supply a deficiency of the crops, to draw on the rich man's purse, — to have recourse to the fatal assistance of the usurer. In later times the usurer was a plebeian knight or a freed man. At this epoch he was almost always a patrician,[3] for to the incomes derived from their estates the patricians united the profits of maritime commerce, which they had perhaps reserved to themselves. The insolvent debtor had no pity to expect, for movable property was as strictly protected as landed property. "If he pay not," said the law, "let him be cited into court. If illness or age hinder, let him be provided with a horse, but not a litter. The debt being acknowledged and judgment given, let there be thirty days' grace. If he still fails to pay, the creditor shall cast him into the *ergastulum*, bound with straps or chains weighing 15 pounds. At the end of sixty days let him be produced on three market days and sold beyond the Tiber. If there be several creditors, they may divide his body; it matters not whether they cut more or less."[4] This was a dangerous and

---

[1] Plutarch, *Marcell.* 5.

[2] To Numa, however, is attributed the formation of nine corporations (Plut., *Numa*, 17): the flute-players, goldsmiths, carpenters, dyers, shoemakers, turners, copper-workers, and potters; all the other artisans were united in a single corporation.

[3] Dionys., iv. 11; Livy, vi. 36. *Nobiles domos . . . ubicumque patricius habitet, ibi carcerem privatum esse.*

[4] *. . . Secanto, si plusve minusve secuerunt, se* (for *sine*) *fraude esto.* (Frag. of XII. Tables.) It may possibly be that in the fifth century before our era, the *sectio* no longer referred to more than the price of the sold debtor; but for earlier ages it must certainly be taken in its literal sense, although, according to Dion. (Frag. xxxii.), who knows nothing of it, it was never practised.

impolitic cruelty, for the crowd could not always remain indifferent to the sight of a corpse, or the appearance in the Forum of a man of the people half dead under the lash for the sake of a little money which he could not pay.

To sum up, the history of the early age of Rome shows us a cold and melancholy people, eager for gain, disdaining the ideal which returns no interest — without fire, without youth. But this nation, which seems never to have lived its teens, owed to its origin, and the circumstances of its historic existence, the most severe discipline in the family, in religion and in the state. If during centuries it never knew aught of poetry or art, it had more than any other the sentiment of duty: its citizens knew how to obey. That is why, in later times, they knew how to command. Moreover, the aristocratic constitution which resulted from its customs permitted it to be prudent in designs and persevering in action; and a military organization, already excellent, henceforth provides it with the means of carrying out everything which it undertakes. When the endless strifes of the Forum and the outer world come, it can apply itself to them with the energy which insures victory, with the political ability which preserves the state.

[1] The Lares, each holding a rod and caressing a dog; above, a head of Vulcan, and pincers; on the right and left the letters LA RE (*Lares*). Reverse of a silver coin of the Caesian family.

L. CAESI.[1]

SECOND PERIOD.

ROME UNDER THE PATRICIAN CONSULS (509–367 B. C.).

STRUGGLES WITHIN — WEAKNESS WITHOUT.

CHAPTER VI.

INTERNAL HISTORY FROM 509 TO 470.

I. ARISTOCRATIC CHARACTER OF THE REVOLUTION OF 509: THE CONSULSHIP.

THE Kings of Rome had not been more fortunate than the Caesars were afterward. Of seven of them, five had died, as so many Emperors did, a violent death. The reason was that both had the same enemy, — a powerful aristocracy. Moreover, the abolition of royalty is a very common historical incident. Throughout the whole Graeco-Italian world, the kings of the heroic age give place sooner or later to the nobles, who, at Rome, were called patricians. *Superbus* does not, perhaps, merit the reputation that legend has affixed to him; but the nobles did not wish for another chief who could, like Servius, prepare for political life the crowd of plebeians whom they held in subjection, or, like Tarquin, strike off the higher heads. They replaced the King by two consuls or praetors, chosen from their midst and invested with all the rights and all the insignia of royalty, except the crown and the purple mantle worked with gold.

At once the ministers and presidents of the Senate, — administrators, judges, and generals, — the consuls had sovereign power, *regium imperium*,[1] but only for one year. In the interior of the city the nobles did not allow them both to exercise the prerogatives of their magistracy at the same time. Each had the authority, and the twelve lictors with their fasces, for a month. If they differed in opinion, the opposition of one, *intercessio*, arrested the decisions of the other, — a conservative measure; for the interdict prevails over the command, that is, the old order prevails against the new. For a sudden attack on the institutions they would have needed a military force; now Rome had no soldiers but her citizens, and no one could appear in arms within the pomerium. As the consuls were responsible for their acts, they were exposed, on quitting office, to formidable accusations. Thus the royal authority was divided, without being weakened; it remained strong without the power of again becoming dangerous, since it was renewed yearly; and by the *intercessio* it was self-restraining. But should a danger arise demanding the rapid concentration of power, it reappeared complete in the dictatorship.

CONSUL BETWEEN TWO LAUREL-CROWNED FASCES.[2]

FASCES.[3]

The nobles did not desire that the revolution should extend to the gods. Custom required that certain sacrifices should be offered by a king, so they appointed a *rex sacrorum* to perform them; but all ambition was forbidden him, he was declared incapable of filling any other office.

Finally, the centuries of Servius were re-established, or became for the first time the great political assembly of the Roman people, under guaranties which prevented all encroachment. In memory of their early character they met outside the

---

[1] *Uti consules potestatem haberent . . . regiam.* (Cic., *de Rep.* ii. 32.) Livy (i. 60) says that the consuls were elected *ex Commentariis Servi Tulli.*

[2] Consular coin of Cn. Piso. The fasces, the insignia of victory, were surrounded with wreaths of laurel; the victor and his soldiers wore laurel too, for it was considered a preservative against evils, and a guaranty against the shocks of Fortune, which is wont to strike more particularly at happy people. This coin, given by Morell, after Goltzius, is no longer to be found in any collection.

[3] Consular coin of C. Norbanus: a fasces with an axe, a caduceus, and an ear of wheat.

pomerium, in the Field of Mars, not at the call of the lictors, like the comitia of the Curiae, but at the sound of the trumpet. Before they met it was necessary to consult the auspices, so that religion kept them in dependence on the patrician augurs. The convocation must be announced thirty days beforehand (*dies justi*), that none might be unaware of it; and to avoid all chance of surprise by the enemy, a red flag floated over the Janiculum, which a picket occupied while the comitia lasted.[1]

The government really remained in the hands of the patricians. They were masters of the Senate, the supreme council of the city, wherein most of the propositions afterward laid before the comitia must first be discussed, and they were predominant in the assembly of centuries by their wealth and the number of their clients. If any plebeians, who had by their fortune reached the highest classes, threatened to render the vote of the centuries unfavorable, the patrician magistrate, who presided over the comitia, could always, by means of the augurs, break up the assembly or annul its decisions; or, if ill omens failed, cause a popular resolution to be rejected by the Senate.

Rome had, then, an upper house, which discussed the law twice, once before and once after it had been laid before the comitia, and a lower house, composed of the whole people, which voted, but did not discuss. It was somewhat like our three readings. But the largest share of influence was accorded to maturity of mind and to experience in public affairs, since by its preliminary authorization the Senate had the initiative in proposing laws, and, by their right of confirmation or rejection, the power to arrest the proceedings of a magistrate who had presented to the comitia, and caused them to pass, a revolutionary bill.

All was done with the same precautions in the elective comitia: the president proposed to the people the candidates whom the Senate and the augurs preferred, and the assembly

---

[1] Livy, xxxix. 15 . . . *nisi quum vexillo in arce posito comitiorum causa exercitus eductus esset*. Cf. Aulus Gellius, xv. 27; Dionys., vii. 59. . . . ὥσπερ ἐν πολέμῳ, and Macrob., *Sat*. i. 16. The comitia could be held only on set days, *dies fasti*, during which it was allowable to engage in state affairs. There were about 190 of these days in the year. The *dies nefasti*, or ferial days, were those on which religion closed the tribunals and forbade all public transactions. (Varro, *de Ling. Lat.* vi. 29; Festus, s. v. *Dies comitiales*.)

could only vote on these names. If a flatterer of the masses succeeded in obtaining a nomination displeasing to the great, the assembly of the Curiae, composed of patricians only, had the right of refusing to grant the chosen magistrate the *imperium*,—that is, the powers necessary for the exercise of his office;[1] and this assembly also formed the supreme tribunal of the city.[2]

It was really, then, the patricians who made the laws and appointed to public offices, all of which they themselves filled, *jus honorum*. They held the priesthood and the auspices; they were priests, augurs, and judges; and they carefully hid from the eyes of the people the mysterious formulae of public worship and of jurisprudence. Finally, they alone had the *jus imaginum*, which fed the hereditary pride of family, while at the same time the prohibition of marriages between the two orders seemed likely to bar forever the people's access to the positions held by the nobles, and entry into that Senate which was their fortress.[3]

But the plebeians had in their favor their numbers, and even their very misery, which soon drove them into successful revolt. They were no longer a stranger people, they were a second order in the State, which grew unobserved and unceasingly in face of the other, and which the patricians were obliged to arm in order to resist Tarquin, the Aequi, Volsci, and Etruscans. This assistance must earn its reward. Already the people had received judges of their own, who decide in most civil suits, and religious festivals, at which the assembled plebeians could reckon their numbers; and it was from the military centuries, or the two orders united, that the nomination of the consuls[4] proceeded, as Servius Tullius is said to have proposed. Henceforth the comitia centuriata makes the laws which the Senate proposes, and the elections which the Curiae confirm, and decides for peace or war. These serious innovations satisfied popular ambition for the time, for the

---

[1] *Ut pauca per populum, pleraque Senatus auctoritate . . . gererentur . . . Populi comitia, ne essent rata, nisi ea patrum approbavisset auctoritas.* (Cic. *de Rep.* ii. 32.) *Ergo . . . nec centuriatis, nec curiatis comitiis patres auctores fiant.* (Livy, vi. 41.)

[2] It will be seen further on that it was the XII. Tables which gave the *centuries* their high criminal jurisdiction.

[3] . . . *Servili imperio patres plebem exercere, de vita atque tergo regio more consulere, agro pellere et ceteris expertibus soli in imperio agere.* (Sall. *Hist. fr.* i. 11.)

[4] Dionys., v. 2.

plebeians saw men of their own order in the first classes, and patricians in the last, like Cincinnatus, who, after his son's lawsuit, had only six acres of land for his own property.[1]

The Roman plebs was not, however, like that populace of great cities which is seen chafing, struggling, and calming down at random, — a blind force, which only becomes formidable when it finds a leader. The plebeians, too, had their nobility, their old families, and even royal families; for the patricians of conquered towns, like the Mamilii, the Papii, the Cilnii, and Caecinae in later times, had not all been received into the Roman patriciate. Other families, of patrician origin, but whom circumstances unknown to us drove out of the Curiae or hindered from entering them — the Virginii, the Genucii, the Menii, the Melii, the Oppii, the Metelli, and the Octavii, placed themselves at the head of the people; and these men, who could vie in nobility with the proudest senators, by joining their fortunes with the order into which they had been driven, furnished the plebs with ambitious leaders, and its efforts with skilful direction.[2] As the price of the help afforded to the nobles against Tarquin, they

---

[1] Val. Max., IV. iv. 7.

[2] The Metelli claimed descent from Caeculus, son of Vulcan and founder of Praeneste. They were plebeians, and yet Livy calls them patricians (iv. 4). The *gens* Furia, on the other hand, was patrician, yet he calls the Furii plebeians (ix. 42 and xxxix. 7); the Melii and Menii were plebeians: he calls them patricians (v. 12); the Virginii (v. 29) and the Atilii (iv. 7) were patricians: he makes them plebeians (v. 13, and x. 23); the Cassii, Oppii, and Genucii are in like manner called by turns patricians and plebeians, consuls and tribunes. One branch of the *gens* Sempronia, the Atratini, are patricians; another branch, the Gracchi, are plebeians. The explanation of this peculiarity, which occurs too often to be due to an error on the part of Livy, may perhaps be found in the supposition that, out of regard for [traditional] numbers (see · p. 189), there remained outside the original Senate certain families who were yet held in as high consideration as those whose chiefs, having become senators, conferred on their descendants the name of patricians. In that case the Curiae must have comprised families which had the auspices, all the rights of the sovereign class of citizens, and admission to office, without being patrician, and yet not plebeian. When two orders only came to be recognized in the city, some of these families re-entered the aristocratical body; others must have been thrown back upon the people, whose strength they constituted. Members of these uncertain families may have even been placed by the censors on the list of the Senate. This would explain the phrase of Livy (v. 12) about the plebeian Licinius Calvus, before the year 367 B. C.: *vir nullis ante honoribus usus, vetus tantum senator.* Dionys. (Frag. xlvi.) asserts that it was through fear of tribunitian accusations (see p. 164) that some patricians had caused themselves to be inscribed among the plebeians. The reason is a poor one; for an *adoption* was necessary in order to change one's family, and in that case the person adopted took the name of the adopter. Whatever explanation is accepted, however, this much is certain, and we only insist on this important point, that there were, either between patricians and people, or at the head of the people, noble and wealthy families interested in overthrowing the distinction between the two orders.

had obtained the enforcement of the constitution of Servius. Hereafter they will extort further concessions; for Etruria is arming in the King's cause, and behind the Veientines and Tarquinians may be already seen the preparations of Porsenna. A common misfortune may bring the two orders nearer by humbling the military pride of the nobles.

Aristocracies die out when they are not renewed, especially in military republics, where the nobles are found in the first ranks of battle, and pay for their privileges with their blood. Decimated by warfare and by that mysterious law of development in the human species which causes the extinction of old families,[1] every aristocracy which does not receive recruits from without its pale is soon exhausted and destroyed by the action of time alone. The 9,000 Spartans of Lycurgus were no longer more than 5,000 at Plataea, fewer still at Leuctra and at Sellasia. But the nobility of Rome never closed its "golden book." Under Tullus the great families of Alba, under Tarquin a hundred new members, had been admitted to the Senate. After the abolition of royalty, the fathers felt the need of strengthening themselves by drawing towards them all the men of consideration in the city to whom the Curia had hitherto been closed.[2] Brutus or Valerius restored the Senate to the usual number of 300 members, as it had been deprived of many by the cruelty of Tarquin and the exile of his partisans.[3] At the same time the Senate distributed among the people the lands of the royal domain, abolished customs, and lowered the price of salt,[5] — a clever

COIN REPRESENTING BRUTUS.[4]

---

[1] The pestilences so frequent at Rome also contributed to the extinction of families. After the plague of 462 B. C., which carried off both the consuls, several patrician families disappear. After that epoch there is no mention of the Lartii, Cominii, and Numicii, and we no longer, or only rarely, meet with patricians of the name of Tullius, Sicinius, Volumnius, Aebutius, Herminius, Lucretius, and Menenius.

[2] I cannot possibly admit the strange theory, originating in Germany, of the constitution, after the year 509, of a plebeio-patrician Senate. The whole internal history of Rome up to 367 B. C. protests against this supposition.

[3] The exiles were so numerous that they fought in separate bodies. (Dionys., v. 6.) A passage in Cicero (*de Rep.* i. 40) shows that there was a violent reaction against the friends of the last King.

[4] Denarius of the Junian family.

[5] Livy, ii. 9. For these proceedings Brutus had re-established, or caused to be confirmed by the Curiae, the quaestors established by the kings. (Tac., *Ann.* xi. 22.) Plutarch refers their creation to Valerius.

move in two ways, for by satisfying the ambition of the chiefs, it separated them from the masses, which remained without leaders, while at the same time it interested the latter, by increasing their material welfare, in the cause of the nobles.

To the first year of the Republic, too, are said to belong the laws of Valerius, who, being left sole consul for some time after the death of Brutus, exercised a kind of dictatorship, and made use of it to pass laws which the *intercessio* of a colleague would perhaps have prevented. These laws punished with death whosoever should aspire to royalty, and authorized disobedience to a magistrate who should continue his office beyond the appointed term. He caused the fasces to be lowered before the popular assembly, and recognized its sovereign jurisdiction by carrying the law of appeal (*provocatio*),[1] which was to Rome what the *habeas corpus* has been to England. In order to show clearly that the power of life and death was taken away from the consuls, he took the axes out of the fasces within the city and within a mile of its walls. Beyond that they were restored to the lictors, for the consuls on passing the first milestone[2] recovered that unlimited power which was

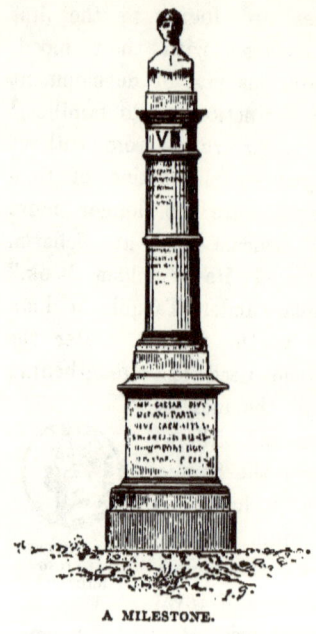

A MILESTONE.

[1] *Neque enim provocationem longius esse ab urbe mille passuum.* (Livy, iii. 20.) "This was," says Cicero (*de Rep.* ii. 31), "the first law voted by the centuries." The appeal forbade *eum qui provocasset virgis caedi securique necari.* (Livy, x. 9.) Compare Val. Max., iv. 1, and Cic., *de Rep.* ii. 31. Dionysius (v. 19) extends the prohibition to fines. But if this occurred, it could only be after the decemvirate. There is attributed to Valerius, too, a law which would throw open the candidature for the consulship. Ὑπατείαν ἔδωκε μετιέναι καὶ παραγγέλλειν τοῖς βουλομένοις. (Plut., *Popl.* ii.) It is, of course, understood that this refers only to patricians who might demand of the Senate or consuls to be inscribed on the list of candidates.

[2] The value of the Roman mile is about 1615 yards (1481.75 metres). Upon the roads which issued from Rome, each mile was marked by a numbered post, and the distances counted from the gate of the circuit wall of Servius. The post represented by the engraving, after a restoration of Canina, was the first upon the Appian Way. It is much later in date than our present epoch,

as necessary to them in the army as it was dangerous in the city.

Thus the patricians and the plebeians remained two distinct orders, widely separated by the inequality of their condition: the one, descendants of the early conquerors and guardians of the ancient worship; the other, a mixed mass of men of all kinds of origins and religions, long kept in subjection by the ruling people, the Quirites, and still placed, as having neither the same blood nor the same gods, under the insulting prohibition against intermarriage with patricians. Fortunately the assembly of centuries united them in a single people, and this union saved them. At first, it is true, it benefited only the patricians, who appropriated the lion's share of the royal spoils. But the plebeians little by little forced them to an equitable division. The establishment of the tribuneship was their first and surest victory; for before attacking they must learn how to defend themselves.

II. The Tribunate.

At Rome, as at Athens, and in all the states of antiquity wherein handicrafts did not support the poor people of free condition, debts were the primary cause of democratic revolutions. Rome, being an exclusively agricultural state, would have needed, in order to profit by the advantages of that condition, a long period of peace or a vast territory, which might save the greater portion of the land from undergoing the ravages of war. Now warfare was constant, and after the conquest of Porsenna and the rising of the Latins, the frontier was so near the town, that the lands of the enemy might be seen from the top of the walls.[1] There was, then, neither repose nor safety to be had; whence it resulted that everywhere there was crowding and bad husbandry. Called to arms every year, the plebeian neglected his little farm; moreover

---

as it bears the names of Vespasian and of Nerva. The use of these posts must be much more ancient than Gracchus, who is supposed to have established them. (Plut., *C. Gracc.* 6-7.) The post was at first a rough-hewn stone, which, by degrees, in the vicinity of Rome and large towns, assumed the shape of a monument.

[1] For the military history of this epoch, see next chapter.

he must equip himself at his own expense, provide his own food in war time, and yet pay the tax, which was relatively heavier for the poor than the rich, because, being based upon landed property, it did not allow for the debts of the one class or the credit of the other. But if the war was not successful; if the enemy, who could in a single day traverse the whole territory of the Republic, came and cut down the crops and burned the farms; if to the pillage of the people of Latium and the Sabine land there were added inclemency of weather, — how was the farmer to support his family or rebuild his burned home?

There were means of coming to some understanding with the gods. A temple was promised, it might be to some foreign deity whom they felt guilty of having neglected; or they offered a sacrifice, and thought they had set themselves right with the celestial powers. Thus, a famine having broken out during the Latin war, the dictator Postumius promised a sanctuary to a Greek divinity, Demeter, who caused the fruitfulness of the Campanian plains, whence the Senate, no doubt, procured corn. She took, on the banks of Tiber, the name of an old Etruscan deity, Ceres;[1] and to minister at her altar a woman was summoned from Naples or Velia, who on her arrival received the rights of citizenship, because a Roman tongue only could invoke the gods in favor of Rome.

The usurer's account was a more difficult matter to settle. All the hard-earned savings went first, then the booty won in previous campaigns, and finally the hereditary patrimony, — the last pledge on which the poor man had raised a loan at an enormous rate of interest. Thus a great number of plebeians had, within a few years after the expulsion of the kings, become the debtors of the wealthy, like their descendants, the peasants of the Roman Campagna, who, ruined by usury and monopolies, sell their crops before they have been sown. But the wealthy were to be found especially among the patricians. Being possessed of vast estates, and holding the lands of the public domain, which, as it was usually left for pasturage, had little to fear from the enemy's ravages, they could still export to foreign countries the wool of their flocks

---

[1] Servius, *ad Aen.* ii. 325. The name Ceres has no meaning in Latin.

and the produce of their land. Their fortune was less dependent on a bad season or a hostile incursion. Thus they always had money for that lucrative business[1] which brought in more than the best land or the most dogged work. At Rome, as at Athens before the time of Solon, and as in all the ancient states of Asia and the North, the law assigned to the creditor the liberty and life of the debtor; it was a pledge, a mortgage held on his person. If the debtor did not fulfil his obligations within the legal period, he became *nexus*,[2] that is to say, he bound his person to pay his debt by labor. He was not a slave; but his creditor could impose servile duties upon him, and even keep him imprisoned in the *ergastulum*. His children, unless he had previously emancipated them, shared his fate, for they were his property; and his property, like his person, belonged to his creditors until he had freed himself from his debt.

CERES FOUND AT OSTIA IN 1856. (MUSEUM OF THE VATICAN.)

It was not necessary that many plebeians should find themselves under the action of this severe law, to cause a widespread

---

[1] Usury was a national vice at Rome. Polybius knew this so well, that he honors Scipio for not having been guilty of it (xxxii. fr. 8). We know that Cato the Censor carried on the most disreputable form of it,—maritime usury; and we see in Plutarch the parsimony of Crassus, notwithstanding his immense fortune.

[2] See page 31. The *nexum* was the verbal agreement undertaken by the creditor, in the presence of witnesses, to pay back the loan.

irritation; its very existence was sufficient. The people soon saw that the revolution had merely substituted patrician for royal authority; and they conceived a violent hatred for these haughty masters, who treated them with the violence they themselves had suffered at the King's hands.[1] At first they peaceably demanded the abolition of debts; then they refused to obey the conscription for service against the Latins. The situation seemed so critical to the Senate that they revived royalty with all its power for a time. In 501 B. C. they created the dictatorship, the powers of which were unlimited. Elected, on the invitation of the Senate, by one of the consuls, and chosen from among the *consulares*, the dictator (*magister populi*)[2] had, even in Rome, twenty-four lictors bearing the axes in the fasces, as a sign of absolute authority. The ordinary magistrates were under his orders, and the right of appeal to the people was suspended; it was like our declaration of martial law. He was nominated for six months, like his lieutenant, the *magister equitum*, but none ever retained these formidable powers so long. So soon as the danger had passed which had caused the suspension of public liberty and the legal establishment of this provisional tyranny, the dictator abdicated.[3] The Senate had thus reserved an extraordinary magistracy for those critical times from which states often emerge only at the cost of their liberty. More than once, indeed, did the dictatorship save the Republic from the enemy without and from the agitations of the Forum within. If for nearly three centuries Rome never felt the stormy vicissitudes of the Hellenic

---

[1] *Propter nimiam dominationem potentium.* (Cic., *pro Corn.* fr. 24.) Sallust speaks similarly. (*Hist. frag.* i. 21.)

[2] *Lars*, in Etruscan, means lord and master. (Plutarch, *Quaest. Rom.* 51.) The expression *magister populi* has the same meaning, and the dictatorship was probably an imitation of what took place in Etruria when, in grave circumstances, she appointed a *lars*, like Porsenna or Tolumnius.

[3] Varro, *de Ling. Lat.* v. 82; Fest, s. v. *optima lex*. A tradition, reported by Livy, would assign another cause for the creation of this magistracy, — that the two consuls were partisans of the King. The Greeks translated the word dictator by μόναρχος and αὐτοκράτωρ. Zonaras (vii. 13) says: τὴν δ' ἐκ τῆς μοναρχίας ὠφέλειαν θέλοντες ... ἐν ἄλλῳ ταύτην ὀνόματι εἶχον. Machiavelli made the following remark, which is confirmed by Montesquieu (*Esp. des Lois*, ii. 3:) "Without a power of this nature, the state must either be lost in following the ordinary lines of proceeding, or else quit them, in order to save itself. But if extraordinary means do good for the moment, they leave a bad example, which is a real evil." The dictatorships of Sulla and Caesar have, of course, nothing in common with the ancient dictatorship.

republics; if those movements, which otherwise would have degenerated into revolutions, only resulted at Rome in the regular development of the constitution, — it was owing in a great measure to this office, this unlimited power of which moderated the public excitement, while at the same time it arrested ambitious designs.

Startled by these menacing displays, by this unlimited power, the plebs stifled its murmurs for some years, and the consuls were able to count on its support in the regal wars. But in 495 B. C., Appius Claudius, the most pitiless of patricians, was appointed consul with Servilius. His pride, which chafed even at a complaint, was already exciting sullen anger, when a man suddenly appeared in the Forum, pale and fearfully emaciated. He was one of the bravest centurions of the Roman army; he had been in twenty-eight battles. He told how, in the Sabine war, the enemy had burned his house and his crops, and carried off his flock. In order to live he had borrowed money, and usury, like an odious sore, devouring his patrimony, had even invaded his body. His creditors had led away himself and his son, loaded with irons and lacerated with blows; and he showed his body still bleeding. At this sight the public fury knew no bounds, and a messenger having come to announce an incursion of the Volscians, the plebeians refused to take arms. "Let the patricians go and fight," said they; "let them have all the perils of war, since they have all its profits!" They only yielded when the consul Servilius had promised that after the war their complaints should be examined, and that all the time it lasted, debtors should be free. On this assurance the people took arms. Before this, the Volscians had given three hundred hostages; Appius had them all beheaded. Then Servilius marched on Suessa Pometia, which was taken, and the booty distributed among his soldiers. But when the victorious army returned to Rome, the Senate refused to fulfil the consul's promises. The poor found themselves again at the mercy of the pitiless Appius, and the *ergastula* were filled anew. In vain the people exclaimed loudly against it; Appius was inflexible. In order to frighten the multitude, he caused a dictator to be appointed. The choice fell upon a man of a popular family, Manlius Valerius, who renewed the pledges of Servilius, and with an army of 40,000 plebeians defeated the Volscians, Aequians, and Sabines. The people thought that they had this time secured the execution of the consular promises; again they were deceived. A few poor men only, it is said, were sent as colonists to Velitrae. The indignant Valerius resigned, calling to witness Fidius, the god of pledged faith, which had been broken.

BRIDGE OF NOMENTUM.

ANNA PERENNA.[1]

To avert a revolt in the Forum, the consuls of the year 493, availing themselves of the military oath taken to their predecessors, forced the army to go out of the city. But outside the gates the plebeians abandoned the consuls, and crossing the Anio, probably at the spot where the bridge of Nomentum was built, they marched, under the leadership of Sicinius Bellutus and Junius Brutus, to the Sacred Mount,[2] and encamped there; those of

---

[1] C. ANNI. T. F. T. N., that is, C. Annius, son of Titus, grandson of Titus Annius. Head with a diadem, attributed by Cavedoni to Anna Perenna: to the right, a caduceus; on the left, a pair of scales. Silver coin of the Annian family.

[2] The *mons sacer* is an elongated hill, separated from the Anio by a meadow, in which there still exists the ancient bridge, surmounted by a pontifical building of the fifteenth century. (See cut.)

Rome withdrew at the same time with their families to the Aventine.[1] Tradition had it that an old woman of Bovillae brought them every morning smoking hot cakes, which she had sat up all night to bake: it was the Goddess Anna Perenna.[2] Under this legend lies hidden a remembrance of the assistance given to the plebeians by the neighboring cities.

Some time passed in delay and in fruitless negotiations. At last the patricians, frightened by the menacing position of the legions, nominated two consuls, friends of the people, and sent ten consulars as a deputation to the soldiers. Among them were three former dictators, also Lartius Postumius, Valerius, and the plebeian Menenius Agrippa, the most eloquent and popular of the senators. He told them the fable of the belly and the members, and brought back their demands to the Senate. They were remarkably moderate. All slaves for debt were to be set free; the debts themselves, at least those of insolvent debtors, to be cancelled.[3] They did not even demand that the criminal law should be altered; fifty years later, we shall find it still inscribed by the decemvirs on the Twelve Tables. But they would not consent to come down from the Sacred Mount until they had nominated two tribunes, Sicinius and Brutus, whose right the Senate should recognize of assisting the harshly used[4] debtor, and of staying by their veto the effect of the consular judgments. In this way those Romans who remained without patrician protection, and had no one to defend them, would henceforth have two official patrons with whom it would be necessary to reckon.[5]

These representatives of the poor had neither the laticlave with a border of purple, nor lictors armed with fasces. No external mark distinguished them from the crowd, and they were preceded by a single apparitor in plain dress. But, as fetials in an enemy's territory, their person was inviolable. They devoted to

---

[1] Cic., *de Rep.*, ii. 37; Livy, ii. 32; App., *Bell. Civ.* i. 1.
[2] Ovid, *Fast.* iii. 654.
[3] Dionys., vi. 83.
[4] At first the tribune could only protect the plebeian who had been insulted or struck in his presence.
[5] Zon., vii. 15: προστάτας δύο; and Livy, ii. 33; iii. 55. The tribunes were not allowed, except during the Latin games, to be away from Rome at night, and their door always remained open. Their power ended one mile from the walls, where the *imperium* of the consuls began.

the gods any one who struck them, by saying *sacer esto*,[1] and his goods were confiscated to the profit of the temple of Ceres. No patrician could become a tribune (493 B. C.).

By this creation of two leaders of the people (soon afterward five, still later ten) the revolt, purely civil, if I may so term it, in principle became almost a revolution, and turned out to be the greatest event in the domestic history of Rome. "It was," says Cicero,[2] "the first reduction of the consular power, in constituting a magistrate independent of it. The second was the help which it afforded to the other magistrates, as well as to the citizens who refused obedience to the consuls."

The rich plebeians adopted the chiefs of the poor as being those of the entire order. Thus supported, this protective power soon became aggressive; and we shall see the tribunes, on the one hand, extending their veto to all acts contrary to popular interests,[3] and on the other politically organizing the people, outside the *auctoritas patrum*, and causing the *concilia plebis* to assert as their own the rights of deliberating, voting, and electing. Later on, we shall see them effacing the distinction between the orders by proclaiming the principle that the sovereignty resides in the whole people; and then will come the time when no one is so powerful in Rome as a tribune of the people. This power doubtless committed many excesses. But without it, the Republic, in subjection to an oppressive oligarchy, would never have fulfilled its great destinies. "Rome ought either to have continued a monarchy," said even Cicero,[4] who had much personal ground for complaint against the tribunate, "or there was no need to grant the plebeians a liberty which was not made up of mere empty words." This liberty now begins for them, since there is no freedom apart from strength, and there is no strength in societies except in discipline. Disciplined by its new chiefs, the people were soon able to maintain a regular struggle against the great,

---

[1] Zon. (*ibid.*) explains this expression, which occurs so often in legislation. The victim, led to the altar as a sacrifice, was *devoted*, *i. e.* given up to death; so also the man declared *sacer*.

[2] *De Leg.* iii. 7. The question how the tribunes were nominated between the years 493 and 471 is very obscure. I do not doubt, however, that it had been from the first reserved to the *concilium plebis*. See p. 295.

[3] Val. Max., ii. 7; Dionys., x. 2.

[4] *De Leg.* iii. 10; . . . *re non verbo*.

and obtain, one after the other, all the magisterial offices. The patrician city, forced to receive them, will be opened to the Italians also; later on to the world; and a great empire will be the recompense of this union, demanded and secured by the tribunes.[1]

It was with the most solemn ceremonies, by sacrifices and the ministry of the fetials, as if the matter in hand were a treaty between two different peoples, that the peace was concluded and celebrated. Every citizen swore to keep eternally the sacred laws, *leges sacratae*,[2] and an altar, erected to Jupiter Tonans on

B, LEFT SIDE.   A, ALTAR OF THE TEMPLE, THOUGHT TO BE THAT OF QUIRINUS, AT POMPEII.[3]   C, RIGHT SIDE.

the site of the plebeian camp, consecrated the mountain where the people had acquired their earliest liberties. Public veneration surrounded, to the day of his death, the man who had reconciled the two orders, and when Agrippa died the people gave him, as well as Brutus and Poplicola, a splendid funeral.

As the consuls had two quaestors, so the tribunes had under them, to guard the material interests of the plebeian community, two aediles, whose rights increased, as did those of the tribunes, and who finally had the care of all public buildings (*aedes*), especially that of the temple of Ceres, where were kept the senatus-

---

[1] On the successive additions to the tribunes' power, see Zonaras, vii. 15.
[2] Livy, ii. 33; Dionys., vi. 89.
[3] The altar of Mons Sacer was certainly very simple and unornamented, whilst that we give is much ornamented. It shows, at any rate, the general form of Roman altars, and how religious art decorated them. On one of its sides (Fig. A) is to be seen a sacrificial ceremony; on the other sides (Figs. B, C) are grouped different articles used in worship, — the *lituus* or augur's staff, the box for perfumes, etc.

consulta, and the right of controlling the supply of Rome with provisions.[1] In the second century B. C. the aedileship was, according to Polybius, a very illustrious office,[2] and Cicero calls the great Architect of the world *the Aedile of the Universe.*

It is certain that the plebeians had already their own special judges, *judices decemviri*, and their public assembly, *concilium plebis;* the patricians were naturally excluded from them, or, to speak more exactly, did not condescend to enter them.[3]

We shall close with two remarks: the tribunate is the most original of Roman institutions, for nothing like it has existed either among ancients or moderns; and the revolution whence it proceeded did not cost one drop of human blood.

III. THE AGRARIAN LAW.

THE beginnings of the tribunate were humble and obscure, like those of all the plebeian magistracies.[4] But a patrician who had been consul and celebrated a triumph three times — Spurius Cassius — revealed to the tribunes the secret of their power, viz. popular

[1] Dionys., vi. 90.
[2] Polyb., x. 4.
[3] Livy, iii. 55, and ii. 56, 60; Dionys., ix. 41.
[4] To fill up the interval void of acts which intervenes between the years 493 B.C. and 486 B.C., there are usually placed, immediately after the establishment of the tribunate, the trial of Coriolanus and the disputes of the tribunes with the consuls respecting the colonies of Norba and Volitrae,—that is to say, the conquest for the tribunes of the right of speaking before the people without interruption, of convoking the comitia of tribes, of declaring plebiscita, of judging and condemning to death patricians. Thus we fail to recognize the humble beginnings of this magistracy, which in the first year of its existence was certainly not strong enough to brave the Senate, the patricians, and the consuls. Besides this consideration many circumstances in the story are actually false. Thus Norba and Velitrae were not then Roman colonies, but independent Latin cities, as the treaty of Cassius with the Latins proves; Corioli was not a Volscian city taken by the Romans, but one of the thirty Latin republics. Then Coriolanus is said to have borne when very young his first arms at the battle of Lake Regillus, in 496 B.C., and in 492 B. C. he demands the consulship and is father of several children. The tradition of Coriolanus has no doubt a historical basis; but this proscription of one of the most illustrious patricians, this vengeance of a chief among the banished, ought to belong to the epoch which saw the condemnation of Menenius and Appius, the exile of Caeso, and the attempt of Herdonius. Niebuhr also believes the Icilian law to be posterior to that of Volero, and Hooke had previously proved it. It was, in truth, a plebiscitum, and the people were only able to pass it after the adoption of the Publilian law in 470 B. C. Besides, the first use of the Icilian law was made only in 421 B. C. in connection with Caeso (*hic primus vades publico dedit*); the tribunes would thus have remained more than thirty years without using it.

agitation. He was the first to start amongst the crowd that grand watchword, "the agrarian law;" and the tribunes after him had only to pronounce it to raise in the Forum the most furious storms. In the Middle Ages, to possess land was to take rank among nobles; at Rome, it was to become truly a citizen, to have true riches, such as alone brought honor, possessed endurance, and the only kind that Rome, without industry and with but little trade, could know and respect. Hence the importance of the agrarian laws; for, political rights being in proportion to fortune, to diminish that of some and increase that of others amounted, in the order of the social system, to raising the latter and bringing down the former. By touching property they touched also the very constitution of the state, — they laid a hand on that which religion had consecrated. Of course the upper classes repelled always, by either force or deception, those laws which sought to give the people, at their expense, a little fortune and power.

The agrarian laws did not, however, attack hereditary patrimonies, ordinarily of small extent, but property usurped from the state, and which could be recovered in its name from the dishonest holder. Like the territory of all the peoples in Italy and Greece, the *ager Romanus* had been primitively divided into equal parts among all the citizens; these *assigned* lands, the limits of which the augurs themselves drew, formed the inviolable and hereditary property of the Quirites. But in this division of the soil there had been reserved for the wants of the state a certain extent of land, generally pasturage and forests, which continued to be the common domain, the *ager publicus*, and on which every one had the right of pasturing his flocks (*pecus*), for the payment of a small rent (*pecunia*). This public domain grew with the conquests made by Rome; for by the right of war all conquered lands belonged to the conquerors, who generally made of them a twofold division, — the one, restored to the old inhabitants or assigned, as property of the Quirites, to particular Roman citizens (*coloni*); the second, without doubt the more considerable, attached to the public domain.

If the *ager publicus* had continued wholly communal, it would have yielded but a slight profit. To increase its value, a part of it was enclosed; and the state, as proprietor, received from the farmers of it a tenth part of the produce. This tithe formed, down to the time of the Veian war, along with the rent for pasturage, the principal revenue of the city; hence the importance of all questions relating to the *ager publicus*. But the farmers, at first, were all patricians,[1] and the Senate, forgetting the interests of the state in behalf of those of their own order, neglected, little by little, to demand the tithes and rents. This was, however, the mark which distinguished these leaseholds, and, at all times, revocable possessions, from full *quiritary possession*. So, on this mark disappearing, the farms became changed into freeholds, and the state lost doubly, by the diminution of the rents paid to the treasury and by the loss of the public domain, transformed into private domains,[2] without the possessor paying for these usurped lands the *tributum ex censu* which was levied on all quiritary (freehold) property.

However, ancient jurisprudence declared that there was never any statute of limitation against the state;[3] which, therefore, retained all its rights over these usurped domains, and was able to resume them, whoever might be the holder, the original farmer, his heirs, or any one who had bought from them for ready money. For, in the case of both parties, the unjust possessor or the *bona fide* purchaser, it was nothing else than a property held without title.

During the monarchy, agrarian laws had been frequent, because it was the interest of the kings, surrounded by a jealous aristocracy, to keep friends with the partisans of the people; but since the exile of Tarquin there had been no other assignment than that of Brutus. How much misery, however, had not the plebeians borne, during those twenty-four years, from war and usury! So the most illustrious of the patricians, the only one of this epoch who, with Valerius, had been three times decorated with the consular purple,

---

[1] A passage of Cassius Hemina, in Nonius (ii. s. v. *Plebitas*) leads to the belief that plebeians could not be admitted to the occupation of domain land. There is certainly reason to believe in the principle here implied, since the plebeians were considered as a foreign people. But the same passage proves that there were also plebeians holders of domain land: *Quicumque propter plebitatem agro publico ejecti sunt*; and Sallust (*Hist. frag.* 11) says also, that some time after the expulsion of the Tarquins, they were driven from the public lands, *agro pellere*. We shall see Lucinius Stolo in the possession of 700 acres.

[2] Cf. Aggenus Urbicus, *de Controv. agror.*, ap. Goes., *Rei agrariae scriptores*, p. 69. *Negant illud solum, quod solum populi Romani esse caepit, ullo modo usicapi a quoquam mortalium posse.*

[3] Cic., *de Rep.* ii. 14.

Spurius Cassius, desired to restore to the state its revenues and lands, and to give the poor the means of becoming useful citizens. He proposed to divide a part of the government lands amongst the most needy; to compel the farmers of the state to pay their tithes regularly; and to use this revenue in paying the troops.[1] If these were indeed the demands of Cassius, we know not how to rate too highly the unrecognized glory of this great citizen, who after having consolidated abroad the tottering fortunes of Rome by his double treaty with the Latins and Hernicans,[2] wished, at home, to prevent trouble by helping the poor, and who, almost a century before it was adopted, had proposed the important measure for the settlement of the soldiers' pay (486).

But these popular and patriotic demands aroused the indignation of the Senate. The usurpation of the *ager publicus*, against which Cassius protested, was the principal source of patrician fortunes. A long possession seemed, besides, to have established a right, and the great number of possessors of domain land no longer distinguished their hereditary estates from the fields which they kept from the state. However, it would have been dangerous, at a moment when the people saw a consul at their head, to reject the law: the Senate accepted it without seeing it carried out, but hastened to be avenged on Cassius. The multitude once appeased, dark rumors spread about the city: "Cassius was only a false friend to the people. To obtain allies he had already sacrificed the interests of Rome to the Latins and Hernicans; but he wished to stir up the poor against the great, and profit from their quarrels to get himself declared king." The tribunes, jealous of their popularity, and the people, whom it is so easy to frighten with empty shadows, deserted him, when, on retiring from the consulship, the nobles accused him of treason in the comitia curiata, *ex more majorum*. Condemned to be beaten with rods and beheaded (486), he was executed by order of his father in his ancestral home.[3] Thus have

---

[1] This law is not that of Cassius, but that of Sempronius Atratinus, who very probably did no more than reproduce the principal provisions of Cassius, excluding, however, the Latins, whom Cassius, in order to strengthen the alliance of Rome with them, admitted to a share of the lands which they had recently conquered in concert with the Romans. (Dionys., viii. 68, 69; Livy, ii. 41.)

[2] See p. 307.

[3] Dion Cassius (*Frag.* 19) regards him as a victim of the nobles : οὐκ ἀδικήσας τι ἀπώλετο.

perished so many popular patricians, victims of a powerful aristocracy. The favor of the people is dangerous: it has slain more tribunes than it has crowned.

The nobles, once rid of Cassius, sought to preclude the return of the danger. The powerful house of the Fabii was signalized by its zeal for the interests of the Senate, and it was one of its members that had pronounced sentence of death against Cassius; the nobles desired no other consuls, and during seven years (484 – 478) a Fabius forms a member of the consulate. In vain, also, did the tribunes call for the acceptance of the agrarian law. C. Maenius even wished, in 482, to oppose his veto to the raising of troops, since the Senate would not proceed to a division of the lands. But the consuls conveyed their tribunal out of the city, where the tribunitian protection did not extend, and summoned the citizens to the enrolment, causing, by their lictors, the farms to be burned, the fruit-trees to be cut down, and the fields laid waste of those who did not give their names. These violent acts might prove dangerous: the Senate preferred fighting the people with its proper weapons, by gaining some members of the college of tribunes, whose opposition stopped the veto of Sp. Licinius in 480, and of Pontificius[1] in 479. But the soldiers took it on themselves to avenge the feebleness of the tribunate, and in 480 the legions refused to gain a victory over the Veientines, so as not to secure to Caeso Fabius the honor of a triumph.

Here the history becomes obscure. The Fabii, chiefs of the Senate, pass over to the people, and then are forced to leave Rome. We cannot but see in this change one of those frequent revolutions in aristocratic republics. Without doubt, the patricians were alarmed at seeing the consulate become the heritage of one family, and the Fabii were obliged to seek among the people, notwithstanding their ambition, that support which the Senate intended to withdraw. Won over by the popular words and conduct of M. Fabius (479), the soldiers promised him, this time, the defeat of the Veientines. The battle was bloody; the consul's brother perished: but the soldiers kept their word: the Etruscans were crushed.[2] On their return the Fabii received the wounded plebeians into their houses,

---

[1] Livy, ii. 43, 44.   [2] Livy, ii. 44 ; Dionys., ix. 6.

and henceforth no family was more popular. The next year, Caeso Fabius, having owed the consulate "rather to the people's votes than those of the nobles,"[1] forgot that he was the accuser of Cassius, and wished to extort from the patricians the execution of the agrarian law. Since all hope of obtaining justice for the people was lost, the whole *gens*, with its clients and partisans, left the city, where it was uselessly compromised in the eyes of the patricians, and in order to be still useful to Rome in its voluntary exile, it established itself before the enemy[2] on the banks of the Cremera. Later on, the pride of the Fabian *gens* insisted in seeing in this exile the devotion of three hundred and six Fabii, who sustained, with their four thousand clients, on behalf of tottering Rome, the war against the Veientines. One Fabius only, left at Rome because of his tender age, prevented, it is said, the extinction of the whole clan.[3]

After conquering in many encounters, they allowed themselves to be drawn into an ambuscade in which the greater part perished. The rest took refuge on a steep hill, and fought there from morning till evening. "They were surrounded by heaps of dead; but the enemy was so numerous that the arrows rained on them like flakes of snow. By dint of striking, their swords had become blunt and their bucklers had been shattered. Yet they never ceased fighting, and snatching arms from the enemy, they fell on them like wild beasts."[4] While these heroic scenes were going on, which remind us of the exploits sung in the *chansons de geste*, the consul Menenius came by chance into the neighborhood with an army; he did nothing to save the Fabii. Perhaps this family, so proud, which had tried to rule in Rome by its consular office, and afterward by the favor of the people, was sacrificed to the jealous fears of the Senate, as afterward Sicinius and his band to the terrors of the decemvirs (477).

The pontiffs inscribed among the *dies nefasti* that on which

---

[1] *Non patrum magis quam plebis studiis . . . consul factus.* (Livy, ii. 48.)
[2] *Cum familiis suis.* (Aul. Gell., xvii. 21.)
[3] Dionys., ix. 15; Livy, ii. 50; Ovid, *Fast.* ii. 195, *seq.* Dionysius says four thousand clients and ἑταῖροι; Festus, five thousand clients. The Vitellii pretended also, aided only by their clients, to have defended against the Aequicolae a town which took their name, Vitellia. (Suet., *Vitell.* i.)
[4] Dionys., ix. 21.

the Fabii had perished, and the gate by which they had left was cursed; no consul would ever cross the entrance on an expedition.[1] Rome preserved the memorial of its misfortunes, and by this mourning, perpetuated through centuries, she prevented its repetition.

IV. Right of the Tribunes to accuse the Consuls and to bring forward Plebiscita.

THE people had not been able to prevent the exile of the Fabii; they wished at least to avenge them. The tribunes accused Menenius of treason (476 B. C.); shame and grief overcame him, he starved himself to death. This was a considerable success.[2] Until then the power of the tribunes had been confined to their veto, and this the consuls well knew how to render illusory; but we see them now adopting a new weapon. The disaster at Cremera and the public mourning helped them to gain the right of citing the consuls to the bar of justice. Henceforth the tribunitian accusers waited for those magistrates who are opposed to the agrarian law, till they gave up office. Excluded from the Curiae, the Senate, and the magistracies; annulled in the centuries by the preponderating influence of the patricians; deprived by the dictatorship of the tribunitian protection, — the plebeians now found the means of intimidating their most violent adversaries by summoning them before their tribes, *concilium plebis*. For meeting and acting the tribunes had need neither of the permission of the Senate nor the consecration of the augurs;[3] and the patricians who could not pretend to the tribunate did not vote in the popular assembly, just as English peers do not in the elections for the Lower House of Parliament. In less than twenty-six years, seven

---

[1] Dion., *Fr.* 21.

[2] From the texts of Dionys. (ix. 44, 46) and of Lydus (i. 34, 44) we might conclude that a law conferred on the tribunes this right of accusing the consuls; but we cannot understand how this law could have been made. We must rest content to be ignorant of many things respecting these old times.

[3] Μήτε προβουλεύματος . . . μήτε τῶν ἱερῶν. (Dionys., ix. 41.) *Plebeius magistratus nullus auspicato creatur.* (Livy, vi. 42.)

consuls and many patricians of the most illustrious families were accused, condemned in penalties, or escaped this shame only by exile or voluntary death.[1]

In 475 B.C. Servilius, and in 473 L. Furius and C. Manlius were accused by the tribunes, the former for a mismanaged attack in the war against the Veientines, the others for not having executed the agrarian law. Servilius escaped; but Manlius and Furius had as their opponent the tribune Genucius, who had sworn before the people to allow no obstacle to stand in his way. On the day of the trial he was found dead in his bed (473).[2]

This assassination spread terror among the people and its chiefs, and when the consuls forced the plebeians to enlist, arbitrarily distributing the ranks, and disdaining to heed any complaints, not a voice arose from the tribunes' seat. "Your tribunes are deserting you," cried Publilius Volero, a brave centurion who refused to serve as a common soldier. "They prefer to allow a citizen to perish under the rods than expose themselves to assassination." On the lictors approaching to lay hold on him, he pushed them away, took refuge in the midst of the crowd, stirred it up, roused it to action, and drove from the Forum the consuls and the lictors with their fasces broken.

The year following he was named tribune (472). He could have taken revenge by an accusation against the consuls: he preferred employing for the popular cause the courage which a successful rising had just aroused in the people. It was the army which, on the Sacred Mount, had elected the first tribunes; but this army, in a state of revolt against the consuls, was the plebeian part of the comitia centuriata; and whilst it had, without doubt, been decided that the new chiefs of the plebs should be designated in the popular assembly of the tribes, the patricians well knew that if they succeeded in carrying the election back to the centuries,[3] the revolution would be abortive. Efforts

---

[1] Menenius and Servilius (Livy, ii. 52), the consuls of the year 473 (ii. 54); Appius (ii. 56), Caeso (iii. 12), the consuls of the year 455 (iii. 31). Cf. Dionys., x. 42. He says elsewhere (vii. 65): 'Ενθὲν δὲ ἀρξάμενος ὁ δῆμος ἤρθη μέγας ἡ δὲ ἀριστοκρατία πολλὰ τοῦ ἀρχαίου ἀξιώματος ἀπέβαλε. Livy (ii. 54) says the same thing.

[2] According to Dion Cassius there were many more murders.

[3] Cicero (pro Corn. 19) and Dionysius (vi. 89) say that the first tribunes were chosen by the curies. But we cannot understand how the victorious plebs could consent to receive its new leaders from the hands of the patricians.

were certainly made to effect this end. Volero wished to decide the matter by demanding that the designation by the tribes should be definitely established. This law would restore to the tribunate its democratic vigor. The patricians succeeded during a year in preventing it from passing. But Volero was reelected, with Laetorius as colleague, who added to the Publilian proposal: that the aediles should be named by the tribes, and the tribes should take cognizance of the general affairs of the state, that is to say, the plebeian assembly should have the right of making *plebiscita*.[1] On their part, the Senate took care that Appius Claudius should secure the consulship, as being the most violent defender of patrician privileges.[2] The struggle was sharp; it was the most serious contest since the creation of the tribunes. "This man," said the colleague of Volero, of Appius, "is not a consul, but an executioner of the people." Then, sharply attacked by Appius at the assembly: "I speak with difficulty, Quirites, but I know how to act: to-morrow I will have the law passed or I will die under your very eyes." The next day Appius came to the Forum, surrounded by the whole patrician youth and by his clients. Laetorius again read his rogation, and before calling on the tribes to vote, ordered the patricians, who had not the right of voting in these comitia, to retire. Appius opposed this: "The tribune has no right over the patricians." Besides he had not used the customary formula: "If you think it good, withdraw, Quirites." To discuss law and legal forms in the midst of a revolution was to increase further the popular ferment. Laetorius, instead of answering, sent against the consul his *viator*; the consul, his lictors against the tribune; and a bloody fight took place. Laetorius was wounded; but, in order to save Appius, the consulars were obliged to hurry him away into the senate-house. He entered, calling the gods to

---

[1] Dionysius, ix. 43; Zonaras, vii. 17. As Heaven was not consulted for the holding of *comitia tributa*, so neither were they preceded by solemn sacrifices, like the *comitia centuriata*; they were beyond the control of the augurs. (Dionysius, ix. 41, 49.) They were held on market days, in order that members of the rustic tribes might attend; if the debate had not closed with sunset, it could not be resumed till the third market day following. The patricians, having in the curies their own proper assembly, and all the influence in the Senate and the centuries, did not vote in the *comitia tributa*. (Livy, ii. 60.)

[2] *Propugnatorem senatus, majestatisque vindicem suae, ad omnes tribunicios plebeiosque oppositum tumultus*. (Livy, ii. 61.)

witness the weakness of the Senate, who were allowing laws to be imposed more severe than those of the Sacred Mount (471).[1]

Nevertheless, the people remained masters of the Forum, voted the Publilian law, and forced the Senate to accept it by seizing the Capitol. Twenty-four years ago, they had compelled the patricians to grant the creation of the tribunate only by leaving the city; now, to complete the victory begun on the Sacred Mount, it was the very citadel of Rome that they held by arms. What boldness in men so recently enfranchised! What strength in this people, lately so humble! The defeat of the aristocracy has, sooner or later, become certain; for the people will find in the tribunate, henceforth free from the influence of the nobles, a sure protection; in the assemblies which have the right of making plebiscita, a means of action; lastly, in their numbers and discipline, an ever-increasing power.[2]

Among the tribunes nominated after the adoption of the Publilian law was Sp. Icilius. To prevent the return of fresh acts of violence, he made use of the right which had just been recognized as belonging to the commonalty, and had this law passed:[3] "that no one should interrupt a tribune when speaking before the people. If any one infringed this prohibition, he was to find security to come up for judgment; if he failed to do so, he was to be punished with death and his goods confiscated."

In the struggle, Laetorius had been wounded, perhaps killed.[4] But Appius had been humbled as patrician and consul; the death of a tribune did not satisfy his wounded pride. An invasion of Aequians and Volscians placed the plebeians at his mercy, by obliging them to leave Rome under his command. Never had authority been more imperious or arbitrary. "My soldiers are so many Voleros," said he, and he seemed to try, by dint of his unjust severity, to drive them into revolt. Whether it was treason, or a panic, or the vengeance of soldiers who wished to dishonor

[1] Dionys., ix. 48.
[2] These plebiscita were not then obligatory on the two orders; but in formulating the wishes of the people, they gave them a force which it was difficult to resist for long. Legally, these plebiscita required the sanction of the Senate and the Curiae.
[3] Dionys., vii. 17. This Icilian law is commonly assigned to the time of the trial of Coriolanus (see p. 288, note 4). We conform, in placing it here, to the opinion of Niebuhr and the logical concatenation of facts.
[4] At least he does not appear again.

their general, is uncertain; but at the first charge against the Volsci, they threw down their arms and fled to the Roman territory. There they again encountered Appius and his vengeance. The centurions, the officers who had abandoned the standards, were put to death, and the soldiers decimated. This bloodshed atoned for the last plebeian victories.

Appius re-entered Rome, certain of the fate which awaited him, but satisfied with having, at the price of his life, once at least subdued this people. Summoned, on quitting his consulship, before the popular comitia, he appeared in the character of accuser and not of suppliant, inveighed against the tribunes and the assembly, and made them yield by his haughtiness and boldness. The day of judgment was put off: he did not wait for it; a voluntary death forestalled his condemnation, and the crowd admiring, in spite of itself, this indomitable courage, honored the funeral of Appius by an immense attendance (470). Livy makes him die of sickness: this is less dramatic, but more probable.[1]

In 493 the tribunes had only their right of veto; in 476 they acquired the right of accusing consulars, and in 471 that of passing plebiscita by the people. Thus twenty-three years had sufficed for organizing the political assembly of the plebeians, and for making it already, within certain limits, a legislative and judicial power. As regards the agrarian law, it had been rejected, and, in spite of so many high-sounding words and promises, the people continued in poverty. But it was in exciting the crowd by this delusion about the equality of property that the tribunes had gained their place in the state and some trustworthy guaranties. So it has been, and always will be.

---

[1] Dionys., ix. 54; Livy, ii. 61.
[2] AED. Pl. (*aediles plebis*). Head of Ceres. The reverse, M. FAN. L. CRT. P.A. Marcus, Fannius, and Lucius Critonius, aediles of the people. Silver moneys of the families Fannia and Critonia. We shall return to this matter when the creation of the curule aedileship takes place.

PLEBEIAN AEDILES.[2]

CHAPTER VII.

MILITARY HISTORY OF ROME FROM THE DEATH OF TARQUIN TO THE
DECEMVIRS (495-451).

I. THE ROMAN TERRITORY IN 495; PORSENNA AND CASSIUS.

MONARCHY had given to Rome a grandeur which the treaty of Tarquin with Carthage testifies,[1] and to the plebeians a well-being which resulted from the commerce which this treaty shows,[2] as well' as by successful wars made under the kings, and the immense works carried out by Ancus, Servius, and the two Tarquins. The aristocratic revolution of 509 caused the Romans to lose this power and prosperity. The people sank into misery, and Rome was almost reduced to its own walls.

The most dangerous of the wars called forth by this revolution was that which Porsenna, the powerful Lars of Clusium, conducted. He conquered the Romans and took from them the territory of the ten tribes established north of the Tiber. Rome hid her defeat under heroic legends, and it was only after she had become mistress of the world that she did not blush to avow the acceptance from Porsenna of harder conditions than she herself ever imposed after her most brilliant victories. He forbade the use of iron, except for agricultural purposes,[3] and exacted as sign of submission that the Senate should send him a curule chair or ivory throne, a sceptre, and a crown.[4] Rome being overcome,

[1] See p. 251.
[2] *Dedita urbe* . . . (Tac., *Hist.* iii. 72) *defendit ne ferro nisi in agricultura uterentur.* (Pliny, *Hist. Nat.* xxxiv. 39.)
[3] Dionys., v. 34.
[4] There remains a curious proof of the extent of this commerce. It is a cup in silver *repoussé* work, recently found among a large number of other gold, silver, and bronze objects at Praeneste (Palestrina), and preserved in the Kircher Museum [Collegio Romano] at Rome. All the objects which compose this treasure differ greatly both from Etruscan and from Greek

Porsenna aimed at conquering Latium, which three centuries earlier the Etruscans had victoriously traversed, and at opening

PHOENICIAN CUP FOUND AT PRAENESTE.

up a route towards the lucumonies of the Vulturnus. The Greeks of Campania saw with terror the preparations for this new invasion, and to prevent it they came to the help of the Latin cities which were resisting the Etruscans. Aricia, which has

art. They recall, by their Oriental stamp, other finds made in Cyprus or Greece. Our patera is an imitation of the Egyptian. The centre is filled with a war scene. A prince is in the act of putting to death some captives. Before him stands the God Horus; behind a warrior in arms, who brings other victims. Above, a sparrow-hawk with outspread wings. The border is filled with symbolic scenes. Four sacred barks are symmetrically disposed; on two of them bequeathed its name to the picturesque village of Laricia on the southern slopes of the Alban Mount, near the charming Lake of Nemi, was then the most flourishing city in Latium. It had resisted Tarquin Superbus, and when the son of the King of Clusium, Aruns, appeared before its walls with a powerful army, the inhabitants met him bravely in the field with their Latin and Greek allies. But they were unable to withstand the charge of the Etruscan phalanx, and they were already retiring in disorder, when the men of Cumae, by a skilful manœuvre, charging the enemy in the rear, changed his victory into defeat.[1] Aruns was slain, and there are shown near Laricia the ruins of a tomb, built in the Etruscan manner, where they allege that he was buried.[2] The *débris* of his army took refuge in Rome, which profited from this reverse to rise in insurrection; the Etruscan rule was driven back again beyond the Tiber.

Rome recovered its liberty, but not its power;[3] for the Etruscans continued masters of the right bank of the river, and

is the scarabaeus, symbol of the sun and immortality; in the two others some divinity. Between the ships are thickets of lotus and a woman who is nursing a boy.

"Two circles of hieroglyphic writing are round these scenes; but the whole is coarsely imitated; the hieroglyphs give no sense.

"The sparrow-hawk is surmounted by a Phoenician inscription which M. Renan reads: *Eschmunjaïr ben Ischeto* (Eschmunjair, son of Ischeto).

"These words are engraved in a very delicate character. They determine conclusively the Phoenician origin of the treasure of Praeneste and of other similar finds. But, besides, they help to fix the date with all but certainty.

"The character of the letters does not permit us to carry down the composition of the inscription lower than the sixth century B. C. The hieroglyphics lead to the same conclusion. M. Maspero finds among them no sign which appears in the texts from the twenty-seventh dynasty on (about the fifth century). The inscription furnishes us again with an indication of another sort. M. Renan translates the last proper name by 'the work of Ilim' (of God), and compares it to analogous names such as Abdo (the servant of Ilim), etc., etc. Now the pronoun suffix 'of Ilim,' which is written in Phoenician by a *vav*, the Carthaginians render by *alef*. Our inscription writes it by the latter letter. Then again, on a cup of the same sort, but without inscription, found in the same place, are seen following, in a circular design, the different events of a royal hunt. Now among the animals hunted by the King is a large ape, probably the gorilla, unknown in Egypt and in Syria. It results from this that these plates or cups are most likely of Carthaginian origin." As our manufacturers imitate for the slop trade the products of China and Japan, so the Carthaginian merchants had made gold and silver articles badly copied from the Phoenician or Egyptian styles. Our imitation Poeno-Egyptian cup, bought from the sailors of the coast by some rich inhabitant of Palestrina, is a proof of the activity of the Carthaginian commerce with the Latin cities. [Cf. M. Clermont-Ganneau's remarkable tract on the second cup, representing the adventure with the colossal ape. — *Ed.*]

[1] Dionys., v. 36.
[2] Canina has given the restoration of it.
[3] This clearly results from the war against Veii in 483, and from the reduction of the

on the left bank was recovered only the old *ager Romanus*, limited on the south by the lands of the Latins of Gabii, Bovillae, Tellenae, and Tusculum.

From the lofty citadel of this last-named city, which rises 15 miles off from the walls of Servius, can be seen all who leave Rome by the *porta Capena;* but from that distance also

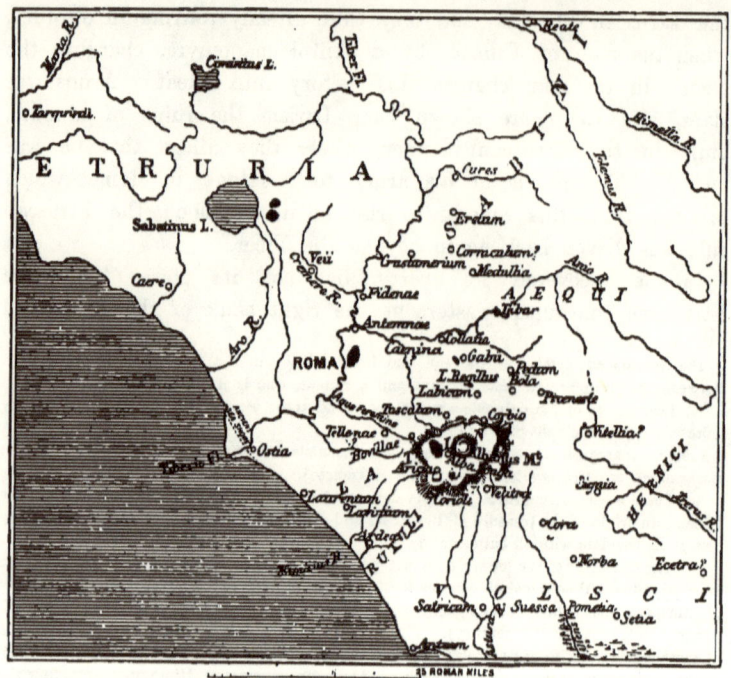

MAP OF THE "AGER ROMANUS"

the Tusculans, their faithful allies, signalled, by two beacon-fires on their ramparts, the approach of the Aequians and Volscians.

On the east some successful expeditions into the Sabine territory extended the Roman frontier to the neighborhood of

---

30 tribes of Servius to 20, the number which is found after the expulsion of the kings. In 495 are named 21 (Livy, ii. 21); a new tribe, called Crustuminian, from the name of a conquered city, having been formed after the Sabine war. Fidenae, which was reduced only in the year 426, is two leagues from Rome.

TOMB, CALLED THAT OF ARUNS.

Eretum, which remained free.[1] Tibur, nearer Rome, from which it was separated only by 20 miles, also kept its independence, and promised to defend it bravely by the worship which it paid to its civic divinity, Hercules of the Rocks, *Hercules Saxanus*, whose temple rose above the Falls of the Anio. And it did in reality defend it for more than a century and a half.[2] On the north the frontier reached scarcely beyond the Janiculum. Rome was at

TUSCULUM. RESTORED BY CANINA.

that time no longer a great state, but it was always one of the greatest of the Italian cities, and this made its fortune. Within its circumference, and on this territory of only a few leagues in extent, were reckoned, if we believe Dionysius of Halicarnassus,[3] 130,000 fighting men, — 130,000 men under the command of the consuls, directed in times of peril by one will, and always under

[1] Since the war during which the Sabine Attus Clausus settled at Rome (see p. 177, n. 1), there was no independent Sabine town nearer Rome than Eretum.
[2] It was not taken till 335.
[3] Dionys., v. 20; he says, according to the census-lists.

excellent discipline. Thanks to the concentration of their forces, the Romans were able to attend safely to their internal disputes; for, though they expended in their Forum the energy which they should have transferred more advantageously to fields of battle, yet they were too strong to be overwhelmed by any enemy who might attack them,—a serious war always bringing back union, and with it invincible power. Thus they never ceased having

TUSCULUM. — PRESENT STATE.

confidence in their good fortune; from the earliest days of the Republic they had raised a temple to Hope.

Their enemies were above all the Aequians and Volscians. Mountaineers, poor and fond of pillaging, always threatening and yet inaccessible, to-day in the plain burning the crops, to-morrow strongly entrenched or hidden among the mountains, the Aequians were, if not the most dangerous, yet at least their most troublesome enemy. The Volscians, numerous, rich, and possessing a fertile territory, ought to have caused more alarm, had they not been divided into a multitude of small tribes, which never united either for attack or defence, and showed neither plan nor perseverance in their expeditions, which the impatience of some and the sluggishness of others generally foiled. This state of division; the want of a capital, the loss of which might by one blow end the struggle; as well as the nature of the country, intersected with mountains and marshes, should have made the war interminable. With such enemies there was no other way of finishing it than that which, but recently, the Pontifical Government employed against the brigands of the Roman States: to raze the cities and exile or exterminate the population. This is what Rome did. But when the war was ended, the country of the Volscians was nothing but a mere solitude.

HOPE.[2]

In Etruria, the enemy was different; Veii, a commercial and industrial city,[1] was only 4 leagues from the Janiculum. On this side they knew where to strike: it was simply to march directly against the city, besiege it and take it. But the danger for Rome was the same as for Veii, for the two cities found themselves existing under very similar conditions: both large, populous, strong in situation, protected by strong walls, and able to put considerable forces on foot. So Rome was not in a state for undertaking this siege, which would end the war, till a century more had elapsed.

Among these enemies we have reckoned neither Latins nor Hernicans, whom their position necessarily rendered allies of the Republic. It was by the burning of the Latin farms that the incursions of the Aequians and Volscians always became known at Rome; and the Hernicans, established between these two people,

---

[1] Dionys. (ii. 52) calls it as great as Athens, and Livy (v. 24) finer than Rome. It was situate where the Isola Farnese is now, on a height which overlooks a magnificent valley, through which runs the Cremera, a short way from the first posting station on the route from Rome to Florence, 11 miles from the walls of Servius.

[2] This statue is reproduced in the Atlas of the *Bull. arch.* 2, vol. ix. pl. 3, under the title of *Statua archaica*.

306   ROME UNDER THE PATRICIAN CONSULS.

in the valley of the *Trerus*, had to suffer daily from their depredations. This alliance dated from ancient times (*feriae Latinae*).

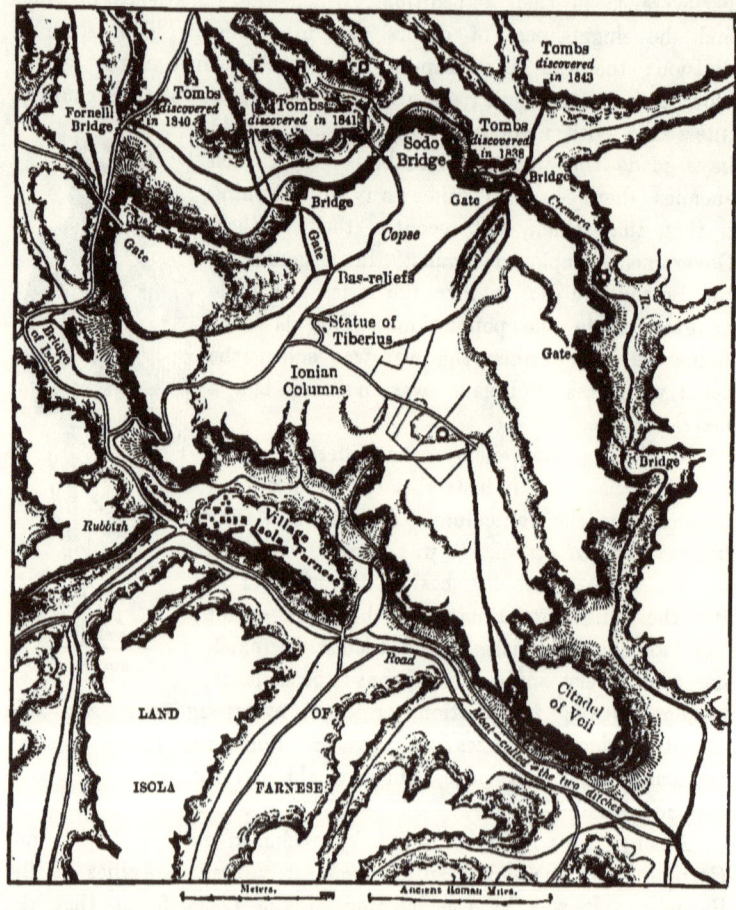

PLAN OF THE CITY OF VEII.[1]

Under the last Tarquin it was changed on Rome's side into a domination which the exile of the kings removed, and which the

[1] This plan has been drawn up by Canina, who has marked on it the tombs discovered in the Necropolis, and the part of the city where were found some columns, bas-reliefs, and a colossal statue of Tiberius, which is in the Chiaramonti Museum. Veii, which remained deserted till Cæsar's time, received from him, and later on from Augustus, a colony, and New Veii seems to have continued several centuries.

battle of Lake Regillus did not re-establish. Rome and the Latins continued separate, but the increasing power of the Volscians and the ravages of the Aequians drew them closer. In 493 B. C., during his second consulate, Sp. Cassius signed a treaty with the 30 Latin cities, either designedly omitted, or misunderstood by the Roman historians, because it bears witness to their feebleness after the wars of the kings; but there could still be read, in the time of Cicero,[1] on a bronze column: "There shall be peace between the Romans and the Latins so long as the sky remains above the earth and the earth under the sun. They shall never arm against each other; they will not afford any passage to the enemy across their territory, and they will bring aid with all their force whenever they are attacked. All booty and conquests made in common are to be divided." Another witness[2] enables us to add: "The command of the combined army shall alternate each year between the two peoples."

Seven years later, during his third consulship, some time before proposing his agrarian law, Cassius concluded a like treaty with the Hernicans.[3] From that time the Aequians and Volscians could make no movement which Hernican or Latin messengers did not at once announce at Rome, and the legions hastening either up or down the Valley of the Trerus were able to threaten the very heart of the enemy's country. These two treaties added more to the grandeur of Rome than any of those which it signed ever after; for they assured its existence at a time when its power might have been nipped in the bud. The whole weight of the war against both Aequians and Volscians fell upon its allies, and on this side it generally played the part of a mere auxiliary. Hence the little importance of these wars, in spite of the acts of heroism and devotion, the great names, and the marvellous stories with which the annalists have adorned them.

[1] Cic., *pro Balbo*, 23; Livy, ii. 33.
[2] Cincius, mentioned by Festus, s. v. *Praetor ad portam* . . . *Quo anno Romanos imperatores ad exercitum oporteret.* . . .
[3] It is by virtue of this treaty that the colony of Antium was divided between the Romans, Latins, and Hernicans: ἔδοξε τῇ βουλῇ . . . ἐπιτρέψαι Λατίνων τε καὶ Ἑρνίκων τοῖς βουλομένοις τῆς ἀποικίας μετέχειν. (Dionys., ix. 59.)

II. Coriolanus and the Volscians; Cincinnatus and the Aequians.

The Volscians, established among mountains (*monti lepini*), which reach a height of 5,000 feet, and whose waters form the Pontine Marshes, had the twofold ambition of stretching at once along the fertile Valley of the Tiber and along that of the Liris. After the fall of Tarquin, they had retaken the cities which that King had conquered from them. Stopped, on the south, by the strong position of Circei, which, nevertheless, fell into their power, and by the impassable and sterile country of the Aurunci, they threw themselves upon the rich plains of Latium, took Velitrae and Cora, in spite of their powerful fortifications, and carried their outposts within ten miles of Rome.[1] The most fortunate of their invasions, and that to which all their conquests have been attached, was led by an illustrious Roman, an exile of the *gens* Marcia.

CERES.[2]

He was, says the legend, a patrician distinguished for his

---

[1] At Bovillae, which they took (Plut., *Cor*. 29), as well as Corioli, Lavinium, Satricum, and Velitrae. (Livy, ii. 39.)

[2] Taken from an ancient painting in the museum at Naples.

courage, piety, and justice.[1] At the battle of Lake Regillus he had won a civic crown, and gained at the taking of Corioli the surname of Coriolanus. Once, when the plebeians refused to give levies of troops, he had armed his own clients, and sustained alone the war against the Antiates. Yet the people, whom he wounded by his pride, refused to give him the consulship, and Coriolanus conceived a feeling of hatred which he showed by some hasty words. During the retreat to the Sacred Mount the lands remained uncultivated; to fight against famine, a temple was vowed to Ceres, and what was of greater service, they bought corn in Etruria and Sicily, where Gelon refused to take money for it. The Senate wished to distribute it gratuitously to the people: "No corn or no more tribunes," said Coriolanus. This expression was understood by the tribunes, who instantly cited him before the people. Neither the threats nor entreaties of the patricians could move them, and Coriolanus, condemned to exile, withdrew to the Volscians of Antium, a powerful and rich maritime city. Tullius, their chief, forgot his jealousy and hatred, that he might arouse in the heart of the exile a desire of revenge; he consented to be simply his lieutenant, and Coriolanus marched upon Rome at the head of the Volscian legions. No army, no fortress stopped him, and he encamped at last near the Cluilian ditch, ravaging the lands of the plebeians, but sparing purposely these of the nobles. In vain did Rome try to bend him. The most venerable of the consulars and the priests of the gods came to him as suppliants, to receive only a harsh refusal. When the deputation returned in despair, Valeria, sister of Poplicola, was praying with the matrons at Jupiter's temple. As if by an inspiration, she led them to the house of Coriolanus and prevailed on his mother Veturia to endeavor to touch the heart of her banished son, whose proud spirit had not been broken by the prayers of his country and his gods. At the approach of these ladies, Coriolanus maintained his fierce aspect. But they told him that amongst them were his aged mother and his young wife leading her two children by the hand. Too Roman still to fail in filial respect, he advanced

[1] Dionys., viii. 62 : Ἄδεται καὶ ὑμνεῖται πρὸς πάντων ὡς εὐσεβὴς καὶ δίκαιος ἀνήρ. This legend has been much discussed, and Shakespeare has utilized it, without clearly sifting out the element of truth it contains. [Was this to be expected?— *Ed.*]

to meet Veturia, and ordered the fasces to be lowered in her presence: "Am I face to face with my son, or with an enemy?" said the dignified matron. The wife did not dare to speak, but threw herself weeping into the arms of her husband, and his children clung to him: he was overcome, and withdrew. The Roman women had saved Rome the second time.

The story is beautiful, but scarcely credible. Tired of war and laden with booty, or finding that resistance grew stronger as they approached Rome, the Volscians withdrew to their cities. The legend adds that they did not pardon Coriolanus for thus stopping them in the middle of their revenge, and that they condemned him to death. According to Fabius, he lived to an advanced age, exclaiming: "Exile is very hard upon an old man."

We can hardly refuse to believe that Rome was reduced to the last extremities, and that the Volscians were established in the centre of Latium; but it was a patrician who had conquered, and thus honor was saved.

Coriolanus, on his part, had reason to find a stranger's bread very bitter, for exile at Rome was both a civil and religious excommunication. The exile lost not only his country and property, but his household gods, his wife, who had the right of re-marrying, his children, to whom he became a stranger, his ancestors, who were no longer to receive funeral sacrifices at his hands. Our civil death is less terrible.[1]

The mountains which separate the basins of the rivers Liris and Anio descend from the borders of Lake Fucinus to Praeneste, where they terminate at Algidus by a sort of promontory which commands the plain and valley of the Tiber. By following the hidden mountain paths, the Aequians could reach Mount Algidus unperceived, the woods of which still covered their march and ambuscades.[2] Thence they burst unexpectedly on the Latin lands;

---

[1] Cicero wishes that he could be put to death, for the reason that this is a more suitable end for the brave: *Huic generi mortis potius assentior*; but Atticus answers: "It is true that rhetoricians are allowed to lie in history if their art gains by it!" (*Concessum est rhetoribus ementiri in historiis ut aliquid dicere possint argutius!*) If we compare this with what is cited from Livy above, p. 185, we shall find that these Romans had a strange idea of the duties of an historian.

[2] *Nigrae feraci frondis in Algido.* A few years ago Algidus was still the haunt of brigands who infested the neighborhood of Palestrina and Frescati.

and if they were in sufficient numbers, or the enemy too cautious, they were soon in the midst of the Roman territory. Every year these incursions were renewed. It was not war; but it would have been far better to have serious engagements than these unceasing acts of brigandage. The Latins were rendered so weak that the Aequians were able to take several of their cities.[1] According to the treaty of Cassius, Rome was bound to send all their forces to their help. Their internal dissensions and the dangers they ran on the side of Veii, kept the legions in the city or to the north of the Tiber. However, the Senate felt alarmed when it saw the Aequians established on Mount Algidus, and the Volscians on the Alban Mount, separating the Latins from* the Hernicans and threatening two peoples at the same time.[2] A forty years' truce, which the Veientes had just signed (474), and the adoption of the Publilian law (471), by ending for a time the Etruscan war and the troubles of the Forum, enabled them to listen to the complaints of their allies.

Two members of the *gens* Quinctia, Capitolinus and Cincinnatus, gained the honors of this war.

T. Quinctius Capitolinus, a popular patrician, had been the colleague of the imperious Appius. While the Voleros of the latter allowed themselves to be beaten by the Volscians, Quinctius seized the booty gained by the Aequians and re-entered Rome with the title of *Father of the Soldiers*. Consul a second time in 467, he took possession of Antium, a part of whose territory was distributed amongst some Roman colonists, and he had on his return so brilliant a triumph that he obtained the surname of Capitolinus. The Aequians continued in arms. Four times their active bands audaciously penetrated into the Campagna of Rome: one day they even surrounded the consul Furius in a narrow gorge. Two legions were on the point of destruction: Capitolinus saved them. At the news of the danger, the Senate had invested the other consul with dictatorial power by the formula: *Caveat consul ne quid detrimenti respublica capiat*, and it was

---

[1] In the legend, all these towns, even Corbio, beyond the Anio, are taken by the Volsci; all the successive conquests of both Volsci and Aequi were attributed to the Roman exile.

[2] These two mountains are the watershed between the basins of the Tiber and the Liris, and they dominate the whole Latin plain.

employed only to charge Capitolinus with the difficult duty of delivering the consular army.

Never had Rome, since Porsenna, been so seriously threatened; internal troubles had begun again respecting the proposal of Terentillus. The pestilence was raging with a violence so much more fatal because the inroads of the enemy filled the city, during the heat of summer, with men and troops accustomed to the pure mountain air.[1] In 462 an army of Aequians and Volscians encamped only three miles from the Esquiline Gate; three years later a night attack delivered the Capitol for a moment into the hands of the Sabine Herdonius; the year following Antium revolted, and the consul Minucius allowed himself once more to be shut into a defile by the Aequians. Cincinnatus alone seemed able to save the Republic. He retook the Capitol, and restored to the Romans the fortress which was also their sanctuary. In this matter he made himself conspicuous by a severity which gained the confidence of the Senate: he was made dictator.

The senators who were sent to inform him of this election found him across the Tiber in the field which was named for a long time the meads of Quinctius. He was digging a ditch, and he received them resting on his spade. After the accustomed salutations, they requested him to assume his toga, in order to receive a communication from the Senate. "He is astonished, asks if all is not well, and sends his wife Racilia to find his toga in the hut. Having put it on, after having brushed off the dust and perspiration, he returns to the deputies, who salute him dictator, present their congratulations, and press him to return to the city."[2] If this scene is not historic, it is at least according to the manners of the time and the character of the man. What follows shows the patrician, so proud of his descent, taking possession of power with the same simplicity which he had shown in quitting his plough and displaying the activity and energy of men born to command. A boat awaited him on the Tiber; he embarked and was received on the left bank by his three sons, his relatives, and the greater part of the senators.

---

[1] Livy, iii. 6. [2] Ibid., iii. 26.

MILITARY HISTORY OF ROME FROM 495 TO 451. 313

Before the end of the day he went to the Forum, and then named as his cavalry chief another patrician as poor as himself, and ordered all business to be suspended, all shops closed, and all men able to take arms to meet on the Field of Mars before sunset, each with five stakes and enough bread for five days. Evening being come, he set out and marched six leagues in four

SEZZE.

hours; before daybreak the Aequians were themselves enclosed by a ditch and a palisade work: they were compelled to pass under the yoke. On his return in triumph to Rome, followed by the consul and the army that he had saved, he compelled Minucius to set him free from his special charge, had the consular fasces[2] broken before him, and on the seventh day laid down the dictatorship, in order to return to his own fields.

[1] Setia was on a hill, difficult of access, which rose above the Pontine Marshes; the town of Sezze has kept the name, and occupies the same site.
[2] Dionys., x. 22; Livy, iii. 26–30: *Vi majoris imperii*. The school of Niebuhr regards this story as legendary.

In spite of this success, which national vanity has thus embellished, as is the case in so many other points of Rome's military history, the war was not ended; the Aequians kept possession of Algidus, as did the Volscians of the Alban Mount.

During the half century that had elapsed since the expulsion of the kings, the decadence of Rome's power was not arrested one instant. In 493 its territory was at least protected by the

RUINS OF A TEMPLE NEAR SEZZE.

Latins; but of the thirty Latin cities which had signed the treaty of Cassius, thirteen were now either destroyed or held by the enemy, and among them some of the strongest places of Italy, such as Circeii, at the foot of its promontory, Setia, Cora, and Norba,[1] all three in the mountains of the Volscian territories and surrounded by strong walls. If the *ager Romanus* was not yet encroached upon, the barrier which ought to have protected it had been partly destroyed. Was Rome more fortunate in the north against the Etruscans?

---

[1] Other Latin cities taken or destroyed: Velitrae, Tolina, Ortona, Satricum, Labicum, Pedum, Corioli, Carventum, Corbio. (Dionys. and Livy, *passim*.)

III. WAR AGAINST VEII.

A GREAT part of Etruria had taken part in the expedition of Porsenna; since that time the invasions of the Cisalpine Gauls and the increasing power of the Greeks and Carthaginians had divided the attention and forces of the Etruscan cities; some of them watching, on the north, the passes of the Apennines; others, in the west, on the coasts threatened by the Ligurian pirates, and on the southwest over their own colonies, which, one by one, were slipping from their hands. The old league was dissolved, and all idea of conquest in the direction of Latium had been abandoned. But Veii, at a distance from the Gauls and the sea, was too near Rome not to profit by its weakness. The war, however, did not break out till 482 B. C. It lasted nine years.

Two incidents only have been preserved of this war, far more serious for Rome than the incursions of the Aequians and Volscians, — the foundation by the Romans of a fortress on the banks of the Cremera, from whence they extended their ravages for two years up to the walls of Veii, and the occupation of the Janiculum by the Veientines. We have already seen that the Roman annalists do great honor to the patriotic devotion of the Fabii for having held in check all the enemy's forces, till the day when, surprised by an ambuscade, the whole *gens* perished.[1] The Veientines in their turn burned up everything along both banks of the Tiber, and established themselves on the Janiculum, from whence they saw Rome at their feet. One day they crossed the stream and ventured to attack the legions on the Field of Mars. A vigorous effort repulsed them; the next day they were caught between two consular armies, and at last driven from the dangerous post which they held. The war was carried up to the very walls of Veii; a forty years' truce left the two peoples in the position which they held before hostilities began (474 B. C.)

In this war Veii had not been supported by the great lucumos of the north, whose attention was at that time called

---

[1] See p. 294.

elsewhere, where the fate of their rivals was being decided. While in fact Rome was rehearsing her part for future greatness by these obscure contests, and for the pillage of the world by the carrying off some rustic plunder, the armies of Xerxes were shaking Asia, and three hundred thousand Carthaginians, his allies, made a descent on Sicily (480). The ability of Themistocles at Salamis saved Greece; that of Gelo at Himera assured the welfare of Syracuse and of the Italiot Greeks who disputed with the Etruscans the commerce of the Tyrrhenian Sea and the Adriatic. At first the Greeks closed against them the Straits of Messina; then in the year which preceded the forty years' truce they annihilated their fleet in the vicinity of Cape Misenum.[1] Hiero established in the Isle of Ischia a station for his galleys, which cut the communications between the Etruscan cities of the Vulturnus and those of the Arno. Thus the most dangerous enemies of the ancient subjects of Porsenna were wasting their forces in these distant wars, and this enabled the Romans to indulge with impunity in all the disorders which accompany growing liberty.

During these first years of the Republic, so fruitful for Rome's institutions, nothing had been done to extend its power. Rome, at all events, had lasted, gaining daily strength and confidence. Its territory, properly so called, had not been impaired, and the population grew warlike in these struggles which were not really dangerous. The soldiers whom Appius decimated without resistance, whom Cincinnatus loaded with five stakes, their arms, and their victuals, for a march of nearly twenty miles in four hours, were already the legionaries who could conquer the Samnites and Pyrrhus. Rome need no longer fear for her existence, as in the time of Porsenna, and she has the right to great expectations.

HOPE.[2]

---

[1] See p. 79.
[2] *Cabinet de France*, No. 94 in the Catalogue: cameo of archaic style, representing Hope standing, with a diadem, lifting up the skirt of her tunic with the left hand, and holding in her right the flower which promises to bear fruit.

SOUTHERN ETRURIA (TERRITORY OF VEII).

CHAPTER VIII.

THE DECEMVIRS AND CIVIL EQUALITY (451-449).

I. BILL OF TERENTILIUS.

UP to the time of Volero and Laetorius, the people had only won the means of fighting; and the struggle, in spite of the violences which had already taken place, had not yet seriously begun. The aristocracy preserve all the offices which they held after the exile of the kings, the supreme command, the magisterial offices, religion, justice; but the plebeians were formerly without guidance and object: now their chiefs are measuring the distance which separates them from power.

The internal history of Rome is truly of an admirable simplicity. First of all, an aristocracy which forms by itself the whole state, and below, far below, strangers, fugitives, men without family and almost without gods. But then the plebeians, used as instruments for conquests, see their number as well as their worth and their strength increase by these conquests. It comes to pass that they help the nobles to drive out a tyrant; next day they are forgotten: they fly to the Sacred Mount from their misery and servitude, and discover chiefs who discipline this mob, hitherto untrained, exercise it in the conflict, and gradually arm it at all points. Presently they pass from the defensive to attack their foe.

In 462 the plebeians demanded the revision of the constitution and a written code.[1] This was too much to ask at once, for they were not strong enough to triumph at once. So then victory was gained piecemeal, so to speak, and needed more than a century

---

[1] *Legibus de imperio consulari scribendis* (Livy, iii. 9); and further on (iii. 34): *Fons omnis publici privatique est juris;* and Dionys., x. 3: τοὺς ὑπὲρ ἁπάντων νόμους, τῶν τε κοινῶν καὶ τῶν ἰδίων. Lastly, Zonaras, vii. 18: τὴν πολιτείαν ἰσωτέραν ποιήσασθαι ἐψηφίσαντο.

to complete it. In 450 they extorted civil equality; in 367 and 339 political equality; in 300, religious equality. The decemvirate was the conquest of equality in civil and penal law.

In the constitution nothing was written or determined; no one knew where the jurisdiction of the magistrates, where the powers of the Senate ceased. Law was not right, *rectum*, or, as the jurisconsults of the Empire defined it, the good and the just, *ars boni et aequi*: it was the order imperiously given, *jus*, by the stronger to the weaker, by the priest to the layman, by the husband to the wife and children.[1] Besides, to fulfil their duty, to protect the plebeians against iniquitous handling of the law, the tribunes needed to know it, and it continued in the uncertain and floating state of custom. The judge gave sentence, "according to the usage of their ancestors," *ex more majorum*, that is, after the particular law of an ancient sovereign people of whom the new people knew nothing. The tribune C. Terentilius Arsa was determined to destroy this uncertainty and the arbitrary conduct it authorized. Abandoning the agrarian law, which was becoming stale, he demanded in 462 that five men should be nominated to draw up a code of laws, which should determine, by limiting it, the power of the consuls.[2] A plebiscitum had no force over the *populus*; the Senate was then able to avoid considering this proposition, but it attempted to stop the tribune by the veto of one of his colleagues. But they had all sworn to remain united, and neither threats nor evil omens could turn them from their purpose.

The leader of these acts of patrician violence was the son of Cincinnatus, Caeso, a young man proud of his power, his exploits, and his high rank. At the head of the young patricians he disturbed the deliberations, attacked the crowd, and more than once drove the tribunes from the Forum. This man seemed to contain in himself all dictatorships and consulates, and his audacity made the tribunitian power useless. A tribune dared nevertheless to make use of the Julian law. Virginius accused Caeso of having struck one of his colleagues in spite

---

[1] For the aristocratic idea of order, *jus* from *jubeo*, we have substituted the idea of justice. The French word *droit* comes from the Latin *rectum* and *directum*, in Italian *diretto*, in Spanish *derecho*, in German *recht*, in English *right*, among the Scandinavians *ret*. The Slavs start from another idea, not that of rectitude, but of truth, *prawda*.

[2] Livy, iii. 9.

of his inviolable office, and a plebeian bore witness that he had knocked down, on the Suburan road, an old man, his brother, who died some days after of his wounds. The people were much excited by this murder, and Caeso, set free on bail, would have been condemned to death at the next comitia, had he not voluntarily gone into exile to Etruria. He had been compelled to find bail to the amount of 30,000 lbs. of bronze; to pay it, Cincinnatus sold all his property except four acres (461 B.C.).[1]

Like Coriolanus, Caeso determined to be avenged, and the tribunes came one day to denounce before the Senate a conspiracy he had organized. The Capitol was to be surprised, the tribunes and chiefs of the people to be massacred, the sacred laws abolished. The Capitol was in fact, in the following year, seized during the night by the Sabine Herdonius, at the head of 4,000 adventurers, slaves or exiles, among whom probably was Caeso (460).[2] This bold stroke frightened the Senate as much as the people, to whom the consul Valerius promised the acceptance of the Terentilian bill in return for their help. The Capitol was retaken by the aid of the dictator of Tusculum, C. Mamilius,[3] and not one escaped of all those who were holding it. But Valerius, the popular consul, had fallen during the attack, and was replaced by Cincinnatus, who thought the Senate released from its promises by his death: "So long as I am consul," said he to the tribunes, "your law shall not pass, and before leaving office I will nominate a dictator. To-morrow I lead the army against the Aequians." They announced their opposition to the enrolment. "I do not want fresh soldiers; the legionaries of Valerius have not been disbanded; they will follow me to Algidus." He wished to take the augurs there, in order that they might consecrate a place for deliberation and compel the army, as representative of the people, to revoke all the tribunitian laws.[4] The Senate dared not follow their consul in this violent reaction. They merely rejected the law; but the same

---

[1] Livy, iii. 13; Dionys., x. 4–8.
[2] Dionys., x. 9, 14; Livy, iii. 15 : *tribunorum interficiendorum, trucidandae plebis.*
[3] He received, in recompense, the freedom of the city. It was, without doubt, a descendant of Tarquinius Superbus, who had a son-in-law a dictator of Tusculum; his family was reckoned among the more illustrious plebeian families.
[4] Livy, iii. 20.

tribunes were re-elected for the third time. So they were in the years following, up to the fifth time; and with them was brought forward the hateful bill, in spite of a new dictatorship of Cincinnatus, who employed his authority to exile without appeal the accuser of his son (458 B. C.).

This state of things kept men's minds in such a continual ferment, that the Senate thought it prudent to consent to nominating for the future ten tribunes, two for each class (457). The people, above all those of the lower classes, expected from this increase more efficacious protection, the patricians greater facility for bribing some members of the college. Other concessions followed.

In 456 the tribune Icilius demanded that the lands of the public domain on the Aventine should be distributed among the people.[1] In vain the patricians troubled the assembly and upset the voting-urns; the tribunes, supported by the brave Sicinius Dentatus, condemned several young patricians to confiscation of their property as authors of these violent acts. The Senate secretly bought back their lands and restored them. But the tribunes had proved their strength; they secured the acceptance of the law by the tribes, compelled the consuls to take it to the Senate, and Icilius obtained the right to enter the curia to defend his plebiscite. From this innovation sprang the right for the tribunes to sit and speak in that assembly; later on, they had even, as had the consuls and praetors, that of calling it together.[2] The law passed. Many of the poor who lived outside the city went to live on the Aventine, and the force of the plebs increased by the number of those who were able to hurry to the Forum at the first call of the tribunes. The popular hill was covered with plebeian houses. The citizens too poor to build one from their own resources united with others; each flat had in this way its proprietor, — a custom which still exists at Rome, in Corsica, and even in some cities of France. As the public domain retained not

[1] Dionys., x. 31. The condition of *ager publicus*, preserved by the Aventine up to 456, contradicts the tradition relative to the establishment, on this hill, of the Latins conquered by Ancus. (Cf. p. 156.)

[2] We see them, after the decemvirs, in full possession of this right. Cf. Livy, iii. 69; v. 1, 2, 3, 6, 26, 36, etc. *Tribunis plebis senatus habendi jus erat, quamquam senatores non essent, ante Atinium plebiscitum.* (Aul. Gell., xiv. 8.)

DECEMVIRS AND CIVIL EQUALITY FROM 451 TO 449. 323

a foot of soil, there the patricians could not stay; and this hill became a sort of fortress of the people. Under the decemvirs it was the asylum of plebeian liberty.[1]

WALL OF THE AVENTINE.[2]

In 454 a law presented to the centuries by the consul Aternius recognized in all the magistrates, even in the tribunes and aediles, the right of punishing by fine those who did not show

[1] The Icilian law was placed among the number of the *leges sacratae*, following Livy (iii. 32); but Lange (*Römische Alterthümer*, i. 519 and 532) thinks with reason that Livy has confounded this *lex Icilia* with the Icilian plebiscitum of 471, which was in fact a *lex sacrata*. (See p. 297, n. 3.) Up to that time a great number of plebeians inhabited, as tenants, houses belonging to the patricians; the latter lost by this law the influence they used to exercise, under the title of landlords, over a certain number of the plebs.

[2] After a photograph by Parker. The Aventine, formerly covered with temples and thickly populated, would be a mere solitude without two or three convents which rise on it above the Tiber.

to them the respect and obedience which their office demanded.[1] The lowest fine was fixed at one sheep, and the maximum, which could be reached only by an increase of a head for each day of refusal, at two oxen and thirty sheep. At the same time this law put a limit to the arbitrary manner in which the consuls had up to that time fixed the amount of the fines.

A short time after an official coinage began. The state had at first only certified the quality of the metal[2] by stamping the pieces of bronze, *aes*, the weight of which was afterward determined by the buyer's balance, whence the form of purchase called *mancipatio per aes et libram:*[3] "I take this object bought with this bronze duly weighed." To this first warranty there was added another in the time of the decemvirs,[4] — the evidence of weight; they ran in a mould pieces of bronze of a circular form, bound to weigh twelve ounces.[5] This was the *as librale*, which carried a stamp with a figure indicating its value, and which was divided as follows: —

As	= 1	pound, bearing the head of	Janus.
Semis	= ½	"	Jupiter.
Triens	= ⅓	"	Minerva.
Quadrans	= ¼	"	Hercules.
Sextans	= ⅙	"	Mercury.
Uncia	= ounce 1/12	"	Rome.

The appearance of money is one of the great events in history. For more than a century and a half, to the year 268 B. C. the Romans were satisfied with their heavy bronze money, while for

---

[1] Dionys., x. 50; Cic., *de Rep.* ii. 35.
[2] The primitive bronze was of almost pure copper: 93.70 of copper and 6.30 of tin.
[3] The Roman pound, which was divided into 12 ounces, weighed 327.4 grammes.
[4] In the Twelve Tables the penalties are given in *ases;* cf. Gaius, iii. 223.
[5] It is believed that no single *as* reached this weight; the greater number in reality weighed 9 to 10 ounces. But in 1852 there were found at Cervetri 1575 *ases*, many of which weighed 312 grammes; whence it must be inferred that the greater part of the ancient *ases* had about the normal weight (see p. 630, No. 2). Respecting the successive reductions of the weight of the *as*, which fell to 4 ounces at the end of the Samnite War; to 2 ounces at the end of the First Punic War; to 1 ounce in 217; and later on to ½, ⅓, during the early Empire; even in the middle of the 3d century to ⅙ and 1/12 of an ounce, — see Pliny, *Hist. Nat.* xxxiii. 5; Festus, s. v. *Sextantarii ases;* Mommsen, *Hist. of Rom. Money;* and Marquardt, *Handb.* ii. p. 9 *et seq.* It is easy to tell by a cursory inspection of the table on p. 630 and by the finish of the work of the stamped *ases*, that these coins are of much later date than the *ases* which were cast. The former date, in fact, only from the second century B. C.

THE AVENTINE (PRESENT STATE).

a long time Greece, Sicily, and South Italy were coining silver money, which is the most beautiful yet known. How wretched the commerce for which such means of exchange sufficed! Let the as cast at Rome be compared with the coins of Thurii and Syracuse, and we can measure the distance which then separated the Romans from the Greeks!

The division of the lands of the Aventine was a true agrarian law, and the *lex Aterna* repressed one of the most crying abuses[1] which Terentilius had attacked. The Senate hoped in this way to impose upon the people, and to delay, by these partial satisfactions, two formidable demands, the agrarian law and the *lex Terentilia*. But the tribunes would not tolerate either truce or respite; the two proposals were immediately resumed, and to get them passed there was elected to the tribunate the most renowned and popular of the plebeians, Sicinius Dentatus, an old centurion who had been present in 120 battles, followed 9 triumphs, slain 8 of the enemy in single combat, received 45 wounds, all in front, earned 183 necklaces, 160 gold bracelets, 18 lances, 25 suits of armor, and lastly 14 civic crowns for the same number of citizens whom he had saved.[3] Employing a means of intimidation which his predecessors had already employed, Sicinius condemned two consuls to fines. The Senate saw the necessity of giving up force without excluding diplomacy, in order to divert the revolution. It accepted the proposition of Terentilius, which the tribunes had changed into a demand for a complete revision of the constitution.[5] One of the consulars condemned, Romilius, had supported the bill, no doubt hoping that the new legislation would take from

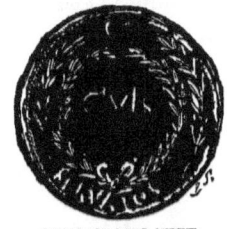

CIVIC CROWN WITH LAUREL LEAVES.[2]

CIVIC CROWN.[4]

---

[1] The importance of this law will be felt if we recall the effect that was produced in England by the penalties enforced by the Government of Charles I. At Rome in 430 the penalties in kind were converted into penalties in money.

[2] OB CIVIS SERVATOS, a large bronze of Augustus' time.

[3] Aul. Gell., ii. 11.; Dionys., x. 37.

[4] AVGVSTO OB C.S. (*ob cives servatos*) in a crown of oak. Reverse of a gold coin of the family *Petronia*.

[5] The lawgivers were to seek *quae aequandae libertatis essent*. (Livy, iii. 3.)

the hands of the tribunes, if it did not destroy the tribunate itself, this terrible right of accusation before the people.[1] The astonished Dentatus praised his courage, abjured their old hatred, and in the name of the people remitted the penalty which ought to have been paid into the treasury of Ceres. "This money," replied Romilius, "belongs now to the gods; no one has the right to dispose of it;" and he refused the boon.

However, three commissioners were named, Sp. Postumius, A. Manlius, and P. Sulpicius, to go, perhaps to Athens,[2] at any rate to the Greek cities of Italy, to collect the best laws. To give the strangers a high idea of the Roman people, the quaestors caused the vessels in which the ambassadors sailed to be richly decorated.

Rome was at peace during the absence of the three deputies. On their return (452) some discussion arose respecting the composition of the legislative commission. This was where the nobles determined to face the tribunes. The question was indeed very serious, for all antiquity thought that the legislator ought to be invested with unlimited power. The consuls, the tribunes, the aediles, the quaestors were then to give way to ten magistrates charged with drawing up the new code. The most precious of the republican conquests, the *provocatio*, was even suspended; but the rights acquired by the plebeians during the last 50 years were reserved![3] Besides, before the new laws could be put in force they would have to receive the approbation of the Senate and the sanction of the people. Rome did not then give up her liberties. In pleading their acquaintance with law, the patricians kept the ten places of legislators for themselves. This first choice decided that the reform should not have a political character.

---

[1] Dionys., x. 48 and 58.

[2] Livy affirms it, *Atticis legibus* (iii. 32); Tacitus (*Ann.* iii. 27) says only . . . *et accitis quae usquam egregia*. [The nature and duties of the censorship (cf. below, p. 345, *seq.*) make it very probable that the financial measures of the decemvirs were borrowed directly from those adopted by the Athenians, who then ruled over a great maritime power. — *Ed.*]

[3] The law *de Aventino publicando* and the *leges sacratae* were, however, removed from the right of general revision granted to the decemvirs. The sentence was terrible for any who should have violated these laws: *Sacer alicui deorum sit cum familia pecuniaque.* (Cf. Fest., s. v., and Livy, iii. 32.)

II. THE DECEMVIRS (451–449).

IN the year 451 B. C., on the Ides of May, the decemvirs, who had all served as consuls, entered on their duties. They were: App. Claudius, T. Genucius, P. Sestius, T. Romilius, C. Julius, T. Veturius, P. Horatius, and the three commissioners.[1] Each day one of them held the presidency, the government of the city, and the twelve lictors. Unanimous in their acts, just and affable towards all, they kept the Republic in a state of profound peace, diminishing rather than exceeding their powers. A dead body had been found in the house of the patrician Sestius; not only did the decemvir Julius follow up the prosecution, but though he had the right of judgment without appeal, he sent the case to the people's assembly. At the end of the first year, ten tables were set up in the Forum, that any one might propose amendments, to be afterward reviewed by the decemvirs, then approved by the Senate, accepted in the comitia centuriata, and sanctioned by the Curiae under the presidency of the Pontifex Maximus. The gods seemed to give their assent by sending favorable auguries.

These ten tables were the old customs of Rome, or of primitive Italy, modified by some things borrowed from the legislation of the Greek cities, which the Ephesian Hermodorus had explained to the decemvirs.[2]

However, the code was not yet complete. In order to finish it, the powers of the legislative commission were continued, but with the aid of other men, in accordance with the spirit of the Roman constitution. Among the resigning decemvirs was Appius Claudius, who during the first year had concealed his pride and ambition under popular appearances. Called upon to preside at the comitia of election, he opposed the candidature of Cincinnatus and Capitolinus, whom he would not have been able to mould to his designs,

---

[1] I follow Dionysius; the list in Livy differs somewhat.
[2] As a reward, they erected a statue to Hermodorus in the Comitium. He had been exiled from Ephesus by the jealousy of the populace, who had caused this law to be passed: *Nemo de nobis unus excellat; sin quis exstiterit, alio in loco et apud alios sit.* Heraclitus said that by reason of this decree: *universos Ephesios esse morte mulctandos.* (Cic., *Tusc.* v. 36.) Envy is at the root of every democracy.

and only allowed those to be nominated who were devoted to him. He did not fear to collect votes for himself, though, as president of the comitia, custom forbade his re-election. His new colleagues, obscure men, submitted to his ascendency. Preceded by 120 lictors [an innovation], with the rods and axes, they seemed to be ten kings,[1] and they were so in pride.

Like their predecessors, they were unanimous, for they had mutually promised that the opposition of none of them should check the acts of his colleagues;[2] and this agreement consolidated their power. Henceforth, the fortune, honor, and the lives of the citizens were at their mercy. The Senate might now have played a splendid part, that of defending the public liberties. It preferred giving way to the old spirit of rancor, and hailed this tyranny arising from a popular law. The patrician youth, for a long time accustomed, under Appius and Caeso, to violence, became for the city a sort of decemviral army, and the senators, deserting their posts in the senate-house, retired to their country houses.

However, the decemvirs published two new tables, "filled," says Cicero,[3] "with unjust laws," and the year ended without their expressing any intention of abdicating. Rome had given herself masters. There existed, in fact, no legal means of depriving a magistrate of his *imperium*, if he did not, of his own accord, come to the Forum and declare that he resigned his office, and swear that he had done nothing contrary to the laws: *jurare in leges*. Fortunately, the Sabines and Aequians renewed the war. The Senate had to be convoked.

Free states, which change character and sentiments by force of external or short-lived impulses, owe their stability to the existence of houses in which the principles and opinions of their forefathers are perpetuated, as a heritage transmitted to the latest posterity. The popular patricians did not on this occasion fall short of their name. A Valerius rose, as soon as the session was opened, and in spite of Appius, who refused to let him speak, he denounced the conspiracy formed against liberty. "These are the Valerii and Horatii who expelled the kings," said Horatius Barbatus; "their

---

[1] Dionys. (x. 58) pretends that three were plebeians; Livy (v. 7) makes them all patricians.
[2] Livy, iii. 36: *intercessionem consensu sustulerant*.
[3] *De Rep.* ii. 37: *duabus tabulis iniquarum legum additis*.

descendants will not stoop their head under the Tarquins." The decemvirs interrupted and threatened him; they threatened to hurl him from the Tarpeian rock; but even the uncle of Appius declared against him. Still timid counsels prevailed, and, at the end of a stormy sitting, ten legions were intrusted to the decemvirs. Two armies left Rome; being badly led, and disloyal to their chiefs, they were beaten. In one Dentatus served, who did not hide his hate. In order to get rid of him, the decemvirs sent him to choose a site for a camp, and gave him as escort some soldiers ordered to assassinate him. The Roman Achilles only succumbed after having killed fifteen of the traitors. The report was circulated that he had perished in an ambuscade; but no one doubted that he had been sacrificed to the fears of the decemvirs. Another crime at last brought about their fall.

From the elevation of his tribunal Appius had seen, several times, a beautiful young girl, hardly grown up, going to one of the public schools, held by freedmen in the Forum; and a criminal passion seized him. She was the daughter of one of the highest plebeians, Virginius, who was then with the army of Algidus, and the affianced of the former tribune Icilius. The decemvir suborned one of his clients, Marcus Claudius, and charged him to lay before him a suit which would bring Virginia into his power. The scene is very Roman, and well told by Livy. No seduction, no abduction or open violence: the iniquity is accomplished with the observance of legal forms which disguise the violation of the law. A stranger, ignorant of the real motive of the suit, would have admired in Appius the imperturbable magistrate in the midst of popular clamor.

One day Claudius seized the maiden under pretence that she, being the child of one of his slaves, belonged to him. The tears of Virginia, the cries of her nurse, stirred up' the crowd. Her father's friends protested against this insolent and false pretence; but Claudius called on Appius to have his rights respected, and the iniquitous judge, contrary to the very law which he had himself passed, adjudged provisional possession to his accomplice. Icilius cried out, and the crowd grew agitated; Appius, with a hypocritical appearance of legality, consented to let Virginia free till the morrow, to hear the father's deposition, and determine the question of her paternity. But at the same time he despatched a secret emissary to the chiefs of the legions of the Algidus to enjoin them to prevent Virginius leaving the camp. The friends of Icilius forestalled the messenger, and in the morning the father was at the Forum with his daughter and neighbors dressed in mourning. His presence did not stop Appius. All the available fighting men were in the armies; in Rome there remained only women, old men, and infants; and the decemvir believed that his lictors and clients would be able to keep in check this timid crowd. So when Claudius had explained his case, he declared, without allowing the father to speak, that the proof was complete, and that Virginia was a slave. Claudius wished to carry her off; the women who surrounded the damsel repulsed him, and Virginius, raising against Appius his arms menacingly, cries: "It is to Icilius that I have affianced my child, and not to you! It is for marriage, and not for shame, that I have brought her up!" And he added, pointing to the unarmed citizens: "Will you permit it? Perhaps; but surely those who have arms will not!"

Appius, carrying out his part as magistrate occupied only with administering justice and order in the city, deigns to answer. "Secret meetings," said he, "are held the whole night long in the city to stir up sedition; I know it, not by the insults of Icilius yesterday, by the violence of Virginius to-day, but by sure proofs. Therefore I am prepared for the struggle, and have come down to the Forum with men-at-arms to check, in a manner worthy of my powers, those who disturb the public peace." And he ended by saying: "Citizens, keep quiet, it is the wisest course; and you, lictor, go, disperse the crowd, and make way for the master to seize his slave."

At these threatening words the multitude dispersed of its own accord. Then Virginius, despairing of aid, addressed the decemvir: "Appius," said he, "pardon the grief of a father, and permit me, here in the presence of my child, to ask her nurse the whole truth!" And he led Virginia towards a corner of the Forum where was a butcher's stall: he takes up from it a knife, and strikes her to the heart, preferring to see her dead than dishonored; then, covered with her blood, he fled to the army encamped on Algidus. The soldiers rose in revolt, marched upon Rome, where they seized the Aventine, and then, followed by all the people, united on the Sacred Mount with the legions of the Sabine army.

For some time the decemvirs hesitated, supported by a party in the Senate who dreaded the results of a plebeian revolution. But if it had been necessary to yield forty-six years before, when the patricians were still powerful and the plebeians without leaders, how was it possible to resist now when the people had the experience derived from their last struggles and the consciousness of their strength? The decemvirs abdicated (449 B. C.).

Is this story of Appius in all parts credible? and has not Livy been, this time also, the echo of this bitterness, which for ten years had checked the great popular reform—the drawing up a code of written law? Appius has been represented as a friend of the people: in proof of this it is asserted that he it was who gave three places to the plebeians in the second decemvirate; that he continued to hold office for the purpose of crushing the opposition of the irreconcilables in the Senate who refused to accept the last two tables,—in short, that the story aimed at perpetuating, by the blood of a virgin, the victory of the plebeians, as the blood of Lucretia, sixty years earlier, had perpetuated that of the nobles. This is possible; but with such confirmed scepticism no history at all can exist; and it being impossible to prove a negative, the old story preserves a part at least of its rights.

III. THE TWELVE TABLES.

THE Twelve Tables made little change in the old rights of individuals. Aristocratic customs were too deeply rooted to permit them yet awhile to become modified by that spirit of equality and justice which the tribunes by degrees infused into the Roman constitution. The decemvirs preserved to the paterfamilias absolute power over his slaves, children, wife, and property.

If no will was left, the inheritance passed to the *agnati*;

if they failed, to the *gentiles:* the law did not as yet recognize the *cognati,* or relations of the wife.[1]

The Twelve Tables did not introduce, as has been sometimes maintained, any new law concerning the family, granting more liberty to the wife and son. The emancipation of the son by these pretended sales freed him, it is true, from the paternal authority, but deprived him of his inheritance; for he suffered by emancipation a diminution of civil rights, *capitis diminutio,* which indicated certain disabilities; as, for example, inheriting from his father, being guardian of his nephews, posterity, etc., since the *capitis diminutio* destroyed the *jus agnationis.* Marriage, on the contrary, by cohabitation or purchase, *coemptio,* was raised, so far as the husband was concerned, to the strictness of the patrician marriage: *usu anni continui in manum conveniebat.*[2] The plebeian had from this time, over wife and children, the paternal and conjugal power which the patrician had hitherto possessed, and which later on the provincial could obtain only by the gift of civic freedom. It is the *civil* marriage which receives the sanction of the law, and which is placed, so far as its results are concerned, on a level with the *religious* marriage,[3] which will ultimately quite disappear. In four years Canuleius made use of the rights recognized in the plebeian marriage to suppress the interdiction preserved in the Twelve Tables, of unions between the two orders. Thus the gates of the patrician city will open first to the plebeians of Rome, then to the Italian allies, and finally to their subjects in the provinces.

The ancient patrician *gens* must have been copied early in the families of rich plebeians; but the bonds of the *clientela* being gradually relaxed, the Twelve Tables tried to strengthen this social institution of old Italy. "If the patron does an injury to his client," it is said therein, "let him be accursed." It was a last effort to tie up to his condition the client, who, finding in the law that protection which he had formerly sought from the great

---

[1] As regards property, the omnipotence of the father was, in the 2d century B. C., restrained by *lex Furia,* which forbade making a bequest of more than 1,000 ases to the same person, in order to prevent the abuse of legacies, which cut up properties and impoverished the old families.

[2] Gaius, i. 111, and Cic., *pro Flacco,* 34.

[3] On the marriage by *confarreatio,* see p. 196, n. 2.

man, drifted away from the *gens* into the common crowd, where he found more liberty. Soon he espoused its interests and passions, as the clients of Camillus did, who voted against him. This was an unfelt and yet profound revolution, for a part of the forces belonging to the aristocracy thus passed over to the plebeian camp.

Property remained also under the same conditions: it was either public or private. As to the first, there was never any freehold, because the state could not lose its rights; as for the second, two years sufficed to acquire it, for the state was interested in this, that the land should not remain without culture. If it was a question of personal property or of slaves, one year was enough. But against a foreign possessor the law was always open: *adversus hostem aeterna auctoritas*.[1] Hence the efforts of provincials, when Rome had extended her conquests to a distance, to obtain the title of citizen, which, among other privileges, gave, after an enjoyment for two years, the right of property over those uncertain lands, so numerous everywhere where the legions had passed.

In the heroic ages the law protected persons but little, because they knew how to defend themselves, and because courage was respected even to the extent of violence. The Twelve Tables have, then, comparatively light penalties for attacks on the person. But — and this is characteristic of Rome — attacks against property are severely punished. Theft becomes in them an impiety; for property is not only the power of the rich and the life of the poor, but all the goods which the house contains are a gift of the Penates, and the harvest is even Ceres herself. "Any one who shall have bewitched or used magical arts (*excantasset, pellexerit*) against another's crops, or who shall have carried off, during the night, the pasture of the flocks of his neighbor or cut his crop,[2] let him be devoted to Ceres, *Cereri necator*. At night let the robber be killed with impunity; during the day, if he make resistance. Let him who shall set fire to a shock of corn be bound, beaten with rods, and then burned. The insolvent debtor

---

[1] On the synonymy of *hospes*, or *peregrinus*, and of *hostis*, cf. Cic., *de. Off.* i. 12; Varr., *de Ling. Lat.* v. 1. The stranger is an enemy: this was for the Romans the first principle of the law of nations.

[2] In the Twelve Tables, says Pliny (xviii. 3), it is a more serious crime than homicide.

shall be sold or cut in pieces."[1] Yet the Twelve Tables had moderated the severity of Numa's law respecting the removal of boundaries. It was no longer a capital crime;[2] soon it became simply a misdemeanor; and the Mamilian law (239 or 165 B.C.) limited the punishment of the offender to a fine. It was inevitable that time and the revolutionary spirit of the plebeians should alter the sacred character of property of former times.

For offences regarded as less grave, two modes of punishment were in use among all barbarous peoples: the *lex talionis*, or corporal reprisals, and the private indemnity. "He who breaks any one's limb shall pay 300 ases to the injured party; if he do not compound with him, let him submit to the talio."

Let us remark that this severe people yet had relatively speaking some very mild laws. It knew nothing as yet of torture, nor condemned either to imprisonment or penal servitude. All offences, even a good part of what we should call crimes, were compounded for by fine, — a punishment not liked by us, because it affects not only the guilty, but the family; a punishment which the Romans preferred, because all the members of a family were conjointly responsible. In regard of crimes they troubled themselves only with those which affected the public peace, and they had only two forms of punishment for them: death and banishment. The condemned were thrown from the Tarpeian rock, strangled in the *Tullianum*, or beaten with rods and beheaded. The Porcian law in the next century suppressed punishment by death for the citizen.

Cicero has preserved for us some curious directions about funerals. "You remember," says he, "that in our infancy we were made to recite the Twelve Tables, which now hardly any one knows." After having reduced luxury to three mourning robes, three bands of purple, and ten flute-players, they put down the lamentations: "Let the women no longer tear their cheeks; let them no longer use the *lessus* at funerals[3] . . ." Praiseworthy directions, for they applied alike to rich and poor, which is very

---

[1] See p. 270.

[2] Cf. Trotz, *de Termino moto*. It is the establishment of the *iter limitare*. By means of this arrangement the need of applying Numa's law occurred but rarely, and this law fell into disuse.

[3] . . . *Neve lessum funeris ergo habento.* Cicero adds: *Lessum quasi lugubrem ejulationem, ut vox ipsa significat.* (*De Leg.* ii. 23.)

proper, since death effaces every difference. There are other regulations: "Let no one be buried within the city," — a religious prohibition which caused, sepulture to take place in the country or along the high roads leading to the city. "Let no gold be put into the graves," — a useless expense, which the Etruscans incurred voluntarily, but which the Romans spared. However, "any one whose teeth are bound with gold wire may be

THE TARPEIAN ROCK.[1]

buried or burned with this gold," — a respect for the corpse which the hand must not profane, and which must be consigned to the flame of the pile or the earth of the tomb. "Let the pile be erected sixty feet at the least from the house of another," — a precaution against fire, in order that the dead hurt not the living.

[1] "Travellers are shown a bare piece of rock at Rome and told: This is the Tarpeian rock; and they are astonished at its small height, not reflecting that the rock which is pointed out to them by the cicerone at random is only a small part of the Tarpeian rock. This name used to be given to the whole southern ridge. I live on this summit, and understand very well what would happen to me if they threw me out by the window into Strada di Consolazione; it would be a fall of 100 feet. Besides, the side of the Tarpeian rock bristled with projections, against which the bodies of those who were thrown down were mangled and smashed before reaching the bottom." (Ampère, *Hist. Rom. à Rome*, ii. 569, notes.)

"Let not the wood be polished with iron," — a useless luxury.[1] "Let funeral feasts be suppressed, as well as the throwing of perfumes into the flames; incense-boxes[2] and chaplets, except that which the deceased shall have gained by his courage, and which may, on the day of the funeral, be placed on his head," — precautions to restrain the pomp used by the great in these ceremonies. "Let not the bones of the deceased be kept for the purpose of performing the obsequies later on," — a prohibition against celebrating several times the obsequies of the same person, and of drawing, by this repeated show, the attention of the city to the same house.

A PRIEST PRESENTING THE INCENSE-BOX.

The greater part of these regulations were borrowed from the laws of Solon, who himself also had aimed at diminishing the influence of the Eupatridae by restraining show at funerals. But we shall see that the severities of the law will not prevail over manners. The funerals of the great were always at Rome among the most pompous ceremonies of the city, and by their tombs the Romans have created a kind of architecture, which we still copy.

Two questions of more importance from an historical point of view are: the introduction of several laws more favorable to the poor or the entire order of plebeians, and the general character which law takes in the Twelve Tables.[3]

Here were arrangements favorable to the plebeians: "Whoever shall lend money at more than 8⅓ per cent shall restore it fourfold;" that the *nexus* (the slave for debt) be not considered

---

[1] And perhaps a religious idea. We have seen that not a single nail was used in the construction of the Sublician bridge.

[2] *Acerra*, incense-box; one of those is represented in the engraving, which has been copied from a painted vase in the Naples Museum, which represents the preparations for a sacrifice.

[3] In the text, so far as it has been made out, there is much uncertainty in the order of the contents; but the order, which has much importance for the jurisconsult, has none for the historian.

infamous. This was a protection for the debtor against the usurer. "In state matters let them adjudge provisionally in favor of liberty," — a protection for the weak against the strong. "That it be permissible to form corporations or colleges, provided that nothing be done against the laws and the public weal." This was the right to the lower classes to form associations. "Let the false witness and the judge who has taken bribes be thrown from the rock," — a protection to the poor defendant against the rich suitor and the patrician judge. "That there be always right of appeal to the people from the sentences of the magistrates." This is a fresh sanction to the Valerian law, and a restriction put on the unlimited power of the dictatorship.[1] "That the people only, in the *comitia centuriata*, have the power of condemnation to death." This was a grant to the people of criminal jurisdiction, taken from the consuls, to whom the *lex Valeria de provocatione* had left the judgment in the first instance.[2] It was to the assembly of the centuries, where all patricians and plebeians are mingled according to scale of property, that the power passes. The Twelve Tables call it *maximum comitiatum*, the true assembly of the Roman people.

This was the general character of the law: "No more personal laws; *ne privilegia inroganto.*" The civil legislation of the Twelve Tables recognizes Roman citizens only. Its regulations are made neither for an order, nor a class, and its formula is always: *si quis,* — if any one; the patrician and the plebeian, the senator and the pontiff, the rich and the proletarian, are equal in its eyes. *Forti sanatique idem jus esto.*[3] Thus by this blotting out of distinctions, formerly so deep, the final union of the two peoples is at last proclaimed, and this new people, formed by the entirety of the citizens, has now the sovereign authority which had till then remained in the hands of the patrician *populus.* "What the people shall have ordained finally shall be law."

---

[1] Fest., *Optima lex;* Livy, iii. 55; Cic., *de Rep.* ii. 31 : *ab omni judicio paenaque provocari licere.*

[2] Cicero said of this law: *admirandum, tantum majores in posterum providisse.* The Senate declared in 310 B. C. *judicium populi rescindi ab senatu non posse.* (Livy, iv. 7.) The elections and the laws were alone submitted to the *auctoritas patrum.*

[3] Let the strong and the weak have the same right. See in Festus, v. *Sanates*, the explanation of this word.

Two remarks must be made on this axiom: the first is that the law is no longer the revelation of the nymph Egeria or the inspiration of gods which should continue mysterious and unchangeable; the people who have made it can unmake it. The second is the clear and simple definition which is given of it. The Romans have not sought for it in philosophical considerations. They do not define a principle: they assert a fact, — a new proof of that practical spirit which demands from life and society only those useful results which they may afford.

The people had also obtained by the Twelve Tables some material ameliorations, and, if not political equality — from which the poor could scarcely profit, at least equality before the civil and criminal law, which gives even to the most wretched the feeling of dignity as a man.

The aristocratic spirit transpires, however, in this code drawn up by patricians: "Let the rich plead for the rich; for the poor any one who will."[1] This is only contemptuous; but the law is very severe against authors of scurrilous verses, and those who meet secretly at night;[2] and in one of the last articles added by Appius it sanctioned the invidious exclusiveness of former days: "Let there be no marriages between patricians and plebeians." It is a protest of the old masters of Rome against the new character of the law, in the name of their ancestors, of the nobility of their race, the religion of their families, and the special protection which the gods granted them. Let there be equality, since they could not prevent it; let the same judges, the same law, the same penalty strike Fabius and Icilius; but no mésalliances. Outside the tribunal let the one return to the crowd from which he came, the other to the *curia*, the temples of the gods, the hereditary atrium!

The patricians had, in fact, allowed nothing to be changed in the constitution: they remained consuls and senators, augurs and pontiffs, judges especially; and by the multifold forms of procedure of which the plebeians were ignorant, they were able to

---

[1] *Assiduo vindex assiduus esto; proletario quivis volet vindex esto.*

[2] *Qui caetus nocturnos agitaverit, capital esto.* For all these citations from the Twelve Tables I have followed the text given by Reiske in his edition of Dionysius of Halicarnassus, pp. 2366-2381.

nullify this publication of the law and this civil equality which they had been compelled to proclaim.[1]

In the populous cities of Italy and Greece neither law nor custom would suffer that state of war in peace — the right of taking justice into one's own hands — which so long decimated the modern nobility; and public good sense was sufficiently strong, in spite of blind superstition, to prevent referring the decision of a cause to the judgment of God, as was the case in the trial by ordeal in the Middle Ages.[2] In every case human justice adjudicated. But at Rome the judges were not a class of men whose life was devoted to the religious duty of affording justice. For every trial the consul named judges, always patricians; and these judges sat only on days fixed by the secret calendar of the Pontiffs, which changed yearly. They did not admit the litigants to set forth simply the matters in dispute;[3] mysterious formulae, gestures, and *actions* were necessary. It was required to hold in one hand a bit of straw as a memento of the lance of the Quirites, to touch with the other the object at stake, to declare his right in the established terms, to throw the straw at the object; then to defy the adversary; if the question related to a theft, to enter naked into the house of the suspected thief, girt with a linen band, a dish in the hand, etc.; and especially to avoid making any mistake, any error in this judicial drama, for then the suit could no longer proceed.[4] In this unknown labyrinth of legitimate acts and formulae of action, the plebeian easily strayed from the legal road, at the least hint from the judges; and the judge was so often his political adversary!

---

[1] Dionys., ii. 27: φανεροὺς ἅπασι. As regards equality before the civil law, it is still proved by these expressions: *aequatae leges* (Livy, iii. 31, 63, 67); ἰσονομία, ἰσηγορία (Dionys., x. 1); νόμους κοινοὺς ἐπὶ πᾶσι (x. 50). Appius says: *Se omnibus, summis infimisque jura aequasse.* (Livy, iii. 34.)

[2] [Nevertheless the legend of the combat of the Horatii and Curiatii is distinctly an appeal to the same principle, which we find in old Jewish history, and which was proposed by the Argives to the Spartans in Thucydides' time (cf. Thuc., v. 41). The Spartans thought it folly (μωρία), but thought it politic to agree. Of course the duel never came off. The Argives quoted the story of Othryades as an old decision in this way. In later Roman times a personal quarrel was settled characteristically by a sort of legal bet *ni vir bonus esset*, where a man's character was investigated in court, and if cleared, his opponent lost his stakes. — *Ed.*]

[3] Cf. Cic., *pro Murena*, 12, and Gaius, iv. 13-17. There were 5 formulas of actions: *sacramento, per judicis postulationem, per conditionem, per manus injectionem, per pignoris captionem.* The *acta legitima* were numberless; cf. Brisson, *de Formulis.*

[4] See p. 268.

Still, the new legislation had founded the civil law of Rome; four centuries after, Cicero still recommended its study, *carmen necessarium*,[1] and Gaius, under the Antonines, drew up a long commentary on the Twelve Tables. This reform did not satisfy all the hopes of the people; but the decemvirs had nevertheless given an impulse to the plebeian power, if not by their laws, at least by the acts of violence of their closing days.

[1] *De Leg.* ii. 4, 23.
[2] A woman holding a balance and a stick, which is doubtless a measure, the *pertica*, or perch (= 10 Rom. ft. = 3 yds. 8 in.).

SILVER PENNY OF ANTONINUS PIUS.[2]

CHAPTER IX.

EFFORTS TO OBTAIN POLITICAL EQUALITY (449-400).

I. RE-ESTABLISHMENT OF THE TRIBUNATE AND CONSULATE.

THE revolution of 510 B. C., made by the patricians, had benefited the aristocracy; that of 449, made by the people, profited the people. The decemvirs had abdicated, and two popular senators, Valerius and Horatius, had gone to the Sacred Mount to promise the re-establishment of the tribunate and right of appeal, extended to all the citizens, with an amnesty for those who had taken part in the revolt. The people returned to the Aventine, and in order to be assured that these promises would be kept, occupied once more the Capitol.[1] But no one dreamt of disputing the victory. The Pontifex Maximus held the comitia for the election of ten tribunes, then Horatius and Valerius were appointed consuls, who by several laws guaranteed the recovered liberty.

The first of these laws prohibited, under pain of death, the creation at any time of a magistracy without appeal.[2] The second gave the force of law to the *plebiscita*, that is to say, that resolutions passed in the assembly of the tribes should no longer need the sanction of the Senate, as did the resolutions of the centuries, to become general laws.[3] The third renewed the anathema pronounced against any who outraged the tribunitian inviolability.

[1] Cic., *pro. Cornel.* i. *Fr.* 25.
[2] Livy, iii. 55.
[3] Τὴν αὐτὴν ἔχοντας δύναμιν τοῖς ἐν ταῖς λοχίτισιν ἐκκλησίαις τεθησομένοις. (Dionys., xi. 45.) M. Willems (*Le Droit public Romain*, p. 61) thinks that from this moment the patricians and their clients were admitted, if not by *right*, yet at least in *fact*, to the *concilia plebis*. The centuries preserved judgments for capital crimes, election to the chief magistracies, the right of making the most general laws, and of deciding for peace or war. The legislative power of the tribes was put in force respecting questions of internal order, and especially for the maintenance

The fourth ordered that a copy of all the Senatus-consulta, countersigned by the tribunes with the letter T,[1] to prevent all falsification, should be intrusted to the plebeian aediles and kept by them in the temple of Ceres on the Aventine. Another copy was, without doubt, kept by the quaestors in the temple of Saturn. The tribune Duilius had this law passed: that the magistrate who neglected to hold the comitia at the end of the year, for the election of the tribunes of the people, should be punished with the rod and axe.[2]

Liberty was assured; but the blood shed called for vengeance. Virginius accused the decemvirs. Appius, their chief, killed himself in prison before the trial; Oppius, the second in unpopularity, died in the same way. The others were exiled; their property was confiscated to the temple of Ceres. The people were satisfied with these two victims, and Duilius declared that he would oppose his veto to any further accusation.

However, the two consuls had resumed military operations against the Aequians and Sabines, and the latter were so thoroughly beaten by Horatius, that they remained at peace with Rome for a century and a half. On their return the consuls demanded a triumph; up to that time the Senate alone had the right to grant it, and refused. The tribune Icilius had it decreed by the people, and "the consuls triumphed not only over the enemy, but the patricians also." It was the tribunes also who, gradually bringing the people into the most important state affairs, decided in the debate between Ardea and Aricia.[3]

This matter is worth a moment's delay, for it has given occasion to one of those very rare stories which show us the interior of the Italian cities. Ardea, a very old Latin city, four miles from the sea, and Aricia, celebrated in antiquity for its terrible temple of Diana, and in modern times by its charming Lake Nemi, disputed about the territory of the city of Corioli,

and extension of public rights. Aul. Gellius (*Noct. Attic.* X. xx. 6) defines the plebiscitum: *lex quam plebes, non populus, accipit.*

[1] Val. Max., II. ii. 7; Livy (ii. 55) says: *Senatusconsulta quae antea arbitrio consulum supprimebantur vitiabanturque.*

[2] Livy, iii. 55 ; Diod., xii. 25. Another law, proposed by Trebonius, required the appointment of ten tribunes and forbade co-optation.

[3] Livy, iii. 71.

EFFORTS TO OBTAIN POLITICAL EQUALITY.

destroyed in one of the wars against the Volscians. After many battles, they chose Rome as umpire. The Senate referred the matter to the people, who, at the instigation of the nobles, played the part of judge in the fable of the Pleaders: they adjudged to themselves the contested territory. The Ardeates, more pleased with the discomfiture of Aricia than annoyed at having lost their case, or at least their nobles, who had need of a foreign alliance against the people of Ardea, made a treaty with Rome which gave some fertile lands to the Romans. Did this convention seem an act of treason to the plebeians of Ardea, or were they hurt in some other way? We know not; but a little while after they left the city, and in place of observing, in this *secession*, the patriotic moderation which the Roman historians confess in the seceders of the Sacred Mount or the Aventine, they returned to Ardea with a Volscian army. The patricians and their clients, incapable of defending themselves, invoked the help of their new allies. Those whom they termed rebels were conquered by a Roman army, and their chiefs perished under the axe. To re-people the city, now half desert, Rome sent there a colony; but the triumvirs put in charge by it of the division of the lands gave the best to their friends of Ardea; so the anger against them was so hot among the Roman people that, not daring to appear before them, they stayed in the colony, where doubtless they obtained a good number of *jugera* well selected. This history enables us to see in the Latin cities the same divisions as at Rome, and, among all those peoples, modes of action which prove that the ancients understood justice differently from us, or at least otherwise than as our moral treatises define it.

The year 449 had not taken from the patricians all their privileges. Rome has still two classes, but only one people; and the chiefs of the plebs, sitting in the Senate, are meditating, after the struggle to obtain civil equality, to commence another to gain political equality.

In a revolution, in fact, the party which has conquered opposition cannot stop short; its momentum carries it beyond the goal, and it preserves for a long while an impetus by which its leaders know how to profit — sometimes in the public interest, more often for their ambition. After the victory, the tribunes employed the rest of their energy to complete the work of the decemvirs and carry out the Terentilian law. The patricians had more than once tried to slip into the tribunate; the Trebonian law closed it against them for ever. They had reserved to themselves the judicial power, except in the case of a capital sentence against a citizen, and the administration of the finances, by leaving to the consuls the right of appointing quaestors of the treasury. The tribunes obtained in 447 B. C. that the *quaestores parricidii* et *quaestores aerarii* should be for the future elected in the comitia tributa, although these two offices remained patrician.[1]

Two things maintained the insulting distinction between the two orders: the prohibition of marriage between patricians and plebeians, and the tenure of all the magisterial offices by those who formed since the origin of Rome the sovereign people of the *patres*. In 445 B. C. the tribune Canuleius demanded the abolition of the prohibition relative to marriages, and his colleagues a share in the consulate. This was a demand for political equality.

II. — NEW CONSTITUTION OF THE YEAR 444.

WE know now that every aristocracy which closes its ranks soon perishes, because time and power quickly exhaust political families. Without knowing it, the Roman patriciate acted as if it comprehended this truth, and this perception of public necessities made the greatness of Rome. After a resistance skilfully calculated for opposing to the popular torrent a dam which broke its force without exciting it, the nobles always yielded; but, like a disciplined army which never becomes broken, they retreated in order to make a strong defence at the next point. Thus was prolonged this internal war, which moulded the robust youth of the Roman people.

When the *patres* heard this new and audacious demand of the tribune, their indignation burst forth. "Thus then," said Claudius, with his hereditary pride, "thus nothing will remain

---

[1] Tac., *Ann.* xi. 22.

LAKE NEMI.

pure: plebeian ambition will pollute everything, — time-honored authority, and religion, and family rights, and auspices, and the images of our ancestors." But the people used the method which had already been used twice before: they withdrew in arms to the Janiculum;[1] and the Senate, thinking that customs would be stronger than law, agreed that henceforth there should be legal marriages between patricians and plebeians.

When this barrier was once broken down, it was not possible to forbid the access of the plebeians to curule offices. However, by mere adroitness, the patriciate, though half conquered, defended itself for forty-five years longer; for it had in this struggle the gods themselves as allies, from the belief, deeply rooted in the people, that the hand of a noble was alone able to offer favorable sacrifices for the state. The colleagues of Canuleius asked, in the name of the plebeians, one of the consulships and two of the quaestorships of the treasury. The Senate granted that the quaestors of the treasury should be chosen without distinction[2] in the two orders; and thanks to this latitude, for a long time only patricians held this office. As regards the consulship, no concession was possible; rather than relinquish that also, the Senate preferred to dismember it. This royal power had already lost the right of performing certain sacrifices (*rex sacrorum*), the care of the treasure (*quaestores aerarii*), and the direction of criminal affairs (*quaestores parricidii*); and two new magistrates, *sine imperio*, that is, without military authority or jurisdiction, the CENSORS, created in 443 B. C., at first for five years, then for eighteen months (434), obtained the consular right of making the census, of regulating the classes, of administering the public domain, of farming out to the highest bidder the tax on the public lands, of watching over public morality, and, later, of drawing up the

[1] Flor., i. 25. *Tertiam seditionem . . . in monte Janiculo . . . duce Canuleio.* The patricians alone were able to take the auspices. This privilege, necessary for acquaintance with all the mysteries of religion and law, gave them a religious character, which the plebeians in the long run would share by the mixing of families. Hence the keen opposition of the Senate to a law which would lead to the mingling of the two orders. When Cleisthenes wished to strengthen, at Athens, the democratic element, he suppressed the *sacra privata; . . . καὶ τὰ τῶν ἰδίων ἱερῶν συνακτέον εἰς ὀλίγα καὶ κοινὰ καὶ πάντα σοφιστέον, ὅπως ἂν ὅτι μάλιστα ἀναμιχθῶσι πάντες ἀλλήλοις* . . . (Arist., *Pol.* VI. ii. 11.)

[2] Livy, iv. 43; *promiscue.* The quaestors were treasurers of the public funds; they it was who opened and closed the treasury, in which were also deposited the standards of the legions.

list of senators and knights.[1] In this way they gradually attained the first rank in the state, and re-election to an office which became the highest honor in the city was presently forbidden.

There remained of the consular power its military functions, civil jurisdiction, the designation of new senators, the presidency in the Curiae and the comitia, the care of the city and the laws. These powers were given, but sub-divided, without curule honors, with six lictors in place of twelve, and under the plebeian name of tribune, to three, four, or six generals. To these *military tribunes*, elected without auspices,[2] religion forbade at first one of the most important prerogatives of the consuls, viz., the designation of a dictator.[3] Mere lieutenants, so to say, of an invisible magistracy, but which the Senate knows and inspires, they did not fight under their own auspices, and never did they obtain the most envied of military rewards, the triumph.[4] What power they have is also divided among them according to their number. One marches at the head of the legions, another commands the reserve, another the veterans, another again watches over the arsenals and provisioning of the troops. One only is invested with the religious and judicial functions of the consuls, viz., the *praefectus urbis*, president of the Senate and the comitia, guardian of religion, the laws, and all the interests of the city.[5] Also the Senate took care that these prerogatives, including the duties given later on to the *praetors*, with the important privilege of naming the

---

[1] Pastures, woods, fisheries, salt mines, mines, harbor dues, etc. (Livy, xxxii. 7; xl. 51.) On the duties of the censors, see Cic., *de Leg.* iii. 3; Hist. Aug. Valer. 2. But all these duties were not theirs from the beginning. Livy says (iv. 8) *Res a parva origine orta.* The first mention of a *lectio senatus* by the censors is from the year 312 B. C. (Livy, viii. 29-30), which, however, does not mean that there had never been one before. [It appears from the researches of Soltau at the Carlsruhe Congress of Philologists (1882), that the censorate was directly imitated from the chief administrator (ὁ ἐπὶ τῆς διοικήσεως) of the Athenian tributes. The direct influence of Greece on Rome is probably older and greater than is usually thought. — *Ed.*]

[2] This can be inferred from the speech of Appius (Livy, vi. 41), *nullus auspicato.* At least they had not the *maxima auspicia.* (Aul. Gell. xiii. 15.) Livy even says (v. 18) that they were nominated in the profane assembly of the tribes; but he contradicts himself elsewhere (v. 13).

[3] *Religio obstaret* . . . (Livy, iv. 31.) However, in 423 B. C., in a pressing danger, the augurs removed this prohibition, and the consular tribune, *praefectus urbis*, Corn. Cossus, nominates a dictator.

[4] Zonaras, vii. 19, confirmed by the silence of the triumphal fasti. The triumph was accorded to those only who had conquered *suis auspiciis.*

[5] Livy, vi. 5. In 424, four tribunes, *e quibus Cossus praefuit Urbi;* the same in 431 B. C., in 383, etc.

judges, remained in the hands of a patrician.[1] When the plebeians ultimately gained entrance into the consular tribunate, one place at least was always reserved for a candidate of the other order.[2]

Out of the consulate three offices are formed: the quaestorship, the censorship, and the consular tribunate. The two former are exclusively patrician. The military tribunes, in reality proconsuls confined, with one exception, to the command of the legions, could now be chosen without distinction from the two orders. But the law, in not requiring that every year a fixed number of them be plebeians, allowed them to be all patricians; and they remained so for nearly fifty years.[3]

In spite of such skilful precautions, the Senate did not give up the consulate. It held in reserve and pure from all taint the patrician magistracy, hoping for better days. The dictatorship, which was not effaced from the new constitutional code, and the right of opposition from the *patres*, remained as a last resource for extreme cases. Religion in fine always furthered the interests of the aristocracy; and if, in spite of the influence of the nobles in the assemblies, in spite of the arbitrary power of the president of the *comitia*, who had the right to refuse votes for a hostile candidate, the majority of votes were in favor of a new man, his election could still be quashed by an adverse decision of the augurs. If necessary, Jupiter thundered.

JUPITER.[4]

---

[1] Once, in 396, Livy names six plebeians. But in the place of P. Maelius the new fragments of the Fasti and Diodorus (xiv. 90) name Q. Manlius.

[2] As regards the frequent variations in the number of the consular tribunes, a thing so strange in Roman antiquity, they are explained by making the consular tribunes to be only generals. Their number grew according to the need. From 443 B. C. to 432 they are three, two for the legions, one to remain as prefect in the city. In 425, after the declaration of war against Veii, four are named. If the number reaches six in 404, it is still for the Veian war. When they are eight, it is perhaps, as Perizonius has maintained, because the censors were included.

[3] From 444 to 400 B. C.

[4] Jupiter with the sceptre and thunderbolt. Antique intaglio from the French National Collection, No. 1,420.

III. STRUGGLE FOR THE EXECUTION OF THE NEW CONSTITUTION.

WHATEVER skill had been exhibited by the Senate, the principle of political equality had just triumphed, and the division of the curule magistracies was only a question of time. This time was long; for the question here was no longer to satisfy general interests, but only the ambition of some chiefs of the people. Thus the attack, though spirited, was ill-sustained; and the plebeians, content with the name of equality, neglected for a long time to grasp the reality.[1] We shall see them at the crisis ready to abandon Licinius Stolo and the consulate for a few acres of land.

The constitution of 444 B. C. authorized the appointment of plebeians to the consular tribunate; down to 400 B. C. none obtained it; and during the seventy-eight years that this office continued, the Senate twenty-four times appointed consuls; that is to say, it succeeded, one year in three, in its attempts to re-establish the ancient form of government.[2]

These perpetual oscillations encouraged the ambitious hopes of a rich knight, Spurius Maelius (439 B. C.). He thought that the Romans would willingly resign into his hands their unquiet liberty, and during a famine he gave very liberally to the poor. The Senate became alarmed at this almsgiving, which was not at all in accordance with the manners of that time, and raised to the dictatorship Cincinnatus, who, on taking office, prayed the gods not to suffer that his old age should prove a cause of hurt or damage to the Republic. Summoned before the tribunal of the dictator, Maelius refused to appear, and sought protection against

COIN OF SERV. AHALA.[3]

---

[1] Livy says, it is true, *imperio et insignibus consularibus usos;* but all that precedes, shows without doubt the inferiority of the tribunes to the consuls. If the name alone had been changed, the tribunes of the people would not have shown such obstinacy in demanding the consulate itself. "It was never a mere quarrel of words," says Madame de Staël.

[2] It was on the proposition of the Senate that the centuries decided each year whether they would elect military tribunes or consuls. It did not generally propose tribunes except when they were threatened with war: the ordinary formula at the time of the election of consuls was, *pax et otium domi forisque.*

[3] AHALA. Head of Servilius Ahala on a silver coin of the Servilian family.

www.ingramcontent.com/pod-product-compliance
Lightning Source LLC
Chambersburg PA
CBHW051246300426
44114CB00011B/904